The Developer's Guide to Social Programming

The Developer's Guide to Social Programming

Building Social Context Using Facebook, Google Friend Connect, and the Twitter API

Mark D. Hawker

✦ Addison-Wesley

Upper Saddle River, NJ • Boston • Indianapolis • San Francisco
New York • Toronto • Montreal • London • Munich • Paris • Madrid
Cape Town • Sydney • Tokyo • Singapore • Mexico City

Many of the designations used by manufacturers and sellers to distinguish their products are claimed as trademarks. Where those designations appear in this book, and the publisher was aware of a trademark claim, the designations have been printed with initial capital letters or in all capitals.

The author and publisher have taken care in the preparation of this book, but make no expressed or implied warranty of any kind and assume no responsibility for errors or omissions. No liability is assumed for incidental or consequential damages in connection with or arising out of the use of the information or programs contained herein.

The publisher offers excellent discounts on this book when ordered in quantity for bulk purchases or special sales, which may include electronic versions and/or custom covers and content particular to your business, training goals, marketing focus, and branding interests. For more information, please contact:

U.S. Corporate and Government Sales
(800) 382-3419
corpsales@pearsontechgroup.com

For sales outside the United States please contact:

International Sales
international@pearson.com

Visit us on the Web: informit.com/aw

Library of Congress Cataloging-in-Publication Data:

Hawker, Mark D.
 The developer's guide to social programming : building social context using Facebook, Google friend connect, and the Twitter API / Mark D. Hawker.
   p. cm.
 ISBN 978-0-321-68077-8 (pbk. : alk. paper) 1. Online social networks. 2. Entertainment computing. 3. Internet programming. 4. Google. 5. Facebook (Electronic resource) 6. Twitter. I. Title.
 HM742.H39 2010
 006.7'54—dc22
                            2010020866

ISBN-13: 978-0-321-68077-8
ISBN-10: 0-321-68077-4

Text printed in the United States on recycled paper at RR Donnelley Crawfordsville in Crawfordsville, Indiana.

First printing, August 2010

To Mam and Dad, I am forever grateful for your patience, understanding, love, and support. More than you will ever know. And to my brother, Dale, who continues to pleasantly surprise us all. I will love you always.

"Some dreams are dressed in gossamer and gumboots; ethereal hope undergirded by practical endeavour."

SarahJayne Vivian

❖

Contents at a Glance

I: **Twitter**

    1 Working with the Twitter API   **1**

    2 Diving Into the Twitter API Methods   **21**

    3 Authentication with Twitter OAuth   **45**

    4 Extending the Twitter API: Retweets, Lists, and Location   **61**

II: **Facebook Platform**

    5 An Overview of Facebook Platform Website Integration   **77**

    6 Registration, Authentication, and Translations with Facebook   **99**

    7 Using Facebook for Sharing, Commenting, and Stream Publishing   **115**

    8 Application Discovery, Tabbed Navigation, and the Facebook JavaScript Library   **137**

III: **Google Friend Connect**

    9 An Overview of Google Friend Connect   **165**

    10 Server-Side Authentication and OpenSocial Integration   **193**

    11 Developing OpenSocial Gadgets with Google Friend Connect   **209**

IV: **Putting It All Together**

    12 Building a Microblog Tool Using CodeIgniter   **235**

    13 Integrating Twitter, Facebook, and Google Friend Connect   **267**

Table of Contents

I: Twitter

1 Working with the Twitter API 1

Twitter API Essentials 1

   Twitter API Methods 3

   Twitter API Parameters 6

   Twitter API Return Formats 10

Accessing the Twitter API 11

   cURL 12

   Twitter-async 14

   Twitter API Rate Limiting 17

   Twitter API Error Handling 18

Summary 19

2 Diving Into the Twitter API Methods 21

Twitter API Methods 21

   User Objects 23

   Status Objects 26

   Direct Message Objects 28

   Saved Search Objects 29

   ID Objects 30

   Relationship Objects 31

   Response Objects 32

   Hash Objects 33

Twitter Search API 34

   Introducing the Atom Syndication Format 34

   Twitter Search API Methods 38

Summary 43

3 Authentication with Twitter OAuth 45

Introducing Twitter OAuth 45

   OAuth Benefits 46

   OAuth Definitions 46

Implementing Twitter OAuth   48

    Twitter OAuth Workflow   48

    Test Tube: A Sample Twitter Application   50

Summary   59

4 Extending the Twitter API: Retweets, Lists, and Location   61

Extending Twitter's Core Functionality   61

    Retweet API   62

    Lists API   64

    Geolocation API   68

Twitter Community Evolution   71

    Platform Translations   71

    Spam Reporting   72

    Future Directions   74

Summary   76

II: Facebook Platform

5 An Overview of Facebook Platform Website Integration   77

Facebook Platform for Developers   77

Facebook Platform   78

    Registering a Facebook Application   79

    Referencing a Facebook Platform Application   81

Facebook API, FQL, and XFBML   84

    Facebook API and FQL   84

    XFBML   97

Summary   98

6 Registration, Authentication, and Translations with Facebook   99

User Authorization and Authentication   99

    Logging In and Detecting Facebook Status   101

    Logging Out, Disconnecting, and Reclaiming Accounts   107

Connecting and Inviting Friends   109

Translations for Facebook   111

   Preparing Your Application and Registering Text   111

   Administering and Accessing Translations   113

Summary   114

7 Using Facebook for Sharing, Commenting, and Stream Publishing   115

Content-Sharing and Live Conversation   115

   Facebook Share   116

   Facebook Widgets   118

Social Commenting and Stream Publishing   120

   Comments Box   120

   Open Stream API   123

Summary   135

8 Application Discovery, Tabbed Navigation, and the Facebook JavaScript Library   137

Application Dashboards and Counters   138

   News and Activity Streams   139

   Games and Applications Counters   143

Navigating and Showcasing Your Application Using Tabs   145

   Configuring and Installing an Application Tab   146

   Extending an Application Tab   149

Dynamic Content and the Facebook JavaScript (FBJS) Library   157

   Facebook Animation Library   157

   Facebook Dialogs   160

   Handling Events with an Event Listener   162

Summary   164

III: Google Friend Connect

9 An Overview of Google Friend Connect   165

Components of Google Friend Connect   165

   Google Friend Connect Gadgets   166

Google Friend Connect JavaScript API   167

Server-Side Integration   167

Google Friend Connect Plug-ins   168

Using the Google Friend Connect JavaScript API   169

Installing and Configuring the JavaScript Library   169

Working with Google Friend Connect Data   171

An Overview of the OpenSocial API   173

OpenSocial API Methods   173

The `DataRequest` Object   174

Fetching People and Profiles   176

Fetching and Updating Activities   177

Fetching and Updating Persistence   178

Color Picker: A Google Friend Connect
Application   181

Summary   191

**10   Server-Side Authentication and OpenSocial
Integration   193**

Server-Side OpenSocial Protocols and Authentication
Methods   193

Google Friend Connect Authentication Methods   194

OpenSocial Client Libraries   196

Using the PHP OpenSocial Client Library
with Google Friend Connect   197

Google Friend Connect Authentication Workflow   197

Setting Up a Server-Side Application   198

OpenSocial Data Extraction Principles   201

Summary   207

**11   Developing OpenSocial Gadgets with Google
Friend Connect   209**

An Overview of Google Gadgets   209

Anatomy of an OpenSocial Google Gadget   210

OpenSocial v0.9 Specification   214

Advanced OpenSocial Gadget Development   217

Creating a Google Gadget   222

Color Picker, Revisited   222

Testing, Tracking, and Directory Submission   230

Summary   233

IV: Putting It All Together

12 Building a Microblog Tool Using CodeIgniter   235

An Overview of CodeIgniter   235

The Model-View-Controller Architectural Design   236

Installing, Configuring, and Exploring CodeIgniter   237

CodeIgniter Libraries   240

CodeIgniter Helpers   245

Building the Basic Sprog Application   246

Stage 1: Creating the Registration, Login, and Home Pages   247

Stage 2: Extending the Sprog Application with Updates, Comments, and Likes   257

Summary   266

13 Integrating Twitter, Facebook, and Google Friend Connect   267

Implementing Twitter Functionality   267

Setting Up Twitter and Twitter-async Support   268

Stage 3: Extending the Sprog Application with Twitter Functionality   270

Updating a User's Twitter Account   276

Implementing Facebook Functionality   279

Registering a Facebook Application and Adding Facebook Support   279

Stage 4: Extending the Sprog Application with Facebook Functionality   281

Implementing Google Friend Connect Functionality   292

Registering and Adding Google Friend Connect Support   292

Stage 5: Extending the Sprog Application with Google Friend Connect Functionality   294

Summary   301

Index   303

Preface

The World Wide Web is in constant flux and, since the introduction of utilities such as Facebook and Twitter, has only recently had social interaction at its core. Currently, Facebook and Twitter have more than 400 million active users, and the Facebook Platform alone is integrated with more than 250,000 websites and applications, engaging over 100 million Facebook users each month. These numbers continue to increase each day. Another dominant force is Google, who introduced their Friend Connect, which enables users to add social functionality to any of their websites. All three companies continue to roll out massive changes to their development platform, rendering previous best practices obsolete.

However, just knowing the technical aspects of each platform is not a guarantee that it will succeed. It is important to also see how each is distinct and to prepare you for changes through examples and sample code. The purpose of these examples is to provide a springboard to build applications on, so there is plenty of room for extending and adapting to suit your own needs. This book is one of the first of its kind to bring together three of the most popular social programming platforms under one hood. Welcome to social programming.

Who This Book Is For

This book is written for beginner or intermediate developers who are comfortable with PHP and the major technologies of the Web: (X)HTML, JavaScript, and Cascading Style Sheets (CSS), as well as Atom, JavaScript Object Notation (JSON), Really Simple Syndication (RSS), and Extensible Markup Language (XML). The reader should also have access to a web server, such as Apache or Internet Information Services (IIS), to test code examples.

No prior experience of social programming is required, although some familiarity and active user accounts with Facebook, Google, and Twitter is assumed. To be a good developer for a platform, it helps to understand it from a user's perspective.

This book will help the reader understand what makes a good Facebook, Google Friend Connect, and Twitter application; explain and show how to use the core technologies of each platform; and build your confidence to develop engaging social applications.

How This Book Is Structured

This book is divided into four main parts:

Part I, "Twitter," provides an overview of the methods, authentication workflows, and components of the Twitter API. It explains what is contained within the Twitter API, including search, retweets, lists, and geolocation using code examples supported by a PHP client library, twitter-async.

Part II, "Facebook Platform," provides an overview of the service, including authentication, sharing, commenting, and publishing. A sample application is created, Test Tube, highlighting key features of the platform through both client- and server-side scripting using the Facebook Platform.

Part III, "Google Friend Connect," showcases the service and its integration with OpenSocial through client- and server-side scripting and the creation of a Google gadget. A sample application, Color Picker, is created to demonstrate Google Friend Connect in action.

Part IV, "Putting It All Together," pulls each of the three social platforms together into a coherent whole and demonstrates how to create your very own microblog from scratch. A sample application, Sprog, is created using a popular web application framework, CodeIgniter, which is extended using select functionalities from Twitter, Facebook, and Google Friend Connect.

Contacting the Author

If you have any questions or comments about this book, please send an e-mail to socialprogramming@gmail.com. You can also visit the book's website, http://www. socialprogramming.info, for updates, downloadable code examples, and platform news. An active code repository will be maintained, http://github.com/markhawker/Social-Programming, which you can use to post issues you have with the code and to download future updates.

Acknowledgments

Writing this book has been one of, if not the, greatest and most thrilling experiences of my life. This adventure has been supported by a great number of people. First, I want to thank my acquisitions editor, Trina MacDonald, who was always there to listen and support me when I had queries and really helped shape the book. I appreciate the encouragement given through some tough and challenging times. Second, I'd like to thank my development editor, Songlin Qiu, for her advice and insight; my technical editors, Joshua Gross, Ben Schupak, and Joseph Annuzzi, who did an excellent job testing and correcting my source code; and Olivia Basegio for keeping us all in check. Others who offered excellent advice and direction include Doug Williams at Twitter, Patrick Chanezon, Arne Roomann-Kurrik, Bob Aman and Chris Schalk at Google, and Jaisen Mathai. Thanks also to my connections on Twitter and Facebook for being with me from the beginning, including Kevin Makice and Dusty Reagan, and to Raj Anand and Dr. Lydia Lau for their input on my original proposal.

A final, special mention goes to SarahJayne Vivian for keeping me inspired and motivated, and for showing me the true meaning of friendship. Thank you. It truly has been an amazing journey and one that I will never forget.

About the Author

Mark Hawker is a social applications developer and consultant focused on developing for social platforms such as Facebook and Twitter. He is a graduate from the University of Leeds, United Kingdom, with a First-class Honors degree in Informatics. A researcher in the field of health informatics, Mark focuses his time on how to innovatively apply social networking technologies in a wide variety of consumer health scenarios.

Working with the Twitter API

The beauty and success of Twitter lies in its simplicity. It's simple not just for its users but also within its rich application programming interface (API), which provides you the tools required to interact with Twitter's internal services. The Twitter API is responsible for more than 90% of Twitter server traffic and provides the gateway to much of Twitter's core functionality, such as status updates, direct messaging, and searches. As the Twitter platform evolves, more features will be added to the Twitter API, so this book will serve as a complement to the expanding online Twitter documentation. Recent enhancements include the Geolocation API, Lists API, and the Retweet API (each of which is covered in Chapter 4, "Extending the Twitter API: Retweets, Lists, and Location").

This chapter explains a number of building blocks, such as methods, authentication, return formats, and status codes that will enable you to start interacting with the service. Interaction with the Twitter API is described using a command-line interface (cURL), and in this chapter, you are introduced to a PHP client library developed by Jaisen Mathai called twitter-async, which supports basic authentication as well as Twitter OAuth, which is covered in Chapter 3, "Authentication with Twitter OAuth." At the end of this chapter, you will have gained an understanding of the Twitter API and developed the necessary skills to start interacting with the service. From here, Chapter 2, "Exploring the Twitter API and Search API," will guide you through Twitter API return objects to give you an in-depth understanding of how to interpret responses to suit all of your applications.

Twitter API Essentials

The Twitter API enables desktop and Internet-enabled third-party applications to interact with Twitter services in a standard and easy-to-use way. An API is a conduit that enables data from one application or service, in this case Twitter, to be shared with the outside world. By making requests to the Twitter API, data is returned in a structured format that makes it easy to parse and extract information from that data. The Twitter API separates the functionality of the site into small, manageable functions, such as "get a list of followers" or "change a profile background" via a number of methods.

Counting to 140

Twitter imposes a limit of 140 characters, or more technically 140 bytes, to updates (primarily because of the size restrictions of cell text messages). Although the Twitter API accepts longer strings of text, those messages are truncated. Because Twitter uses the UTF-8 character set, it is possible to represent each of the 128 ASCII characters, which consume 1 byte, plus special Unicode and international characters, which can consume up to 4 bytes. This is why tweets with special characters are truncated even though they are technically 140 characters in length. Twitter uses the Normalization Form C (NFC) convention for counting update length, which can be evaluated using the `Normalizer` class in PHP.

The Twitter API is a Representational State Transfer (REST)-based resource exposed over HTTP(S), which means that "accessor" methods (those that retrieve data) require a GET operation and "mutator" methods (those that create, update, or destroy data) require a POST operation.

However, the Lists API methods require that you use a PUT operation for updating data and also a DELETE operation for destroying data. This is discussed in Chapter 4 because it is slightly removed from the conventional structures of the other Twitter API methods. The DELETE operation instructs the Twitter servers to remove the requested resource and does not return a response value to guarantee that this has been performed successfully. It is recommended that applications use the POST operation wherever possible because both successful and unsuccessful attempts will be reported to the requestor.

REST-based web services such as the Twitter API consist of three elements:

- **HTTP operation**

   How the request is being transferred to the Twitter API. The transfer operations are GET, POST, PUT, and DELETE, as described earlier, and which operation is appropriate depends on the method being executed. Supplying an incorrect operation will result in an error.

- **Method**

   A URL that points to the location of a resource on Twitter's servers. A list of methods appears in the next section, and Chapter 2 further describes these methods. Methods can also include a number of parameters for customizing requests (for example, returning only a certain number of values) or for supplying update text.

- **Return format**

   The format in which to return data back, which must be supported by that method. Twitter accommodates Extensible Markup Language (XML), JavaScript Object Notation (JSON), Really Simple Syndication (RSS), and Atom return formats depending on the method that has been executed. For example, changing the URL extension of a request from `.xml` to `.json` will adjust the return format.

The Twitter API has many different components. For example, the REST API and Search API include methods for accessing Twitter services (for instance, updating timelines, status data, and user data), for searching timelines and trend data, and for user authentication (see Chapter 3). Three other components of the Twitter API are the

Retweet API (for accessing and creating retweets), the Lists API (for accessing and creating lists), and the Geolocation API (for geotagging tweets). These components are discussed more fully in Chapter 4. Each Twitter API component functions in a similar way, sharing parameter conventions and returning data in standard file formats, which makes each component an intuitive service.

Twitter API Methods

Twitter API Versioning

The Twitter API supports versioning, which means that Twitter will be able to provide beta functionality without compromising stable code. There are currently two method address conventions: one for search methods, http://search.twitter.com/; and one for other methods, https://api.twitter.com/<<version>>/. In the second case, you can replace `<<version>>` with the version number that you intend to use, which should be set to 2 (the latest release version as of this writing). Twitter expects that deprecation between old and new versions will take approximately six months, and so you have plenty of time to update code before changes become permanent.

The official Twitter API documentation groups methods into "categories" which can be identified by the method stub. For example, the `users/show` method is part of the User method category. The method stub will help you translate methods back into the language used by Twitter to describe the methods in their official documentation. Most categories are organized logically and include methods to perform each of the standard CRUD (Create, Read, Update, and Delete) operations. The Search API methods that have the stubs `search` and `trends` use the https://search.twitter.com/ prefix, and all other methods use the https://api.twitter.com/2/ prefix. The Lists API methods have been deliberately excluded here because they use a slightly different structure and are detailed in Chapter 4.

Where methods show an `<<id>>` parameter, this must be replaced with a valid Twitter user identifier, such as a screen name, as explained in the next section. All methods should be appended with a `.<<format>>` to denote which format the method should return.

Accessor Methods

These methods require a `GET` operation for extracting data from Twitter and are split into the following categories:

- **Account methods**

    The `account/rate_limit_status` method returns the number of requests that a user has remaining before his limit is refreshed. At the time of this writing, users had approximately 150 requests available to them per hour. The `account/verify_credentials` method checks whether a user's credentials, in the form of a username and password or OAuth tokens, are valid and returns an error or User object (see Chapter 2) if successful.

- **Block methods**

  The `blocks/blocking` method returns a collection of users that a user has blocked on Twitter. The `blocks/blocking/ids` method returns the same collection of users as the `blocks/blocking` method, although you are given only their user identifiers. The `blocks/exists/<<id>>` method checks whether a specified user has been blocked by the authenticated user.

- **Direct messages methods**

  The `direct_messages` method retrieves a number of messages that a user has received and works alongside the `direct_messages/sent` method, which refers to the messages that the authenticated user has sent.

- **Favorites methods**

  The `favorites` method returns a number of updates that a user has marked as a favorite. Favorites in Twitter are similar to bookmarks in a web browser.

- **Friendships methods**

  The `friendships/exists` method returns a simple true or false if two users are following each other. In addition, the `friendships/show` method can be used to extract more detailed information, such as whether the follow is reciprocated.

- **Help methods**

  The `help/test` method can be used to check whether the Twitter API is up and running and does not count toward a user's rate limit.

- **Saved searches methods**

  The `saved_searches` method returns a list of search terms that the authenticated user has saved. A particular search can be retrieved via the `saved_searches/show/<<id>>` method.

- **Search methods**

  The `search` method is used to perform powerful searches and is covered in detail in Chapter 2.

- **Social graph methods**

  The `followers/ids` and `friends/ids` methods return the identifiers of all the followers and friends a user has. For users with large numbers of connections, this can be iterated over to retrieve them all.

- **Status methods**

  The `statuses/retweets/<<id>>` method retrieves a number of statuses that have "retweeted" the original `<<id>>` update. The `statuses/show/<<id>>` method simply returns the Status object (see Chapter 2) for a given `<<id>>`.

- **Timeline methods**

  The `statuses/friends_timeline`, `statuses/home_timeline`, `statuses/public_timeline` and `statuses/user_timeline` methods return a collection of Status objects (see Chapter 2) for a user's friends, everyone on Twitter, or a specific user. In addition, mentions (updates that reference a particular user) of the authenticated user can be retrieved through the `statuses/mentions` method. Three retweet methods exist and are covered in Chapter 4: `statuses/retweeted_by_me`, `statuses/retweets_of_me`, and `statuses/retweeted_to_me`.

- **Trends methods**

  The `trends` method can be used to return the topics that are currently "trending" on Twitter. To refine this search, you can also use the `trends/current`, `trends/daily`, and `trends/weekly` methods. In addition to these three methods, Twitter has two "local trends" methods—`trends/available` and `trends/location`—which return trends for a given area (for example, the buzz in London or San Francisco).

- **User methods**

  The final set of methods is for returning details about users such as extracting the details of followers (`statuses/followers`) and friends (`statuses/friends`), but also for specific users via the `users/show` and `users/lookup` methods. Twitter enables you to search for users via the `users/search` method, and to access suggested users through the `users/suggestions` and `users/suggestions/<<category>>` methods.

The next group of methods is contained within the same categories but is now for creating, updating, and deleting Twitter data.

Mutator Methods

In addition to the accessor methods described in the preceding section, you might also want to manipulate Twitter data. These methods require a POST operation for mutating Twitter data and are split into the following categories of methods:

- **Account**

  Twitter maintains a concise profile for every user that can be updated via the `account/update_profile` method. This can be used to update their name, description, and location. You can also update colors and images via the `account/update_profile_background`, `account/update_profile_colors`, and `account/update_profile_image` methods. For users who want updates to be sent to their cell phone, you can set the `account/update_delivery_device` method. Finally, for ending a Twitter session, you should use the `account/end_session` method, which logs your user out of your application and Twitter.

- **Block**

  One method exists for blocking nuisance users (`blocks/create/<<id>>`), and another exists for unblocking should a user change his mind (`blocks/destroy/<<id>>`).

- **Direct messages**

  Some applications may want to send or delete messages on behalf of their users. The `direct_messages/destroy/<<id>>` and `direct_messages/new` methods exist for such a use case.

- **Favorites**

  If you want to manage a user's favorite tweets in your application, both the `favorites/create/<<id>>` and `favorites/destroy/<<id>>` methods should come in handy. Simply supplying an `<<id>>` will add or remove a favorite from a user's profile.

- **Friendships**

  For managing a user's friends list, the `friendships/create/<<id>>` and `friendships/destroy/<<id>>` methods are particularly useful for creating and destroying connections. Like the methods for manipulating favorites, all you need to provide is an `<<id>>` of the user to follow or un-follow.

- **Notifications**

  If users request to receive updates to their cell phone, you can use the `notifications/follow/<<id>>` and `notifications/leave/<<id>>` methods to set which friends they receive updates from.

- **Saved searches**

  Users sometimes may want to store frequently requested searches into their profile so that they are easy to access at later dates. The `saved_searches/create` and `saved_searches/destroy/<<id>>` methods make this action seamless.

- **Statuses**

  You can use status methods to create statuses (`statuses/update`) and to delete them (`statuses/destroy/<<id>>`). You can also use a status method to retweet a status (`statuses/retweet/<<id>>`).

Instead of describing each method (and its parameters) in any more detail in this chapter, this discussion will follow an object-oriented approach, describing each return value as an "object" (see Chapter 2). From just the methods listed here, you can perhaps start to understand the size of the Twitter API and get an idea about which methods can be accessed when connecting to the Twitter API later in this chapter. The remainder of this section defines the many parameters available to tailor Twitter API method requests. Some methods require parameters to be set, such as user identifiers or update text, but most do not (and function just fine).

Twitter API Parameters

Parameters are particularly important because they can be used to customize the outputs of requests and they affect data sent to the Twitter API in update, create, or delete operations. Twitter promotes the use of parameters such as `since_id`, `max_id`, and `cursor` in timeline requests to reduce the burden of requests on its servers (not that a full result set does not have to be returned each time the method is executed). You can set parameters by either appending them to the method request if using GET operations such as https://api.twitter.com/1/users/show.xml?id=markhawker and by adding additional parameters separated by an ampersand (&) or by including them within POST, PUT, or DELETE operations. The following section explores both approaches.

Coverage and Deprecation

Not all parameters are available for each of the Twitter API methods and may change over time. Chapter 2 covers each parameter in detail. Parameters for the Lists API are defined in Chapter 4 because this is a newer component that uses different naming conventions.

The Twitter API uses UTF-8 character encoding for all parameters, which means that special characters such as the ampersand (&) and equals (=) characters must be encoded before being sent to Twitter. Most programming languages contain functions for performing this conversion for you; for example, `htmlentities()`. Encoding special characters will take up more storage than a single-byte character, which means that some requests may be rejected if they are over Twitter's 140-character limit. A list of the most popular parameters that you can use when interacting with the Twitter API have been gathered and categorized into parameters that affect input and parameters that affect output. Parameters that can be used in both Search API methods and in other Twitter API methods are denoted by an asterisk (*) character, whereas parameters exclusive to the Search API are denoted by a caret (^) character.

Parameters Affecting Input

These parameters affect data that is sent to the Twitter API:

- `description, email, location, name, url`

  These parameters can be any set of alphanumeric characters and should be limited to a maximum length of 20, 40, 100, 30, and 160 characters, respectively. The `email` parameter must be a valid e-mail address.

- `follow`

  Boolean `true` or `false` parameter used when you want to enable notifications for a target user and to follow that user.

- `image`

  Used for setting a user's profile image or background and requires multipart form data rather than a URL or raw image bytes. The content-type must be a valid GIF, JPEG, or PNG image. In addition size restrictions apply: < 2,048 pixels and 800KB for backgrounds and < 500 pixels and 700KB for profile images.

- `in_reply_to_status_id`

  Used for associating a mention with an original status. If the identifier is not valid, or not the username mentioned within the update, the parameter is just ignored.

- **lat, long**

  The latitude and longitude of the update, which must be a number set within the range `-90.0` to `+90.0`, and where north and east are positive. These parameters are ignored if outside that range, if not a number, if `geo_enabled` is disabled, or if they are not sent in pairs.

- **profile_background_color, profile_link_color, profile_ sidebar_border_color, profile_sidebar_fill_color, profile_text_color**

  Used for setting a user's profile colors and must be set to a valid hexadecimal value. Values may be either three or six characters in length; for example, `fff` and `ffffff` are equivalents for the color white. You do not need to include the hash (#) character when using this parameter.

- **query**

  The saved search query that the user would like to save.

- **source**

  To help users identify which tool has published a tweet, Twitter has provided this parameter, which can contain a short string for identifying your application. The parameter will be returned as a URL-encoded string containing a hyperlink to your application. Applications that use OAuth have this parameter set by default.

- **status, text**

  Used for setting a user's status or within a direct message. To avoid truncation, the string of text should be within 140 characters when encoded.

- **tile**

  Boolean parameter used to set whether a profile background image should be "tiled" onscreen. Otherwise, it will remain in a fixed position in the top-left corner of a profile page.

Parameters That Affect Output

These parameters affect data requested from the Twitter API:

- **callback***

  For client-side JSON requests, the `callback` parameter can be set to a JavaScript function name, which will automatically be sent the return data to parse.

- **count, page*, rpp^**

  Twitter imposes pagination limits, but you can combine `count` and `page` parameters to retrieve the maximum number of results. For example, by setting `count` to `100`, you can iterate through pages `1–32` to extract all available status updates. Note that the `page` parameter begins with `1`, not `0`. These parameters are scheduled to be deprecated in favor of cursor-based pagination. The `rpp` parameter is specific to the Search API and is akin to the `count` parameter. The default is `15`, but this can be increased to 100 entries.

You can use the page parameter in conjunction with rpp to extract the maximum number of results, which is currently 1,500. If you exceed Twitter's pagination limits, an empty result set will be returned. Currently, the Search API will return results up to 1.5 weeks in the past, but this might increase or decrease in the future as the number of updates per day continues to increase. These parameters are set to be replaced by the cursor parameter.

- **cursor**

  Setting a cursor breaks requests into "pages," each with 100 results. Providing a value of -1 begins paging, and the Twitter API will then return next_cursor and previous_cursor parameters within responses so that you can "scroll" through requests. Twitter also returns next_cursor_str and previous_cursor_str, which are the string-based equivalents of the next and previous integers.

- **geocode^**

  For returning updates within a given radius (mi or km) of a latitude/longitude in the format latitude,longitude,radius. Remember to URL-encode commas (,) to code %2C.

- **id, user, user_a, user_b**

  When referencing a user, the id parameter can be set to either the integer user_id or alphanumeric screen_name of a user or an integer identifier of a valid status, direct message, or saved search.

- **lang^, locale^**

  To search for updates in languages other than English, use this parameter along with the country's two-letter ISO 639-1 code.

- **lat, long**

  The latitude and longitude of the location to return trending topics for which must be a number set within the range -90.0 to +90.0, where north and east are positive.

- **max_id*, since_id***

  An integer used to return status updates or direct messages that have identifiers greater or less than that integer. For example, to show all statuses published more recently than a particular status, say 12345, you set the since_id to 12345. However, if you want to show all of the statuses that were posted before that particular status, you set the max_id to 12345 instead.

- **per_page**

  An integer used to control the number of results returned when searching for users. This must be less than 20.

- **q***

  The search query or username to be requested, which must be URL-encoded and no larger than 140 characters.

- **screen_name, source_screen_name, target_screen_name**

  The "friendly" alphanumeric name or username of a Twitter user, which is not the same as a user_id, but it is possible that a screen_name may contain just numeric characters. In this case, the screen_name parameter would be set to distinguish it from a user_id. For example, a valid screen_name may be 1234567890, which could also be interpreted by Twitter as a valid user_id value.

- **show_user^**

  When set to true, this parameter is used to prefix updates with <user>: for readers that do not display Atom's author element. The default value for this parameter is false.

- **source_id, target_id, user_id**

  The numeric identifier for a user, which remains fixed, unlike the screen_name parameter, which can be changed by the user. It is recommended that you work with and store this parameter rather than screen_name for your applications.

- **woeid**

  For retrieving location-specific trending topics, a Where on Earth IDentifier (WOEID) is required.

The final part of this section looks at the return formats accepted by the Twitter API. With this final piece of knowledge, you can start accessing and interacting with the Twitter API to retrieve data.

Twitter API Return Formats

For successful requests, you should expect the Twitter API to return data back in the format that you requested. The Twitter API supports four MIME types for formatting returned data:

- **JSON**

  JavaScript Object Notation is a lightweight data-interchange format favored in AJAX applications and is considered a simpler and faster alternative to XML. Defined in a structured format, JSON is object based, and simple text can be used to represent many different data types and relationships. It is the favored MIME type of the twitter-async client library, which is used throughout Chapters 2, 3, and 4. JSON is the only data format supported by all the Twitter API methods, and so it's particularly important for you to understand it.

- **RSS and Atom**

  Really Simple Syndication is a standard form of XML commonly used on blogs and news sites. Atom was created as an alternative to RSS to accommodate some of the flaws in the RSS protocol and to improve international support. Both RSS and Atom are used to accommodate people who want to "subscribe" to Twitter information streams, such as the public timeline or a particular user's timeline.

- **XML**

  Extensible Markup Language is a general-purpose language for specifying custom markup languages. The language is extensible in that users can define their own tags and structure. XML is used to structure data in a way that separates content from presentation: a guiding principle of Web 2.0.

Not all methods support all of these data formats. Support for each of the methods will be clearly identified as you explore the Twitter API in more detail in Chapter 2. As a comparison to XML, JSON returns a set of "key/value" pairs nested within curly braces. For example, using the `users/show` method with the `screen_name` parameter set to "markhawker" with JSON output would produce the following, which has been snipped for brevity because we're just comparing the two formats:

```
{
 "screen_name":"markhawker", ..., "status":{
 "text":"Testing JSON and XML output formats.", ... }
}
```

Whereas the same `users/show` request in XML would produce the following:

```
<user>
 <screen_name>markhawker</screen_name>
 ...
 <status>
 <text>Testing JSON and XML output formats.</text>
 ...
 </status>
</user>
```

As you can see, the two formats are comparable and return exactly the same data. It is easy to "translate" JSON into a PHP object by using the `json_decode()` function, which can then be manipulated in your applications. This complexity is handled for you if you choose to use the twitter-async client library, which handles JSON responses by default. The basics of the Atom file format are described in Chapter 2 when interacting with the Search API, although it is not a requirement to use the format at all (because JSON is supported by all Twitter API methods).

Accessing the Twitter API

Most Twitter API requests require user authentication to access data that is not otherwise open to the public, such as direct messages or favorites, and to control Twitter rate limiting. Historically, Twitter has implemented Basic Authentication, whereby user credentials in the form of a username and password combination are sent in the header of a request. Although this method is easy to use, it is prone to security risks, even if sent over a secure connection, due to usernames and passwords being transferred across the Internet. A better, and safer, method that which implements open authentication (OAuth) has been developed (see Chapter 3).

Authorized Connections

The "Connections" tab inside a Twitter profile lists OAuth applications that users have authorized on their Twitter account. From there, users can choose the "Revoke Access" option to de-authorize unwanted applications.

Twitter has not set a deadline for deprecating Basic Authentication, but it is only a matter of time. For this reason, it is important that you get to grips with OAuth as soon as possible. You can enable Basic Authentication by either typing the methods into your browser's address bar or by using a command-line application known as cURL. For production applications, you will require something more sophisticated, and so this section also details how to make Twitter API requests using a client library called twitter-async. If you intend to use another client library or programming language, the platform-independence of cURL should help guide you more than being taught how to interact with the Twitter API using a specific programming language. The elegance and simplicity of twitter-async makes it a great choice for developing Twitter applications from the ground up.

cURL

The cURL application provides a way of accessing URL resources from the command line and functions much like a text-based web browser. If cURL is not already installed on your computer, you can download it for free from http://curl.haxx.se/download.html for almost any operating system. If you download the version with Secure Sockets Layer (SSL), you need to ensure that all the necessary files are included in the package. You can find whether you have all the necessary files by navigating to the directory where you have saved the cURL files and trying to run the command `curl`. If you get the following response, you've succeeded:

```
curl: try "curl --help" or "curl --manual" for more information
```

If you get an error response saying that your operating system was unable to find a specified component, it is recommend that you try another download source (of which there are usually multiple sources for each version of cURL). Alternatively, search for the component online or check the cURL FAQ (http://curl.haxx.se/docs/faq.html). You can also run any of the method URLs directly from your web browser, although it is recommended that you change the file format from JSON to XML because browsers display XML more elegantly inline. The web method works only for accessor methods, those that pull data from Twitter, and cannot be used for actions such as creating tweets or sending direct messages, which is why cURL is recommended.

If you are happy to try out cURL, here are some useful commands to help you interact with the Twitter REST API from the command line:

- `curl`

   After you have navigated to the directory where you installed cURL, you can use this command in the command line to initiate a cURL request.

- `-A "Name Of Your User Agent"`

  This is used to set the user agent of the request. Twitter requires that you set this parameter so requests can be attributed to particular applications and debugged by the applications' respective programmers.

- `-d`

  The `-d` switch is used to send unencoded data via POST. If you want to send a POST request without parameters, just use `-d ""`.

- `--data-urlencode "status=Hello, world."`

  The `--data-urlencode` switch is used to send URL-encoded messages—ones including special characters and spaces—via a POST request.

- `-G`

  The `-G` switch is used to send `-d` data as a GET request so that parameters can be set in the same way as in the switches described earlier (instead of appending them to method URLs).

- `-H "Expect:"`

  The Twitter API may reject some cURL requests because it sometimes sets the header parameter to `Expect: 100-continue`. This needs to be set to an empty field to be valid.

- `-k`

  You might receive an error message when using the `https://` prefix with requests stating that the "certificate verify failed." This verification process can be disabled by supplying the `-k` switch.

- `-u <<username>>:<<password>>`

  Used for authentication where `<<username>>` can be a Twitter `screen_name`, `id` or `email`, and `<<password>>`. Although cURL provides some security when sending these details across the network, they might not be 100% secure. Using cURL with SSL will help reduce the risk of a third-party phishing your Twitter credentials.

- `-v`

  Standing for verbose, this command-line switch will return the full HTTP headers and additional server debugging information (for example, port names, user agent, and cookie details).

As an example, you can run the following via cURL to display the public timeline (which does not require authentication):

```
curl -k https://api.twitter.com/2/statuses/public_timeline.xml
```

Returning the timeline of your followers requires user authentication. Remembering to replace <<username>>:<<password>> with your actual username and password, try the following:

```
curl -k -u <<username>>:<<password>>
https://api.twitter.com/2/statuses/home_timeline.xml
```

Getting more complex, to post an update which requires user authentication and a status parameter using a POST request, try this:

```
curl -k -u <<username>>:<<password>> --data-urlencode "status=Testing updating my
status with cURL."
https://api.twitter.com/2/statuses/update.xml
```

In addition to using the cURL command-line function, code examples using the twitter-async client library are provided in the next section to hint at how the Twitter API functions inside a programming language such as PHP.

Twitter-async

You can download the twitter-async client library, which requires PHP 5.2+, from http://github.com/jmathai/twitter-async. It contains just three files, enabling you to execute (a)synchronous calls to the Twitter API using Basic Authentication or OAuth. The asynchronous element of twitter-async means that multiple requests can be executed in parallel, instead of waiting idly for them to be executed serially (for example, sending multiple direct messages to a number of followers and then returning the results of each back to the client application). The simplest twitter-async application you can make is one that makes an unauthenticated call to the Twitter API, such as retrieving search trends:

```
$twitter = new EpiTwitter();
$trends = $twitter->get_trends();
echo $trends->responseText;
```

The preceding code shows the creation of the $twitter object, which is one of three methods of initiating a request. The second is Basic Authentication, which is achieved by supplying username and password parameters within the request. For example:

```
$user = $twitter->get_basic("/account/verify_credentials.json", null, "username",
"password");
```

The third method is using OAuth, discussed in detail in Chapter 3, which is the use of a consumer key and consumer secret. The EpiTwitter object that was just created has only two methods, one of which is constructing it! The second is executing the Twitter API methods, which use the following naming convention:

- The operation in lowercase, such as get, post, or delete, plus an underscore (_). Operations that end in _basic are specifically for Basic Authentication or no authentication and must not be used for OAuth.

- The path to the Twitter API method that is in lowercase except for when there needs to be a forward slash (/), which is denoted by a capital letter (for example, usersShow). Underscores must be retained where appropriate, such as in the account/verify_credentials method.
- Parameters can be added by including an array inside the request, as follows: usersShow(array("screen_name" => "markhawker")).

For example, the account/verify_credentials method can be called by using the following:

```
$response = $twitter->get_basic("account/verify_credentials.json",
null, <<username>>, <<password>>);
```

Or, if you are using OAuth, you could use this:

```
$response = $twitter->get_accountVerify_credentials();
```

The client library also supports image uploading and exposing response headers, and it provides additional functionality for exception handling. The following code can be used to initiate the twitter-async library, assuming that it is stored within a directory called twitter-async, which should be above your test page, which can be saved as index.php:

```
<?php
require_once "twitter-async/EpiCurl.php";
require_once "twitter-async/EpiOAuth.php";
require_once "twitter-async/EpiTwitter.php";
$username = "INSERT YOUR TWITTER USERNAME"; // Edit Me
$password = "INSERT YOUR TWITTER PASSWORD"; // Edit Me
$twitter = new EpiTwitter();
try {
 $response = $twitter->get_basic("/account/verify_credentials.json",
 null, $username, $password);
 if($response->code == 200) {
   echo "<p>Username: ".$response->screen_name."</p>";
   echo "<p>Description: ".$response->description."</p>";
 }
}
catch(EpiTwitterException $e){ echo $e->getMessage(); exit; }
catch(Exception $e) { echo $e->getMessage(); exit; }
?>
```

The preceding code uses Basic Authentication, which you can replace with OAuth code after reading through Chapter 3. You should replace the $username and $password parameters with your own Twitter credentials. The example shows how a GET request can be initiated using your Twitter credentials and how exceptions can be handled. If the request for verifying a user's credentials is successful, a status code 200 will be returned along with a User object (see Chapter 2), which is why you can extract their screen_name and description. With a verified account, you can then extend the example index.php file to also retrieve a user's latest friends by using the following:

```
1  echo "<h1>Latest Friends</h1>";
2  echo "<ul>";
3  $friends = $twitter->get_basic("/statuses/friends.json", null,
   $username, $password);
4  foreach($friends as $friend) {
5    echo "<li>".$friend->screen_name.": ".$friend->status->text."</li>";
6  }
7  echo "</ul>";
```

Another way to access the $friends details is to use a for() loop and access each friend using $friends[$i]["screen_name"], ensuring that your counter is set to $i. Notice that you can also extract a user's status via the embedded Status object accessible via $friend->status->text. The second parameter for this example was set to null, but you could also insert an array containing the parameters that you want to set. If you want to extract all the user's friends, you must set "cursoring" by adding array("cursor" => -1) and then extracting the value of the next cursor and rerunning the request:

```
1  echo "<h1>All Friends</h1>";
2  echo "<ul>";
3  $cursor = -1;
4  do {
5    $friends = $twitter->get_basic("/statuses/friends.json",
     array("cursor" => $cursor), $username, $password);
6    foreach($friends->users as $friend) {
7      echo "<li>".$friend->screen_name.": ".$friend->status->text."</li>";
8    }
9    $cursor = $friends->next_cursor_str;
10 } while ($cursor > 0);
11 echo "</ul>";
```

This do-while() loop initiates cursoring on Line 3 and then proceeds to return friends' details until the cursor returns 0, which means that all the user's friends have been returned. The foreach() loop should also be updated to replace $friends with $friends->users because cursoring places subsequent results within an array called users. A final example uses the asynchronous capabilities of twitter-async, which delays accessing results from requests for as long as possible. This might prove useful if you want to update a number of user accounts simultaneously or send multiple direct messages:

```
$twitter->useAsynchronous(true);
$users = array("user1", "user2", "user3", "user4"); // Edit Me
$responses = array();
foreach($users as $user) {
  $responses[] = $twitter->post_basic("/direct_messages/new.json",
```

```
    array("user" => $user, "text" => "Hey, {$user}. What's up?"),
    $username, $password);
}
echo "<h1>Direct Messages</h1>";
echo "<ul>";
foreach($responses as $response) {
  echo "<li>Direct Message: {$response->id}</li>";
}
echo "</ul>";
```

This code, alongside the other elements of `index.php`, should be uploaded to your web server. You'll need all this in Chapter 2 when you experiment with more of the Twitter API methods.

Twitter API Rate Limiting

Rate limiting is Twitter's way of controlling and regulating access to their servers, to provide equitable performance to all application developers and users. You may have seen the Fail Whale when you tried to access Twitter on the Web, and perhaps you've also seen "Rate Limit Exceeded" errors appearing on third-party applications that you may be using to access Twitter. This was their server's way of saying they were overcapacity and needed a brief pause for breath.

Two different limits apply to the number of requests per hour made to the Twitter API. For the Twitter API, the default rate is 150 requests per hour, through a mixture of account- and IP-based rate limiting. Therefore, if you reach the Twitter API limit on one third-party application, other applications will also be subject to that limit. In which case, you should access your account through the Twitter web client until your limits have been reset. The Search API is limited by IP address, but the rate limits are considered sufficient to not warrant a number being released on the number of requests per hour.

> ### POST and GET Rate Limiting
> Rate limiting affects only methods that request information via a GET request. This means that methods that use the POST, PUT, or DELETE requests to submit, update, or delete data (such as tweets) are not affected. Requests to the `account/rate_limit_status` method to check limit status are not charged, to provide developers access to how many free requests a user has.

If you think your application might exceed those rate limits—for instance, if you intend to send out multiple messages or tweets—you can request to be "whitelisted" by filling out a request form (http://twitter.com/help/request_whitelisting) to increase your limits to 20,000 requests per hour. This process may take up to a week, but you will receive confirmation from the Twitter team if you have been whitelisted. Applications that repeatedly abuse their rate limits can also be "blacklisted" and are required to e-mail Twitter Support with further details as to why they keep reaching the limits. You can avoid the rate limiter in several ways, including caching results, prioritizing active users, and reducing the number of times a particular search is requested.

Twitter API Error Handling

For error handling, methods that require a particular request will return a meaningful status code indicating whether the request was successful or not. If you've ever encountered a "404 – Page Not Found" or a "501 – Internal Server Error," you've experienced status codes. These are just fancy "user-friendly" ways to present a status code error back to the browser in a meaningful way. The Twitter API uses a similar method of returning response codes and friendly error messages should a problem arise with a request.

Twitter uses the following three-digit codes to report whether a request was successful and provides a description of the error encountered within a construct known as a Hash object (see Chapter 2), which is a simple structure containing the error code and a description from the Twitter API:

- **200 – OK**

  Your request was successful, and so you should receive back exactly what you requested from the Twitter API in the data format that you specified.

- **304 – Not Modified**

  There was no new data to return, and so you already have the most up-to-date data. This will occur if you make a request to a timeline in a period sooner than once per minute.

- **400 – Bad Request**

  The request was invalid. This could be because a method that required parameters may have been missed, formatted incorrectly, or a rate limit has been exceeded.

- **401 – Not Authorized**

  Authentication failed for the user details you provided. This means that a password has been supplied incorrectly. Check that it is correct and try again.

- **403 – Forbidden**

  The request was understood, but it was refused. Check the returned error text for an explanation. This may be due to rate limits being reached.

- **404 – Not Found**

  The method URL requested is invalid or does not exist.

- **406 – Not Acceptable**

  The method was formatted incorrectly when being requested from the Search API. Check that you have properly encoded the URL.

- **500 – Internal Server Error, 502 – Bad Gateway, 503 – Service Unavailable**

  Something is broken with Twitter; try again later. It may be that it is down or being upgraded, or perhaps its servers are overloaded with requests.

As an example, Twitter API error messages are returned in the requested format with an error message. For example, an XML error may look like this:

```
<?xml version="1.0" encoding="UTF-8"?>
<hash>
 <request>/direct_messages/destroy/456.xml</request>
 <error>No direct message with that ID found.</error>
</hash>
```

When you are using twitter-async, you can retrieve an error message from a response by using the `$response->code` and `$response->error` variables to return both the status code and error message, respectively. It is assumed that any request that does not return a status code 200 will need to be reformatted and requested again. This model makes it simple to enclose a request within a conditional statement to test for this occurrence. You can then choose whether to return this error message directly back to users or return a meaningful response indicating that they must resubmit their request. The most common error message will be that a rate limit will have been exceeded, and so sending a request for this data before submitting the response may be preferable, storing a cached value for the number of remaining requests for the duration of the session so that it is not being requested each time.

Summary

This chapter provided an overview of the Twitter API and its many methods, parameters, and return formats. Two tools that you can use to access the Twitter API were described: a command-line tool, cURL; and a PHP client library called twitter-async, which is used throughout Chapters 2, 3, and 4. This chapter also briefly explained how Twitter handles errors by returning meaningful status codes with requests, which you can use to either manipulate the data or manage a failed request. The next chapter identifies the types of data you can expect to retrieve from the Twitter API, including user data and status updates.

2

Diving Into the Twitter API Methods

Chapter 1, "Working with the Twitter API," explored the Twitter application programming interface and provided essential information you need when interacting with the Twitter API, such as return formats and response codes. The Twitter API is split into several method categories, but these are grouped together in this chapter, except for the Retweet API, Lists API, and Geolocation API (which are explored in Chapter 4, "Extending the Twitter API: Retweets, Lists, and Location"). The Twitter API contains a number of methods, including ones for sending updates, direct messages, following and unfollowing users, and account management. The Search API contains methods for extracting search and trend information from Twitter as a means of filtering, finding, and sorting the huge volumes of data.

This chapter explores the numerous Twitter API methods in detail, illustrating them using an object-oriented approach focusing on their return values, and giving examples of each alongside sample output and source code. You can test the examples using the command-line cURL interface or via twitter-async, as described in Chapter 1. If you do not want to use cURL, you can access many of the Twitter API methods directly via the Twitter web interface by typing the commands into your web browser's address bar and providing your Twitter username and password when prompted.

Twitter API Methods

Beware, Deprecation!

As the Twitter API evolves, you may find that some attributes become deprecated. Instead of removing the attributes from their outputs, Twitter will set them to `null` where applicable. There is also the possibility that methods will become deprecated, which will result in an error being returned for method calls.

To understand the methods that the Twitter API provides in conjunction with the parameters described in Chapter 1, it is important to explore the various outputs that you can expect when interacting with the service. These return "objects" include several useful pieces of data about a status or direct message, a user, or even an error or simple Twitter response. There are eight main objects in the Twitter API:

- User objects
- Status objects
- Direct Message objects
- Saved Search objects
- ID objects
- Relationship objects
- Response objects
- Hash objects

Alongside sample XML responses for each of these methods to illustrate these return objects, a form of UML (Universal Modeling Language, a universal language and diagramming technique) is used to illustrate these return objects and the methods that can be used to expose them. Figure 2.1 provides an example of an object and the conventions that have been adopted in this chapter.

Object Name
+Attribute 1: Type +Attribute 2: Type #Attribute 3: Type
+<<HTTP_REQUEST>> Method 1(Parameter 1:Type,   Parameter 2:Type=20): Return File Format -<<HTTP_REQUEST>> Method 2(): Return File Format

Figure 2.1   Skeleton that will be used to
describe Twitter API objects.

Several conventions have been adopted to fit in with the nature of the Twitter API, as follows:

- Objects are divided into three "compartments": a class name; attributes, which include types such as `integer`, `string`, or `true`/`false` Boolean values (and attributes can also be other objects; for example, in some instances, a User object also includes a Status object); and operations or methods, which will return back that object.

- `#element` defines a protected element that requires user authentication for it to be returned (for example, when users have protected their status). Methods denoted with a hash (#) character mean that they can be executed without authentication but may not return all values.

- `-method` defines a private method that must be executed with user authentication or will fail and return an error Hash object.

- `+method` defines a public method that does not require any user authentication to return all data.

- `<<HTTP_OPERATION>>` denotes what operation is required by the method, which can be one of GET, POST, PUT, or DELETE.

- Parameters are enclosed in brackets, and default values are identified with an equals (=) character. For example, `count=20` means that the default value for the `count` parameter is `20`. So, if the parameter is omitted, 20 values will be returned.

- Return formats appear after the method name and colon (:) and must be set to one of `json`, `xml`, `atom`, or `rss`.

For each of the Twitter API objects, you'll see an illustration of the object, a description, and example of what values to expect back from the service. In Chapter 1, a sample file was created, `index.php`, which is extended in this chapter with more calls to the Twitter API.

User Objects

User objects (see Figure 2.2) are full of interesting data about an individual or a set of individuals when wrapped inside a `users` array, such as when using `statuses/friends` or `blocks/blocking` methods. With any of the methods that use cursors for pagination, you should expect the return format to look like the following skeleton code block, which includes a collection of User objects plus indicators of the values of the next and previous cursors, which can be used to retrieve subsequent results:

```
<users_list>
 <users type="array">...</users>
 <next_cursor>...</next_cursor>
 <previous_cursor>...</previous_cursor>
</users_list>
```

User objects are also embedded within Status objects to help reduce the number of calls made to the Twitter API. In this instance, they do not contain the embedded Status object as shown above. In Direct Message objects, there are also `sender` and `recipient` objects that are exactly the same as User objects but without the embedded Status object, which is why it defaults to a `null` value.

```
                              User
+created_at: Date
+description: String
+favourites_count: Integer
+followers_count: Integer
+following: Boolean = null
+friends_count: Integer
+geo_enabled: Boolean = false
+id: Integer
+location: String
+name: String
+notifications: Boolean = null
+profile_background_color: String
+profile_background_image_url: String
+profile_background_title: Boolean
+profile_image_url: String
+profile_link_color: String
+profile_sidebar_border_color: String
+profile_sidebar_fill_color: String
+profile_text_color: String
+protected: Boolean
+screen_name: String
#status: Status = null
+statuses_count: Integer
+time_zone: String
+url: String
+utc_offset: String
+verified: Boolean = false
--<<GET>> account/verify_credentials(): json/xml
--<<GET>> blocks/blocking(page:Integer): json/xml
--<<GET>> blocks/exists/<<id>>(): json/xml
--<<GET>> statuses/followers(cursor:Integer,
                  id:String,screen_name:String,
                  user_id:Integer): json/xml
--<<GET>> statuses/friends(cursor:Integer,
                  id:String,screen_name:String,
                  user_id:Integer): json/xml
#<<GET>> users/lookup(screen_name:String,
                  user_id:Integer): json/xml
#<<GET>> users/search(page:Integer,per_page:Integer=20,
                  q:String): json/xml
#<<GET>> users/show(id:String,screen_name:String,
                  user_id:Integer): json/xml
--<<POST>> account/update_delivery_device(device:String): json/xml
--<<POST>> account/update_profile(description:String,
                        email:String,
                        location:String,
                        name:String,
                        url:String): json/xml
--<<POST>> account/update_profile_background_image(image:Image,
                        tile:Boolean=false): json/xml
--<<POST>> account/update_profile_colors(profile_background_color:String,
                        profile_link_color:String,
                        profile_sidebar_border_color:String,
                        profile_sidebar_fill_color:String,
                        profile_text_color:String): json/xml
--<<POST>> account/update_profile_image(image:Image): json/xml
--<<POST>> blocks/create/<<id>>(): json/xml
--<<POST>> friendships/create/<<id>>(follow:Boolean): json/xml
--<<POST>> notifications/follow/<<id>>(): json/xml
--<<POST>> notifications/leave/<<id>>(): json/xml
--<<POST>> report_spam(id:String,screen_name:String,
                  user_id:Integer): json/xml
--<<POST/DELETE>> blocks/destroy/<<id>>(): json/xml
--<<POST/DELETE>> friendships/destroy/<<id>>(): json/xml
```

Figure 2.2   Twitter API User object including Status object.

An example of a User object returned by requesting the
https://api.twitter.com/1/users/show.xml?id=markhawker method currently contains the
following keys and values in XML:

```
<user>
 <id>15397909</id>
 <name>Mark Hawker</name>
 <screen_name>markhawker</screen_name>
 <location>West Yorkshire, United Kingdom</location>
 <description>Health informatics researcher and social application
  developer. Creator of @omnee.</description>
 <profile_image_url>http://a3.twimg.com/profile_images/
 234974305/me_normal.jpg</profile_image_url>
 <url>http://markhawker.tumblr.com/</url>
 <protected>false</protected>
 <followers_count>1139</followers_count>
 <profile_background_color>001313</profile_background_color>
```

```
<profile_text_color>00131e</profile_text_color>
<profile_link_color>1d8395</profile_link_color>
<profile_sidebar_fill_color>e3f0f2</profile_sidebar_fill_color>
<profile_sidebar_border_color>1d8395</profile_sidebar_border_color>
<friends_count>185</friends_count>
<created_at>Fri Jul 11 23:02:14 +0000 2008</created_at>
<favourites_count>131</favourites_count>
<utc_offset>0</utc_offset>
<time_zone>London</time_zone>
<profile_background_image_url>http://a3.twimg.com/profile_background_
images/35364101/collage.gif</profile_background_image_url>
<profile_background_tile>true</profile_background_tile>
<statuses_count>13859</statuses_count>
<notifications/>
<geo_enabled>false</geo_enabled>
<verified>false</verified>
<following/>
<status>...</status>
</user>
```

Notice the Status object that is returned inside the `status` element for all nonpro-tected accounts, and keys, such as `<notifications/>`, which contain no data and use a shorthand opening and closing tag. The `created_at` key is used to show when an individual first started using Twitter. In this case, it was on July 11, 2008. By default, the majority of methods will return 100 users per page, so the `cursor` parameter is required to return details of all followers. Here are two examples using the twitter-async library and the sample code created in Chapter 1:

```
$user = $twitter->get_basic("/users/show.json", array("screen_name" =>
"markhawker"), $username, $password);
// $user = $twitter->get_usersShow(array("screen_name" => "markhawker"),
$username, $password);
$followers = $twitter->get_basic("/statuses/followers.json",
array("cursor" => -1, "screen_name" => "markhawker"), $username,
$password);
// $followers = $twitter->get_statusesFollowers(
array("cursor" => -1, "screen_name" => "markhawker"), $username,
$password);
```

If successful, each request should return a User object or an array of User objects, which can be accessed using a `foreach($followers->users as $follower)` or `for()` loop. Note that there are two distinct ways of forming the queries using either `get_basic()` or by using the Twitter API method name in the name itself, which will return equivalent results. In some instances, you might want to use the longhand version to extract data other than in JSON format. From the `$followers` data, the relevant `next_cursor_str` and `previous_cursor_str` parameters can be retrieved by using `$followers->next_cursor_str` or `$followers->previous_cursor_str`, respectively, which was demonstrated in Chapter 1. Each element of the `$user` can be accessed by using `$user->` followed by the name of the element; for example, `$user->id` or `$user->friends_count`. If you want to access the Status object, you just use `$user->status->id`, where the `id` field can be replaced by any of the elements contained within the Status object (as described in the following section).

The two variants to these methods are the `users/suggestions` and `users/suggestions/<<category>>` methods, which were not included in Figure 2.2. They can be used to access Twitter's suggested user lists—such as users who are recommended from Business, Health, or Technology categories—and can be accessed as follows:

```
$users = get_basic("/users/suggestions/health.json", null, $username,
$password);
echo "<ul>";
foreach($users->users as $user) {
 echo "<li>".$user->screen_name."</li>";
}
echo "</ul>";
```

If you are unsure of category names, you can use the `users/suggestions` method to extract a list of categories and their associated "slugs," which you can then use in the `users/suggestions/<<category>>` method.

Status Objects

Status objects (see Figure 2.3) contain data about the user's latest status update as well as geolocation data, which is explored in Chapter 4. The `truncated` key denotes that a status update was larger than the 140-character limit imposed by Twitter and has been truncated. The `favorited` key denotes whether the authenticated user has bookmarked that update, which can be accessed using any of the `favorites` methods. Other information contained within Status objects is the `source` of the update and information as to whether it was also a mention.

Each Status object contains a User object minus its nested Status object. Multiple Status objects are enclosed inside a `statuses` array and can be accessed in the same way as the collection of User objects. An example of a Status object returned by requesting the https://api.twitter.com/2/statuses/show.xml?id=5327214528 method currently contains the following keys and values in XML:

```
<status>
 <created_at>Sun Nov 01 01:08:45 +0000 2009</created_at>
 <id>5327214528</id>
 <text>Now, I really must sleep. Good night.</text>
 <source><a href="http://mobileways.de/gravity" rel="nofollow">
 Gravity</a></source>
 <truncated>false</truncated>
 <in_reply_to_status_id/>
 <in_reply_to_user_id/>
```

```
<favorited>false</favorited>
<in_reply_to_screen_name/>
<geo/>
<user>...</user>
</status>
```

```
+-----------------------------------------------------------------+
|                            Status                               |
+-----------------------------------------------------------------+
| +created_at: Date                                               |
| +favorited: Boolean                                             |
| +geo: String                                                    |
| +id: Integer                                                    |
| +in_reply_to_screen_name: String                               |
| +in_reply_to_status_id:Integer                                 |
| +in_reply_to_user_id: String                                   |
| +source: String                                                 |
| +text: String                                                   |
| +truncated: Boolean                                             |
| +user: User = null                                              |
+-----------------------------------------------------------------+
| #<<GET>> favorites(id:String,page:Integer): atom/json/rss/xml   |
| -<<GET>> statuses/friends_timeline(count: Integer=20,           |
|                             max_id:Integer,                     |
|                             page:Integer,                       |
|                             since_id:Integer): atom/json/rss/xml|
| -<<GET>> statuses/home_timeline(count:Integer=20,               |
|                            max_id:Integer,                      |
|                            page:Integer,                        |
|                            since_id:Integer): atom/json/rss/xml |
| -<<GET>> statuses/mentions(count:Integer=20,                    |
|                       max_id:Integer,                           |
|                       page:Integer,since_id:Integer): atom/json/rss/xml|
| +<<GET>> statuses/public_timeline(): atom/json/rss/xml          |
| -<<GET>> statuses/retweeted_by_me(count:Integer=20,             |
|                             max_id:Integer,                     |
|                             page:Integer                        |
|                             since_id:Integer): atom/json/rss/xml|
| -<<GET>> statuses/retweets_of_me(count:Integer=20,              |
|                            max_id:Integer,                      |
|                            page:Integer                         |
|                            since_id:Integer): atom/json/rss/xml |
| -<<GET>> statuses/retweeted_to_me(count:Integer=20,             |
|                             max_id:Integer,                     |
|                             page:Integer                        |
|                             since_id:Integer): atom/json/rss/xml|
| -<<GET>> statuses/retweets(count:Integer,                       |
|                       id:Integer): json/xml                     |
| #<<GET>> statuses/show/<<id>>(): json/xml                       |
| -<<GET>> statuses/user_timeline(id:String,                      |
|                            screen_name:String,                  |
|                            user_id,count:Integer=20,            |
|                            max_id:Integer,                      |
|                            page:Integer,                        |
|                            since_id:Integer): atom/json/rss/xml |
| -<<POST>> favorites/create/<<id>>(): json/xml                   |
| -<<POST>> statuses/update(in_reply_to_status_id:Integer,        |
|                      lat:String,long:String,                    |
|                      status:String): json/xml                   |
| -<<POST/DELETE>> favorites/destroy/<<id>>(): json/xml           |
| -<<POST/DELETE>> statuses/destroy/<<id>>(): json/xml            |
| -<<POST/PUT>> statuses/retweet/<<id>>(): json/xml               |
+-----------------------------------------------------------------+
```

Figure 2.3   Twitter API Status object including User and Retweet objects.

You will notice that within some Status objects (such as the statuses/home_timeline method, which replaces the deprecated statuses/friends_timeline) there are Retweet objects denoting that a particular status was retweeted. These are explained in more detail in Chapter 4. Like User objects, these may not be included in all situations, and so they may be null or unavailable. Here is an example using the twitter-async library to update a status:

```
$status = $twitter->post_basic("/statuses/update.json",
array("status" => "This is a test status."), $username, $password);
```

Again, this could also be achieved by using the $twitter->post_statusesUpdate() convention with equivalent outcomes. The results of this request can be extracted by either using `$status->responseText` or by accessing fields directly such as `$status->id`, which returns the identifier for the new status update.

Direct Message Objects

Direct Message objects (see Figure 2.4) contain all you need to know about the message, the `sender`, and the `recipient`. The `sender` and `recipient` elements are User objects without embedded Status objects, which were discussed earlier in this chapter. This is one of the advantages of adopting an object–oriented approach: Structures can be reused multiple times.

```
┌─────────────────────────────────────────────────────────────────┐
│                        Direct Message                           │
├─────────────────────────────────────────────────────────────────┤
│ +created_at: Date                                               │
│ +id: Integer                                                    │
│ +recipient: User                                                │
│ +recipient_id: Integer                                          │
│ +recipient_screen_name: String                                  │
│ +sender: User                                                   │
│ +sender_id: Integer                                             │
│ +sender_screen_name: String                                     │
│ +text: String                                                   │
├─────────────────────────────────────────────────────────────────┤
│ -<<GET>> direct_messages(count:Integer=20,                      │
│                          max_id:Integer,page:Integer,           │
│                          since_id:Integer): atom/json/rss/xml   │
│ -<<GET>> direct_messages/sent(count:Integer=20,                 │
│                          max_id:Integer,                        │
│                          page:Integer,                          │
│                          since_id:Integer): atom/json/rss/xml   │
│ -<<POST>> direct_messages/new(user:String,                      │
│                          screen_name:String,                    │
│                          user_id:Integer,                       │
│                          text:String): json/xml                 │
│ -<<POST/DELETE>> direct_messages/destroy/<<id>>(): json/xml     │
└─────────────────────────────────────────────────────────────────┘
```

Figure 2.4   Twitter API Direct Message object.

A sample Direct Message object that can be obtained from any of the methods from Figure 2.4 looks like this:

```
<direct_message>
 <id>154217109</id>
 <sender_id>15397909</sender_id>
 <text>Testing out the @twitterapi and Direct Message Objects.</text>
 <recipient_id>XXXXXXXX</recipient_id>
 <created_at>Wed Jun 03 19:49:27 +0000 2009</created_at>
 <sender_screen_name>markhawker</sender_screen_name>
 <recipient_screen_name>XXXXXXXX</recipient_screen_name>
 <sender>...</sender>
 <recipient>...</recipient>
</direct_message>
```

Multiple Direct Message objects are enclosed within a `direct-messages` array, and individual message elements are listed as `direct_message`. Notice the subtle use of an underscore (_) for individual elements and a hyphen (-) for the array name if you are looking to parse results using regular expressions or other means. As an example, you should add the following code to your `index.php` file:

```
echo "<h1>Direct Message Objects</h1>";
$direct_messages = $twitter->get_direct_messages(array("count" => 2),
$username, $password);
echo "<ul>";
foreach($direct_messages as $direct_message) {
 echo "<li>".$direct_message->text."</li>";
}
echo "</ul>";
```

What this code will print out is the text from the authenticated user's latest two direct messages. You can modify this by adjusting the `count` parameter and by adding a `page` parameter to view older direct messages.

Saved Search Objects

Four methods enable you to manipulate information about searches that users have saved to their profile. For example, a search could be saved for a specific keyword (for example, `healthcare`), which saves the user time inputting the keyword multiple times across different applications to perform the same search. Saved Search objects (see Figure 2.5) contain five keys for defining a search query that a user has saved: `id`, `name`, `query`, `position`, and `created_at`.

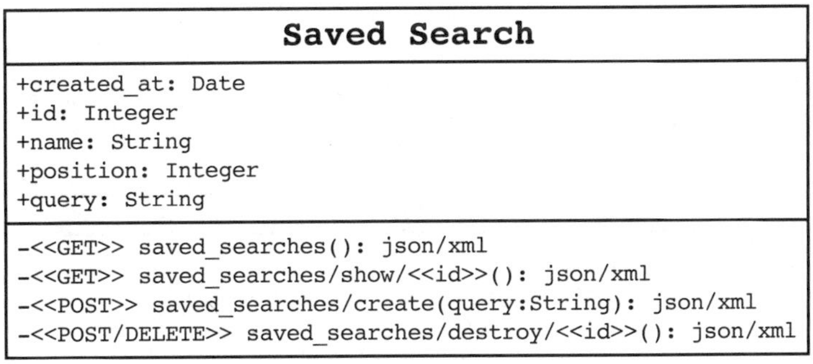

```
                    Saved Search
+created_at: Date
+id: Integer
+name: String
+position: Integer
+query: String

-<<GET>> saved_searches(): json/xml
-<<GET>> saved_searches/show/<<id>>(): json/xml
-<<POST>> saved_searches/create(query:String): json/xml
-<<POST/DELETE>> saved_searches/destroy/<<id>>(): json/xml
```

Figure 2.5   Twitter API Saved Search object.

A sample Saved Search object in XML looks like this:

```
<saved_search>
 <id>333753</id>
 <name>healthcare</name>
 <query>healthcare</query>
 <position/>
 <created_at>Sun Jun 07 13:36:37 +0000 2009</created_at>
</saved_search>
```

The `position` key denotes the absolute position of a Saved Search object in the saved_searches array, which is returned from the `saved_searches` method. This value can be empty or an integer starting from 1. In the instance above, it is empty because it is the only saved search available. To retrieve a collection of saved searches, you should modify `index.php` to include the following:

```
echo "<h1>Saved Search Objects</h1>";
$saved_search = $twitter->post_saved_searchesCreate(array("query" =>
"test"), $username, $password);
echo "<p>Saved Search: ".$saved_search->id."</p>";
$saved_searches = $twitter->get_saved_searches(null, $username,
$password);
print_r($saved_searches->responseText);
$delete_saved_search = $twitter->post_basic("/saved_searches/destroy/
{$saved_search->id}.json", null, $username, $password);
echo "<p>Deleted Search: ".$delete_saved_search->id."</p>";
```

The preceding code will create a Saved Search object using the keyword `test` and then prints out all the authenticated user's saved searches. The `test` search is then deleted, and its identifier is printed.

ID Objects

ID objects (see Figure 2.6) contain multiple `id` elements wrapped inside an `ids` array and a cursor-based `id_list`.

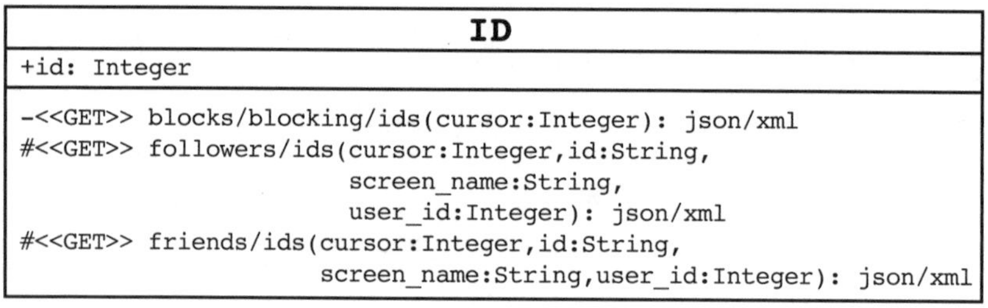

```
┌──────────────────────────────────────────────────────────────────────┐
│                                  ID                                    │
├──────────────────────────────────────────────────────────────────────┤
│ +id: Integer                                                           │
├──────────────────────────────────────────────────────────────────────┤
│ -<<GET>> blocks/blocking/ids(cursor:Integer): json/xml                 │
│ #<<GET>> followers/ids(cursor:Integer,id:String,                       │
│                        screen_name:String,                             │
│                        user_id:Integer): json/xml                      │
│ #<<GET>> friends/ids(cursor:Integer,id:String,                         │
│                      screen_name:String,user_id:Integer): json/xml     │
└──────────────────────────────────────────────────────────────────────┘
```

Figure 2.6   Twitter API ID object.

The two "social graph" methods friends/ids and followers/ids used for retrieving all followers and people who a user is following are more lightweight than the statuses/friends and statuses/followers methods, in that they return only a list of identifiers, not detailed information about the set of users:

```
<id_list>
 <ids>
  <id>XXXXXXXX</id>
  <id>XXXXXXXX</id>
  <id>XXXXXXXX</id>

  ...
 </ids>
 <next_cursor>0</next_cursor>
 <previous_cursor>0</previous_cursor>
</id_list>
```

Remember to enable "cursoring" by setting cursor=-1 in the friends/ids or followers/ids method calls; otherwise, no results will be returned. In the preceding example, the next_cursor and previous_cursor elements are set to 0 because all the data was successfully returned by the query. To extract all of a user's friends, you use the following code:

```
echo "<h1>ID Objects</h1>";
$cursor = -1;
do {
 $ids = $twitter->get_basic("/friends/ids.json", array("cursor" =>
 $cursor, "screen_name" => $username), $username, $password);
 foreach($ids->ids as $id) {
  echo "<li>".$id."</li>";
 }
 $cursor = $ids->next_cursor_str;
} while ($cursor > 0);
```

For this method to work, you must set the initial cursor parameter to -1; otherwise, Twitter will return an error. As with other methods that require cursors, the twitter-async library adds next_cursor_str and previous_cursor_str elements as the other cursor elements are converted to floating-point numbers by PHP.

Relationship Objects

Relationship objects are generated from the method friendships/show for detailing the relationship between two users known as the source and target. With authentication, the source parameter is attributed to the logged-in user unless either a source_screen_name or source_id is provided. A target user must be supplied by setting the target_screen_name of `target_id` parameters. A sample Relationship object using the `friendships/show` method is shown here:

```
https://api.twitter.com/2/friendships/show.xml?target_screen_name=socprog&
source_screen_name=markhawker
```

The XML response from this query looks like this:

```
<relationship>
 <target>
  <followed_by type="boolean">true</followed_by>
  <following type="boolean">true</following>
  <screen_name>socprog</screen_name>
  <id type="integer">109892189</id>
  </target>
 <source>
  <followed_by type="boolean">true</followed_by>
  <following type="boolean">true</following>
  <notifications_enabled nil="true"/>
  <screen_name>markhawker</screen_name>
  <blocking type="boolean">false</blocking>
  <id type="integer">15397909</id>
  </source>
</relationship>
```

The `notifications_enabled` and `blocking` elements will be empty unless user authentication is provided because this is not publicly available data. This can be re-created using the sample file by adding the following:

```
echo "<h1>Relationship Objects</h1>";
$relationship = $twitter->get_basic("/friendships/show.json",
array("target_screen_name" => "socprog", "source_screen_name" =>
$username), $username, $password);
print_r($relationship->responseText);
```

In this example, the `source_screen_name` is set to your own username, but this can be the credentials of any Twitter user. The `target_screen_name` is set to this book's account, but could be any valid user identifier.

Response Objects

Similar to ID objects in that they only return one element, Response objects return a Boolean value of `true` or `false`. Two methods return this response: `friendships/exists` and `help/test`, returning a `<friends>true</friends>` or `<ok>true</ok>`. The `friendships/exists` uses a GET operation and both `user_a` and `user_b` parameters to be set; these parameters are screen names or identifiers of users, which requires authentication for protected users. The `help/test` method does not require any parameters and uses a GET operation:

```
echo "<h1>Response Objects</h1>";
```

```
$friendship = $twitter->get_basic("/friendships/exists.json",
array("user_a" => $username, "user_b" => "socprog"), $username, $password);
echo $friendship->responseText;
```

The `$friendship->responseText` should return either `true` or `false` for this method depending on whether you follow this book's Twitter account.

Hash Objects

The final sets of objects are Hash objects. Two methods will return a Hash object as a sign of success (`blocks/exists/<<id>>` and `account/end_session`), whereas the other methods return a Hash object to notify you of an error. The `blocks/exists/<<id>>` and `account/verify_credentials` methods both return a Hash object to signify that a block or user does not exist. Although you can check the status codes for successful and unsuccessful requests, it is possible to use the Hash object to get a description of the particular problem. Hash objects contain two elements `error` and `request`. For example, executing the `account/end_session` method will return the following:

```
<hash>
 <error>Logged out.</error>
 <request>/account/end_session.xml</request>
</hash>
```

Other popular `error` messages include "Not found," "Could not authenticate you," and "This method requires authentication." Even though other error messages may be added in the future, they will conform to the key/value pair given above. The `account/rate_limit_status` method is the only exception to this rule; it returns the following response:

```
<hash>
 <remaining-hits type="integer">86</remaining-hits>
 <hourly-limit type="integer">100</hourly-limit>
 <reset-time type="datetime">2009-06-01T21:05:01+00:00</reset-time>
 <reset-time-in-seconds type="integer">1243890301</reset-time-in-seconds>
</hash>
```

The key `remaining-hits` indicates the number of requests left to the Twitter API until the counter is reset and should always be less than or equal to the `hourly-limit`. Both `reset-time` and `reset-time-in-seconds` are two ways of saying when the user's rate limit will be reset. First, `reset-time` is a Greenwich mean time (GMT) `datetime` stamp in the format `YYYY-MM-DDTHH:MM:SS+00:00`, and reset-time-in-seconds is the equivalent UNIX timestamp measured in seconds since January 1, 1970. By subtracting the current UNIX timestamp from `reset-time-in-seconds`, you will see that it is equivalent to `reset-time`. To access these elements programmatically, you use the following:

```
echo "<h1>Hash Objects</h1>";
$rate_limit_status = $twitter>get_basic("/account/rate_limit_status.json",
```

```
null, $username, $password);
echo "<p>Remaining Hits: ".$rate_limit_status->remaining_hits."</p>";
echo "<p>Hourly Limit: ".$rate_limit_status->hourly_limit."</p>";
echo "<p>Reset Time: ".$rate_limit_status->reset_time."</p>";
echo "<p>Reset Time (Secs): ".$rate_limit_status->reset_time_in_seconds.
"</p>";
```

One thing to note is that twitter-async has converted the minus character (-) of each element to an underscore (_), which was discovered by printing out `$rate_limit_status->responseText`.

Twitter Search API

The Search API is used to perform Twitter searches and for extracting trend data. Unlike the methods discussed previously, which support multiple return formats, the Search API supports only two formats, Atom and JSON, which is why the JSON format is recommended. The Atom syndication format is described in the following section so that you can see how it compares to JSON before exploring the Search API methods and search operators. The Twitter API and Search API are separate entities, which means that date formats, User and Status objects, and `screen_name` capitalization are not standard across both, although this is one of the goals of the new version of the Twitter API.

Introducing the Atom Syndication Format

The Atom syndication format is an XML-based data standard considered to be an alternative to Really Simple Syndication (RSS), which you may have been exposed to through newsfeed subscriptions. The Atom format is the reason you can subscribe to Twitter searches in your browser via the web interface. To get you started, here is an example of a Search API Atom feed for the search term markbook, which is the hashtag used during the production of this book:

```
<?xml version="1.0" encoding="UTF-8"?>
<feed xmlns:google="http://base.google.com/ns/1.0" xml:lang="en-US"
xmlns:openSearch="http://a9.com/-/spec/opensearch/1.1/"
xmlns="http://www.w3.org/2005/Atom"
xmlns:twitter="http://api.twitter.com/">
 <id>tag:search.twitter.com,2005:search/markbook</id>
 <link type="text/html" rel="alternate"
 href="http://search.twitter.com/search?q=markbook"/>
 <link type="application/atom+xml" rel="self"
 href="http://search.twitter.com/search.atom?q=markbook&rpp=1"/>
 <title>markbook - Twitter Search</title>
 <link type="application/opensearchdescription+xml" rel="search"
 href="http://search.twitter.com/opensearch.xml"/>
 <link type="application/atom+xml" rel="refresh"
```

```
href="http://search.twitter.com/search.atom?q=markbook&rpp=1&
since_id=2452360691"/>
<twitter:warning>since_id removed for pagination.</twitter:warning>
<updated>2009-07-02T21:47:02Z</updated>
<openSearch:itemsPerPage>1</openSearch:itemsPerPage>
<link type="application/atom+xml" rel="next"
href="http://search.twitter.com/search.atom?max_id=2452360691&
page=2&q=markbook&rpp=1"/>
<entry>
 <id>tag:search.twitter.com,2005:2443841666</id>
 <published>2009-07-02T21:47:02Z</published>
 <link type="text/html" rel="alternate"
 href="http://twitter.com/markhawker/statuses/2443841666"/>
 <title>Been working on #markbook tonight. Getting a skeleton
 chapter ready. Funny how Atom and JSON are *so* different in
 @twitterapi.</title>
 <content type="html">
 Been working on &lt;a href="http://search.twitter.com/
 search?q=%23markbook"&gt;#&lt;b&gt;markbook&lt;/b&gt;&lt;/a&gt; tonight.
 Getting a skeleton chapter ready. Funny how Atom and JSON are *so*
 different in &lt;a href="http://twitter.com/
 twitterapi"&gt;@twitterapi&lt;/a&gt;.</content>
 <updated>2009-07-02T21:47:02Z</updated>
 <link type="image/png" rel="image" href="http://s3.amazonaws.com/
 twitter_production/profile_images/234974305/me_normal.jpg"/>
 <twitter:source>&lt;a href="http://www.tweetdeck.com/"&gt;TweetDeck
 &lt;/a&gt;</twitter:source>
 <twitter:lang>en</twitter:lang>
 <twitter:geo></twitter:geo>
 <author>
  <name>markhawker (Mark Hawker)</name>
  <uri>http://twitter.com/markhawker</uri>
 </author>
</entry></feed>
```

The first thing you will notice is that you are given a wealth of meta-data stored inside the feed element and related Twitter update information embedded within an entry element (or multiple entry elements). Note that in this example, one entry element has been included by setting the rpp parameter to 1; typically, however, multiple elements are returned, with the default being 15 entries.

Feed Elements

All feed elements contain meta-data associated with the search query to enable it to be repeated or traversed programmatically. This includes preformatted links to display the next results and refresh the page plus any Twitter warning information. They also contain information regarding the OpenSearch specifications used by Twitter (for example, in the link http://search.twitter.com/opensearch.xml). The attributes within a `feed` element are as follows:

- **`entry`**

  Each result is contained within its own `entry` element, which is described in the next section.

- **`id`**

  Unlike numeric identifiers in Twitter API objects, the `id` element of the Search object contains a text string describing the search query in general terms.

- **`link`**

  Several link elements are contained within a `feed` element, each including three common attributes detailing their `type`, `href` and `ref`. The `link` element tagged with the `self` attribute details the query that was run along with XML pointers for OpenSearch, which facilitates the syndication of results. Both the `next` and `refresh` references enable results to be automatically refreshed if desired.

- **`openSearch:itemsPerPage`**

  This element contains the number of search results returned and should be identical to the `rpp` parameter supplied in the query. The default is 15 but can be increased up to a maximum of 100 entries returned in an instance.

- **`title`**

  Containing the query appended with the `- Twitter Search` label, this element may be useful in saving you time creating an appropriate page title yourself.

- **`twitter:warning`**

  Any warning messages provided by Twitter will be contained within this element (in this instance warning that the `since_id` parameter was excluded). Although this element can be useful when debugging your applications, it is important to note that not all Search API responses will contain this element.

- **`updated`**

  This element describes when the search results were last updated and is in the format `YYYY-MM-DDTHH:MM:SSZ`. This can be useful if caching results in a database, because you can test whether an update needs to be performed based on whether the data has been refreshed.

Entry Elements

Each update matching the query string is encapsulated within its own `entry` element. Although some basic information is returned referencing the update, it is nowhere near as complete as the data returned in Status or User objects from the Twitter API. In this case, should additional information be required by your application, sufficient information is provided to enable you to make requests using the Twitter API to extract that information:

- **author**

  This value contains a nested set of two elements, `name` and `uri`. The `name` element contains the `name` and `screen_name` of the user enclosed in parentheses and `uri` links to the author's Twitter profile page.

- **content, title**

  Both elements contain the body of the update but the `content` element also contains HTML that can be used to reconstruct the Status object. Depending on whether you want to re-present the update or analyze its text will help you decide which element to use.

- **id**

  Similar to `feed` elements, the `id` is a text string used to identify the update in the search results. The trailing integers of this value are the Status object `id` of the update, which provides an opportunity to extract further details using the Twitter API. The Status object `id` and full URL is provided in one of the `link` elements.

- **link**

  Containing the same attributes as in `feed` elements, the two `link` values give the URL to the Status object and a link to the author's profile image stored by Twitter.

- **published, updated**

  These two values give the creation date of the Status object in the same `YYYY-MM-DDTHH:MM:SSZ` format as in `feed` elements.

- **twitter:geo**

  This element will be populated with status location data if explicitly enabled by the user.

- **twitter:lang, twitter:source**

  The `twitter:source` value is the encoded link to the application used to publish the update and matches the `source` attribute of the Status object. The `twitter:lang` value is the language of the update stored in the two-letter ISO 639-1 format.

Contrasting Atom and JSON Outputs

In contrast to the Atom syndication format the Search API, JSON output returns a set of "key/value" pairs enclosed within a parent `results` object. For the same query for `markbook` that was executed earlier, the following JSON data is returned:

```
{"results":[
 {
  "text":"Been working on #markbook tonight. Getting a skeleton
```

```
chapter ready. Funny how Atom and JSON are *so* different in
@twitterapi.",
 "to_user_id":null,
 "from_user":"markhawker",
 "id":2443841666,
 "from_user_id":924649,
 "iso_language_code":"en",
 "geo":null,
 "source":"&lt;a href=&quot;http:\/\/www.tweetdeck.com
 \/&quot;&gt;TweetDeck&lt;\/a&gt;",
 "profile_image_url":"http:\/\/s3.amazonaws.com
 \/twitter_production\/profile_images\/234974305\/me_normal.jpg",
 "created_at":"Thu, 02 Jul 2009 21:47:02 +0000"
 }
],
"since_id":0,
"max_id":2452360691,
"refresh_url":"?since_id=2452360691&q=markbook",
"results_per_page":1,
"next_page":"?page=2&max_id=2452360691&rpp=1&q=markbook",
"completed_in":0.027692,
"page":1,
"query":"markbook"
}
```

In this example, you can see a `results` key with entries placed within square brackets
and each enclosed within a pair of curly braces and separated by a comma: `"results":`.
You will also notice there is meta-data returned similar to `feed` elements: `since_id`,
`max_id`, `refresh_url`, `results_per_page`, `next_page`, `completed_in`, `page`, and `query`.
The attributes returned for each entry are similar to `entry` elements with a few aesthetic
exceptions. Forward slashes (/) are "escaped" by a backslash (\), because in JavaScript a forward slash is used as an escape character. By escaping the character, it prevents the inter-
preter from performing the action typically associated after the forward slash. You are also
explicitly given the Status object `id` attribute and a `to_user` attribute if a user is mentioned in the update. Finally, the date format between both outputs is inconsistent, but the
JSON output is comparable to that of the JSON output of the Twitter API.

Twitter Search API Methods

There are two categories in the Search API: Search and Trends. Search allows you to supply a query and retrieve results based on search terms and a mix of operators and parameters. The Trends category shows you what's hot or "trending" in the community currently
or for any given date or week.

Search

In its simplest form, a query in the Search API consists of the stem https://search.twitter.com/search.<<format>>, where <<format>> can be replaced with json or atom, a q parameter, and a keyword (for example, https://search.twitter.com/search.json?q=twitter). This will return in JSON format the default number of updates, 15, that include the twitter keyword. Note that keywords must be URL encoded. So, for example, if you want to find updates mentioning a particular user, an @ symbol is encoded as %40; for a hashtag, the hash character (#) is encoded as %23; and for searching for an update containing a question, the question mark character (?) is encoded as %3F.

> ### Set a User Agent
>
> You *must* supply a user agent to prevent the Twitter API returning a status code 403 for requests. You can do so by setting the -A switch in cURL, or if you are using twitter-async this will be set automatically for you.

To conduct a simple search within the index.php sample code, you just add the following:

```
echo "<h1>Search Objects</h1>";
$query = "test";
$search = $twitter->get_search(array("q" => urlencode($query),
"rpp" => 2), $username, $password);
echo "<p>Query: ".$search->query."</p>";
echo "<ul>";
foreach($search->results as $result) {
 echo "<li>".$result->from_user.": ".$result->text."</li>";
}
echo "</ul>";
```

Twitter Search is about more than just simple keywords and parameters, which were discussed in Chapter 1. You can also use a wealth of operators to customize results or control how results are returned from the Search API. Operators are similar to the parameters that you were shown in Chapter 1 and the main operators are listed here. You can find a full list at http://search.twitter.com/operators, which mirrors some, but not all, of the functionality of an advanced Twitter search.

There are numerous content-based operators, including those for phrase matching, hyperlink and source filtering, and word negation. Here is a description of some content-based operators:

- To search for multiple keywords, you can separate words with a plus (+) character. For example, twitter+api would find status updates containing both twitter and api.

- Exact phrase matches can be found by enclosing the words within quotation marks (""), which are URL encoded using `%22`. For example, `%22twitter+api%22` would find status updates containing the phrase `twitter api`.

- To search for one word *or* another word (or both), you use the logical `OR` operator (for example, `twitter+OR+api`).

- If you want to exclude a word from a search you prefix the word with a minus (-) character. For example, `twitter+-api` searches for updates containing `twitter` but not `api`.

- You can return status updates that must include a hyperlink. For this, you would use the `filter:links` operator. For example, `twitter+filter:links` returns status updates containing `twitter` and that include a hyperlink.

- If you want to find updates sent from a particular source, such as TweetDeck, you can use the `source:application` operator (for example, `twitter+source:tweetdeck`). This could prove useful if you have set your own `source` parameter and want to track how users are interacting with your application.

In addition to content-based operators, a number of meta-content operators exist for filtering updates to or from a particular user and updates sent from a geographic region or before or after specific dates. The operators are as follows:

- To filter by updates sent to or from a user, you can use the `from:username` and `to:username` operators. For example, `twitter+from:markhawker` would search for updates containing `twitter` and sent by `markhawker`. For filtering updates sent to `markhawker`, you would use `to:markhawker`.

- As devices begin to be supported by the Geolocation API, the `location:place_name` operator and `geocode` parameter will become increasingly useful for location-based searches (for example, `party+location:London`).

- Dates can be used to filter updates using `since:YYYY-MM-DD` or `until:YYYY-MM-DD`. For example, you may be running a competition that only accepts entries after a specified date, or even before a closing date (for example, `vote+until:2009-07-04`). Note that Twitter Search currently only provides results up to a week and a half in the past.

You can experiment with any of these operators by modifying the `$query` parameter, which was used in the search example. By outputting the `$search->responseText`, you can also start to build up a picture of what elements are returned by the Search API and how you can use them in your own applications.

Trends

Although search is good for filtering and extracting information at an individual level, you need `trends` methods to provide aggregate-level data across the Twitter ecosystem.

Local Trends Methods

Twitter has two `trends` methods for providing trends specific to a particular location. The `trends/available` and `trends/location` methods will return trending topics using the Yahoo! Where On Earth ID (WOEID) convention and will make trend results more relevant to a user's specific location.

There are four `trends` methods. They output in JSON format only and are summarized here:

- To extract the ten topics currently trending on Twitter, use the `trends` method. This method will return a `trends` element containing a `name` and `url` for performing the related Twitter search. An `as_of` attribute is also included, which gives the date and time that the results were valid. An example date is `Sat, 01 Aug 2009 18:00:00 +0000`.

- The `trends/current` method displays similar information to the ten topics but uses a non-URL-encoded `query` attribute in place of a `url` and provides the `as_of` element as the number of seconds since January 1, 1970. This method permits the use of an `exclude` parameter, which can be set to `hashtags` to remove all hashtags from the trends list. An example date is `2009-08-01 18:00:00`.

- The `trends/daily` method allows for a `date` parameter to be supplied in the format `YYYY-MM-DD` to extract top topics for a given date. If no date is provided, results are returned for today's date. The `exclude` parameter can be supplied to exclude hashtags.

- The `trends/weekly` method returns the top 30 topics for each day in a given week by providing a `date` parameter and optionally setting the `exclude` parameter. If no date is provided, results are returned for the current week.

All methods apart from the `trends` method return results in a somewhat strange manner. Comparing the two, the trends method will return the following JSON results, which have been truncated to show only two trends:

```
{"trends":[
 {
  "name":"Roger Federer",
  "url":"http:\/\/search.twitter.com\/search?
  q=%22Roger+Federer%22+OR+%23Federer"
 },
 {
  "name":"A-Rod",
  "url":"http:\/\/search.twitter.com\/search?q=A-Rod"
 }
],
"as_of":"Sun, 05 Jul 2009 18:34:58 +0000"
}
```

In comparison, all three `trends/current`, `trends/daily`, and `trends/weekly` methods return results in the following format, which (again) has been truncated and generalized for the sake of brevity:

```
{"trends":{
 "2009-07-05 19:30:00":[
  {
   "query":"Wimbledon OR #Wimbledon",
   "name":"Wimbledon"
  },
  {
   "query":"\"Roger Federer\" OR Federer",
   "name":"Roger Federer"
  }
  ]
 },
 "as_of":1246822183
}
```

These short examples demonstrate the varied outputs of the `trends` methods in terms of both their structure and date formats. To access the same trends programmatically, you should add the following code:

```
echo "<h1>Trends Objects</h1>";
echo "<h2>Current Trends</h2>";
$trends = $twitter->get_trends(null, $username, $password);
print_r($trends->responseText);
echo "<h2>Current Trends</h2>";
$trends_current = $twitter->get_trendsCurrent(array("exclude" =>
"hashtags"), $username, $password);
print_r($trends_current->responseText);
echo "<h2>Daily Trends</h2>";
$date = date("Y-m-d");
$trends_daily = $twitter->get_trendsDaily(array("date" => $date,
"exclude" => "hashtags"), $username, $password);
print_r($trends_daily->responseText);
echo "<h2>Weekly Trends</h2>";
$trends_weekly = $twitter->get_trendsDaily(array("date" => $date,
"exclude" => "hashtags"), $username, $password);
print_r($trends_weekly->responseText);
```

In addition to these examples, the two local trends methods can be accessed by supplying `lat` and `long` parameters or a `woeid`. The `lat` and `long` is used to sort results from the `trends/available` method by distance from that particular location. These methods are accessible via the following code:

```
echo "<h1>Local Trends Objects</h1>";
```

```
$trends_available = $twitter->get_basic("/trends/available.json",
array("lat" => 37, "long" => -122), $username, $password);
print_r($trends_available->responseText);
```

This should return the closest matches to San Francisco (the town specified by the `lat` and `long` parameters), which is contained within this JSON response:

```
"country":"United States",
"url": "http://where.yahooapis.com/v1/place/2487956",
"placeType": {"code": 7, "name": "Town"},
"woeid": 2487956,
"countryCode": "US",
"name": "San Francisco"
}, ...]
```

The response will return a number of potential matches, starting with the closest, which was an exact match to San Francisco. The next stage is to extract the WOEID by using `$trends_available[0]["woeid"]`, which can then be entered into the `trends/location` method:

```
$trends_location = $twitter->get_basic("/trends/".
$trends_available[0]["woeid"].".json", null, $username, $password);
print_r($trends_location->headers);
```

The results from this query should return the following JSON data:

```
"as_of": "2010-03-15T22:10:03Z",
"locations": ,
"trends":
```

This response will return a regular Trends object with an embedded `locations` element for extracting the initial `woeid` and `name` of the location.

Summary

This chapter illustrated a number of Twitter API methods that enable you to perform a multitude of actions to access and mutate data, such as sending updates and exploring a user's social graph. You were also given an overview of the Search API, including the Atom syndication format, methods, and operators that you can use to extract both individual-level search data and also aggregate trends data. The next chapter explores how to use OAuth for user authentication so that you can begin to put your knowledge of Twitter methods to practical use.

3

Authentication with Twitter OAuth

Chapter 2, "Exploring the Twitter API and Search API," covered the various Twitter API and Search API methods using cURL and twitter-async using Basic Authentication. Basic Authentication is by no means unique to Twitter, and many sites and social services also use the same mechanism for user authentication. However, requiring a user's password even over a secure connection such as HTTPS can present security concerns. Although the barrier to entry is higher for an OAuth implementation in comparison to Basic Authentication, it is an essential tool for accessing the Twitter API because Basic Authentication will be deprecated in the future.

This chapter investigates Twitter's implementation of OAuth as an alternative to Basic Authentication and describes the workflow of Twitter OAuth, with a focus on web applications. OAuth is a method for interacting with Twitter on behalf of users without requiring them to supply a password every time they want to use an application. Twitter OAuth takes the form of the "Sign in with Twitter" service, which enables users to sign in to your website or application using their Twitter credentials. The chapter then provides a walkthrough of how to implement Twitter OAuth using twitter-async to create a very simple application called Test Tube. You can then use the code in this example as a basic template for your own Twitter application ideas.

Introducing Twitter OAuth

OAuth is an open protocol to facilitate a standard, secure authorization method for desktop, mobile, and web applications. The idea behind OAuth is similar to that of valet keys provided in some of today's luxury cars. The valet keys give parking attendants access to certain features of the car but may restrict them to driving only a limited number of miles or may prevent them from opening the trunk. In this instance, you are giving someone limited access to your car via a special key, while using another key to unlock everything else. This is in contrast to Basic Authentication, through which users are giving you their keys, and thus not only exposing their passwords to prying eyes but also giving you unrestricted access to their accounts.

In February 2009, Twitter released the first implementation of OAuth as a closed beta for developer experimentation. This has now been opened up to all developers through a new registration process for OAuth applications, available at http://twitter.com/oauth_clients. (You must have a Twitter account to access this URL.) All the applications that you have previously registered with Twitter will appear here. Clicking an application name will give you further details about the application and will enable you to edit your application settings, reset your consumer key and consumer secret (described in the next section), or delete your application.

During registration, you are prompted with a series of fields that you must fill out, including application name, description, and website. You are also asked whether you are creating a desktop or browser application (because the authentication steps are slightly different) and whether you require read/write or just read-only access to user data. Read-only access is just "pulling" data from Twitter, as you have seen with Twitter API accessor methods, and would include reading a user's updates, direct messages, or favorites. Read/write access includes pulling data from Twitter but also "pushing" data back, as you have seen with mutator methods of the Twitter API. This includes updating a user's status, sending a direct message, or marking a favorite. The callback URL is a location where users are redirected after successfully authenticating your application. For unsuccessful attempts, a user is returned to the Twitter home page.

OAuth Benefits

In addition to avoiding the impending deprecation of Basic Authentication, both users and developers can gain a number of benefits by adopting OAuth. For users, they no longer need to hand out their passwords to applications, and they can view authorized applications by visiting the Twitter "Connections" tab in their profile. From the Twitter "Connections" tab, users can de-authorize or "Revoke Access" to unwanted applications, which was previously subject to a user trusting an application to remove users' profile details from their data store or required users to change their password to "break" the relationship. In the case of "Sign in with Twitter", users can also use their Twitter credentials to authenticate themselves on third-party websites (using their Twitter details to post comments, for example). Permissions are also granular, allowing users to select whether they want to permit read-only or read/write access to an application. For developers, you will no longer need to worry about users changing their password or storing password details securely. Adopting OAuth will also show that you care about the progression and evolution of the Twitter API, which gives users greater confidence in your application.

OAuth Definitions

Before delving into the Twitter OAuth workflow, you need to understand a few terms so that you can start speaking the OAuth lingo:

- **Consumer**

  A website or application that uses OAuth to access Twitter on behalf of the user: your application. Consumers are created and developed by individuals or organizations known as consumer developers (*you*). Access by the consumer to a user's protected resources is controlled by a consumer key and consumer secret, which are used by Twitter to identify the consumer. The consumer key and consumer secret are given to a consumer developer when registering a consumer and can be reset at any time. For brevity, throughout this chapter, the word *application* is used rather than the word *consumer.*

- **OAuth protocol parameters**

  Parameters with names beginning with `oauth_` (for example, `oauth_consumer_key`, `oauth_token`, `oauth_nonce`, `oauth_timestamp`, `oauth_version`, `oauth_signature_method`, and `oauth_signature`). These parameters are handled internally via the twitter-async client library to ensure that OAuth exchanges are validated.

- **Protected resources**

  Data stored by Twitter that an application can access through authentication (for example, account data, updates, direct messages, favorites).

- **Service provider**

  A web application that allows access to protected resources via OAuth. In this chapter, Twitter is the service provider.

- **Tokens**

  Used by the application rather than a user's username and password to gain access to protected resources on Twitter. Tokens are random strings of letters and numbers paired with a token secret. There are two types of token: request and access. Twitter supports the HMAC-SHA1 signature base string. The Twitter OAuth workflow has two phases: authorization and access. The authorization phase is when the users give permission to Twitter that an application can "impersonate" them. The access phase is when the application actually does the impersonating.

  In terms of tokens, a request token is required only once during the authorization phase to generate an access token and token secret, which can then be stored and used multiple times during action phases. Twitter tokens currently do not expire, and so once users authorize an application, it will be granted infinite access to their information unless they choose to revoke access. Access can also be revoked if Twitter suspends an application.

- **User**

  This is an individual or organization that has signed up for a Twitter account. Users create protected resources, which they can share with a consumer. For example, their direct messages or updates can be read (and written) by an application.

The next section explores the full Twitter OAuth workflow, using all these terms in context (so don't worry if they don't make much sense just yet).

Implementing Twitter OAuth

After you have registered your application, you are ready to begin implementing Twitter OAuth. The Twitter API includes four OAuth methods: `oauth/request_token`, `oauth/authorize`, `oauth/authenticate`, and `oauth/access_token`. The official Twitter documentation for these methods is complex and is best described using workflows and by giving an example.

Twitter OAuth Workflow

A simplified workflow for browser-based applications is as follows:

1. A user visits an application, and a request token is generated by Twitter by calling the `oauth/request_token` method and using the application's consumer key and consumer secret.

2. A request can be made to `oauth/authorize` by following a URL appended with the request token to request user authorization. The `oauth/authenticate` method is reserved for applications using the "Sign in with Twitter" feature, which can be used to provide "one-click" user authentication. For desktop applications, you must set the parameter `oauth_callback=oob` in the `oauth/authorize` method to initiate PIN-based authorization. Where desktop authorization differs is that after obtaining approval from the user, Twitter displays a seven-digit PIN that must be recorded by the user and then entered into the application to be used as the `oauth_verifier` parameter. Steps 4 and 5 are the same as web-based authentication. The twitter-async library does not support this desktop application workflow.

3. Following the URL, the user is redirected to Twitter where the request token is verified. If not logged in to Twitter, the user is required to log in to grant access to the application. At this stage, the user is reminded of which application is requesting access by being shown its logo, description, and developer information, and is then prompted to allow or deny access to their protected resources. If access is denied, a prompt will be displayed by Twitter but the user will not be redirected back to the application.

4. If allowed, Twitter marks the request token as authorized and redirects the user back to the application using the callback URL together with the request token and other OAuth protocol parameters.

5. An access token is then generated by passing the request token and OAuth protocol parameters to the `oauth/access_token` method, which can then be stored alongside the token secret by the application.

6. Whenever applications want to access a user's protected resources, they use the access token and token secret along with their consumer key and consumer secret for each request.

Figure 3.1 shows this workflow, specifically the transition between your application and Twitter in terms of authentication and redirects. If a user is already signed in to Twitter and they have authorized your application, this will appear like a "one-click" process. If users close down their browser window before authenticating their details, the next time they visit the Twitter site they will be prompted with an error saying that their request token has expired.

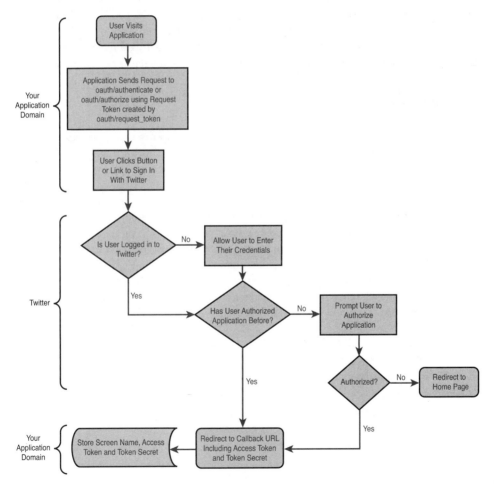

Figure 3.1   Workflow of a "Sign in with Twitter" session.

A number of OAuth client libraries are available to help reduce the complexity of this workflow. Client libraries are generally supplied by third parties and are tested quite rigorously by hundreds, if not thousands, of developers. One such library is twitter-async, which is used in the sample application described in the next section, Test Tube, which you can use as a template for your own Twitter applications.

Test Tube: A Sample Twitter Application

Twitter-async is a PHP client library that enables you to integrate with the Twitter API and Search API using OAuth. Twitter-async was written to maximize the efficiency of making HTTP requests over cURL using a mixture of synchronous and asynchronous methods. The twitter-async client file (`EpiTwitter.php`) has two dependencies contained within `EpiOAuth.php` and `EpiCurl.php` that handle all the authentication and URL signing relevant to Twitter and for handling the cURL requests. If you like, take some time to familiarize yourself with them; you will be using them later in this section.

Class Methods

Twitter-async has two methods: `__construct` and `__call`. The constructor takes a minimum of two parameters and a maximum of four. The first two parameters are the consumer key and consumer secret that were generated by Twitter during application registration. The last two are the access token and token secret, which are generated during the authorization phase and should be stored to allow requests to be made on behalf of users. The `__call` method handles the majority of other requests and uses a simple naming convention to map onto Twitter API and Search API method names known as API endpoints. As an example, the `account/verify_credentials` method maps to `get_accountVerify_credentials`, which consists of a lowercase GET request, an underscore (_) and a lowercase URL which has the forward slash (/) omitted and the first letter of the preceding method name capitalized. Parameters can be added by adding an array inside the method call. For example, for `statuses/update`, you would use `post_statusesUpdate(array("status" => "This is my new status."))`.

Uploading Images Using Twitter-async

Twitter-async supports the uploading of images via the `account/update_profile_image` and `account/update_profile_background_image` methods. This is achieved by using the following:

```
post_accountUpdate_profile_image(
  array("@image" => "@filename.png;type=image/png")
)
```

Remember to prefix the key and value with an "at" (@) character and that the image must be an absolute path to a file on your server.

When using OAuth, you should not use the `get_basic()`, `post_basic()`, and `delete_basic()` methods; these were reserved for Basic Authentication. Instead, twitter-async provides `get()`, `post()`, and `delete()` methods that require an application's consumer key and secret to access Twitter resources. For these methods, you are not required to supply the user's screen name and password; these are already catered for when using OAuth.

Accessing Responses

When you use twitter-async to make a call to the Twitter API, you will be returned an object with properties. The properties are named identical to what you have previously seen in both of the Twitter APIs, and dimensions of two or more are returned as arrays (for instance, when a collection of users or statuses is returned). For example, the following code snippet is a JSON response from the `account/verify_credentials` method that has been stored in the `$user` variable:

```
{
 screen_name: "markhawker",
 name: "Mark Hawker",
 status: {
  text: "This is my last status.",
  created_at: "Sat Aug 01 12:00:00 +0000 2009"
 },
}
```

In this example, you can access properties in two ways, either directly as member variables such as `$user->screen_name` or `$user->status->text` or through the response property by using `$user->response["screen_name"]` or `$user->response ["status"]["text"]`. For methods that return multiple responses, you can either access them through the `$user[0]->screen_name` syntax (remembering that PHP uses zero-based indexing, and so zero is actually the first response) or via using a looping function such as `for()`, `foreach()` or `while()`. If you are having trouble accessing data, you should return the response text via `$user->responseText`, which will give the full data set. In some instances, Twitter wraps data within arrays, so instead of using `$response->element`, you would use `$response[0]->element` instead.

Creating a Twitter-async Application

As a developer, it is generally easier to understand a new concept by experiencing it, so in this section you will develop a simple application to show your ten latest Twitter friends along with their profile image and a link back to their profile. You can demonstrate both the `oauth/authorize` and the `oauth/authenticate` or "Sign in with Twitter" workflows using similar codes, but the only difference between the `oauth/authenticate` and the `oauth/authorize` workflow is that in the former the user is only prompted to allow or deny access to the application once. In the latter, users are prompted to allow or deny access each time that they use the application.

> **"Sign in with Twitter" Buttons**
>
> Twitter provides a number of ready-made buttons that you can use to standardize the sign-in experience of users. You can find these on the Twitter API wiki (http://apiwiki.twitter.com/ Sign-in-with-Twitter).

Downloadable source code for this chapter is available via the book's code repository (http://github.com/markhawker/Social-Programming/). If you want to start from scratch, however, it is assumed that you have downloaded the twitter-async client library and have uploaded the files `EpiCurl.php`, `EpiOAuth.php`, and `EpiTwitter.php` to your web server inside a `twitter-async` directory. There are four steps to getting your application up and running: registering your application with Twitter, creating a "landing page," creating a "master page," and then testing your application. Although only a simple application, you should be able to quickly make modifications to test what you have learned so far about the Twitter API methods.

Registering Your Application

At the start of every project, you must register your application with Twitter by going to http://twitter.com/apps/new. From there, the required fields should be self-explanatory up to callback URL field, which will point to a "master page," which is the page that the user will be sent back to once a request token and token secret have been granted, `master.php`. For example, if your domain name is http://mytwitterapp.com/, you set your callback URL to http://mytwitterapp.com/master.php. Because you are just going to be accessing protected resources and not mutating them, you should select read-only access and also check the Use Twitter for Login option (because you will be using this feature). Click Save and create a new PHP file called `functions.php`, which will be a utility file for all your Twitter functions, and enter the lines shown in Listing 3.1 using the consumer key and consumer secret that Twitter has just generated for your application during the registration process.

Listing 3.1   **The `functions.php` File**

```php
1  <?php
2  include "twitter-async/EpiCurl.php";
3  include "twitter-async/EpiOAuth.php";
4  include "twitter-async/EpiTwitter.php";
5  define("TWITTER_CONSUMER_KEY", "XXXXXXXXXXXXXXXXXXXX");
6  define("TWITTER_CONSUMER_SECRET", "XXXXXXXXXXXXXXXXXXXX");
7  define("INDEX", "index.php");
8  define("MASTER", "master.php");
9  define("TITLE", "Test Tube - Sign In With Twitter");
10 function init($oauth_token = null, $oauth_token_secret = null) {
11   return new EpiTwitter(TWITTER_CONSUMER_KEY,
     TWITTER_CONSUMER_SECRET, $oauth_token, $oauth_token_secret);
12 }
13 function login() {}
```

```
14 function logout() {}
15 function verify() {}
16 function check() {}
17 function printFriends() {}
18 ?>
```

The INDEX, MASTER, and TITLE variables can be modified should you want to use different filenames. Remember that if you change the value of MASTER you should also edit the callback URL from within Twitter. Be sure to add the consumer key and consumer secret that Twitter generated for your application on lines 5 and 6. The init() function on lines 10 to 12 is used to create the EpiTwitter object using the consumer key and consumer secret but also handles being passed an OAuth token and token secret upon a user successfully authorizing the application. Methods on lines 13 to 17 are intentionally left empty because they will be updated later in this section. Now that you have saved your configuration details within functions.php, you are ready to create the landing page.

Creating the Landing Page

The landing page will serve a single purpose: generating a valid request token, which can be then passed to the Twitter OAuth authorization and authentication URLs for a user to click to be taken to Twitter. Twitter-async handles all this complexity for you, so a simple landing page can be created using the code in Listing 3.2.

Listing 3.2 **The index.php File**

```
1  <?php
2  include "functions.php";
3  $twitter = init();
4  try {
5    $authorize_url = $twitter->getAuthorizeUrl();
6    $authenticate_url_forced = $twitter->getAuthenticateUrl(null,
       array("force_login" => true));
7    $authenticate_url_unforced = $twitter->getAuthenticateUrl();
8  }
9  catch(EpiOAuthException $e) { echo "There was an error"; exit; }
10 catch(EpiTwitterException $e) {
11   echo "There was an unknown exception"; exit;
12 }
13 ?>
14 <!DOCTYPE html PUBLIC "-//W3C//DTD XHTML 1.0 Strict//EN"
     "http://www.w3.org/TR/xhtml1/DTD/xhtml1-strict.dtd">
15 <html xmlns="http://www.w3.org/1999/xhtml">
16 <head>
17   <title><?php echo TITLE; ?></title>
18   <link href="static/css/style.css" rel="stylesheet"
     type="text/css" />
19 </head>
```

```
20 <body>
21 <div id="main">
22  <h1>Test Tube</h1>
23  <p>This application uses Twitter's "Sign in with Twitter"
    feature to demonstrate what is possible in only a few lines of
    code.</p>
24  <p id="authorize"><a href="<?php echo $authorize_url; ?>">
     Authorize with Twitter</a></p>
25  <h2>Forced Login</h2>
26  <p>Whether a user is logged into Twitter or not they will be
    prompted to login and then Allow/Deny the application.</p>
27  <p id="authenticate"><a href="<?php echo $authenticate_url_forced; ?>">
    <img src="static/img/siwt-darker.png" height="24" width="151" alt="Sign
    in with Twitter" /></a></p>
28  <h2>Unforced Login</h2>
29  <p>The currently logged in user will be used and then prompted to
    then Allow/Deny the application.</p>
30  <p id="authenticate"><a href="<?php echo $authenticate_url_unforced;
    ?>"><img src="static/img/siwt-darker.png" height="24" width="151"
    alt="Sign in with Twitter" /></a></p>
31 </div>
32 </body>
33 </html>
34 ?>
```

Line 2 is used to include the `functions.php` file containing the application logic for convenience. The Twitter object is initiated on line 3 and can be used for a number of things, but on the landing page you will use it to create an authorization (line 24) and two authenticate URLs (lines 27 and 30). These URLs map to the Twitter API `oauth/authorize` and `oauth/authenticate` methods. The authenticate URL on line 24 demonstrates how you can pass the `force_login` parameter to the method, thus prompting users to log in to Twitter regardless of whether they are already logged in (which proves useful if they have multiple accounts). Note that Twitter handles the `force_login` rather strangely, in that even if it is set to `false`, it will be accepted and the user will be forced to log in. The "Sign in with Twitter" button has also been used alongside a simple Cascading Style Sheet (CSS) containing the following styles:

```
body { background: #3ea8bc; font-family: Tahoma, Verdana, Arial, sans-
serif; margin: 1em; padding: 1em; }
img { border: 0; }
#main { background: #fff; padding: 1em; border: 5px solid #ccc; text-
align: center; }
.following, .follower { margin: 1em; border: 0; }
.tweet { font-size: 1.5em; color: #ccc; }
```

Save the code in Listing 3.2 as `index.php`, and then upload the file to your web server alongside `functions.php`, the image, and the CSS.

Creating the Master Page

The next page is the master page, which is the page that was set as the callback URL, and will have the following functionality:

- Handling of a "sign-in" process
- Handling of a "sign-out" process
- Handling of users who access the page and who have not signed in
- Accessing a user's protected resources in the form of a friends list
- Handling of simple exceptions to degrade gracefully

For simplicity, you can use cookie-based storage of user credentials, although in practice you might want to store them in a database or in PHP sessions. You can re-create the master page with the skeleton code used in Listing 3.3.

Listing 3.3 **The `master.php` File**

```php
1  <?php
2  include "functions.php";
3  if (isset($_GET["logout"])) {
4    logout();
5  } else {
6    $twitter = login();
7    $user = verify($twitter);
8  if ($user) {
9    ?>
10   <!DOCTYPE html PUBLIC "-//W3C//DTD XHTML 1.0 Strict//EN"
       "http://www.w3.org/TR/xhtml1/DTD/xhtml1-strict.dtd">
11   <html xmlns="http://www.w3.org/1999/xhtml">
12   <head>
13    <title><?php echo TITLE; ?></title>
14    <link href="static/css/style.css" rel="stylesheet" type="text/css" />
15   </head>
16   <body>
17    <div id="main">
18     <h1>Hello, <?php echo $user->screen_name; ?>!</h1>
19     <p><img src="<?php echo $user->profile_image_url; ?>" alt="<?php
        echo $user->screen_name; ?>" height="48" width="48" /></p>
20     <p class="tweet">&quot;<?php echo $user->status->text; ?>&quot;</p>
21     <?php
22     // Print Latest Friends
23     printFriends ($twitter, 10);
24     ?>
25     <p><a href="<?php echo MASTER; ?>?logout">Sign Out</a></p>
26  <?php } else { ?>
27   <h1>Twitter Error</h1>
```

```
28  <p>We were unable to verify your Twitter credentials.</p>
29  <?php } ?>
30    </div>
31  </body>
32  </html>
33  <?php } ?>
```

As with the landing page, you must include the `functions.php` dependency, which will be revisited to add the `login()`, `logout()`, `verify()`, `check()`, and `printFriends()` functions. Lines 3 to 8 contain the workflow that first evaluates whether the `logout` parameter has been set via the link on line 25. If it hasn't, this workflow will attempt to create the Twitter object and verify whether a valid user has visited the page on line 7. If a valid `$user` is available, the application will show his or her Twitter username, profile picture, and latest friends. If not, an error message will display. Save the code in Listing 3.3 as `master.php` and reopen `functions.php`. Edit the `logout()` function so that it contains the following code:

```
function logout() {
  $twitter = init($_COOKIE["oauth_token"], $_COOKIE["oauth_token_secret"]);
  $twitter->post_accountEnd_session();
  setcookie("oauth_token", "", 1);
  setcookie("oauth_token_secret", "", 1);
  header("Location: ".INDEX."?loggedout");
}
```

These lines are used to handle the sign-out process by calling the `account/end_session` method, clearing the cookie that contained the user's credentials, and then redirecting back to the landing page. Next, here's the `login()` function:

```
function login() {
  // An OAuth Token has just been granted from Twitter
  if (!empty($_GET["oauth_token"])) {
    $twitter = init();
    $oauth_token = $_GET["oauth_token"];
    try {
      $twitter->setToken($oauth_token);
      $token = $twitter->getAccessToken();
      $twitter->setToken($token->oauth_token, $token->oauth_token_secret);
      setcookie("oauth_token", $token->oauth_token);
      setcookie("oauth_token_secret", $token->oauth_token_secret);
      header("Location: ".MASTER."?loggedin");
    }
    catch(EpiOauthException $e) { header("Location: ".
    INDEX."?oauthexception"); }
    catch(EpiTwitterException $e) { header("Location: ".INDEX."?exception");
  }
  } else if (
```

```
empty($_COOKIE["oauth_token"]) && empty($_COOKIE["oauth_token_secret"])
) {
 setcookie("oauth_token", "", 1);
 setcookie("oauth_token_secret", "", 1);
 header("Location: ".INDEX);
 } else {
 return init($_COOKIE["oauth_token"], $_COOKIE["oauth_token_secret"]);
 }
}
```

If an authorized request token has been returned from Twitter, you then need to convert it into an access token. This function checks for the token, attempts to create the access token, and then stores it alongside the token secret within a cookie. The user is then redirected or the page is "refreshed" so that the request token cannot be reused. If you do not do this, users might receive an error if they refresh the page manually with the request token still in the URL. If an access token and token secret cannot be found in the cookie, you should redirect the user back to the landing page.

The only case this leaves is if you have a user who has had his credentials stored in the cookie and has just returned from the automatic refresh and is now logged in. In this case, the init() function is called using the access token and token secret. If you store the access token and token secret alongside the user's screen name, you will be able to perform Twitter actions on behalf of the user. In Part IV of this book, you learn how to create your own microblog application from scratch.

Just because you have received an access token and token secret does not mean that the user has been verified as legitimate. This is why you need to call the account/verify_credentials method, which will return a status code 401 if the user credentials are incorrect, which is encompassed within the verify() and check() functions, which will return false for all responses that do not have a status code of 200:

```
function verify($twitter) {
 if(is_object($twitter)) {
  $response = $twitter->get_accountVerify_credentials();
  return check($response);
 } else {
  return false;
 }
}
function check($payload) {
 return ($payload->code == 200) ? $payload : false;
}
```

You now have a test to ensure that you have a verified user and can now work with his protected resources. Remember that a call to the account/verify_credentials method returns a User object if valid, so that is why you can extract their profile_image_url, screen_name, and status on lines 18 to 20 in Listing 3.3. The final function is printFriends(), which calls the statuses/friends method, passing a count parameter to extract the user's latest ten friends. The results from this method are ordered by the latest person added first:

```
function printFriends($twitter, $count = 10) {
 try {
  $friends = $twitter->get_statusesFriends(array("cursor" => -1));
  if (check($friends)) {
   $next_cursor = $friends->next_cursor;
   $previous_cursor = $friends->previous_cursor;
   echo "<h2>Latest ".$count." Twitter Friends</h2>";
   for ($i = 0; $i < $count; $i++) {
    $friend = $friends->users[$i];
    echo "<span><a title=\"".$friend->name."\" href="http://twitter.com/\".
    $friend->screen_name."\"><img class="following" src=\"".$friend->
    profile_image_url."\" alt=\"".$friend->screen_name."\" height="48"
    width="48" /></a>";
   }
  } else {
   return false;
  }
 }
 catch(EpiTwitterException $e) { echo "<p>You have no friends to
 list.</p>"; }
}
```

Save functions.php after adding the new functions, and then upload it alongside master.php to your web server.

Testing Your Application

Before testing, you should ensure that you have all the files uploaded to your web server and have successfully registered your test application on Twitter. Navigate to your landing page in a browser and you should see your landing page with three hyperlinks: "Authorize with Twitter" and two "Sign in with Twitter" buttons, as shown in Figure 3.2.

If you roll your mouse cursor over the links, you should see that you have an oauth_token parameter appended to the URL, which was automatically generated by twitter-async. Clicking the first link should redirect you to Twitter, where you can sign in (if required) and gain access to your application. If all was successful, you should then be redirected to your master page, which is shown in Figure 3.3.

Feel free to now explore the other links and see where they take you. Consider denying access to your application or using the forced and unforced login options. You might also want to be more adventurous and test some other Twitter API methods using the same principles as used to create the printFriends() method. For example, you could update the code created in Chapter 2 to use OAuth rather than Basic Authentication.

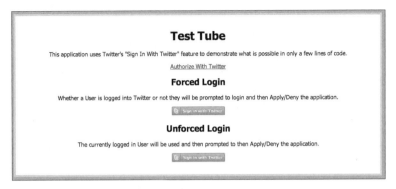

Figure 3.2   Landing page for the Test Tube application.

Figure 3.3   Master page for the Test Tube application.

Summary

This chapter provided an overview of OAuth as a more secure mechanism for obtaining user credentials for accessing their protected resources from Twitter. The example in this chapter used a PHP OAuth client library, twitter-async, to show how you can use OAuth to simplify the Twitter authorization process to create a simple Twitter application. Combining the skills you have learned in this chapter with those you learned in and Chapters 1 and 2, you should now feel confident to go on and develop your own applications. Chapter 4, "Extending the Twitter API: Retweets, Lists, and Location," covers some of the newer Twitter API methods, such as the Retweet API and the Geolocation API.

Extending the Twitter API: Retweets, Lists, and Location

Chapter 1, "Working with the Twitter API," and Chapter 2, "Exploring the Twitter API and Search API," gave an overview of the Twitter API and illustrated the essential Twitter API methods for account maintenance, updating status, searching, and accessing trends using Basic Authentication, cURL, and the twitter-async PHP client library. In Chapter 3, "Authentication with Twitter OAuth," you used OAuth as a means of authenticating user accounts without handling usernames and passwords within your applications and created a simple application using this method. As Twitter evolves, new functionality will be added to the public website and also for developers within the Twitter API. As examples, new features that were implemented during the writing of this book include the Retweet API, Lists API, and geolocation functionality:

- The Retweets API provides core functionality for handling retweets.
- The Lists API enables users to curate lists of users that can be subscribed to and followed and can be either public or private.
- There are many location-based Twitter applications that handle geolocation internally. Twitter now allows developers to "tag" updates on an opt-in tweet-by-tweet basis based on a user's privacy settings.

This chapter takes each of these new functionalities and describes how they work and, with the aid of simple code examples, shows you how you can implement them in your Twitter applications. These examples extend the Test Tube application created in Chapter 3.

Extending Twitter's Core Functionality

As Twitter continues to gain momentum in the personal and business spheres, it is inevitable that they will look to increase their core service functionality to both generate revenue and increase user participation. As has been seen with the introduction of OAuth and the phased deprecation of Basic Authentication, sometimes these changes can affect your applications in major ways, which is why OAuth was explained in detail. Twitter has introduced API versioning, which means that applications can be made to support specific API versions and Twitter will be able to provide beta functionality without compromising stable code. The convention that is being used is as follows:

```
https://api.twitter.com/<<version>>/<<method>>
```

Here, `<version>` can be replaced with the version number that you intend to use, which can currently be set to a `1` or `2`. Twitter intends to keep this version control method simple, and so will not be introducing complex branching and conventional version-control features. Introduced in version 2 of the Twitter API was support for retweets, lists, and geolocation.

Retweet API

The Retweet API enables developers to programmatically create a retweet (an act akin to forwarding an e-mail) and provides several ways to access retweets that users have created, that their followers have created, and tweets of their own that have been retweeted. Five new methods were added, and the `statuses/friends_timeline` method was superseded by the `statuses/home_timeline` method, which includes retweets. The new Retweet API methods are as follows:

- `statuses/retweet`

  Retweets a tweet and requires an `id` parameter of the tweet you are retweeting submitted via `POST` or `PUT`. This method supports only JSON or XML output.

- `statuses/retweets`

  Returns up to 100 retweets of a given tweet using `GET`. An example is https://api.twitter.com/2/statuses/retweets/1234.xml, where `1234` is the value of a valid status id. An optional `count` parameter can be supplied to restrict results. This method supports only JSON or XML output.

- `statuses/retweeted_by_me`, `statuses/retweeted_to_me`

  Returns a default of the 20 most recent tweets made by or to the authenticated user and accepts the `count` and `page` parameters using `GET`. Along with JSON and XML, this method also supports Atom.

Following its initial release to developers, the majority of feedback for the Retweet API addressed how to handle multiple retweets, which saw a change in the way retweet "collapsing" was processed by Twitter. To prevent clutter, a retweet appears only once in the user's home timeline, and subsequent retweets of the same tweet have to be retrieved via the `statuses/retweets` method, which will return up to a maximum of 100 retweets. For example, if you want to return the five most recent retweets for the tweet with identifier `1234`, you make the following call:

```
https://api.twitter.com/2/statuses/retweets/1234.xml?count=5
```

In the initial specification, it was possible that users would see updates from others whom they did not follow appearing in their timeline because of retweets being represented internally as "User B retweeted by User A" rather than "User A retweeted User B." In the latest incarnation of the Retweet API, you will see retweets from users you are following returned as Status objects that have a `retweeted_status` element nested within them from the original tweeter. This way, users will see a familiar face in their timeline but the retweeted tweet will be accredited to the original user. If no `retweeted_status` element is returned within the Status object, the tweet has not yet been retweeted. To see an example using twitter–async, open the `functions.php` file that you created in Chapter 3 and add the `printRetweets()` function as shown in Listing 4.1.

Listing 4.1   **The `printRetweets()` Function**

```php
function printRetweets($twitter, $type = "of", $count = 5, $page = 1) {
 try {
  $method = "get_statusesRetweets_".$type."_me";
  $retweets = $twitter->$method(array("count" => $count, "page" =>
$page));
  if (check($retweets)) {
   echo "<h2>Latest ".$count." Retweets ".$type." Me</h2>";
   echo "<ul>";
   foreach ($retweets as $retweet) {
    echo "<li>".$retweet->id.": &quot;".$retweet-> text."&quot; last
    retweeted by: ";
    $method = "get_statusesRetweets{$retweet->id}";
    $statuses = $twitter->$method(array("count" => 1));
    if (check($statuses)) {
     $retweeters = "";
     foreach ($statuses as $status) {
      $retweeters .= $status->user->screen_name.", ";
     }
    }
    echo substr($retweeters, 0, -2)."</li>";
   }
   echo "</ul>";
  } else {
   return false;
  }
 }
 catch(EpiTwitterException $e) { echo "<p>You have no retweets
to list.</p>"; }
}
```

The function can be called within `master.php` underneath the `printFriends()` function as `printRetweets($twitter, "of", 5, 1)`. The function makes use of the statuses/retweets method to get details of the retweeter and prints a single user as the count parameter is set to 1. The format of the retweeted_status element is exactly the same as with a Status object. When multiple retweets are requested, they are contained within a statuses element as an array of status elements, which can be iterated over using a foreach() loop. In the code listing above, the original status text could be accessed using $status->retweeted_status->text using data from the statuses/retweets method call.

Unfortunately, the way in which retweets are handled by Twitter means that commenting on the original tweet is not permitted (which has caused some upset in the user base, and many clients support both the new method of retweeting plus allowing users to comment and submit as a regular mention). What the Retweet API adds is the ability to quickly retrieve retweets programmatically so that they can be tracked and managed gracefully within all third-party applications that choose to implement the new features.

Lists API

Lists are a feature for organizing and sharing "groups" of Twitter users publicly or privately. These lists are linked through a user's profile and can be subscribed to (if permitted) by everyone, and therefore have the potential to be the new discovery mechanism for new and exciting accounts. For developers, the Lists API contains methods for creating, updating, retrieving, and deleting lists (and their members and subscribers). Another feature exists for retrieving a timeline of updates from a list that gives users greater control over their timelines and how information is filtered to prevent overload (for example, being able to see messages from close friends or work colleagues in a separate timeline from the home timeline). If group preferences are stored within Twitter, this means that other applications can share these preferences to provide a more streamlined user experience (because users will need to create lists only one time rather than multiple times per application). An example is when switching between desktop and mobile clients and synchronization of groups occurs between the two.

List API Limits

The current incarnation of the Lists API limits users to having a maximum of 20 lists, each of which can have up to 500 members. There are no known limits for list subscribers. These numbers may be increased, or decreased, in the future depending on Twitter's resource management and capability.

Unlike other Twitter API methods, the Lists API adheres more strictly to the definition of the Representational State Transfer (REST) design pattern, such as https://twitter.com/<<username>>/lists/memberships.xml, which returns the public lists that a specified <<username>> has been added to (see Table 4.1). This structure will decrease the need for excessive parameters in API method calls and should be a more friendly and understandable format for Twitter users. To demonstrate how the information is returned back to developers in XML the List object looks like this:

```
<list>
 <id>1111</id>
 <name>Example List</name>
 <full_name>@markhawker/example-list</full_name>
 <slug>example-list</slug>
 <description>An example list.</description>
 <subscriber_count>0</subscriber_count>
 <member_count>1</member_count>
 <uri>/markhawker/example</uri>
 <mode>public</mode>
 <user>...</user>
</list>
```

Table 4.1   **Lists Methods, Parameters, and Return Types**

Method	Description	Method	Parameters	Return Type
POST	Creates a new list	lists	description, mode, name	List object
POST/ PUT	Updates an existing list	lists/ <<list_id>>	description, mode, name	List object
GET	Gets the lists that the user has created	lists	cursor	Lists collection
GET	Gets the lists that the user has been added to	lists/ memberships	cursor	Lists collection
GET	Gets the lists that the user subscribes to	lists/subsc riptions	cursor	Lists collection
DELETE	Deletes a specified list	lists/ <<list_id>>	None	List object
GET	Gets the timeline for list members	lists/ <<list_id>> /statuses	max_id, page, per_page, since_id	Statuses collection
GET	Gets the list details.	lists/ <<list_id>>	None	List object

The id element is unique to each list and does not change if elements such as the list name changes. The slug element is an alphanumeric version of the name, which is in low-ercase and uses the hyphen character (-) in place of spaces. The Lists API is split into three categories, each with similar methods: Lists, for creating, reading, updating, and deleting of lists (see Table 4.1); List Members, for adding and removing of users to the list and for checking member status for a user and returning all members (see Table 4.2); and List Subscribers, for subscribing and unsubscribing and for checking subscriber status for a user and returning all subscribers (see Table 4.3).

Table 4.2   **List Member Methods, Parameters, and Return Types**

Method	Description	Method	Parameters	Return Type
POST	Adds a member to a list	<<list_id>>/ members	id	List object
GET	Gets the list members	<<list_id>>/ members	cursor	Users collection
DELETE	Removes a member from a list	<<list_id>>/ members	id	List object
GET	Checks whether a user is a memberf	<<list_id>>/ members/<<id>>	None	User object

Table 4.3   **List Subscriber Methods, Parameters, and Return Types**

Method	Description	Method	Parameters	Return Type
POST	Subscribes the authenticated user to a list	<<list_id>>/ subscribers	None	List object
GET	Gets the list sub-scribers	<<list_id>>/ subscribers	cursor	Users col-lection
DELETE	Unsubscribes the authenticated user from a list	<<list_id>>/ subscribers	None	List object
GET	Checks whether a user is a subscriber of a list	<<list_id>>/ subscribers/ <<id>>	None	User object

The https://api.twitter.com/2/<<username>>/ prefix is used on each of the Lists API methods where <<username>> must be replaced with the logged-in user's screen_name in the methods in Table 4.1 and can be set to any valid screen_name in the methods in Tables 4.2 and 4.3.

Instead of using <<list_id>>, you should use the appropriate identifier of the list that you want to access. For the XML example shown earlier, for example, you would use 1111 as the <<list_id>>. Each of these methods should be appended with a format set to either XML or JSON. The following few examples use twitter-async. In these examples, the <<username>> parameter is set to the value of $list_user, which is equal to $user->screen_name, which can be accessed after calling the verify() function in master.php of the sample code:

- ```
  $new_list = $twitter->post("/{$list_user}/lists.json",
  array("description" => "An example list.",
  "mode" => "private", "name" => "Example List"));
  ```

- ```
  $updated_list = $twitter->post("/{$list_user}/lists/
  {$new_list->id}.json", array("description" => "An updated
  example list."));
  ```

- ```
  $lists = $twitter->get("/{$list_user}/lists.json",
  array("cursor" => -1));
  ```

- ```
  $deleted_list = $twitter->delete("/$list_user/lists/
  {$updated_list->id}.json");
  ```

For each of the examples, you can access the responseText, such as $new_list->responseText, to retrieve the data returned by the Twitter API. In the examples of updating and deleting the list, these also use the id value of the previous lists within their method names. Here is an example of extracting all the lists that the authenticated user has been added to:

```
echo "<h1>List Objects</h1>";
$cursor = -1;
do {
 $lists = $twitter->get("/{$list_user}/lists/memberships.json",
 array("cursor" => $cursor));
 foreach($lists->lists as $list) {
  echo "<li>".$list->id.": ".$list->name." created by ".$list->
  user->screen_name."</li>";
 }
 $cursor = $lists->next_cursor_str;
} while ($cursor > 0);
```

The next set of methods (see Table 4.2) is for updating the members of an existing list.

With the exception of the final method, these methods function in the same way as Lists methods but require a numeric `id` parameter, which is of the logged-in user. In the last method, if the user is not a member of the specified list, an appropriate Hash object will be returned; otherwise, it will be a User object. Each of these methods should be appended with a format set to either XML or JSON. Here are two sample URLs that use the public @twitterapi `team` list:

- https://api.twitter.com/2/twitterapi/team/members.xml
- https://api.twitter.com/2/twitterapi/team/members/3191321.xml

To test the final method using twitter-async, you would use the following:

```
$id = $response->id;
$membership = $twitter->get("/twitterapi/team/members/{id}.json");
if ($membership->code == 200) {
 echo "Yes, the user is a member of this list.";
} else {
 echo "Sorry, the user is not a member of this list.";
}
```

The `$id` parameter will be that of the authenticated user. However, if you replace it with `3191321` (a current member of the Twitter API team), you should receive a successful response. The `$membership` element will also contain a User object if successful, so the message could use `$membership->name` to display the member's name. The methods listed in Table 4.3 enable you to update subscribers to an existing list. Unlike the List Member methods that only allow the authenticated user who created the list to add and remove members, authenticated users can subscribe and unsubscribe themselves to and from any public list. Like the List Member methods, you can use the using the final check method shown in the table to determine whether a user subscribes to a list.

These three categories cover all the current functionalities, but these may be extended in future implementations of the Lists API (perhaps to include bulk adding and removing features).

Geolocation API

Many third-party applications that support geolocation do so by using the user-defined location field within Twitter profiles. This field is not coded in any way and represents an account-level location for the user. Some applications provide functionality to update profile locations by using the Global Positioning System (GPS) within cell phones or location-aware laptops or other Internet-enabled devices. The Geolocation API is the natural extension to this third-party functionality, enabling applications to tag single updates with a user's current latitude and longitude. The feature is an opt-in service, quite understandably, and supports multiple use cases such as providing context-aware advertising or for browsing updates from users around a neighborhood, arena event, or music concert.

Mozilla Geode and Yahoo! Fire Eagle

Several options are available for supporting geolocation within web browsers and mobile devices. Two popular choices are Mozilla's Geode and Yahoo!'s Fire Eagle. In the future, many more will become available as geolocation becomes a mainstream feature. A browser-based extension for Mozilla Firefox named Geode can be used to add geolocation features to the popular web browser through a W3C standards-compliant API. A broker-based solution is Fire Eagle, a service that allows users to update their location and control its privacy and access by other applications. It provides an API to access locations, but requires users to have access to an account.

In terms of the Geolocation API for developers, two new fields were created: one within the User object, which is a read-only field named `geo_enabled`, indicating whether the user has opted-in to the feature; and the geolocation itself, which can be added as `lat` and `long` parameters to a status update request. GeoRSS-Simple is used to specify the return data format of locations in XML and uses GeoJSON for JSON requests. For example, specifying a `lat` of `37.78445` and `long` of `-122.39671` (the approximate location of the Twitter headquarters in San Francisco) will return the following in XML using GeoRSS-Simple:

```
<geo xmlns:georss="http://www.georss.org/georss">
 <georss:point>37.78445 -122.39671</georss:point>
</geo>
```

And the same request will return the following using GeoJSON:

```
"geo": {
 "type": "Point",
 "coordinates": [37.78445, -122.39671]
}
```

If no geolocation data is available, an empty result set will be returned as `<geo />` in XML or `"geo": {}` in JSON. If geolocation data is available, `coordinates` and `place` elements will also be included, with further details about the current location of the user. The place elements will contain all the data described in the Twitter `geo` methods described here. Currently, all geolocation data will be removed from an update after seven days of being posted. Twitter also provides three Geolocation API methods that support adding a location to updates: `geo/reverse_geocode` and `geo/nearby_places`, for returning a set of locations that are closest to a latitude and longitude or IP address; and `geo/id/<<id>>`, which returns detailed information about one specific location. It is recommended that you use the `geo/nearby_places` method for returning location data specific to the authenticated user and `geo/reverse_geocode` for general geographic data. Both methods will return the same data elements, but the former will return results in an order specific to the user. If you use the latitude and longitude of the Twitter headquarters, a call to the `geo/reverse_geocode` method will return the following JSON:

```
{
 "result": {
  "places":
 }.
 "query":{
  "type": "reverse_geocode",
  "url": "http://api.twitter.com/1/geo/reverse_geocode.json?
  lat=37.78445&long=-122.39671&accuracy=0&granularity=neighborhood",
  "params": {
   "granularity": "neighborhood",
   "coordinates": {
    "type": "Point", "coordinates": [-122.39671,37.78445]
   },
   "accuracy": 0
  }
 }
}
```

Additional parameters that you can send to this method include `max_results` (to control how many results are returned), `granularity` (which defaults to `neighborhood` but could also be set to `city`), and `accuracy` (which you can set to a numeric value to denote a radius in meters or a string for feet which must be suffixed by `ft`). For example, to search for results within an 800-foot radius, you set the `accuracy` parameter to `800ft`. For the `geo/nearby_places` method, you can also supply an `ip` parameter rather than a `lat` and `long`. Twitter will convert the `ip` parameter using Geo-IP. Currently, results are limited to the United States, but the Twitter people are working on including other locations eventually. This method returns the coordinates of both the place itself and the neighborhood or city in which it is situated. This could be used if you wanted to plot the location in a Geographical Information System (GIS).

If this same query were executed via twitter-async, you would access variables using the following code:

```
echo "<h1>Geolocation Objects</h1>";
$response = $twitter->get("/geo/reverse_geocode.json", array("lat" =>
37.78445, "long" => -122.39671, "max_results" => 3));
echo "<ul>";
foreach($response->result->places as $geo) {
 echo "<li>".$geo->id.": ".$geo->full_name." (".$geo->contained_within[0]
 ->full_name.")</li>";
}
echo "</ul>";
```

The results are accessed from within the `$response->result->places` object, and data from the `contained_within` element must be extracted by using `$geo->contained_within[0]`. As for accessing the initial query, you would use `$response->query` to extract the parameters executed alongside the method. To demonstrate the `geo/id/<<id>>` method, you can use one of the `id` elements returned by the query above. The closest to the Twitter headquarters is `5c92ab5379de3839`, which is South Beach, San Francisco. If you pass this into the `geo/id/<<id>>` method, you'll output the following JSON:

```
{
 "url": "http://api.twitter.com/1/geo/id/5c92ab5379de3839.json",
 "country": "",
 "bounding_box": {
  "type": "Polygon",
  "coordinates": [[...]]
 },
 "place_type": "neighborhood",
 "contained_within": ,
 "polylines": ["ioseFd`_jVhKjKxKkHbFdHhD{DjIhEhLiSnDbUo}@bmAoj@su
 "full_name": "South Beach",
 "geometry": {
  "type": "Polygon",
  "coordinates": [[...]]
 },
 "name": "South Beach",
 "id": "5c92ab5379de3839",
 "country_code": "US"
}
```

The additional information contained within this method gives access to polygon coordinates as well as data for drawing a polyline. Unfortunately, the `id` returned by both of these methods does not relate to a Yahoo! Where On Earth ID (WOEID), which could be used by the Local Trends methods. If you are using your own GIS, you could use these coordinates to plot your own maps or use the Google Maps API to show the locations of tweets in near real time.

Twitter Community Evolution

Alongside major feature extensions, which offer new opportunities for application developers in their own applications, Twitter has also started supporting community-driven tools that promote the growth of its own platform. Currently, these include translations and spam reporting, but could extend to other features in the future. The translate feature has huge potential to be extended to third-party developers for providing internationalized applications based on community submissions of translations, which is something Facebook and Google Friend Connect already support.

Platform Translations

Translations is a new feature to support Twitter in French, Italian, German, and Spanish (FIGS) in addition to English and Japanese, which are currently available on the Twitter website. In the future, this will be extended to other languages, too. For now, however, Twitter hopes to test the platform using these four new languages first. Twitter is recruiting volunteers to provide these translations. If you're interested in contributing, you can visit their official Translate (@translate) page to register to become a translator.

Spam Reporting

The original solution for spam reporting involved following the Twitter spam account (@spam) and sending it a direct message with the screen name of the suspected spammer. However, this was found to be too complicated for most users, who often just retweeted spam messages and therefore were suspected of spamming themselves. As a replacement, a Report for Spam feature has been added to the Twitter actions context menu. So, you can now report a particular user without having to follow the spam account and send it a message.

Twitter also released a new API method for performing this functionality named `report_spam`. It enables developers to incorporate spam control directly within their applications. Spam can be reported by supplying an `id`, `user_id`, or `screen_name` parameter via a POST request to the `report_spam` method, which will return a User object if successful or a Hash object if unsuccessful. For example, if you suspect `iamaspammer13` is a spam account, you can use the following cURL command:

```
curl -k -u username:password -d "screen_name=iamaspammer13"
https://api.twitter.com/2/report_spam.json
```

Calls to this method are limited per user per hour and so should be used sparingly when in batches. As usual, relevant error responses will be returned once this rate has been reached. No automated response will be taken by Twitter as a result of a spam request for reasons such as abuse and mistaken identity, so users should not expect accounts to be suspended immediately upon submitting a request. To test this feature out in code, you can use the Test Tube application from Chapter 3, adding the following line of code to the `master.php`:

```
printFollowers($twitter, 10);
```

The line above will execute the `printFollowers()` function, which will be detailed next, should be placed inside the `functions.php` file. The function will return a list of the last ten (or however many are provided in the second parameter) followers of the authenticated user along with a radio button next to each so that a user can select a potential spammer and click Report Spam to send the request to Twitter. The `printFollowers()` function is shown in Listing 4.2.

Listing 4.2   **The `printFollowers()` Function**

```
function printFollowers($twitter, $count = 10) {
  try {
    $followers = $twitter->get_statusesFollowers(array("cursor" => -1));
    if (check($followers)) {
```

```
    $next_cursor = $followers->next_cursor;
    $previous_cursor = $followers->previous_cursor;
    echo "<h2>Latest ".$count." Twitter Followers</h2>";
    echo "<form name=\"spam\" action=\"".MASTER."\" method=\"post\">";
    for ($i = 0; $i < $count; $i++) {
     $follower = $followers->users[$i];
     echo "<span><a title=\"".$follower->name."\" href=\"
     http://twitter.com/".$follower->screen_name."\"><img class=\"follower\"
     src=\"".$follower->profile_image_url."\" alt=\"".$follower->
     screen_name."\" height=\"48\" width=\"48\" /></a>";
     echo "<input type=\"radio\" name=\"spammer\" value=\"".$follower->
     screen_name."\" /></span>";
     }
     echo "<input type=\"hidden\" name=\"method\" value=\"spam\" />";
     echo "<p><input type=\"submit\" value=\"Report Spam\" /></p>";
     echo "</form>";
    } else {
     return false;
    }
   }
   catch(EpiTwitterException $e) { echo "<p>You have no followers to
   list.</p>"; }
}
```

In this function, the statuses/followers method is called along with a cursor parameter that returns the latest 100 followers. These are then iterated over using the $count parameter that was supplied to the function as a limiter. Each follower has a radio button next to his or her profile picture that will be submitted via the form as a spammer value alongside a hidden method value, which will be parsed by the master.php file. An extension to this could be to use a check box to report multiple spammers. You now need to add the report_spam functionality within the master.php file:

```
if (isset($_POST["method"])) {
 switch($_POST["method"]) {
  case "spam":
   $response = $twitter->post_report_spam(array("screen_name" =>
   $_POST["spammer"]));
   echo check($response) ? "<p>Spam user {$_POST['spammer']} reported
   successfully.</p>" : "<p>Spam user {$_POST['spammer']} reported
   unsuccessfully.</p>";
   break;
 }
} else {
 printFollowers($twitter, 10);
}
```

The name of the case parameter is the same as the hidden method value of the form, and the screen_name parameter is set to the value of spammer. The check() function will validate the method call and return the corresponding User object if successful or false if unsuccessful. For this example, no further processing was completed on the response, but the simple text line denoting either a successful or unsuccessful report attempt indicates where you could add extra functionality. The extensibility of the functions.php library and the power of twitter-async make adding these features relatively easy after you have suitable architectures in place.

Future Directions

As a platform, Twitter is still in its infancy. The introduction of OAuth and Sign In With Twitter is their first real step toward being a worthy "connect" provider. Twitter has already confirmed three features during the writing of this book: the Streaming API, contributions functionality, and Twitter @anywhere.

Streaming API

Twitter has released new Streaming API methods, such as firehose, filter, and retweet, that enable developers to provide almost real time access to large amounts of Twitter data. This is also the service that is used to index public statuses by Google and Microsoft Bing. These methods use streaming HTTP, whereby clients are connected to continuous data streams and will have to explicitly disconnect themselves to stop receiving data. The current Streaming API methods are as follows:

- The statuses/filter method returns all public statuses that match one or more filter parameters. These include follow for mentions, locations for geotagged updates, and track for specific keywords. The default access to this method allows you to track up to 200 keywords, 200 users, and 10 "bounding boxes" for locations. These boxes are a combination of longitude/latitude pairs, such that the first pair is the southwest corner of the box and the second pair is the northeast corner.

- The statuses/firehose method returns all public statuses without any kind of filtering. This is one of the least-used Streaming API methods because of its size and the fact that other methods that return less data can often be used in combination to return a more comprehensive set of data.

- The statuses/links method returns all statuses that contain either an http: or https: link. Like the statuses/firehose method, because of the number of data items retrieved by this method, it is less widely used.

- The statuses/retweet method returns all retweets made by users. It is generally not used, in favor of the statuses/filter method, whereby you can set the follow parameter to track a set of users.

- The `statuses/sample` method returns a random sample of all public statuses, which is a small proportion of the Firehose. For research or data mining, Twitter also allows you to request access to the Gardenhose, which gives access to a larger number of samples.

Only public accounts are made available, and so you will not be able to extract information from protected Twitter accounts. The Streaming API uses Basic Authentication, and access to methods other than `statuses/filter` and `statuses/sample` must be explicitly requested from Twitter to prevent abuse and to track usage. Because of the large amounts of data that will be flowing to your applications, it is recommended that you decouple stream processing and persistence. This just means that as soon as you receive data from Twitter it should be stored and then processed using methods other than attempting to render inline.

An example PHP client for use with the Streaming API is Phirehose (http://code.google.com/p/phirehose/), which is moderately maintained. The library uses a fairly simple structure that conforms to the official Streaming API documentation:

```php
require_once("Phirehose.php");
class MyStream extends Phirehose {
 public function enqueueStatus($status) {
  print $status;
 }
}
$stream = new MyStream("<<USERNAME>>", "<<PASSWORD>>");
$stream->consume();
```

In this example, the `Phirehose` class is extended, and the `enqueueStatus()` function is overridden, and called once for each status successfully retrieved. If you are interested in using the Streaming API, you should read the documentation provided by Twitter (http://dev.twitter.com/pages/streaming_api) and within Phirehose to ensure that your applications run smoothly. Because extracting large amounts of data was not the focus of this book, this section provides just a snapshot of what is possible via the Streaming API.

Contributions

For groups or organizations that have multiple users who post on their behalf from a shared account, Twitter is implementing a "contributors" feature. An account will have to explicitly enable the feature, which will set the `contributors_enabled` parameter within a User object to `true`, and thus enable specified user accounts to update its status. Within a Status object will be a new parameter called `contributors` containing a set of user identifiers who will have "signed" the update. A sample can be accessed at https://api.twitter.com/2/statuses/show/7680619122.xml. The update outputs a regular Status object plus the following:

```xml
<contributors>
 <user_id>8285392</user_id>
</contributors>
```

The feature enables you to append the contributor's username to a tweet (for example, the @twitterapi account invited @raffi to tweet on its behalf) so that users can direct responses back to the person who was referred to in the tweet. At the time of this writing, this feature is not yet available within the Twitter API.

Twitter @anywhere

At the time of this writing, the details about Twitter @anywhere are scarce. As a concept, @anywhere is an attempt to enable Twitter functionality, such as following people, to be embedded within any web page using just a few lines of JavaScript. Like website integration with the Facebook Platform (see Part II) and Google Friend Connect (Part III), this client-side functionality could see new incarnations of Sign In With Twitter and other related Twitter API methods when used in combination with a server-side library such as twitter-async.

Summary

Twitter is a continually moving target. As a developer, not only will you have to contend with existing features being changed, you will also have to react to new features being added or old features being deprecated and removed. During the course of writing this book, Twitter introduced the Lists API, Retweet API, and Geolocation API, and was already underway in the development of the Streaming API. This goes to show the pace of change of the platform in even a short space of time. In this chapter, you were given examples of these new methods and other community features such as translations and spam reporting, which are likely to be included as features in the future. Keeping up-to-date with the Twitter API announcements and blog will ensure you are the first to know of new Twitter enhancements.

5

An Overview of Facebook Platform Website Integration

In today's networked world, Facebook is a household name enabling users to create rich profiles and interact with others across the world through wall posts, status updates, messages, and pokes. For developers, the Facebook Platform has opened up almost infinite possibilities to create engaging applications that have before been mostly restricted to the internal Facebook environment. This is where Facebook Platform integration for websites (previously known as Facebook Connect) is different. It allows developers to hook into the Facebook ecosystem through external applications on the Web, cell phones, and even game consoles.

This chapter explores the fundamentals of Facebook for developers, including the Facebook Platform and website integration. You will learn about core components, including the Facebook API for manipulating Facebook data, the Facebook Query Language (FQL) for accessing data, and the Facebook Markup Language (XFBML) for displaying Facebook components such as profile pictures in your web applications. You will also learn how to create a sample application that you'll use in Chapter 6, "Registration, Authentication, and Translations with Facebook," for registration, authentication, and internationalization and in Chapter 7, "Using Facebook for Sharing, Commenting, and Stream Publishing," for sharing, commenting, and publishing.

Facebook Platform for Developers

On August 15, 2006, Facebook introduced the first version of its Facebook Platform and API enabling users to share their information with third-party websites and applications of their choosing. At the official 2007 f8 press conference, Mark Zuckerberg gave a keynote presentation to 800 developers introducing the next evolution of the Facebook Platform: "Imagine all the things we're going to be able to build together".

This movement was led by the opening of Facebook registration to users outside of the United States and the exploitation of network connections through the social graph. He highlighted three components to the platform:

- **Deep integration**

  Integration points enable applications to create synergies with the Facebook environment. These integration points include boxes, tabs, application info sections, inboxes, bookmarks, the Publisher, activity streams, feed forms, and canvas pages. Not all integration points suit all applications, and so which features you choose to exploit depends on what type of application you are developing. Also, Facebook has deprecated many of these integration points (such as boxes and application info sections), and Facebook is likely to add more in the future.

- **Mass distribution**

  The integration points provide unique ways to distribute your application through the social graph. These include notifications and requests that can push messages to friends, but also serendipitous means (such as via activity streams or via browsing a user's profile page). New features also include application and game dashboards, and counters, which were not available for testing during the production of this book, but are available on the Facebook Developer Roadmap.

- **New opportunity**

  Applications can create new business opportunities, as within canvas pages you can display advertisements or use applications to transact through Facebook. By attracting more users to your application, both your business and Facebook benefit through increased site traffic and creating a richer social graph.

While the Facebook Platform continues to evolve, enabling developers to build within the Facebook ecosystem, a new movement to integrate Facebook data with external applications has already started to mature. This is where Facebook Platform website integration comes into its own.

Facebook Platform

Facebook Platform for websites is the next evolution of the Facebook Platform, enabling you to integrate Facebook functionality into your own site, desktop application, cell phone applications, and beyond. This is not just about users collaborating and sharing within the internal Facebook environment as was the intention of the original Facebook Platform, this is about bringing Facebook to your own product or service. Plug-ins and social widgets, as well as custom programming, can get you up and running with the Facebook Platform in minutes in some cases. Facebook Platform website integration offers three benefits:

1. Increasing registrations because users can register on your application in just two clicks using their Facebook user credentials (see Chapter 6). No longer do they

need to remember yet another password. In addition, through authorized accounts, you get access to their Facebook data such as name, photo, location, and more. This allows you to create a richer personalized experience, such as serving them targeted information based on their location, age, gender, or interests.

2. Driving traffic to your product or service by giving users the opportunity to comment on, share, and stream content through their Facebook social graph and activity streams so that their friends click back to your site and engage with your content, completing the viral loop (see Chapter 7).

3. Increasing activity on your site by adding social context to increase user engagement, not just showing users what's most popular on your site, but what's most popular with their friends on your site. This is known as social filtering and adds to the personalized experience.

Facebook provides a sample application called The Run Around (http://www.somethingtoputhere.com/therunaround/) that demonstrates the service in action. To integrate the Facebook Platform into your site, you need to first set up a Facebook application, get an API key, and add some snippets of JavaScript code to your existing site. The next section focuses on concretizing these steps and requires an active Facebook user account.

Registering a Facebook Application

The process for creating a Facebook application is much the same as for regular Facebook Platform applications. You'll need to ensure that you have the Facebook Developer application enabled on your account by visiting http://www.facebook.com/developers and then clicking "Set Up New Application". You will be presented with a space to enter your application name and agree to the Facebook terms and conditions. The application name entered here will be the one that is used within the Facebook Application Directory and viewable on all correspondence with users. Use a suitable name such as "Test Tube" and click "Create Application".

Facebook Principles and Policies

As a developer, you are obliged to adhere to the Facebook Developer Principles and Policies (http://developers.facebook.com/policy/) to help protect your users, yourself, and Facebook.

The Application Edit page contains seven tabs, containing every setting available to Facebook Platform developers:

- Basic
- Authentication
- Profiles
- Canvas
- Connect

- Widgets
- Advanced
- Migrations

Most of these tabs are applicable to Facebook Platform for website applications with the exception of Canvas, which is used only if you have an internal Facebook application, and Advanced, which is for server whitelisting and mobile integration. The "Sandbox Mode" setting in the "Advanced" tab may prove useful should you only want developers to view the application (for instance, before being made live).

Basic Tab

The "Basic" tab contains options for controlling how your application appears within the Facebook Application Directory, such as name, description, logo, icon and language. From this tab, you can also add other developers to your application (who must be a friend on Facebook), which will give them full access to the application via their own profile. Facebook also strongly supports adding user-facing links to help, privacy, and terms of service URLs, which can contain information such as contact addresses or frequently asked questions. The bookmark URL must be set if you want to allow users to bookmark your application via the `<fb:bookmark>` XFBML element.

The three most important fields on this tab are your application ID, API key, and secret. These parameters are used to authenticate your application with Facebook. (Only you and Facebook should know the secret!) These parameters should be added to a configuration file, which you can create and save as `config.php` and which will be included on each page on which you want to use Facebook Platform for websites functionality:

```php
<?php
define("APP_ID", "XXXXXXXXXXXX");
define("API_KEY", "XXXXXXXXXXXXXXXXXXXXXXXXXXXXXXXX");
define("SECRET", "XXXXXXXXXXXXXXXXXXXXXXXXXXXXXXXX");
?>
```

Should your secret ever be compromised, you can reset it by going to the Facebook Developer application, selecting your application, and clicking the "Reset Secret Key" option. Because the secret is used to "sign" all Facebook requests, resetting it renders the old code useless.

Authentication Tab

The "Authentication" tab contains two important authentication callback URLs, which are "pinged" when a user first authorizes or removes your application. These will be created in Chapter 6, where the authentication process is explained, but should be set to http://myfacebookapp.com/authorize.php and http://myfacebookapp.com/remove.php (where myfacebookapp.com should be replaced by your own web server details).

Profiles Tab

The "Profiles" tab is usually reserved for Facebook Platform applications, but it also contains options for the Publisher interface (see Chapter 7). Set the "Publish Text" option to `Check Mood` and the Publish Callback URL to http://myfacebookapp.com/publish.php and "Self-Publish Text" to "Update Mood" and the "Self-Publish Callback URL" to http://myfacebookapp.com/self_publish.php.

Connect Tab

The "Connect" tab contains settings that are available only to Facebook Platform for websites applications, such as the "Connect URL", which you should set to http://myfacebookapp.com/, and a setting that enables you to add a logo, which will appear when a user first registers for your application or when requesting permissions such as reading or writing to their stream. If you want your implementation to span multiple domains, you can set the base domain to `myfacebookapp.com`, which will enable `foo.myfacebookapp.com` and `bar.myfacebookapp.com`. The account reclamation URL, as explained in Chapter 6, is requested should a user remove his or her account from Facebook and wants to create an independent account on your site without Facebook integration. Access to friend linking is being revamped by Facebook and will be available in mid to late 2010. Further details are available on the Facebook Developer Roadmap and will also be posted on this book's website at http://www.socialprogramming.info.

Widgets Tab

The "Widgets" tab is useful if you intend to use the comment boxes or live stream boxes on your website or application (see Chapter 7). From here, you can control who can administrate and moderate comments and also control who is able to comment. When you are happy with all the settings, just click "Save Changes" to be returned back to the Facebook Developer application. You can make other user-facing changes from here, such as editing your application's profile, which is where users can become fans, viewing application usage statistics, and handling translations (see Chapter 6). The next section explains how to reference your application using both the server-side PHP and client-side JavaScript client libraries.

Migrations Tab

The "Migrations" tab was created to provide backward functionality to help developers transition their applications to use Facebook's new features (for example, the handling of empty arrays in JSON and other potentially application-breaking platform adjustments). From this tab, developers can disable new features until they are happy that their application can support them.

Referencing a Facebook Platform Application

To reference Facebook Platform on your site, you need to upload a small file called a cross-domain communication channel file onto your web server to enable authenticated

communication between your site and Facebook. The file can be created by creating a
new file called xd_receiver.htm and adding the following HTML:

```
<!DOCTYPE html PUBLIC "-//W3C//DTD XHTML 1.0 Strict//EN"
 "http://www.w3.org/TR/xhtml1/DTD/xhtml1-strict.dtd">
<html xmlns="http://www.w3.org/1999/xhtml">
<body>
 <script src="http://static.ak.connect.facebook.com/js/api_lib/v0.4/
XdCommReceiver.js" type="text/javascript"></script>
</body>
</html>
```

Only one of these channel files is required per domain, and so you can specify its location as a relative path using a forward slash (/) to denote relativity to your root directory.
For instance, /example/xd_receiver.htm would look at the location http://www.
example.com/example/xd_receiver.htm, whereas if your root directory were set to
http://www.example.com/example already then you could just use xd_receiver.htm
without the forward slash. After uploading the file and setting its permissions to 644 using
chmod, you then need to add some JavaScript code to each of your pages that use
Facebook. Listing 5.1 shows a simple implementation of this that you can save as
index.php and store in the same directory as config.php and xd_receiver.htm.

Listing 5.1   **A Simple Facebook Platform Page**

```
1   <?php
2   include "config.php";
3   ?>
4   <!DOCTYPE html PUBLIC "-//W3C//DTD XHTML 1.0 Strict//EN"
    "http://www.w3.org/TR/xhtml1/DTD/xhtml1-strict.dtd">
5   <html xmlns="http://www.w3.org/1999/xhtml"
    xmlns:fb="http://www.facebook.com/2008/fbml">
6   <head>
7    <title>Test Tube</title>
8   </head>
9   <body>
10  <h1>Test Facebook Platform Page</h1>
11  <script src="http://static.ak.connect.facebook.com/js/api_lib/v0.4/
    FeatureLoader.js.php" type="text/javascript"></script>
12  <fb:login-button autologoutlink="true" onlogin="login();">
    </fb:login-button>
13  <script type="text/javascript">
14   FB.init("<?php echo API_KEY; ?>", "xd_receiver.htm",
    {"reloadIfSessionStateChanged":true});
15   function login() {
16    alert("Logged into Facebook.");
```

```
17  }
18  </script>
19  </body>
20  </html>
```

The code in Listing 5.1 is the simplest implementation of Facebook Platform website integration utilizing the JavaScript client library to log a user in and out. In Chapter 6, you will learn how to extend this basic authentication to use the post-authorize and post-remove callback URLs so that you can start tracking which users are interacting with your application. This client-side code can be extended to use a server-side library such as the official Facebook PHP Client Library to access the Facebook API.

Using the official client libraries means that a user's session can be shared between client-side and server-side code, but if you want to use a third-party client, you will have to verify the signature of requests yourself by adding the following function to a functions.php file and uploading that to your web server:

```php
function valid_facebook_session($expires, $session_key, $ss, $user,
$valid_signature, $secret) {
  $signature = md5("expires=".$expires."session_key=".$session_key."ss=".
  $ss."user=".$user.$secret);
  return ($signature == $valid_signature ? true :. false);
}
```

The function ensures that parameters sent from Facebook are authentic and have not been tampered with. If you send a request to Facebook and receive a true response, then you know that it is genuine. Adding to the index.php file that you created in Listing 5.1, add the following code below line 2:

```php
include "functions.php";
include "facebook-platform/php/facebook.php";
$facebook = new Facebook(API_KEY, SECRET);
$official_user = $facebook->get_loggedin_user();
$valid_facebook_session = valid_facebook_session(
$_COOKIE[API_KEY."_expires"], $_COOKIE[API_KEY."_session_key"],
$_COOKIE[API_KEY."_ss"], $_COOKIE[API_KEY."_user"],
$_COOKIE[API_KEY], SECRET);
$unofficial_user = ($valid_facebook_session ? $_COOKIE[API_KEY."_user"] :
false);
```

After adding the code into index.php, you can reference the $official_user and $unofficial_user by adding the following code within the <body> tags:

```php
<p>Official Client User: <?php echo $official_user; ?></p>
<p>Unofficial Client User: <?php echo $unofficial_user; ?></p>
```

Notice that both parameters will output the same identifier, but if the Facebook cookie (which is used in the unofficial clients) is tampered with, the signature will not match and will return `false`. With the client-side and server-side libraries now referenced successfully, you can now begin to use the Facebook API to access and manipulate user details and use the Facebook Markup Language (FBML) to display the results.

Facebook API, FQL, and XFBML

The Facebook Platform is split into four core components that comprise its REST-based API and give developers the tools to perform Facebook actions such as creating events, getting a list of friends, or updating a status through accessor (retrieval) and mutator (creating, updating, or deleting) methods and accessing Facebook data through the Facebook Query Language (FQL). For consistent formatting and user experience, you can use FBML for canvas applications and XFBML for `<iframe>` and Facebook Platform applications to replicate the appearance of Facebook controls (for example, displaying usernames and profile photos, creating secure areas through privacy settings, and for hooking into Facebook's integration points).

A client-side version of the REST-based API is provided by Facebook JavaScript (FBJS) for creating rich, interactive user experiences through a sandboxed JavaScript environment. Select uses of the Facebook JavaScript appear throughout this chapter and Chapters 6 and 7, but the majority of requests will be managed using server-side application logic. There is currently an open source version of the Facebook JavaScript SDK in production that is slimmer than the existing client library and will be continually updated throughout 2010 and beyond.

Facebook Platform Developer Roadmap

Facebook has published a roadmap of future developments for developers to keep up-to-date with changes to the Facebook Platform. Because the Platform is constantly evolving, you should keep track of this page to ensure future applications are compatible with new versions. The two features that could not be included in this book but that are important are the creation of an inbox for user content sharing, and invites for inviting friends to applications.

For those of you who want to dive straight into coding, the Facebook Test Console (http://developers.facebook.com/tools/) can be used to test a number of features, such as finding friends and publishing to the stream. The Console is a great resource to begin exploring how the Facebook API works, which can then be extended and customized using the server-side client library. The next two sections cover the Facebook API, FQL, and FBML in more detail.

Facebook API and FQL

Facebook provides two ways to access user data: through FQL (Facebook's own SQL-like query language, which can be used to craft complex queries); or via predefined Facebook

API methods, which are less customizable but provide a user-friendly interface to Facebook data. With the Facebook API, you can add social context to your application by using profile, friend, page, group, photo, and event data. The Facebook API is a REST-based resource that sends data over the Internet using GET and POST operations though the Facebook API REST server http://api.facebook.com/restserver.php.

Facebook Open Graph

At the f8 Developer Conference in 2010, Facebook announced a new evolution of the Facebook Platform, the open graph. The open graph puts people at the center of the Web with the introduction of "social plug-ins" (http://developers.facebook.com/plugins). These plug-ins enable users to add (via one line of HTML) Facebook functionality to their websites that are aware of users' Facebook connection status. These include adding Like or Recommend buttons, which can be used to show site visitors whether their friends have liked a blog post, a photo, or a piece of music (to give just a few examples). This activity can then be streamed via an activity feed plug-in for alerting users to their friends' interactions. The final plug-in that was announced enables recommendations, to highlight content based on popular items generated by site visitors. Implementing these features will allow visitors to take actions on your site and will become more relevant to them and their friends as they find and share what matters most to them. Facebook also announced the Open Graph Protocol (http://developers.facebook.com/docs/opengraph), which is Facebook's move toward a semantically enabled social web and the Graph API (http://developers.facebook.com/docs/api), which simplifies the way in which developers read and write data to Facebook. All of these changes will unfold in time, and so keeping up with the Facebook developer resources and this book's blog, http://www.socialprogramming.info, will help you make the best choices for your applications.

Using the Facebook PHP client library, you can conveniently access many of the Facebook API functions through the $facebook object. For example, to access and display a user's friends, you can use the following within index.php:

```
if($official_user) {
 try {
  $friends = $facebook->api_client->friends_get();
  foreach($friends as $friend) {
   echo '<p><fb:name uid="'.$friend.'" /></p>';
  }
 }
 catch(Exception $e) {
  print_r($e);
 }
} else {
 echo "<p>User not logged in.</p>";
}
```

Many other Facebook API methods are available and can be viewed within the facebookapi_php5_restlib.php file contained within the Facebook PHP client library, which also indicates their return types and optional parameters. These methods are categorized as follows:

- Administration methods
- Login/authentication methods
- Data-retrieval methods
- Publishing methods
- Mobile methods
- Dashboard API methods
- Photos API methods
- Events API methods
- Custom Tags API methods

It's impossible to cover every one of these methods here, because they are too numerous, but we will take a look at some of the most useful methods in this chapter. It is worth checking the facebookapi_php5_restlib.php file itself to see how each method works and what data you can expect to be returned.

Administration Methods

These methods are used to administer your applications and their users—such as using the admin.banUsers and admin.unbanUsers to ban and unban users, admin.getBannedUsers to get banned users, and links.getStats to get Facebook share statistics for a link—and for checking allocation limits using admin.getAllocation, which prevent applications from spamming users. Another useful method is admin.getMetrics, which returns specific metrics for your application, such as active_users, canvas_page_views, and api_calls. An example of this method in action is shown here:

```
$end_time = time();
$period = 86400;
$start_time = $end_time - $period;
$metrics = $facebook->api_client->admin_getMetrics(
$start_time, $end_time, $period, array("active_users",
"canvas_page_views"));
foreach($metrics as $metric) {
 echo "Active Users: ".$metric["active_users"];
 echo "Canvas Page Views: ".$metric["canvas_page_views"];
}
```

Because the UNIX time is being used, the $period in this instance must be set to either 1 day (86,400 seconds), 1 week (604,800 seconds), or 30 days (2,592,000 seconds).

The value of $end_time must not be greater than thirty days after the $start_time parameter. This method proves particularly useful if you want to track your own application statistics for storage automatically within an external database.

Login/Authentication Methods

You can use these methods for advanced session management, particularly for desktop applications. For Facebook Platform for websites, the most useful methods are for session expiration using auth.expireSession, getting a session via auth.getSession (which returns a session key, user ID, and a session expiry time), and creating temporary sessions with the auth.promoteSession method. In particular, you may want to call the auth.getSession method after a user has connected and store the details within a temporary encrypted session for future use. For sessions that have an expiry of zero, this means that the user has granted offline access to his account, meaning that you can perform actions on his behalf irrespective of whether he has logged in to Facebook. For users who want to completely remove your application, the auth.revokeAuthorization method logs them out of Facebook and revokes access to their details until they authorize your application again. The same is true of the auth.revokeExtendedPermission method, which will remove access to a previously authorized extended permission such as offline_access or read_stream.

Data-Retrieval Methods

You can use a number of methods to return Facebook data: from comments, friends, groups, and notes, to accessing a user's stream and profile information. Included in these methods is also the ability to execute FQL, which is explored in the next section via the fql.query and fql.multiquery methods. All of these methods are for retrieving data and contain methods such as comments.get, friends.get, groups.get, notes.get, status.get, and stream.get. Because many of these methods are used throughout later chapters in this book, they are not explored in great detail in this section. However, methods such as friends.areFriends, friends.getAppUsers, users.getInfo, and users.getStandardInfo are useful for extracting data about users and their friends. An example of the user.getStandardInfo method is shown here:

```
$users = $facebook->api_client->users_getStandardInfo(
array($official_user), array("first_name", "last_name"));
echo "<ul>";
foreach($users as $user) {
 echo "<li>Name: ".$user["first_name"]." ".$user["last_name"]."</li>";
}
echo "</ul>";
```

The results from this method must not be displayed to the user (that's what users.getInfo is for), but it can be used to gather analytics data. Other fields that can be used include uid, name, timezone, birthday, sex, affiliations, locale, profile_url,

proxied_email, current_location, and allowed_restrictions. The allowed_
restrictions field is particularly useful for restricting content based on a user's age,
country of residence, and type of content (for example, alcohol-related content). It can be
used in conjunction with admin.setRestrictionInfo and admin.setRestrictionInfo
to set restrictions that prevent users from accessing an application if they fail to meet your
criteria. For example, if the following were set, it would restrict an application to anybody
over the age of 18 from the United Kingdom:

```
$info = array("age" => "18+", "location" => "UK", "type" => "alcohol");
$success = $facebook->api_client->admin_setRestrictionInfo($info);
```

Because the alcohol type was set, this automatically restricts access for each country's
minimum age rather than setting them individually. The allowed_restrictions field
will return alcohol if the user is able to view the content. Another way to restrict content that does not completely prevent users from access is to use the <fb:restricted-
to> XFBML element, which can be wrapped around potentially sensitive material.

Publishing Methods

Unlike data-retrieval methods, these methods are used to create and delete Facebook data
(comments, links, notes, statuses, streams, and such). Most methods require extended permissions, as discussed in Chapter 7. The majority of the publishing methods are described
in Chapters 6, 7, 8, and 13, and so we do not discuss them in this section. However, the
one set of methods that may be of use are for creating and handling notes. Facebook provides three methods for working with notes, which are similar to blog posts and require
the create_note extended permission:

- notes.create
- notes.edit
- notes.delete

A note consists of a suitable title plus a string of content, which can include some
HTML elements (see http://www.facebook.com/notes_cheatsheet.php) for added visual
effect. New lines are supported by either wrapping content within two <p> tags or by
using the <br /> element. An example note would be created as follows:

```
$note_id = $facebook->api_client->notes_create("Test Note", "<b>This is a
bold paragraph.</b><p>This is a normal paragraph.</p>");
```

If successful, a note_id will be returned, which can then be used to make edits or
delete. For retrieving notes, you can use the notes.get method, which includes an
optional note_ids parameter, which accepts an array of note identifiers that you may
have collected via the creation methods.

Mobile Methods

For applications that use the Mobile platform, you can use two methods to check whether a user has enabled Short Message Service (SMS): for an application, via sms.canSend and for sending a message to their cell phone, sms.send.

Dashboard API Methods

A new set of integration points for both applications and games is exposed via the Dashboard API (see Chapter 8, "Application Discovery, Tabbed Navigation, and the Facebook JavaScript Library"). Methods in this category are used for sending users short notifications and displaying counters related to actions generated by users and their friends. These experimental methods were not available to test at the time of this writing, but they were described on the Developer Roadmap.

Photos API Methods

Photos are an important component of the Facebook Platform and user experience. Facebook provides a set of methods for creating and viewing data about albums, uploading and getting photos, and for creating and reading photo tags. The best way to demonstrate each method is by way of example. This will involve creating a new album, uploading a photo, adding a tag, and then retrieving all of this data programmatically:

```
1  $album = $facebook->api_client->photos_createAlbum("Test Album",
   "This is a test album.", "Everywhere", "everyone");
2  $photo = $facebook->api_client->photos_upload("photo.jpg",
   $album["aid"], "This is a test photo.");
3  $tag = $facebook->api_client->photos_addTag($photo["pid"],
   $official_user, null, 50.0, 50.0, null);
4  $albums = $facebook->api_client->photos_getAlbums(null, null);
5  echo "<ul>";
6  foreach($albums as $album) {
7   if($album["name"] != "Profile Pictures") {
8     echo "<li>".$album["aid"].": ".$album["name"]."</li>";
9     $photos = $facebook->api_client->photos_get(null, album["aid"],
      null);
10    echo "<ul>";
11    foreach($photos as $photo) {
12      echo "<li>".$photo["pid"].": ".$photo["caption"]."</li>";
13      $tags = $facebook->api_client->photos_getTags($photo["pid"]);
14      if(is_array($tags)) {
15       echo "<ul>";
16       foreach($tags as $tag) {
17         echo "<li>".$tag["subject"].": (".$tag["xcoord"].", ".
         $tag["ycoord"].")</li>";
```

```
18    }
19    echo "</ul>";
20    }
21    }
22    echo "</ul>";
23    }
24  }
25  echo "</ul>";
```

An album is created on line 1, which includes setting its name, description, and location details. The final parameter is for setting privacy permissions and can be set to one of everyone, friends, friends-of-friends, or networks. Unless you are going to display an advanced user interface for your users to select particular permissions, it is recommended that you set this to null. The resulting $album array includes keys such aid, owner, name, created, and a link to the album on Facebook. Once an album has been created, you can then upload a photo to that album using the returned $album["aid"]. If you do not supply an album identifier, the photo will be uploaded to the application's default album, which can contain up to 1,000 photos. The first parameter should be set to an existing image file located on your web server, which in this instance is called photo.jpg. The $photo array will contain the newly created pid and aid and links to the photo src, src_big, src_small, and link. All applications can upload photos. The photos remain in a "pending" state until the user authorizes them or grants the photo_upload extended permission. The only storable values from this method are aid, pid, and the owner who uploaded the photo.

After a photo has been uploaded to Facebook, users can add tags to specific sections to indicate the locations of their friends or other details. The photos.addTag method is used to reference users and provide the horizontal and vertical coordinates of the tag. In the preceding code, line 3 includes a reference to the authenticated user, but this could be the Facebook identifier of any user. If this were set to null, the next parameter could contain a string of text to identify an object in the photo.

On line 4, an array of albums is extracted, which could be restricted to a particular user by inserting a Facebook identifier as the first parameter, or to a set of albums by supplying an array of aid values as the second parameter. This array of albums is then iterated over and the relevant photos are extracted on line 9 and associated tags for each photo on line 13. Although the photos.getTags uses just a single pid, you could also use an array of multiple pid values, and for the photos.get method you could set the first parameter as a Facebook identifier or the third parameter as an array of pid values.

Events API Methods

As with photos, Facebook provides an extensive Events API for creating, editing, and canceling events and for inviting friends and setting RSVP status. Creating events on behalf of a user requires the create_event extended permission. Setting RSVP status requires rsvp_event, which is explored in Chapter 7. For now, you should visit the following two URLs, replacing <<API_KEY>> with your own API key, which will grant extended permissions to your application:

- http://www.facebook.com/authorize.php?api_key=<<API_KEY>>&v= 1.0&ext_perm=create_event

- http://www.facebook.com/authorize.php?api_key=<<API_KEY>>&v= 1.0&ext_perm=rsvp_event

When handling events, your application will be added as an administrator for the event and the authenticated user as the creator. Therefore, you can edit and cancel events as required. Events created by the events.create method require the creation of an Events object, which must be converted to JSON. The one tricky element with creating events is that Facebook handles time data very strangely. The time is converted to UTC (coordinated universal time) based on the assumption that the date already exists in Pacific time format (Facebook server's time), which could have major implications on your applications if they are using another time zone, such as Greenwich mean time (GMT). However, you can counteract this by creating a function using DateTime and DateTimeZone objects:

```
function prepare_time($time) {
 $date_string = date("r", $time);
 $datetime = new DateTime($date_string);
 $facebook_time = new DateTimeZone("America/Los_Angeles");
 $datetime->setTimezone($facebook_time);
 $offset = $datetime->getOffset();
 $offset = $offset * (-1);
 $datetime->modify($offset." seconds");
 return $datetime->format("U");
}
```

This function will take a time and then reverse the offset that is applied by Facebook so that when it is stored it is translated to the original time. To find the original function, go to http://forum.developers.facebook.com/viewtopic.php?pid=129685.

With this function at hand, you can then create an event using the three required parameters (name, start_time, and end_time):

```
$start_time = gmmktime(22, 0, 0, 3, 25, 2010);
$start_time = prepare_time($start_time);
$end_time = gmmktime(23, 0, 0, 3, 25, 2010);
$end_time = prepare_time($end_time);
$event_info = array(
 "name" => "Test Event",
 "start_time" => $start_time,
 "end_time" => $end_time
);
$event_info = json_encode($event_info);
$event = $facebook->api_client->events_create($event_info,
"event_logo.png");
```

This code creates an event whose date is March 25, 2010, with a start time of 10 p.m. and an end time of 11 p.m. An optional `file` parameter is also passed to the `events.create` method, which must be a file saved on your web server. If successful, the `$event` variable will contain a numeric Facebook event identifier. To demonstrate the other parameters that can be set, you can use the `events.edit` method on the returned `$event`:

```
$event_info = array(
 "name" => "Updated Test Event",
 "category" => 1,
 "subcategory" => 1,
 "location" => "My House",
 "street" => "1 Test Lane",
 "city" => "London",
 "phone" => null,
 "email" => null,
 "page_id" => null,
 "description" => "This is a test event.",
 "privacy_type" => "SECRET",
 "tagline" => null,
 "host" => "Me"
);
$event_info = json_encode($event_info);
$updated_event = $facebook->api_client->events_edit($event, $event_info);
```

The additional values include an event category and subcategory (http://wiki.developers.facebook.com/index.php/Event_Categories). These are set to a "Party > Birthday Party", a `page_id` (which can be used to associate an event with a particular group or page), and `privacy_type` (which can be one of OPEN, CLOSED, or SECRET, depending on how discoverable you want your event to be). Again, an image can be supplied as the third parameter in the call to `events.edit` if you want to update it. If the update was successful, the `$updated_event` value will be set to 1.

After your event has been created and users have granted the `rsvp_event` extended permission, you can set their RSVP status by using the following:

```
$rsvp = $facebook->api_client->events_rsvp("<<EVENT_ID>>", "unsure");
```

The values for status can be one of `attending`, `unsure`, or `declined`. Users attending an event might want to invite their friends. This is catered for via the `events.invite` method, which accepts an event identifier as its first parameter, an array of the user's friends' identifiers, and an optional message to be sent along with the invitation. Another useful method is `events.getMembers`, which helps you display which members have been invited to an event and their RSVP status. You can use this if you want to provide your own events interface and allow users to view others who are attending on your own site. It can be used as follows:

```
$members = $facebook->api_client->events_getMembers("<<EVENT_ID>>");
```

The `$members` variable will contain four array keys: `attending`, `unsure`, `declined`, and `not_replied`. These contain arrays of user identifiers according to RSVP status. If you are unsure about an event identifier, you can use the `events.get` method to extract all the events for a specified user. You can filter this by start and end times and by RSVP status. For example, to find the test event that was just created, you just use the following:

```
$events = $facebook->api_client->events_get($official_user, null,
$start_time, $end_time, "attending");
```

The method will return an array of events that match the query, and any or all the parameters can be set to `null` to include more results. The second parameter can be an array of event identifiers if you want to extract details from a list of known events that have been created by your application or within Facebook. Finally, events can be canceled by calling the following:

```
$facebook->api_client->events_cancel("<<EVENT_ID>>", "This event has been
cancelled by the organisers due to bad weather.");
```

The second parameter is a message that is sent to all users detailing why the event has been canceled. If you do not want to provide an explanation, you can exclude this parameter from the method call. The Facebook API gives access to many of the events functions which can be used within applications to create, update, and delete Facebook events. They also enable you to set RSVP status for users and create simple ways for them to invite a list of friends.

Custom Tags API Methods

The final set of methods can be used for registering, retrieving, and deleting custom tags. Custom tags allow developers to extend existing FBML tags by defining their own and optionally sharing them with others. Tags consist of FBML snippets that are rendered during parse time and can be either private or public. Custom tags can be defined with the `fbml.registerCustomTags` method and are referenced by importing them into a namespace using the `xmlns` attribute of the `<fb:fbml>` tag. Unfortunately, at the time of this writing, there is no way to use custom tags in Facebook Platform for website applications. So, your best option is to keep tracking the Facebook Developer Roadmap for an alert about this addition.

An Overview of FQL

FQL can be used to perform many of the retrieval functions of the Facebook API, but it even enables greater customization such as multiquery support. FQL queries can be made more efficient than Facebook API counterparts because you can specify which fields you want returned, which condenses request outputs, and allows for a standard interface for data extraction. A number of FQL tables are available (and which you'll be using throughout Chapters 6 and 7). With these tables, you'll be able to access the following:

- Application data via the `application`, `developer`, `metrics`, `notification`, and `cookies` tables

- Event data via the `event` and `event_member` tables
- Family and friends data via the `connection`, `family`, `friend`, `friend_request`, `standard_friend_info`, `friendlist`, and `friendlist_member` tables
- Group data via the `group` and `group_member` tables
- Inbox data via the `mailbox_folder`, `message`, and `thread` tables
- Links data via the `link` and `link_stat` tables
- Page data via the `page`, `page_admin`, and `page_fan` tables
- Photo data via the `album`, `photo`, and `photo_tag` tables
- Privacy data via the `permissions`, `permissions_info`, and `privacy` tables
- Stream data via the `comment`, `like`, `status`, `stream`, and `stream_filter` tables
- User data via the `profile`, `standard_user_info` and `user` tables
- Video data via the `video` and `video_tag` tables
- Plus, other data such as notes and translations via the `note` and `translation` tables

Through these tables, you can access almost any element of Facebook data provided that you have sufficient permissions. To get you started, here is what a typical FQL query looks like:

```
$fql = "SELECT uid2 FROM friend WHERE uid1=".$official_user." LIMIT 10";
$friends_fql = $facebook->api_client->fql_query($fql);
foreach($friends_fql as $friend) {
 echo '<p><fb:name uid="'.$friend["uid2"].'" /></p>';
}
```

This query is equivalent to the Facebook API function used in the previous section to retrieve a user's friends using the `friends.get` method, but this one has been limited to ten friends. Note also how the user identifier is extracted using `$friend["uid2"]`, which maps to the fields returned by the FQL query. Table 5.1 provides some examples of the commutability of the Facebook API and FQL queries.

The main difference is that when you are using the Facebook API methods, you must include the `<<UIDS>>` and `<FIELDS>` parameters as an array (but these must be a comma-separated list when using FQL). The `<<FLID>>` parameter exists only in the Facebook API for specifying a friends list identifier and alongside `<<UID>>` must be supplied as a single string. Data from the user information method cannot be stored but can be displayed, whereas the standard information method may be used to store user data for internal analytics but cannot be used to display user information.

Table 5.1   Common Relationships between Facebook API Methods and FQL

Description	Facebook API	FQL
Get user information	`users_getInfo(` `<<UIDS>>,` `<<FIELDS>>` `)`	`SELECT <<FIELDS>>` `FROM user` `WHERE uid IN (` `<<UIDS>>` `)`
Get a user's friends	`friends_get(` `<<FLID>>,` `<<UID>>` `)`	`SELECT uid2` `FROM friend` `WHERE uid1 =` `"<<UID>>"`
Get user standard information (for example, name, birthday, locale, and sex)	`users_getStandardInfo(` `<<UIDS>>,` `<<FIELDS>>` `)`	`SELECT <<FIELDS>>` `FROM` `standard_user_info` `WHERE uid IN (` `<<UIDS>>` `)`

Unlike database SQL, in FQL you can supply only one table name in the FROM clause, which is where you can use the FQL multiquery functionality. For example, suppose you want to get some data about users who are members of a group. You'd have to perform two queries in a row, waiting for the results of the first query before running the second query, because the second query depends on data from the first one. With `$facebook->api_client->fql_multiquery()`, you can run both results at the same time and get all results at once, which is more efficient than running single queries. An example follows:

```
$queries = array(
 "group_members" => "SELECT uid, positions FROM group_member
 WHERE gid='2205007948' LIMIT 5",
 "members_details" => "SELECT id, name, url, pic FROM profile WHERE id IN
 (SELECT uid FROM #group_members)"
);
$queries = json_encode($queries);
$data = $facebook->api_client->fql_multiquery($queries);
```

Notice that your queries need to be JSON encoded before being passed to the multi-query method. Assuming that a valid `gid` was provided, the `$data` variable will return the following:

```
Array (
 [0] => Array (
  [name] => group_members
  [fql_result_set] => Array (
   [0] => Array ([uid] => XX [positions] =>)
   [1] => Array ([uid] => YY [positions] =>)
   ...
  )
 )
 [1] => Array (
  [name] => members_details
  [fql_result_set] => Array (
   [0] => Array ([id] => XX [url] => XX [name] => XX [pic] => XX)
   [1] => Array ([id] => YY [url] => YY [name] => YY [pic] => YY)
   ...
  )
 )
)
```

To access the results, you can use the following code:

```
$group_members = $data[0]["fql_result_set"];
$members_details = $data[1]["fql_result_set"];
$i = 0;
foreach($group_members as $group_member) {
 echo '<fb:name uid="'.$group_member["uid"].'"></fb:name> 
 '.$members_details[$i]["name"].'<br />';
 $i++;
 }
```

The ordering of results is the same as supplied to the query, which is why `$group_members` accesses the first set of data and `$members_details` the second. Inside those arrays, the data is also ordered symmetrically so that the first result in one is also the first result in the other. In the example above, this should produce two identical name values. The multiquery functionality can prove quite useful when used in conjunction with the FQL to get the user's friends who are application users by using the following base and replacing <<UID>> with the logged-in user's Facebook identifier:

```
SELECT uid FROM user
WHERE uid IN (
 SELECT uid2 FROM friend WHERE uid1="<<UID>>"
) AND is_app_user
```

Using this base, an application can use the user's set of friends who have also added the application to make features more prominent to them or to help a user find those friends who have not added the application to invite them to do so. The results can then be wrapped within `<fb:name>` or `<fb:profile-pic>` XFBML tags to reveal the user's friends' names and profile pictures. You can also request other features via the `<fb:prompt-permission>` XFBML element, such as allowing an application to send e-mail to users, updating status, uploading and tagging photos, creating and modifying events, and many other Facebook functionalities. These permissions can then be queried via the `$facebook->api_client->users_hasAppPermission()` method to test whether a user has granted application access before executing Facebook events.

XFBML

XFBML, the Facebook Markup Language for websites, is the Facebook equivalent of HTML and can be used to provide social context to your applications. For example, the `<fb:name>` element can be used to render a user's name if you supply a uid parameter such as `$official_user`. The full list of XFBML parameters is available from the Facebook Developer wiki, and most are explored in Chapters 6 and 7. Here is a sample of common XFBML elements you can use in your applications:

- **fb:bookmark**

  The `<fb:bookmark>` tag renders an Add Bookmark button on your website so that a user can add your application to a user's profile. If the user already bookmarked your application, the bookmark will not be shown. To adhere to Facebook's terms of service, you cannot force a user to bookmark your application but could highlight the additional benefits, such as how a bookmark contributes to applications and game dashboards, as discussed in Chapter 8.

- **fb:name**

  The `<fb:name>` tag can be used to render the user's name and requires a uid parameter to be set. Optional parameters include `firstnameonly`, which can be set to `true` to just display the user's first name, `linked` to add a link to the user's profile, or `possessive` to make the user's name possessive (for example, *Mark's*). You can use other parameters such as `reflexive` and `ifcantsee` to render a string of text for users whose names cannot be retrieved for privacy reasons. As with the `<fb:profile-pic>` tag (described next), this tag ensures that you always have the user's most recent name rendered by your application.

- **fb:profile-pic**

  The `<fb:profile-pic>` tag renders a profile picture of the user supplied in the required uid parameter. For Facebook Platform for websites applications, an optional `facebook-logo` parameter can be set to display a Facebook logo in the bottom corner of the user's profile picture. Using this tag will ensure that whenever you want to show a user's photograph it will be his or her most current one.

- **fb:pronoun**

  For applications that want to display a *he, she,* or *they* within text the `<fb:pronoun>` tag can be used. This option reduces the need to store the user's gender in an application to perform the same logic.

- **fb:user-status**

  The `<fb:user-status>` tag can be used to show the status of the user supplied in the `uid` parameter.

Unlike FBML parameters used within canvas pages, XFBML elements *must* use a closing tag, such as `<fb:name uid="512973464"></fb:name>`. All XFBML tags can contain an optional `condition` attribute, which can be used to hide or show elements such as the following:

```
<fb:container condition="FB.XFBML.Conditions.ifCanSee('512973464',
'profile')">
 <p>This is only visible if the user can see the profile of user
 512973464.</p>
</fb:container>
```

This could be particularly useful to adhere to privacy restrictions set by users if they have blocked access to their details to specific users. As you can see, the extensibility of XFBML means that you can start building applications that use Facebook data with as little data as a user's identifier. When used in combination with the Facebook API and FQL, you can integrate the look and feel of Facebook within your web pages just by including the Facebook libraries. This can also be extended by making use of the dialog and animation libraries provided by Facebook (see Chapter 8) for adding greater functionality to your applications.

Summary

Facebook is one of the most visited sites on the Web, with millions of users coming back each day. Since the release of the Facebook Platform on May 24, 2007, thousands of applications have been developed. As an evolutionary step for the Facebook Platform, you can use Facebook to integrate with your own site, desktop application, Apple iPhone application, and beyond. Now you can leverage your existing user base and attract new and existing users using the power of the Facebook social graph. In this chapter, you were given an overview of the Facebook Platform. This included setting up a new application, Test Tube, which will be used in Chapters 6 and 7. The next chapter explores authentication and application translations in more detail.

6

Registration, Authentication, and Translations with Facebook

Chapter 5, "An Overview of Facebook Platform Website Integration," introduced you to the Facebook Platform as a technology that facilitates identity and friend connection sharing with any Internet-enabled device through client-side and server-side libraries that can be used to access many of the Facebook resources described in this chapter and in Chapter 7, "Using Facebook for Sharing, Commenting, and Stream Publishing." The Facebook Platform for website integration toolset is split into two interrelated sections: one for registration, authentication, and translations (discussed in this chapter); and one for adding social interactions such as commenting, publishing, and for content sharing (see Chapter7).

This chapter explores how to handle the user registration and authentication process via Facebook. This includes handling users logging in and out of Facebook and helping them reclaim accounts if they have deactivated their Facebook account. When users are connected to a site through Facebook, either for the first time or as a returning user, they may want to search for friends. Doing so is facilitated through the Facebook API client libraries, both client and server side. Once registered via Facebook, you can begin to personalize content and publish to a user's stream (as covered in Chapter 7).

User Authorization and Authentication

Facebook can be used as a login mechanism for users of any website or Internet-enabled application such as a cell phone or game console. If a user registers an account using Facebook and already has an account and profile on the third-party application, this can be linked to the user's Facebook account and that user can start finding his or her friends who have already connected their accounts. Three of the main processes for handling Facebook logins will be described in this section:

- Logging users in with Facebook for the first time, registering their details, and when they revisit the application, detecting whether they can be logged in automatically using their Facebook account

- Logging users out of the application using Facebook and handling de-registration if they choose to disconnect their account
- Helping users reclaim their third–party application accounts if they choose to de-activate their Facebook accounts

Both the Facebook API PHP client library and the JavaScript API provide functionality to handle each of these processes, which can be integrated seamlessly into existing code. Most of the functionality is contained within the post-authorize callback URL, post-remove callback URL, and account reclamation URL, which were explained in Chapter 5. In the case of the first two URLs these are "pinged" by Facebook without redirecting the user anywhere. The account reclamation URL should be a branded page that users visit, enabling them to create an independent, non-Facebook account.

The workflow of a Facebook authorization is shown in Figure 6.1. It shows the exchange between your application server, the user's web browser, and Facebook in rendering login buttons and creating a session.

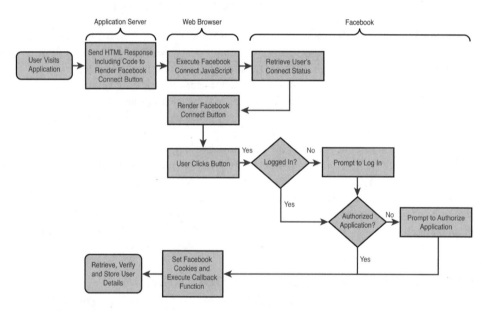

Figure 6.1   Standard Facebook Platform for websites authentication workflow.

The workflow keeps user information secure through several means. These include signing the user's session with a secret key that can be verified within your applications to ensure that the information came from Facebook and not a malicious source. The browser mediates all communication, meaning user identifiers are kept private unless users who have accessed your application have authenticated themselves within Facebook. Finally, during the authentication step, no information about the application is passed to Facebook apart from your API key.

Logging In and Detecting Facebook Status

When users visit a website or application that is using Facebook, they can be in one of three states: *Connected*, which means that they are logged in to Facebook and have authorized the application; *Not Logged In*, which means that they are not logged in to Facebook, and so their Facebook status cannot be evaluated (and so need to be prompted to log in or create a Facebook account); or they are *Not Authorized*, which means they have logged in to Facebook but have not connected to the application. For most applications, the distinction between *Not Logged In* and *Not Authorized* is not important because they both require users to log in to their Facebook account. This detection is handled using the Facebook JavaScript library using the `FB.Connect.get_status()` function:

```
FB.Facebook.init("<?php echo API_KEY; ?>");
FB.ensureInit(function() {
 FB.Connect.get_status().waitUntilReady(function(status) {
  switch (status) {
   case FB.ConnectState.connected:
    loggedIn = true;
    break;
   case FB.ConnectState.appNotAuthorized:
    loggedIn = false;
    break;
   case FB.ConnectState.userNotLoggedIn:
    loggedIn = false;
  }
 });
});
```

For users who are not logged in, Facebook provides an `<fb:login-button>` XFBML element that handles the process of registering users, which can be shown or hidden depending on their connection state. The `<fb:login-button>` element is displayed whether a user is logged in or not, and so its visibility should be handled programmatically to prevent confusion. This could be performed server side by testing whether `$facebook->get_loggedin_user()` or the `FB.Connect.get_loggedInUser()` function returns a user identifier or `null`. If a user is logged in, you can set the `autologoutlink` parameter of the `<fb:login-button>` element to `true` to show logout text instead.

For applications that do not use the XFBML element, the `FB.Connect.require Session()` function can be used. This function contains three parameters for providing a callback: for a successful session creation, for an unsuccessful session creation, and a final parameter that must be set to `true` for registering a user action hint. Usage of this function could be as follows:

```
<a href="#" onclick="FB.Connect.requireSession(function() { alert(true); },
null, true); return false;"> Connect with Facebook</a>
```

Once users are logged in using Facebook, the application can make Facebook API calls on their behalf. If this is the first time they've connected to the site, their details will be pinged to the post-authorize callback URL, which is detailed in the "Using the Post-Authorize Callback URL" section. If they are returning users, they will be connected and a new session created for the application.

Detecting and Handling Facebook State Changes

For sites that generate content using server-side processing, it is often simplest to refresh the page when users connect or log out or redirect them depending on their connection state. This is to prevent having to update all elements using client-side scripts, which may become complex if multiple states are tested. Within the `FB.init()` function, three parameters can be provided to handle state changes: `reloadIfSessionStateChanged`, which can be set to `true` to refresh the current page; `ifUserConnected`, which can be set either to a URL for redirection or to a JavaScript function to perform client-side processing; and `ifUserNotConnected`, which can be set in the same way as `ifUserConnected`. An example, which now includes a URL to the cross-domain communication channel file `xd_receiver.htm` explored in Chapter 5, is as follows:

```
FB.init(
 "<?php echo API_KEY; ?>", "xd_receiver.htm",
 {
  "ifUserConnected":"http://myfacebookapp.com/member.php",
  "ifUserNotConnected":"http://myfacebookapp.com/register.php"
 }
);
```

In the example above, http://myfacebookapp.com/member.php and http://myfacebookapp.com/register.php would need to exist on your web server, and so could be replaced by JavaScript functions such as `onConnected()` and `onNotConnected()` to process the connection client side. A single `user` parameter will be passed to the `onConnected()` function:

```
FB.init(
 "<?php echo API_KEY; ?>", "xd_receiver.htm",
 {
  "ifUserConnected": onConnected(user),
  "ifUserNotConnected":onNotConnectd()
 }
);
```

The `reloadIfSessionStateChanged` parameter could also be set to refresh the page, which promotes the use of the `$facebook->get_loggedin_user()` method to test for user credentials. Listing 6.1 shows a simple skeleton Facebook implementation that includes status change handling and uses both client-side and server-side processing. You should save this as `index.php` and upload it to your web server alongside the Facebook client files.

Listing 6.1   **A Sample Facebook Page**

```php
1   <?php
2   include "config.php";
3   include "functions.php";
4   include "facebook-platform/php/facebook.php";
5   $facebook = new Facebook(API_KEY, SECRET);
6   $user = $facebook->get_loggedin_user();
7   ?>
8   <!DOCTYPE html PUBLIC "-//W3C//DTD XHTML 1.0 Strict//EN"
    "http://www.w3.org/TR/xhtml1/DTD/xhtml1-strict.dtd">
9   <html xmlns="http://www.w3.org/1999/xhtml"
    xmlns:fb="http://www.facebook.com/2008/fbml">
10  <head>
11  <title>Facebook Integration</title>
12  </head>
13  <body>
14  <fb:login-button autologoutlink="true" onlogin="connected(); return
    false;"></fb:login-button>
15  <?php echo "<p>User Identifier: ".($user ? $user : "Unknown").
    "</p>"; ?>
16  <p>Facebook Name: <span id="facebook_name">Unknown</span></p>
17  <p>Facebook Status: <span id="connect_status">Unknown</span></p>
18  <script src="http://static.ak.connect.facebook.com/js/api_lib/v0.4/
    FeatureLoader.js.php/en_GB" type="text/javascript"></script>
19  <script type="text/javascript">
20  function connected() {
21    document.getElementById("facebook_name").innerHTML =
      '<fb:name uid="loggedinuser" useyou="false"></fb:name>';
22    FB.XFBML.Host.parseDomTree();
23  }
24  function not_connected() {
25    document.getElementById("facebook_name").innerHTML = "Unknown";
26  }
27  FB.init("<?php echo API_KEY; ?>", "xd_receiver.htm", {
    "reloadIfSessionStateChanged":true, "ifUserConnected":connected,
    "ifUserNotConnected":not_connected});
28  FB.ensureInit(function() {
29    FB.Connect.get_status().waitUntilReady(function(status) {
```

```
30    switch (status) {
31      case FB.ConnectState.connected:
32        document.getElementById("connect_status").innerHTML =
          "Connected";
33        break;
34      case FB.ConnectState.appNotAuthorized:
35        document.getElementById("connect_status").innerHTML =
          "Not Authorized";
36        break;
37      case FB.ConnectState.userNotLoggedIn:
38        document.getElementById("connect_status").innerHTML =
          "Not Logged In";
39      }
40    });
41    });
42  </script>
43  </body>
44  </html>
```

This sample code demonstrates how to handle a Facebook login using both client-side and server-side code. The `<fb:login-button>` on line 14 uses an additional `onlogin` parameter that links to the JavaScript function on lines 20 to 23. This function simply updates the element `facebook_name` and includes a call on line 22 that is required to parse and render the XFBML. The `connected()` function is also referenced on line 27 along with a `not_connected()` function that will update the `facebook_name` element without having to click the login button. As the page is refreshed on status change, the `$user` variable on line 6 will remain current.

Storable User Data

To adhere to Facebook Platform policies, you cannot cache any user data you receive from Facebook for more than 24 hours. The exception to this rule is if an application is being run on a device controlled by and possessed by the user, such as a desktop or mobile device. However, data cannot be stored remotely and must be stored locally in the absence of a user's Internet connection. There are values that can be stored indefinitely, including `uid`, `aid`, `eid`, `email`, `flid`, `gid`, `page_id`, `pid`, and `post_id`. You cannot store relationships between these values, though, because these must be extracted programmatically via the Facebook API or via FQL tables.

Facebook utilizes cookies upon a user logging in, so you can extract cookie data via the `data.getCookies` method or via the `cookies` FQL table:

```
$cookie = $facebook->api_client->data_getCookies($user, null);
```

This method will return a multidimensional array of cookie parameters, with each including `uid`, `name`, `value`, `expires`, and `path` keys. For added security, and to ensure the cookies remain unique, each value for name is suffixed by your application's API key. For example, you can access the value of the session key by using $cookie[1]["<<API_KEY>>_session_key"] as the session key is returned as the second value in the array. Alternatively, you can supply <<API_KEY>>_session_key as the second parameter of the data.getCookies method, replacing <<API_KEY>> with your application's session key.

It is possible to take advantage of Facebook's cookie mechanism by setting your own values via the data.setCookie method. Although this might be beneficial for small-scale data storage, you must be aware that cookies are embedded within each request. A workaround to storing user preferences is to use the Data Store API, which is Facebook's scalable storage solution.

Storing User Preferences via the Data Store API

The Data Store API is a collection of specialized tables and object-oriented "distributed" tables with associations. Storing user preferences is catered for via a set of specialized tables and methods. The four User Preference API methods are as follows:

- data.setUserPreference for updating one preference
- data.setUserPreferences for updating multiple preferences
- data.getUserPreference for retrieving one preference
- data.getUserPreferences for retrieving all preferences

Applications can store up to 201 preferences for each user. These preferences are given an identifier between 0 and 200. As with other Facebook API methods, these are supported by the client library. An example follows:

```
$preference = $facebook->api_client->data_setUserPreference(0, "male");
echo $facebook->api_client->data_getUserPreference(0);
```

The first parameter in the data.setUserPreference is the numeric identifier for the preference, and the second parameter must be a string that is 128 characters or fewer. To remove a preference, you pass an empty string or a value of 0 to the method. You can set multiple preferences by providing an associative array as the first parameter of the data.setUserPreferences method along with a Boolean parameter for telling Facebook that you want to replace existing preferences or whether they should be merged with existing preferences. For example, if a user has set the first, third, and fourth preferences, you might want to set the second preference at a later stage. The associated data.getUserPreferences will return an array of preferences for an optional user identifier. This means that you can extract preferences for any user as well as the current user via these methods.

User Registration Using the Post-Authorize Callback URL

When a user first connects to an application, Facebook pings its post-authorize callback URL, which was set in Chapter 5, via a POST operation with the following fields so that the user's details can be stored for future reference:

- fb_sig_added, fb_sig_authorize, and fb_sig_in_new_facebook

These three fields will always be set to `1`.

- `fb_sig_api_key`, `fb_sig_app_id`, `fb_sig_expires`, `fb_sig_session_key`, and `fb_sig_ss`

  The `fb_sig_app_id` and `fb_sig_api_key` fields should already be available to the host but can be used if multiple applications are maintained on a single domain to perform customized addition on a per-application basis. The remaining parameters can be used to perform Facebook API actions for the `fb_sig_user` and will remain valid until the value of `fb_sig_expires` or if the user uninstalls. The session secret (`fb_sig_ss`) is a session-only secret key that can be used to perform Facebook API actions in the place of the `fb_sig_session_key` (and should never be revealed to the user).

- `fb_sig_cookie_sig`

  The signature of the cookie saved for the Facebook user.

- `fb_sig_ext_perms`

  This will be set to `auto_publish_recent_activity`, which is a permission to publish entries to the user's wall and which can be extended to `publish_stream` and `read_stream` (described in Chapter 7).

- `fb_sig_locale`

  This is the user's locale—including language, which is a two-character ISO 639-1-alpha-2 code, plus their country, which is an ISO 3166-1-alpha-2 code separated by an underscore (_) character. For example, for a British English user, it is set to `en_GB`.

- `fb_sig_profile_update_time` and `fb_sig_user`

  The UNIX time when the user last updated his profile and the identifier for the user, which should be the identifier stored within the host to link accounts.

- `fb_sig_time`

  The UNIX time in seconds when the callback was performed.

- `fb_sig`

  The signature of the `POST`, which is used to validate that all fields that have been returned from Facebook have not been tampered with maliciously.

Fields have an `fb_sig` prefix that can be accessed via the `$facebook->fb_params` array with the prefix removed. For example, `fb_sig_authorize` becomes `$facebook->fb_params["authorize"]`. The Facebook signature, `fb_sig`, is not accessible via the `$facebook->fb_params` array and must be accessed via `$_POST["fb_sig"]`. Once connected, the user does not get transferred to the post-authorize callback URL, so this must not contain any Facebook-framed processing information. Listing 6.2 shows a typical page using the Facebook API PHP client library, which is used to verify the connect request, which should be saved as `authorize.php` and uploaded to your web server alongside the Facebook client files.

Listing 6.2   **A Sample Facebook Post-Authorize Callback URL**

```php
1   <?php
2   include "config.php";
3   include "facebook-platform/php/facebook.php";
4   $facebook = new Facebook(API_KEY, SECRET);
5   $facebook_parameters = $facebook->get_valid_fb_params($_POST, null,
    "fb_sig");
6   try {
7    if (!empty($facebook_parameters) && $facebook->fb_params["authorize"]
    == 1) {
8     // Add the user's details to storage using $facebook->
      fb_params["user"] as the identifier
9    } else {
10    // Log unsuccessful addition attempt due to incorrect parameters
11   }
12  }
13  catch (Exception $e) {
14   // Log unsuccessful addition attempt due to exception
15  }
16  ?>
```

The `$facebook` object that is created on line 4 can be used to manipulate the
Facebook API and handle all the Facebook processes. With the Facebook API initialized,
the `$facebook` object can be used to validate the parameters sent to the post-authorize
callback URL on line 5. This method passes in the `$_POST` fields and sets the field "slug,"
which in this instance is `fb_sig`, because all fields are prefixed with these characters,
except for the underscore (_) character, which is appended within the function itself. If
the fields are not valid, an empty array is returned; otherwise, a full set of fields is made
accessible via the `$facebook_parameters` variable or `$facebook->fb_params`.

Logging Out, Disconnecting, and Reclaiming Accounts

Logging users out of a website or application also means logging them out of Facebook,
in a process known as *single sign out*. The single sign out process is used because users may
log out of a third-party application but forget to log out of Facebook where their session
is still active. If you are using the `<fb:login-button>` element with the `autologoutlink`
parameter set to `true`, this process is automatically catered for. If this is not convenient,
Facebook provides two JavaScript functions, `FB.Connect.logout()` and `FB.Connect.
logoutAndRedirect()`, that you can place within an `onclick` parameter of a link or but-
ton. The former accepts a `callback` parameter that is executed on a successful logout, and
the latter requires a URL string that redirects users after they have been logged out. In
PHP, a logout can be performed by the `$facebook->logout()` method, which also
accepts a URL redirection URL.

User Disconnection Using the Post-Remove Callback URL

Disconnecting users from a website or application takes a bit more care and processing. Users can either de-authorize applications via the Facebook Edit Applications page or this can be achieved programmatically via the `$facebook->api_client->auth_revoke Authorization()` method passing in a user identifier; otherwise, the currently logged-in user will be selected. The method will return a 1 if successful or 0 if unsuccessful.

Setting a post-remove callback URL is important because if users want to disassociate their Facebook account with a website or application that has stored details about them, this removal request must be honored. If users choose to sever the link between an application and their Facebook account, the post-remove callback URL will be pinged via a POST operation, which will return the following fields:

- **fb_sig_uninstall**

  This field will always be set to 1, indicating removal.

- **fb_sig_added, fb_sig_api_key, fb_sig_app_id, fb_sig_in_new_facebook, fb_sig_locale, fb_sig_time, fb_sig_user and fb_sig**

  These fields will be the same as those returned by the post-authorize callback URL, except for `fb_sig_added`, which will be set to 0.

Listing 6.3 shows a post-remove callback URL page using the Facebook API PHP client library, which is used to verify the disconnect request and should be populated with code to remove a user's details from the host. Save this code as `remove.php` and upload it to your web server alongside the Facebook client files.

Listing 6.3   **A Sample Facebook Post-Remove Callback URL**

```
1  <?php
2  include "config.php";
3  include "facebook-platform/php/facebook.php";
4  $facebook = new Facebook(API_KEY, SECRET);
5  $facebook_parameters = $facebook->get_valid_fb_params($_POST, null,
   "fb_sig");
6  try {
7   if (!empty($facebook_parameters) && $facebook->fb_params["uninstall"]
   == 1) {
8    // Remove the user's details from storage using $facebook->
     fb_params["user"] as the identifier
9   } else {
10   // Log unsuccessful removal attempt due to incorrect parameters
11  }
12 }
13 catch (Exception $e) {
14  // Log unsuccessful removal attempt due to exception
15 }
16 ?>
```

With the Facebook API initialized, the `$facebook` object can then be used to validate the parameters sent to the post-remove callback URL on line 5. The remaining lines 6 to 15 are the skeleton code suggesting where to place code to remove a user's details or to log an exception.

Reclaiming Deactivated User Accounts

In the unlikely event that users deactivate their Facebook account, there must be adequate controls in place to help them recover their profile on sites that they have already connected to using Facebook. When users deactivate their Facebook account, they are sent an e-mail that includes any Facebook accounts they have linked to and which have provided an account reclamation URL in their application settings. Alongside the application's logo and name, they are given a URL that directs them to the site and that includes two parameters:

- A user identifier (u) containing the Facebook ID of the user wanting to set up the independent account on the site
- An MD5 hash (h) of the user identifier and the application's secret, which should be used for validating legitimate requests

These parameters can be conveniently validated using the `$facebook->verify_account_reclamation($_GET["u"], $_GET["h"])` method, which returns a `true` or `false` depending on the result of the validation. You could then prompt users to create a new account and update their entry in your database using the validated user identifier parameter.

Connecting and Inviting Friends

After users have connected their Facebook account to an application, they may also want to recommend that their friends connect. A special connect request can be sent to friends to encourage them to sign in via Facebook. Facebook provides this functionality via the `<fb:connect-form>` XFBML element, which renders an invitation widget on a page, or via the recommended `FB.Connect.inviteConnectUsers()` function, which renders the same information but within a Facebook pop-up that allows users to select their unconnected friends. Before rendering these options, an application should first test whether a user has any friends whom to invite, which can be displayed via the `<fb:unconnected-friends-count>` XFBML element or the `$facebook->api_client->connect_getUnconnectedFriendsCount()` method. Note that these two features are set to be deprecated but will be replaced by similar methods in the future. A suggested implementation follows:

```
if($user) {
 try {
  $unconnected_friends_count =
  $facebook->api_client->connect_getUnconnectedFriendsCount();
  echo "<p>You have <fb:unconnected-friends-count>
```

```
</fb:unconnected-friends-count>friends who have not connected
their Facebook accounts.</p>";
if($unconnected_friends_count > 0) {
  echo '<p><a href="#" onclick="FB.Connect.inviteConnectUsers();
  return false;">Invite Facebook Friends</a></p>';
  }
}
catch (Exception $e) {
  // There was an exception
  }
}
```

An alternative is to use `<fb:connect-form>` in place of the `FB.Connect.invite ConnectUsers` function link, which you could do as follows:

```
<fb:serverfbml style="width: 350px;">
 <script type="text/fbml">
  <fb:connect-form action="connect_request.php"></fb:connect-form>
 </script>
</fb:serverfbml>
```

The `<fb:connect-form>` must be placed within an `<fb:serverfbml>` XFBML element, which renders FBML inside an `<iframe>` for security reasons. The optional `action` parameter will be pinged with a list of invited friends via an `ids[]` array within a `POST` operation. This can be used to track the individual invitation habits of Facebook users or to analyze invitation conversions. Facebook intends to transition invitations to a tab in their inbox that will display along with private messages and other updates. The inbox will also be the place where users can send shared content to their friends rather than displaying it in their stream.

Facebook Friend Linking

Specific details of friend-linking capabilities were not available at the time of this writing because Facebook was updating its deprecated `$facebook->api_client->connect_registerUsers()` and `$facebook->api_client->connect_unregisterUsers()` methods. You can find further information on the Facebook Developer Roadmap. As new details emerge, code will be added to this book's repository and to the blog at http://www.socialprogramming.info.

As Facebook registration also requires users to enter their e-mail address. These functions could be extremely useful for linking Facebook accounts with existing accounts on your website. For example, if you have collected the e-mail addresses of users on your site, you can register these with Facebook, which will then prompt them to link their accounts. An example without using these friend-linking methods is demonstrated in Chapter 13, "Integrating Twitter, Facebook Connect, and Google Friend Connect."

Translations for Facebook

Translations for Facebook is a free tool for developers. It provides a simplified process to translate a website or application into any of the languages currently supported by Facebook. There are more than 65 locales available, which can be constructed by taking the two-letter ISO 639 language code and joining it with an underscore (_) character to a two-letter ISO 3166 country code. For example, en_US represents U.S. English. Locales generally follow these standards, but there are two exceptions: ar_AR and es_LA, which are "umbrella" locales for Arabic and Spanish. Developers have complete control over the translation process, from registering text for translation to administering and accessing translations. Translations are still a work in progress as Facebook reaches out to communities to provide additional translations for the platform. They are also looking to incorporate translations into other elements with internationalization set for stream attachments (as described in Chapter 7, "Using Facebook Connect for Sharing, Commenting, and Stream Publishing").

Preparing Your Application and Registering Text

To prepare an application for translation, you must set a default locale via the Application Settings panel, which is found on the "Basic" tab of the Application Settings page, which then allows a developer to access the Translations Administration panel (http://www.facebook.com/translations/), as shown in Figure 6.2.

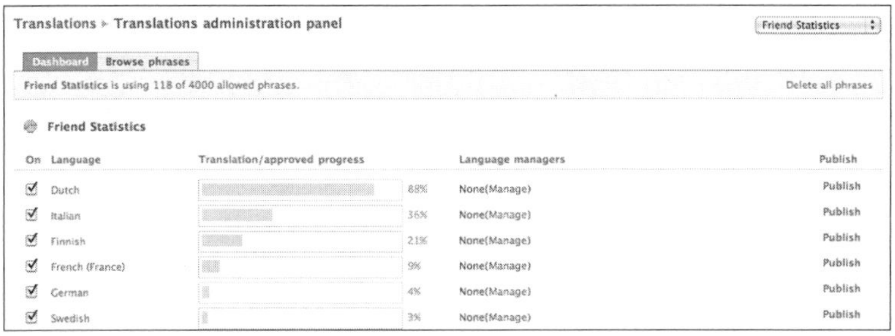

Figure 6.2   Facebook Translations Administration panel.

From this Administration panel, you can enable a language for translation, which will make text strings available to connected users. Translation progress can be reviewed by administrators or designated language managers, and existing translations can be made live, which makes the application appear in the Facebook Application Directory in the new locale.

Once enabled, text that is to be translated can originate from many different sources. Facebook automatically registers the application name, description, and the publish and self-publish text alongside any text contained within `<fb:intl>` elements. Additional strings such as static text contained within databases or within stream stories can be uploaded via the `$facebook->api_client->intl_uploadNativeStrings()` method, translated from within Facebook and then retrieved via the `$facebook->api_client->intl_getTranslations()` or via the Translation FQL table. An example using XFBML follows:

```
1   <fb:intl desc="Label displaying a location that a user has visited">
2     <fb:name uid="loggedinuser" useyou="false" firstnameonly="true">
      </fb:name> has visited {location}.
3     <fb:intl-token name="location"><fb:intl desc="United States of
      America">United States</fb:intl></fb:intl-token>
4   </fb:intl>
```

The code demonstrates how a description can be used (on line 1) that will be shown to the users translating the string. On line 2, the `<fb:name>` element is included alongside a `location` token, which is contained within curly parentheses ({ }). This is accompanied by an `<fb:intl-token>` XFBML element on line 3 containing a country name. This arrangement means that if a different country is submitted, the whole string does not need to be translated again. A list of country names from a database would be submitted to Facebook via the `$facebook->api_client->intl_uploadNativeStrings()` method:

```
$locations = array(
 array(
 "text" => "United States",
 "description" => "United States of America"
 )
);
$uploaded_strings = $facebook->api_client->intl_uploadNativeStrings(
$locations);
```

If successful, the `$uploaded_strings` will contain the number of strings uploaded (1) to Facebook, which will then be made available within the Translations Administration panel. Another example using the `<fb:intl>` and `<fb:intl-token>` tags follows:

```
<fb:intl desc="Label for my favorite number.">
 My favorite number is {number}
 <fb:intl-token name="number">5</fb:intl-token>
</fb:intl>
```

If you are rendering a button or text field that uses a prepopulated `value` attribute, use the `<fb:tag-attribute>` XFBML element:

```
<input type="submit">
 <fb:tag-attribute name="value">
 <fb:intl desc="Button: Submit Form">Submit</fb:intl>
 </fb:tag-attribute>
</input>
```

Finally, if you want to translate the title of your application, use the `<fb:window-title>` XFBML element within the `<body>` tag:

```
<fb:window-title>
 <fb:intl desc="Page Title">Test Tube<fb:intl>
</fb:window-title>
```

The source code for this chapter, which is available from this book's code repository at http://github.com/markhawker/Social-Programming/, includes the internationalized version of the sample application created in the previous section.

Administering and Accessing Translations

After you have registered all of your text for translation, you can guide your users to the Translations Administration panel for your application via the following:

```
http://www.facebook.com/translations/index.php?translate?app=<<APP_ID>>
```

The `<<APP_ID>>` parameter should be replaced by the application identifier created in Chapter 5. As the application creator, you can follow the progress of translations via the Administration panel, and when you have a significant proportion of you application translated, you can publish the translations to make them available to your users (see Figure 6.3). Strings contained within `<fb:intl>` elements will be translated inline translation but could also be retrieved via FQL. For example:

```
SELECT best_string, native_string, translation, approval_status
FROM translation
WHERE locale="<<LOCALE>>"
AND pre_hash_string IN ("United States:::United States of America:")
```

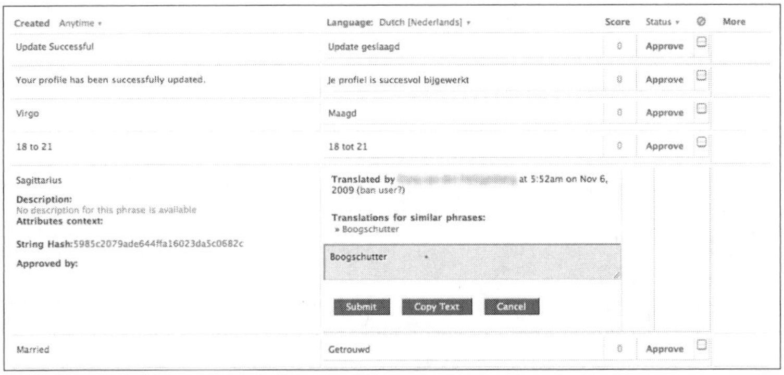

Figure 6.3   Administering, viewing, and publishing user-provided translations.

The <<LOCALE>> should be replaced by the locale of the user, which can be retrieved using the $facebook->api_client->users_getInfo() method and requesting the locale parameter. If the result of the method was stored within a $locale parameter, it can then be extracted by using $locale[0]["locale"]. If the locale parameter cannot be extracted, Facebook will assume that it is en_US. Using the results from this query, you can then decide how to present the translation back to the user. For example, if the approval_status is set to approved, you may want to use that translation. If it is set to unapproved, you might choose to keep the original translation.

As well as using FQL for specific translations, you can retrieve all translations using the $facebook->api_client->intl_getTranslations("all", true) method or for a specific locale by replacing the parameters with the locale code (such as en_GB) and setting the second parameter to false. The approval status for each translated string will be one of auto-approved, approved, or unapproved, which will dictate whether a localized translation is appropriate for use. When you are confident that you have translations ready, you can append FeatureLoader.js.php with a forward slash (/) and the short code for the locale, such as FeatureLoader.js.php/es_LA to display your application in Spanish for a Latin American audience.

Summary

This chapter explored how the Facebook Platform can provide functionality for user authentication and authorization as well as for inviting and connecting with friends across websites and applications. Through the client- and server-side libraries, users can log in, log out, and disconnect seamlessly using only their Facebook account. Facebook can also be used to connect users with their existing Facebook friends, reducing the barrier to entry of mapping their social graph or re-creating networks time and time again. The next chapter describes how the Facebook Platform can be used for content-sharing, commenting, and publishing.

7

Using Facebook for Sharing, Commenting, and Stream Publishing

Chapter 6, "Registration, Authentication, and Translations with Facebook Connect," explained how to use Facebook for user authorization and authentication, which enables users to log in to a website or application using their Facebook credentials. Once connected, it is possible to access users' Facebook details to personalize an application to their needs, such as providing custom content for males or females or international visitors and interacting with their friends. For activity publishing, the Open Stream API can be used to track user activities such as comments, likes, or shares, which can then be retrieved for users and their friends. This creates a "virtuous cycle of sharing" whereby shared content will be made more prominent, thus encouraging further commenting and liking.

This chapter explores how the sharing of multimedia is facilitated using Facebook, which enables users to "push" content to Facebook, and describes how Facebook widgets, such as the Like Box and Live Stream Box, provide scalable solutions for driving traffic and increasing engagement using only a few lines of code. The second section of this chapter discusses social commenting and stream publishing and how you can integrate them into an existing website to enable users to share comments with their friends both inside and outside of the Facebook environment.

Content-Sharing and Live Conversation

Prior to the Facebook Platform for websites, the only option for promoting third-party content was inside Facebook through Facebook pages or groups or by directing users to an external website and attempting to create a custom solution for providing social context. Although users were able to share content such as links, photos, and videos through social bookmarks, e-mail, and other media, there was no easy way for them to share content with their friends on Facebook. There was also no easy way for them to discuss content in real time with friends and others around the world. Facebook Share and widgets attempt to fill this gap by providing easy-to-use services to enable streamlined content sharing and live conversation with Facebook.

Facebook Share

Facebook Share allows you to place a button or link onto a page so that its content can be shared on Facebook. The content can be set to appear in a user's stream or as a message in a friend's inbox. Content can be a link to a page or blog article or other multimedia such as audio, photo, or video, which controls how the content is parsed and displayed when returned to Facebook. You can use either the Facebook `<fb:share-button>` XFBML tag or use the following code, which includes the `FB.Share` library:

```
<a name="fb_share" type="button_count" share_url="http://example.com/">
Share</a>
<script src="http://static.ak.fbcdn.net/connect.php/js/FB.Share"
type="text/javascript"></script>
```

The `<a>` tag contains three attributes: to initialize Facebook Share (`name`), to decide how the button will be rendered (`type`), and the link itself (`share_url`). If the `type` and `share_url` attributes are omitted, the button will default to `button_count` and the URL of the page in which it is placed. Button styles will be explored later in this section, but note that the `Share` text between the anchor tags can be replaced with any text, of any language, to support internationalization of the button. As a comparison to this syntax, the `<fb:share-button>` equivalent looks like this:

```
<fb:share-button class="url" href="http://example.com/"
type="button_count">
</fb:share-button>
<script src="http://static.ak.connect.facebook.com/js/api_lib/
v0.4/FeatureLoader.js.php/en_GB" type="text/javascript"></script>
<script type="text/javascript">
 FB.init("<?php echo API_KEY; ?>");
</script>
```

The `<fb:share-button>` tag contains a `class` attribute, which must be set to `url`, a `href` attribute in replace of `share_url`, and an equivalent `type` attribute. If none of these are supplied, the button will default to the URL for the current page. Whichever method is used to share content, the URL sent to Facebook will be in the format http://www.facebook.com/sharer.php?u=<<url>>&t=<<title>>, where <<url>> and <<title>> must be URL-encoded strings containing the URL of the content that is being shared and its title (for example, http://www.facebook.com/sharer.php?u=www.cnn.com&t=CNN).

Facebook Share can also be used to share other content, such as audio, photo, and video, which can be passed to Facebook so that the content can be accompanied by other meta-data, such as a link to an audio or video file or an album title and artist. Using multimedia tags will enhance the richness of the share because content will be made playable or viewable directly within the user's feed (for example, a YouTube video or an audio track).

Facebook Share and Multimedia Content

As well as links, Facebook Share enables the posting of other multimedia content to Facebook through `<link>` and `<meta>` tags. The process of sharing means that Facebook parses the HTML of the shared content before being published, which means that certain tags can be used to configure its display. To provide a content preview, Facebook will always look for the title of the page, a summary of the content, and an image. These tags must be added within the `<head>` element of pages, such as the following:

```
<head>
 <meta name="title" content="Example Page" />
 <meta name="description" content="This is an example page." />
 <link rel="image_src" href="http://www.example.com/image.png" />
 ...
</head>
```

These basic tags can be extended (depending on the content being shared) by setting the `medium` `<meta>` tag and supplying one of `audio`, `image`, `video`, `news`, `blog`, or `mult`. Additional `<meta>` and `<link>` tags for specific content are as follows:

- **Audio**

  There are two required tags: one `<meta>` tag containing the `audio_type`, which must be set to the content type of the audio (for example, `audio/mpeg3` or `audio/wav`); and a `<link>` to the source of the audio setting the `audio_src`. Optional `<meta>` tags are `audio_title`, `audio_artist`, and `audio_album`, which are all self-explanatory.

- **Video**

  There are four required tags: three `<meta>` tags containing the `video_height`, `video_width`, and the `video_type`, which must be set to the Adobe Flash content type (`application/x-shockwave-flash`), which is the only supported `video_type`; and a `video_src` `<link>` tag provides Facebook with the source URL of the video, which must be registered via the Developer Help Contact Form (http://www.facebook.com/developers/developer_help.php). Providing the domain names that are to be used in the `video_src` attribute ensures that videos will play correctly when content is shared back to Facebook.

Facebook Share tags make it convenient for users to post content back to their feed or via messages. In the examples, the `button_count type` was used to format the button to display a counter with the Facebook Share button, which is 96 pixels wide and 18 pixels high. Other values can be supplied. For example, you can show the counter above the button via `box_count` (57x57px), `button` (56x18px), `icon` (18x15px), or `icon_link` (51x15px). You can find more information about this on the Facebook Developer wiki.

Retrieving Shares, Likes, Comments, and Clicks Using FQL

Although counters can be displayed visually on a page, counts can also be accessed programmatically via the Facebook API. This can prove useful for extracting statistics for a
batch of URLs or for triggering events in applications once a given count has been
achieved. If you reference the `link_stat` table using the Facebook Query Language
(FQL), the following fields can be retrieved from Facebook: `normalized_url`,
`share_count`, `like_count`, `comment_count`, `total_count`, and `click_count`. The
`click_count` is the number of times users have clicked the share on Facebook and
returned back to the original source. Here is what a simple implementation extracting
statistics for two URLs (`facebook.com` and `google.com`) looks like:

```
<?
include "config.php";
include "facebook-platform/php/facebook.php";
$facebook = new Facebook(API_KEY, SECRET);
try {
 $response = $facebook->api_client->fql_query(
 'SELECT url, normalized_url, share_count, like_count, comment_count,
 total_count, click_count FROM link_stat WHERE url IN ("facebook.com",
 "google.com")');
 print_r($response);
}
catch (Exception $e) { print_r($e); }
?>
```

The `$response` from the Facebook API will be a 0-based array of results, which can
then be iterated over using a `foreach()` loop. Note that in FQL you cannot supply an
asterisk (★) for the SELECT clause to return all fields, so these must be entered separately
into the query. Individual fields can be returned by using `$response[n]["field"]`.
For example, `$response[0]["normalized_url"]` would return the normalized URL
http://www.facebook.com. When passing URLs into the WHERE clause of the FQL query,
these must be URL encoded, which can be achieved by wrapping them within the PHP
`urlencode()` function, which ensures that Facebook is able to parse the location. In the
code example above, this was not required because the `http://` prefix was excluded for
brevity. The data returned by queries is cached for 2 minutes by Facebook and is updated
in near real time every 10 to 20 minutes based on network capacity.

Facebook Widgets

Facebook provides a number of widgets that you can use to promote Facebook content
on external websites (for example, the Like Box and Live Stream Box widgets). In comparison to Facebook Share, widgets can be used to "pull" users in to Facebook rather than
push content to it or do both simultaneously, as is the case with the Live Stream Box.
These widgets are highly customizable and use the Facebook Platform library to display
dynamically updated "live" information from Facebook pages. To utilize the functionality

of widgets, you must have access to a Facebook page and administrator privileges. So, this option might not be appropriate in all situations if you are not an administrator (although it is recommended that one is created to supplement the website of an organization, product, or service).

For users' personal profiles, Facebook widgets can also be used to embed a profile badge or photo badge on their web pages, or for sharing their favorite pages via the page badge. These badges are generated dynamically by Facebook and involve adding a chunk of HTML to a web page.

Like Box

Like boxes allow users to become a fan (using the old Facebook terminology which is now being transitioned to mean "those who like a page") of a Facebook page, see how many users are also fans and whether their friends are fans, and to view its activity stream on an external site without having to visit Facebook. A like box can be created using the Like Box Wizard or the `<fb:fan>` XFBML tag. The following example also includes the Facebook Platform library for completeness, which must be omitted if it has already been initialized when using Facebook Share:

```
<fb:fan profile_id="XXXXXXXXXXX" stream="1" connections="10"
width="300"></fb:fan>
<script src="http://static.ak.connect.facebook.com/js/api_lib/
v0.4/FeatureLoader.js.php/en_GB" type="text/javascript"></script>
<script type="text/javascript">
  FB.init("XXXXXXXXXXXXXXXXXXXXXXXXXXXXXXXX");
</script>
```

In the example, the `profile_id` must be replaced by the Facebook page identifier. You can find this by moving your cursor over its profile photo and extracting the `id` parameter of the URL. Alternatively, the `name` parameter can be supplied in replace of `profile_id` if a Facebook page has been secured. The stream parameter indicates whether the page's activity stream is to be included, the `connections` parameter is the number of fans who should be displayed (and can range from 0 to 100), and `width` is used to control the width of the like box. There are also two optional parameters: a `height` parameter that you can use to control the height of the like box (which is 554 pixels high if all features are included and only 64 pixels high if only the "Like" button is shown), and a `css` parameter for setting an external style sheet.

Live Stream Box

The Live Stream Box widget allows users to share activity and comments around an event in real time. As compared to the Comments Box widget, which is explored in the next section, the Live Stream Box widget works best in situations where events are occurring in real time and supports millions of simultaneous users. Users can see comments from their friends as well as others viewing the live stream, which can also be posted back to

Facebook (including a URL link back to the referring website). You can add a Live Stream Box widget by using the `<fb:live-stream>` XFBML tag, as follows:

```
<fb:live-stream event_app_id="<?php echo APP_ID; ?>" xid="default"
width="300" height="500"></fb:live-stream>
```

To identify the live stream box, either the `event_app_id` (the application ID that can be found for your application in the Facebook Developers section of the site) or an `apikey` parameter must be supplied. If multiple live stream boxes exist on the same website, the optional `xid` parameter must be used to help separate the updates and is set to `default` if not supplied. Unlike a comments box, updates from a live stream box cannot be accessed programmatically via the Facebook API.

Social Commenting and Stream Publishing

Facebook widgets are a great way of engaging users and driving traffic to a website, but two additional functionalities can be exploited using the Facebook Platform library: the comments box and stream publishing. Social comments can increase the authenticity and quality of conversation on websites and can increase traffic through the power of the social graph, where users discover new content on Facebook through friends' comments. It is reported that websites that have implemented comments with Facebook Platform integration have seen as much as a 15% to 20% increase in users who register to comment, and even more in total comment activity.

Comments Box

You can use the Comments Box widget to allow users to comment on content from within a website or application. Users have the option of sharing the comment on Facebook, with the comment appearing both on their wall and in their friends' streams. This is a great way to have your users engage in an asynchronous way, whether for a blog, news site, or review application. As with the other Facebook widgets, a comments box can be created through a single `<fb:comments>` XFBML tag that can be customized to suit the particular application. The simplest version of the comments box is using the tag itself, `<fb:comments></fb:comments>`, but the following parameters are available for customization:

- `css`, `numposts`, `width`, `simple`, and `reverse`

  These parameters are used to control the aesthetics of a comments box: `css` for providing an external style sheet; `numposts` for controlling the number of displayed posts (if set to `0`, all comments will be hidden, which allows for comment moderation); `width` for controlling the width of the comments box (and which must include `px` at the end of the value [for example, `600px`]); `simple`, which can be set to `true` to prevent each comment being enclosed within a rounded box; and `reverse` for ordering the comments so that the most recent one appears at the bottom of the list when set to `true`.

- **quiet, title, and url**

  These parameters are used when posting comments back to Facebook and default to the title of the current web page and its URL. The quiet parameter can be set to true so that comments don't send any notifications to Facebook.

- **xid**

  A unique identifier for the comments box if multiple instances exist on the website and can contain alphanumeric characters plus any that are created by the urlencode() function; for example, hyphens (-) or percentages (%).

For administrators, comments can be moderated by clicking the "Administrate Comments" link inline on the comments box (see Figure 7.1). This link gives the option of adding new administrators and moderators as well as enabling settings for global and local comments boxes (such as whitelist and blacklist modes and allowing anonymous comments). Comments that have been entered can also be deleted from here, or this can be done programmatically (as explained in the following section).

Figure 7.1   Sample rendering of a comments
box with inline administration.

One feature is unique to the Facebook Platform: the ability to "listen" for comment submissions via the JavaScript library. You can use the following code within applications that want to trigger an external event upon adding and deleting a comment. It must be placed within the <script> tag with the FB.init() method:

```
1  FB_RequireFeatures(["Comments"],
2   function() {
3    FB.CommentClient.add_onComment(
4     function(comment) {
5      alert("ID: " + comment.user + " Comment Added: " + comment.post);
6     }
7    );
8   }
9  );
```

On line 1, the JavaScript API ensures that the comments feature is loaded, and then the callback function is executed on lines 2 to 8. The function adds a comment listener on line 4 that includes a function to display an `alert()` that accepts a `comment` object containing `user` and `post` values, which hold the unique Facebook identifier for the user and the comment text. Extracting the callback on lines 4 to 6 and instead referencing it by name would mean that the `FB.CommentClient.remove_onComment()` method could also be used to deregister the function. This functionality could be used in conjunction with the detection of whether a user is logged in or out of Facebook (as discussed in Chapter 6) so that functionality can be tailored to non-Facebook users.

Retrieving Comments Using FQL and the Facebook API

As with Facebook Share, comments on Facebook can be accessed programmatically using the Facebook API and FQL. Comments can be retrieved in two ways, both of which have equivalent responses. However, unlike Facebook Share, the Facebook API provides a `comments_get()` method that accepts an `xid` (the unique identifier of the comments box) as its only parameter. Calls to this method will execute the equivalent FQL statement:

```
SELECT xid, object_id, post_id, fromid, time, text, id, username,
 reply_xid
FROM comment
WHERE xid = "<<xid>>"
```

If you are using this Facebook API method, only a single `xid` can be requested at a time. If the `fql_query()` method is used, however, multiple `xid` parameters can be supplied in the same call. The `object_id`, `post_id`, `username`, and `reply_xid` parameters will return `null` values because the `comment` FQL table is also used for returning comments on videos, notes, photos, and other Facebook objects as well as some stream comments. Other returned values include a `fromid`, which is the identifier of the commenter; `time`, which returns a UNIX time stamp of when the comment was posted; and `id`, which is the unique identifier for the comment and local to the `xid`. To add further social context to comments, the `friends_getAppUsers()` can be called. This retrieves a list of the user's friends who have also connected to the calling application. The list can be passed alongside the `xid` inside the `WHERE` clause as a list of `fromid` values.

Adding and Removing Comments Using the Facebook API

As well as retrieving comments, the Facebook API provides functionality for adding and removing comments via the Comments API. You can use the Comments API to integrate an existing comments system with Facebook if the functionality of the comments box is too restrictive (for example, if comments need to be sent in a particular format or external validation checks are required on the inputs). The `comments_add()` method can be used to optionally publish comments to the user's stream (as described in the next section) if it has been granted by the user and contains the following parameters:

- **publish_to_stream, title, and url**

  These optional parameters can be used to publish a comment to the user's stream. The `publish_to_stream` parameter will default to `false` if the user has not granted extended permissions to the calling application. This functionality will be discussed in the following section on stream publishing.

- **text, uid, and xid**

  There are two required parameters, `xid` and `text` (which must be URL encoded) and an optional `uid` parameter that defaults to the identifier of the logged-in user. This parameter can also be accessed by using `$facebook->get_loggedin_user()`, which will return `null` if the user is not logged in. In this instance, the user can be prompted to log in using Facebook.

When you are using the Facebook API PHP client library, there is no need to pass in the extra `session_key` parameter to this method, although this is required for the desktop and JavaScript client library applications.

> **Facebook Developer Principles and Policies**
>
> When using the Comments API to add or remove comments, users should be made aware explicitly of their actions. For example, an application should not post to their stream without their prior knowledge or use any functionality that may deceive them into adding comments inadvertently. A simple "Also Post Comment to Facebook" check box should satisfy this platform policy.

If successful, the `comments_add()` method returns a `comment_id` that can be stored by the calling application, because this is a required parameter for the `comments_remove()` method. The `comments_remove()` method also requires an `xid` parameter and the optional `session_key` parameter. Remember that users can delete their own comments either on Facebook or in the comments box itself. Therefore, this method may return an error if unsuccessful or will return `true` if the comment has been deleted. The three Comments API methods for retrieving, adding, and deleting comments show that aside from the simple installation of the comments box, the Facebook Platform provides greater functionality for administering comments without using the standard tools.

Open Stream API

An accompaniment to the comments box is provided by the Open Stream API. This API allows users to post content, add comments, and create content "likes" (on their profile or on the wall of a Facebook page, group, or event). Not only can the Open Stream API be used to stream content to Facebook (such as that which is provided by Facebook Share or to update their status), but it can also be used to retrieve content, comments, and likes from the user's stream. Using the Open Stream API requires special permissions to be granted by the user in the form of the `publish_stream` and `read_stream` permissions.

Setting these permissions enables applications to publish and read to the user's stream automatically without prompting again unless the user chooses to revoke permissions via his Settings page. Facebook provides the `FB.Connect.showPermissionDialog()` method for streamlining this authorization process, which can be utilized as follows:

```
function get_permissions(names) {
 FB_RequireFeatures(["Connect"],
  function() {
   FB.Connect.showPermissionDialog(names,
   function(response) { alert(response); }, true, null);
  }
 );
}
get_permissions("publish_stream,read_stream");
```

The `get_permissions()` function can be used to show the Permissions dialog box and could be used within a function for writing to or reading from the stream. This is discussed in the next section. On success, the callback function returns a string with a comma-separated list of the permissions that the user has granted. On failure, or if the user cancels the Permissions dialog, a `null` value is returned. Two optional parameters were also supplied to the method: The first is for displaying a drop-down menu so that the user can select pages that they administer and also want the application to write to its stream; and the second parameter can be an array of page or user identifiers to be shown in the drop-down menu. For example, if a user administers two pages, `12345` and `67890`, the method call is as follows:

```
FB.Connect.showPermissionDialog("publish_stream", <<callback>>, true,
[12345,67890]);
```

A list of all the pages where the user is an administrator can be retrieved using the following FQL:

```
SELECT uid, page_id, type
FROM page_admin
WHERE uid = "<uid>"
```

As good practice, the Extended Permissions dialog should be shown the first time the user chooses to publish content from an application rather than the first time it is visited, which is why it has been placed within the `get_permissions()` function. It is also possible to access whether a user has already granted `publish_stream` and `read_stream` permissions by using FQL:

```
SELECT uid, publish_stream, read_stream
FROM permissions
WHERE uid = "<uid>"
```

The result of this FQL query will return a `0` if the user has not granted extended permissions or a `1` if the user has granted permissions. If you are using the `get_permissions()` function, this will always return the permissions that have been granted.

So, if `publish_stream` has been allowed, this will always be returned to the callback. Remember that the `uid` parameter can also be that of a page, and so it can be combined with the FQL for identifying the pages that a user administrates.

Writing Data to the Stream

There are two related processes for writing data to a stream depending on the required workflow of the calling application: via feed forms, which work in a similar way to Facebook Share, where users are first prompted to confirm the content before posting to the stream; or via direct publishing, which requires extended permissions so that content can be streamed directly to Facebook. Generally, it's better to use feed forms rather than direct publishing because feed forms provide users with the most control over what gets posted to their profiles. If using direct publishing, it must be made clear to users that they are publishing to Facebook, and they should always be given the option to opt out of this feature. Both processes use the `FB.Connect.streamPublish()` or `stream_publish()` methods, but their functionality depends on which parameters are supplied to them.

Working with Stream Attachments and Action Links

Stream attachments work in a similar way to the `meta` elements used by Facebook Share in that they give the opportunity to expand on the post by describing what the user did in an application (for instance, sharing a blog post to the stream alongside an image, link, and textual description). Stream attachments are optional, and if one is not supplied the stream function will just update a user's status message. Stream attachments must be JSON-encoded strings and can contain any of the following optional elements:

- **`name`, `href`, and `description`**

  The `name`, `href`, and `description` are used to provide further details about the story and should be as concise as possible so that they are displayed correctly to the user. The `caption` parameter is a subtitle and should describe the action that the user has taken and can contain the `{*actor*}` token, which gets replaced by a link to the profile of the session user. An example caption parameter is `{*actor*}` just posted a new high score!. All these parameters must contain plain text and `href` should be no longer than 1,024 characters.

- **`properties` and `comments_xid`**

  The `properties` parameter can be used to pass in an array of key/value pairs which are shown to the user and are stored by Facebook. These could be used to store data such as high scores for games or ratings for book reviews. To store values that are not shown to the user you would pass in a key/value pair within the method, such as `longitude` and `latitude` values for location-based applications. The `comments_xid` is an application-specific identifier for the comment and can be used to retrieve comments and likes for that comment and for associating it with a comments box.

- **`media`**

  The `media` parameter enables rich media to be associated with the stream post and can be of the type `image`, `flash`, or `mp3`. Only one of these types will be displayed within the stream story, although an array can be supplied, such as for sending multiple photos that can be viewed by clicking a "See More" link that gets appended to the story. Unfortunately, the parameters for each `type` are not the same as with Facebook Share.

Here are three variations of stream attachments shown as PHP arrays and which can be JSON encoded using the `json_encode()` function:

```php
$example_1 = array(
 "name" => "Facebook",
 "href" => "http://www.facebook.com/",
 "description" => "Facebook Home Page",
 "media" => array(
  array(
   "type" => "image",
   "src" => "http://static.ak.facebook.com/images/wiki_logo.png",
   "href" => "http://www.facebook.com/"
  )
 )
);
```

In this example, the user is publishing the Facebook home page to his stream alongside a Facebook logo that directs them to the home page when clicked. The next example demonstrates how the `flash` type can be used within applications:

```php
$example_2 = array(
 "name" => "Facebook Song",
 "href" => "http://www.youtube.com/watch?v=rSnXE2791yg",
 "description" => "Rhett and Link's Facebook Song",
 "media" => array(
  array(
   "type" => "flash",
   "swfsrc" => "http://www.youtube.com/v/rSnXE2791yg&hl=en&fs=1",
   "imgsrc" => "http://i3.ytimg.com/i/bochVIwBCzJb9I2lLGXGjQ/1.jpg",
   "width" => 100,
   "height" => 30,
   "expanded_width" => 320,
   "expanded_height" => 260
  )
 )
);
```

In this example, the user can share a YouTube video, which will be playable within their stream. The user can also share an audio file by using the `mp3` type, which will be rendered using Facebook's MP3 Player widget. (Note that in the third example the `src` parameter is not set.)

```php
$example_3 = array(
 "name" => "Flight of the Bumble Bee",
```

```
"href" => "http://www.last.fm/music/Maksim+Mrvica/_/ The+Flight+of+the+Bumble-Bee",
"description" => "Flight of the Bumble Bee performed by Maksim Mrvica",
"media" => array(
 array(
  "type" => "mp3",
  "src" => "XXXXXX",
  "title" => "Flight of the Bumble Bee",
  "artist" => 'Maksim Mrvica",
  "album" => "The Piano Player"
 )
 )
);
```

As shown by the examples, stream attachments are highly extensible and can be used in multiple ways depending on your needs. They can also be combined with an action link, which is a short string of text that accompanies a stream story and invites the user to take some action related to that story. An example of an action link for an MP3 could be to purchase it via an online store. Like with stream attachments, an action link should be a JSON-encoded string containing two parameters, `text` and `href`, which could be as follows:

```
[{"text":"Buy Song", "href":"<<URL>>"}]
```

Stream attachments and action links are only a small part of the wider scope of publishing and need to be placed in context to be useful. You can see other examples in "The Publisher" section. (The Publisher is used to update a user's status from within Facebook).

Feed Forms and Direct Publishing

Publishing to the stream is achieved through either the `FB.Connect.streamPublish()` or `stream_publish()` methods, depending on whether the application wants to use client- or server-side scripting. Both methods contain similar, but not identical, parameters for publishing to the stream after a user has granted extended permissions to the `publish_stream` functionality. The following optional parameters are shared by both publish methods:

- **`action_links` and `attachment`**

  As detailed above, rich content can be added to a user's stream via the `attachment` and `action_links`, which allows media such as images and video to be added to posts.

- **`target_id`**

  By default, content is published to the logged-in user's stream. By supplying a `target_id`, however, it can be pushed to a page, group, or event or to a friend's wall instead if a valid identifier is provided. This mimics the action of posting on a friend's wall on Facebook.

When you are using the `stream_publish()` server-side method, a `message` parameter should be supplied containing the short update that will be posted alongside any content such as stream attachments or action links. Because this is a direct publishing method, this can be automated if users have granted an application access to post directly to their stream. As an example from the stream attachments, a call to this method may look like the following:

```
$message = "Check out this great song!";
$attachment = $example_3;
$action_links = '';
$target_id = null;
$uid = null;
$response = $facebook->api_client->stream_publish($message, $attachment,
$action_links, $target_id, $uid);
print_r($response);
```

Upon success, the $response parameter will contain a post_id to the published post or will return an error if unsuccessful. As with the Comments API methods, an optional session key or session secret can be supplied to this method, and that is used alongside the uid parameter for posting content on behalf of another user or page. If the user is an administrator of a page and this is supplied in both the target_id and uid parameters, the post will appear as if published by the page itself and not the user.

Removing Stream Posts Programmatically

Removing stream posts is achieved through the stream_remove() method, which requires a post_id parameter and an optional session_key and uid. Posts can be removed only by the application that created them, and therefore it is good practice to save post_id values stored when publishing to the stream. The method returns true if the post was removed or false and an error code if the post could not be removed.

Feed forms can be activated by setting the auto_publish parameter of the FB.Connect.streamPublish() method to false, which prompts the user to add or verify the user_message as advised by the user_message_prompt parameters. Feed forms can be displayed even if the user has not granted extended permissions to the calling application. A callback parameter can be supplied to the method, and this will return post_id, exception and data.user_message values back to the application for further processing. The method uses an actor_id in place of the uid parameter of stream_publish(). Listing 7.1 gives a suggested implementation of a get_write_permission() function.

Listing 7.1 **get_write_permission() Method**

```
1   function get_write_permission() {
2     FB_RequireFeatures(["Connect"],
3       function() {
4       FB.Connect.showPermissionDialog("publish_stream", publish_to_stream,
        false, null);
5     }
```

```
6    );
7    }
8    function publish_to_stream(response) {
9     if(response == "publish_stream") {
10     FB_RequireFeatures(["Connect"],
11      function() {
12       user_message = "This is a test.";
13       attachment = action_links = target_id = actor_id = null;
14       user_message_prompt = "What's on your mind?";
15       auto_publish = false;
16       FB.Connect.streamPublish(user_message, attachment, action_links,
         target_id, user_message_prompt, function(post_id, exception, data)
         { alert(post_id + ", " + exception + ", " + data.user_message); },
         auto_publish, actor_id);
17      }
18     );
19    } else {
20     alert("Extended Permissions Denied");
21    }
22  }
```

Lines 1 to 7 define the `get_write_permission()` function, which will check that the `publish_stream` permission has been accepted and then execute the callback function `publish_to_stream()`. The `publish_to_stream()` function exists on lines 8 to 22 and first checks that a valid `publish_stream` response has been received and if `null` will create an alert box on line 20. A post is then created, and then the `FB.Connect.streamPublish()` method is called on line 16, passing in all the defined parameters. A simple alert box is used as a `callback` to display the response of the request. Functionality can be tested by adding an `onclick="get_write_permission();"` attribute to any HTML link or button. This basic skeleton code can be used to increase complexity such as adding stream attachments or posting to a friend's wall.

Adding and Removing Comments and Likes

As well as posting content to the stream, it is possible for users to both comment and like a post, which can be achieved using the `stream_addComment()` and `stream_addLike()` methods. Both methods require a `post_id` as an identifier, and the `stream_addComment()` method also requires a `comment` parameter containing the user's comment. If successful, the `stream_addComment()` method will return a `comment_id`, whereas the `stream_addLike()` method will return a `true` value. Both methods will return `false` and an error code if unsuccessful. Comments and likes can be removed via the `stream_removeComment()` and `stream_removeLike()` methods, which require a `comment_id` or `post_id` parameter, respectively.

Reading Data from the Stream

Facebook enables you to read users' streams, including content from both their news feed and wall. Reading the stream retrieves all the content of a user's stream, including posts, comments, and likes from the user and their friends (regardless of privacy settings of the posts). Two Facebook API methods that can also be accessed using FQL exist for retrieving posts and comments:

- `stream_get()`

  By default, calls to the `stream_get()` method will return the last 50 posts associated with the logged-in user from the past 180 days. This can be restricted in numerous ways such as supplying `source_ids`, `start_time`, `end_time`, or `limit` parameters but can also contain a `filter_key`. A list of `filter_key` values can be extracted by querying the `stream_filter` FQL table, but it is useful to note that an application-level filter exists in the form `app_xxxxxxxxxxx`, where `xxxxxxxxxxx` is an application identifier. Applying filters will restrict results to the past 9 days.

- `stream_getComments()`

  This method works in an identical way to the `comments_get()` method of the Comments API, but instead indexes the FQL query by `post_id` rather than `xid`. Original posts must have been created by the calling application; otherwise, they will not be retrieved and a successful call will return an array of comments, each containing the fields from the `comment` table.

Both of these methods require the `read_stream` extended permission, so this must be first tested for in the same way as the `publish_stream` permission before requesting the stream or comments. An example call follows:

```
$viewer_id = $source_ids = $start_time = $end_time = $filter_key = null;
$limit = 5;
$metadata = '';
$response = $facebook->api_client->stream_get($viewer_id, $source_ids,
$start_time, $end_time, $limit, $filter_key, $metadata);
print_r($response);
```

A successful `$response` will return an array of `posts` in reverse chronological order, which can be iterated over to extract all of their values. Values include additional `property` and `metadata` that was set using stream attachments, profile data for retrieving thumbnails and URLs, plus access to likes and comment data. To retrieve additional data associated with albums, profiles, and photo tags, you can set the `$metadata` parameter to a JSON-encoded array that includes `albums`, `profiles`, and `photo_tags`. An alternative is to use activity streams, which are Atom-based syndications of user feeds and which can be accessed via the following URL:

```
http://www.facebook.com/activitystreams/feed.php?source_id=<<uid>>
&app_id=<<app_id>>&session_key=<<session_key>>&sig=<<checksum>>&v=0.7&read
&updated_time=<<time>>
```

The `<<uid>>` must set the user identifier that is to be retrieved, `<<app_id>>` is the application identifier, `<<session_key>>` must be a valid session key or session secret for the user, and the `<<checksum>>` is used to verify that the request was sent from a valid application. This parameter is computed by performing the `md5()` function on the combination of an `<<app_id>>`, `<<session_key>>`, and `<<uid>>` appended with the application's secret. For example, if the user identifier is `12345`, application identifier is `67890`, the session key is `ABCDE`, and the application secret is `ZYXWV`, the `<<checksum>>` is as follows:

```
app_id=67890session_key=ABCDEsource_id=12345ZYXWV
```

This would result in a value of `47fdd4fe6cc4f19f58f1485c33749a9b` that should be passed as the `<<checksum>>`. The `<<time>>` parameter is an optional UNIX time stamp indicating that results should be returned only for posts after this time. The functionality of activity streams might not suit all applications and so has not been covered in great detail, although it could be used if you want to subscribe to activity within a news reader.

All of these Open Stream API methods can be used to make rich applications that users and their friends can interact with both inside and outside of the Facebook environment. As you can see, some overlap exists between the Open Stream API and other services, such as the Comments API and Facebook widgets, that you can use to hide some of the complexities of stream publishing for people who are not developers. The extensibility of the methods provided by the Facebook API PHP client library and JavaScript client library reduce the barriers to entry in creating rich device-independent applications, whether client or server side.

The Publisher

The Publisher is the primary feature for users to post information and messages on their own wall or on their friends' walls. Applications can create their own Publisher interface, which enables users to post rich content to profiles and which will appear in their stream. Applications are sorted with default applications first such as for photos, videos, and events, and then by how recently the application was used by the user. The Publisher interface looks similar to users when viewing their own profile as when viewing a friend's profile, but its content may differ if supported by an application. For example, the Photos application allows users to post a photo to a friend's profile, but allows them to create an album on their own profile. An application's Publisher interface can be accessed by using http://www.facebook.com/?pub=<<app_id>> and replacing the `<<app_id>>` parameter with a valid application identifier.

A Publisher can contain custom HTML, CSS, and FBJS for interactive content that is handled by a callback URL. Once a user authorizes an application, its Publisher interface will be shown to that user. Two registration options are available to developers when setting up a Publisher within the "Profiles" tab of an application's settings:

- For publishing content to a user's own profile, a developer can set the self-publish text and self-publish callback URL.

- For publishing content to a user's friend's profile, a developer can set the publish text and publish callback URL.

The Text fields determine the label that is shown to the user (for instance, "Add Photo" or "Update Status"), and an application can set one or both of the callback URLs. A Publisher can be in one of two states: for rendering the Publisher interface, and for posting content to the user's stream. The states can be differentiated by the method value, which is sent as a POST parameter. A skeleton Publisher for displaying on a user's profile would be coded in the following way:

```
1   <?php
2   function render_publisher_css() {
3     return '<style type="text/css">#self_publish_frame { padding: 10px;
      }</style>';
4   }
5   function render_publisher_js() {
6     return '<script type="text/javascript">function enable_publish() {
      Facebook.setPublishStatus(true); }</script>';
7   }
```

These two utility functions generate the CSS and JavaScript for the Publisher interface which must be embedded within the FBML and cannot be references to external files. The JavaScript contains a function to enable the Share button of the Publisher interface, which is disabled by default. This technique proves useful if users are required to input data before publishing to their stream:

```
8   function error_and_exit($error_title, $error_message) {
9     $data = array(
      "errorCode" => 1,
      "errorTitle" => $error_title,
      "errorMessage" => $error_message
      );
10    echo json_encode($data);
11    exit;
12  }
```

If an error occurs in the Publisher, it is appropriate to provide a function that will return an error code and message back to Facebook. Currently, the only supported error code is 1, which is then returned with a title and message as a JSON-encoded string. Further processing is then halted via the exit command. In addition, a developer may want to log the error along with the user who interacted with the Publisher, which is contained within the $_POST["fb_sig_user"] parameter, or if they were interacting with a friend's profile, via the $_POST["fb_sig_profile_user"] parameter:

```
13  if ($_POST["method"] == "publisher_getInterface") {
14    $fbml = render_publisher_css();
15    $fbml .= render_publisher_js();
16    $fbml .= '<div id="self_publish_frame">';
```

```
17   $fbml .= " <form>";
18   $fbml .= '   <label for="mood">How are you feeling today?</label>
     <br /><br />';
19   $fbml .= '   <select name="mood" onclick="enable_publish();
     return false;">';
20   $fbml .= "     <option value="undecided">Undecided</option>";
21   $fbml .= "     <option value="happy">Happy</option>";
22   $fbml .= "     <option value="sad">Sad</option>";
23   $fbml .= "   </select>";
24   $fbml .= " </form>";
25   $fbml .= "</div>";
26   $content = array(
       "fbml" => $fbml,
       "publishEnabled" => false,
       "commentEnabled" => true
     );
27 }
```

This is where the Publisher interface is constructed and contains references to the CSS and JavaScript functions on lines 14 and 15. This simple Publisher will post a "mood" to the user's profile which uses a drop-down menu with three options. On line 19, the enable_publish() function that enables the Share button is called. The content of the interface is packaged into an array on line 26 containing the FBML for the interface alongside settings for whether the publish facility and comments are enabled by default. The enable_publish() function sets the value of the publishEnabled parameter to true when executed:

```
28 else if ($_POST["method"] == "publisher_getFeedStory") {
29   $attachment = array(
       "name" => "I've just updated my mood.",
       "href" => "http://www.example.com/",
       "caption" => "Today, {*actor*} is feeling ".
       $_POST["app_params"]["mood"].".",
       "properties" => array(
         "mood" => $_POST["app_params"]["mood"]
       )
     );
30   $content = array("attachment" => $attachment);
31 }
```

When users select and publish their mood, this branch of code is executed. It contains any submitted parameters within an $_POST["app_params"] array. For this Publisher, this is determined by the mood drop-down box on line 19. For users who also submit a comment with their update, this is packaged within the $_POST["comment_text"] parameter. In this example, the content is then packaged within a stream attachment because these can also contain rich media such as images or video. From here, you might want to store

interactions using the `$_POST["fb_sig_user"]` and `$_POST["fb_sig_profile_user"]`
parameters or perform other Facebook actions using the
`$_POST["fb_sig_session_key"]`, `$_POST["fb_sig_expires"]` and
`$_POST["fb_sig_ss"]` parameters if a user has authorized the application:

```
32 else {
33   error_and_exit("Method Error", "Unknown method passed.");
34 }
```

If the method isn't set to `publisher_getInterface` or `publisher_getFeedStory`, the
error function will be called.

```
35 $data = array("method" => $_POST["method"], "content" => $content);
36 echo json_encode($data);
37 ?>
```

The content is wrapped inside another array that is then JSON-encoded and posted to
Facebook. Figure 7.2 shows how the Publisher would be rendered within a user's profile
on Facebook, and Figure 7.3 shows the same within his stream.

Figure 7.2   Final rendering of the Update
Mood self-publisher.

Figure 7.3   Final rendering of the Update
Mood self-publisher within the stream.

The code provides an example of what a self-publish callback URL may look like, but
the code could also be used for a regular publish callback URL. However, the attachment
on line 29 and any other processing would have to be modified to be made suitable for a
friend interaction.

Summary

This chapter explored how the sharing of multimedia is facilitated using the Facebook Platform through Facebook widgets such as the Like Box and Live Stream Box and how you can use social commenting and feed publishing to enable users to share updates and feedback with their friends both inside and outside of the Facebook environment. The Open Stream API can be an incredibly powerful tool for integrating threaded conversations into websites and Facebook through a multitude of methods for publishing content and enabling comments and likes.

8

Application Discovery, Tabbed Navigation, and the Facebook JavaScript Library

Facebook can be used as a mechanism for sharing content, commenting, and stream publishing, as you learned in Chapter 7, "Using Facebook Connect for Sharing, Commenting, and Stream Publishing." However, the Facebook environment contains three other ways in which users and their friends can interact: application dashboards, which focus on the discovery and reengagement of games and applications; counters, for alerting users that they need to take action on an application or game (perhaps taking their next turn) or that a report is ready for them to view; and application tabs, which can be shown on a user's profile alongside other profile information. These three channels can be used by a Facebook Platform application to engage users both within and outside of Facebook.

This chapter explores how you can use dashboards in your Facebook Platform application through the Dashboard API. Through the Dashboard API, you can post news items to a user's dashboard, promote friends' activities, and utilize activity counters. The second part of this chapter focuses on application tabs as a way of sharing your application's information with users and their friends. Following the deprecation of profile boxes, application tabs are the only mechanism for enabling users to personalize their profiles and showcase their favorite applications. This section includes details about how to configure, install, and develop an application tab through the use of "Mock AJAX". The final section showcases Facebook JavaScript (FBJS) and how you can use it for events, animations, and Facebook dialogs.

Application Dashboards and Counters

Dashboard API

At the time of this writing, the methods from the Dashboard API were not available to test and could be subject to change. When the Dashboard API becomes fully available, examples will be added to this book's code repository. A blog post will also be added to the book's website denoting that the functionality in this section is available.

Because of the popularity of social gaming applications on Facebook, their recent redesigns have started to put more emphasis on highlighting specific features for games. There are now two types of "dashboards": Games (http://www.facebook.com/?sk=games) and Applications (http://www.facebook.com/?sk=apps). These are accessible via a user's home page alongside bookmarks. The goal of each of the dashboards is to make it easier for Facebook users to access games or applications that they or their friends have recently used and to discover new applications through their friends or the Application Directory (see Figure 8.1).

Figure 8.1   Screenshot of the Games dashboard.

Various key features are available within the dashboards:

- Recently used applications or games display right at the top so that users can quickly and easily find applications they use on a daily basis. The number of friends who also use the application is also highlighted next to each application's title.

- News items can be used to allow applications to communicate with users either to display news to all users or alert individual users that they need to take action. For example, a game news item may say "It's your turn to play, Mark!" You can also use news items to mention a user's friends and invite them to play a game with you.

- A user's friends' recent activity is shown, which is used to promote applications and games that a user might not have installed. This can also be toggled to display the activities that an individual has recently completed, which can be privacy controlled.

- A list is maintained of all friends who recently interact with applications that appear below the activities. These take the form of a list and are updated dynamically based on usage.

- The legacy Facebook Application Directory is displayed right at the bottom of the dashboards for searching for applications in particular categories. When submitting your own application to the directory, this will be the category or categories that you have provided.

- Facebook also runs features on particular applications or sponsored applications, which are shown to the right side of a profile. These are generated by combining a users' and their friends' activities to suggest the most suitable applications or games to their profile.

- Counters can be shown alongside an application's name for games or applications that a user has bookmarked. These are discussed further in the "Games and Applications Counters" section, later in this chapter.

When submitting an application to the directory, a developer will choose whether the application should be listed as a "game" or as a regular "application." This designation dictates which dashboard it will be placed within. Both dashboards contain the same functionality and so differ only in content. A new Dashboard API was released in February 2010 to encompass all the features of dashboards (the subject of the remainder of this section), including adding to news and activity streams and updating counters.

News and Activity Streams

As you have seen in the Games and Application dashboards, Facebook has concentrated a lot of their efforts on keeping users updated as to what they and their friends are up to. One of the main ways in which this is achieved is through activity streams. Activities are reported on the Games and Application dashboards in two distinct ways, through news and activities:

- News items can be set to display global and personal items to an individual or set of individuals. These could be that a new feature has been added to your game or application or if a friend has initiated an action involving a particular user.

- Activity items display actions performed specifically by the individual that appear in that individual's stream but could also reference one of their friends. In which case, that individual's activity will also appear in a friend's news items.

The methods for each of these streams are similar to those regarding stream publishing discussed in Chapter 7. The only real difference here is that news and activities are restricted to the dashboards rather than the user's stream, which helps to reduce unnecessary clutter.

Working with News Items

News items are a way of sharing announcements with your users or for indicating that a friend has performed an activity that has referenced them. There are two types of news items, global and personal, depending on what method was called to create the item. Facebook displays just two news items within either the Games or Applications dashboard, and so they also provide a convenient method to clear news items from a user's stream.

Adding News Items

> ### Dashboard API Naming Conventions
>
> Although Facebook lists these methods as including `add` in their name, this might change to `set` in the future. In the most recent version of the Facebook API PHP client library, the `dashboard.addNews` method was actually `dashboard.setNews` but returned an error when executed.

News items can be added using the following methods either individually, globally, or for multiple individuals using the following:

- `dashboard.addNews`

- `dashboard.addGlobalNews`

- `dashboard.multiAddNews`

Each method requires a slightly different set of parameters, such as providing a `uid` (which is that of the user whose dashboard you are updating) for individual news and which is not required for global news items. For updating multiple users, an array of `uids` is required instead. This array contains a number of user identifiers that require updating. Note that you cannot set multiple messages for each of these individuals, so each news item will be the same for each of the identifiers you provide. An array of up to eight `news` items is also required. This must contain a `message` and an optional `action_link` that includes `text` and a `href`. If you want, you can also supply an optional `image` parameter. This must be an absolute URL that is formatted as a 64x64px square. An example of each method is shown here:

```
$user = $facebook->get_loggedin_user();
$users = array("1", "2", "3");
$news = array(
 array(
  "message" => "Hey, {*actor*}. Your friend @ just invited
  you to play chess.",
  "action_link" => array (
   "text" => "Play Now!",
   "href" => "http://myfacebookapp.com/?game=chess"
  )
 )
);
$global_news = array(
```

```
array(
  "message" => "Hey, {*actor*}. There is a new game to play, chess.",
  "action_link" => array (
   "text" => "Play Chess!",
   "href" => "http://myfacebookapp.com/?game=chess"
  )
 )
);
$image = "http://29.media.tumblr.com/avatar_abad48dbd089_96.png";
$individual_news = $facebook->api_client->dashboard_addNews($user, $news,
$image);
$global_news = $facebook->api_client-
>dashboard_addGlobalNews($global_news, $image);
$multi_news = $facebook->api_client->dashboard_multiAddNews($users, $news,
$image);
```

If successful, the $global_news and $individual_news items will return a news_id if the call succeeds, and the $multi_news item will return an associative array of uid keys that contain either a news_id if successful or false if unsuccessful. These news_id values are important and should be stored because they will be required if news items need to be cleared from a dashboard. In addition, two conventions were demonstrated in the message values: You can use the {*actor*} token, which is also available within stream attachments, to be rendered as the user whose dashboard is being updated; and you can use <<USER_ID>>, where <<USER_ID>> can be replaced by any user identifier. In your own applications, this would form part of a two-stage process of updating an individual's activity stream but also updating the news streams of that user's friends that he or she was playing against or wanting to update.

Clearing News Items

As with adding news items, three methods enable you to clear updates that have already been created by an application. Clearing individual news will not remove global news and vice versa, and so these methods may be used alongside each other:

- dashboard.clearNews
- dashboard.clearGlobalNews
- dashboard.multiClearNews

All of an individual's news items can be removed by using the dashboard.clearNews method and supplying their uid as the single required parameter or by additionally passing in an array of news_id values. For global news, the dashboard.clearGlobalNews method can be called without any parameters to remove all news or can include an array of news_id values similar to the individual news item method. Clearing multiple individuals' news items is slightly more complex. Here is an example assuming that the $multi_news parameter that was presented in the "Adding News Items" section above returned the following:

```
$multi_news = array(
 "1" => 111,
 "2" => 222,
 "3" => 333
);
$ids = array(
 "1" => array("111"),
 "2" => array("222"),
 "3" => array()
);
$removed_multi_news = $facebook->api_client->dashboard_multiClearNews($ids);
```

A successful response from the individual and global methods is an associative array of news_id keys and Boolean values depending on whether the news item has been removed. When you are removing multiple individuals' news items, an associative array will be returned equivalent to the individual and global methods if news_id values were supplied. Otherwise, if no news_id values were supplied (such as the last $ids parameter), an associative array will be returned containing the uid as the key and a Boolean value of whether the news item was removed or not.

Getting News Items

The final sets of methods are used to extract a user's or group of users' news streams. Simply put, these methods provide you with the original news and image values that were set when adding news items. The method names are as follows:

- dashboard.getNews

- dashboard.getGlobalNews

- dashboard.multiGetNews

These methods prove particularly useful should you not want to store news_id values within your database of file stores.

Working with Activity Items

Unlike news items, activity items are an experimental feature and may be removed by Facebook in the future. Activity streams are used to broadcast to a user's friends what that user been up to within a game or application (for example, posting high scores or whether the user has uploaded new files or photos). There are only three methods for working with activity items, and these cannot be called for multiple individuals like news items:

- **dashboard.getActivity**
  This method will return the latest 100 activities recorded for the current user. The method can be called with an optional activity_ids array if you have recorded each activity_id for your users.

- **dashboard.publishActivity**

  This method works in exactly the same way as `dashboard.addNews`, but rather than being a `news` object, it is an `activity`. The same conventions for using `{*actor*}` and `<<USER_ID>>` tokens can be used when setting activity items. Successful publishing of an activity will return a numeric `activity_id`.

- **dashboard.removeActivity**

  Activities can be removed by supplying an array of `activity_id` values, which will return an associative array of `activity_id` keys and a Boolean value indicating success or failure.

When setting up your application in Chapter 5, "An Overview of Facebook Platform Website Integration," you may have noticed a setting called Hide User Activity within the "Advanced" tab. This setting can be checked if you think that your application will generate activities that a user might want to keep private and not share with friends. Although further details were not available at the time of this writing, Facebook intends to give users sufficient control over which news and activity items they both send and receive. Like items being posted to their stream, it may be that they want to inform certain friends of their activities but exclude others.

Games and Applications Counters

Before an application or game can utilize counters, it must first be bookmarked by the user. This can be done from within Facebook using the links provided on each of the dashboards. However, it can also be facilitated through embeddable `<fb:bookmark>` FBML and XFBML tags. A bookmark URL must be set. You can find this within the "Basic" tab of an application; otherwise, the application's connect URL or canvas page URL will be used. For Facebook Platform applications, you can set the `type` attribute of the button to `off-facebook`, which will render a blue button in place of the standard gray used within canvas applications. Upon clicking the button, users are prompted with a dialog box to add the application to their profile (see Figure 8.2).

If a user has already bookmarked your application, the button will not appear. You can also check this by querying the `permissions` FQL table, as follows:

```
$bookmarked = $facebook->api_client->fql_query('
SELECT uid, bookmarked
FROM permissions
WHERE uid = "'.$official_user.'"
');
```

The result of this FQL query will be either a `1` or a `0` that can be extracted by using `$bookmarked[0]["bookmarked"]`. New bookmarks will appear underneath the links to the Games and Applications dashboards and can be rearranged by users after clicking the "More" link below their bookmarks. After an application has been bookmarked, you can start exploiting the features of counters via the Dashboard API.

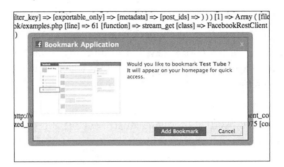

Figure 8.2   Example bookmark dialog for the
Test Tube application.

There are two types of counter methods. One type of method enables you to update an individual's counter. The other type of method can be used to update a number of individuals' counters. Users could utilize this to let a group of friends know of an action they've taken in a game and that it is now their turn. There are four methods for updating the first type of counter for individuals:

- `dashboard.decrementCount`
- `dashboard.getCount`
- `dashboard.incrementCount`
- `dashboard.setCount`

These methods can be run either using the logged-in user's credentials or by supplying a `uid` alongside your application secret. Unlike internal Facebook applications or games, when using website integration you must ensure that every time a user visits your bookmark URL that the user's counter is reset to zero. For applications that want to update a group of individuals' counters at the same time, the second type of counter method, a number of batch methods are available:

- `dashboard.multiDecrementCount`
- `dashboard.multiGetCount`
- `dashboard.multiIncrementCount`
- `dashboard.multiSetCount`

These batch methods all request that an array of `uids` be supplied and will return an array of `uids` as the key and a Boolean value for whether the request was successful. It is suggested that when users visit your application, either on a canvas page or via an external website, that their counter is set to zero to ensure that users do not get confused as to what actions they are required to take.

Navigating and Showcasing Your Application Using Tabs

In the early days of Facebook, a number of "integration points" were available to developers to showcase their applications. These integration points included profile boxes, news feeds, and notifications. As a greater mass of developers started using the platform, Facebook quickly became a dumping ground for spam because insufficient controls and policies failed to prevent malicious developers abusing the platform. Today, Facebook has become a lot more of a controlled environment, which means that many developers have been forced away, but many others have gone on to produce really impressive applications. With the introduction of Games and Applications dashboards alongside a unified stream social application, developers have to focus a lot more of their attention on users' experiences.

Add Application Tab FBML Element

Like the deprecated `<fb:add-section-button>` FBML element, Facebook intends to create a related element for adding an application tab. However, at the time of this writing, no information was available as to its name or related attributes.

Facebook officially deprecated boxes and application info sections, which left application tabs as the only way for users to showcase their favorite applications on their profile. There are still modifications being made to how application tabs will be rendered, but the information in this section should give you enough information to start implementing them in conjunction with your Facebook applications. The deprecation has meant that many methods have been removed from the API, including the following:

- `profile.getFBML`

- `profile.getInfo`

- `profile.getInfoOptions`

- `profile.setFBML`

- `profile.setInfo`

- `profile.setInfoOptions`

If you are a new Facebook developer, the changes will mean that you now only have a single integration point to worry about. For developers who have been working with the platform for a longer period of time, these changes have been met with some negativity. Ultimately, however, these should improve the platform. They also allow you to focus more on users' experience of your applications and will be replaced by newer features as time goes by.

Configuring and Installing an Application Tab

Application tabs are displayed within Facebook next to a user's Wall, Info, and Photos tabs, and must be added explicitly by the user. An application tab is currently 520 pixels wide and can be used to render information pulled directly from your application servers as either an `<iframe>` or FBML. Other features of application tabs are that they can be used to load AJAX but cannot autoplay Adobe Flash, `onload` JavaScript, or use `<iframes>`. When interacting with an application tab on a friend's profile, a user's identifier is passed within an `$facebook->fb_params["user"]` parameter alongside the owner's identifier, which is passed within an `$facebook->fb_params["profile_user"]` parameter. An example of how these two parameters can be used is shown in the next section.

Other Canvas Settings

A number of other canvas settings are available within the Canvas tab that are not used within this book but are essential if you want to create an internal Facebook application. The default setting for Facebook Platform website applications is an `<iframe>` render, which means that any standard page will be wrapped within a Facebook frame and displayed to the viewer. For example, if you set the canvas callback URL to the location where you uploaded your files from Chapters 5–7, you will be presented with your `index.php` page.

Because application tabs are used within the Facebook environment, their location must be set relatively to a canvas page URL. And because Facebook Platform website integration has been the focus of this book, a canvas page URL has not yet been set. We can rectify this by navigating to the "Canvas" tab of your application's settings and by providing a unique base URL prefixed by http://apps.facebook.com/. You should also set a canvas callback URL, which is the file or directory on your web server that will be served by Facebook as content for internal canvas pages. For example, if you set your canvas page URL to http://apps.facebook.com/myfacebookapp/ and your canvas callback URL to http://myfacebookapp.com/canvas/, that means that if a user visits http://apps.facebook.com/myfacebookapp/foo.php, it will be rendered from http://myfacebookapp.com/canvas/foo.php. Before continuing, check that the render method on the "Canvas" tab is set to "IFrame" because the Facebook Platform library will be used in this section.

Modifying Your `config.php` File

The `config.php` file that was used in Chapters 5, 6, and 7 should be updated with two new parameters called `CANVAS_PAGE_URL` and `CANVAS_CALLBACK_URL`. These should be inserted as with the other parameters within that file and without their trailing forward slash (/).

For this chapter, you should create a new directory called `canvas` within your existing file structure from Chapters 5, 6, and 7, and upload two files, `index.php` and `tab.php`, along with an `xd_receiver.htm` file. Ensure that the references to the Facebook API PHP client library in `index.php` and `tab.php` are relative to your existing directory structure. The code in Listing 8.1 demonstrates a sample Facebook canvas page showing a simple greeting along with a user's identifier and name.

Listing 8.1   **The `index.php` File Demonstrating a Simple Facebook Canvas Page**

```
1   <?php
2   include "../config.php";
3   include "../functions.php";
4   include "../facebook-platform/php/facebook.php";
5   $facebook = new Facebook(API_KEY, SECRET);
6   $user = $facebook->get_loggedin_user();
7   ?>
8   <!DOCTYPE html PUBLIC "-//W3C//DTD XHTML 1.0 Strict//EN"
    "http://www.w3.org/TR/xhtml1/DTD/xhtml1-strict.dtd">
9   <html xmlns="http://www.w3.org/1999/xhtml"
    xmlns:fb="http://www.facebook.com/2008/fbml">
10  <head>
11  <title>Test Tube</title>
12  </head>
13  <body>
14  <h1>Canvas Page - Test Tube</h1>
15  <?php echo "<p>User Identifier: ".($user ? $user : "Unknown").
    "</p>"; ?>
16  <?php echo '<p>Facebook Name: <fb:name uid="'.$user.'"
    useyou="false"></fb:name></p>'; ?>
17  <script src="http://static.ak.connect.facebook.com/js/api_lib/
    v0.4/FeatureLoader.js.php" type="text/javascript"></script>
18  <script type="text/javascript">
19    FB.init("<?php echo API_KEY; ?>", "xd_receiver.htm");
20  </script>
21  </body>
22  </html>
```

This basic page will be rendered inside an `<iframe>`, which means that the Facebook PHP client library alongside the client-side Facebook Platform library will be utilized. The PHP library and configuration files are included on lines 2 to 5, and the current user is assigned on line 6. Because any Facebook user can view this page, it might be that you do not have a `$user` available. Therefore, this must be tested on line 15. To require that a user has logged in when visiting your canvas page, you add `$facebook->require_login();` before the call on line 6. The Facebook Platform library is included on line 17 and initialized on line 19, referencing the recently uploaded `xd_receiver.htm` file. Save the code in Listing 8.1 as `index.php` and upload it to your `canvas` directory, which should be set as your canvas callback URL. If you visit your canvas page URL, you should be presented with a page similar to that shown in Figure 8.3.

Unlike pages within a canvas, which can be an `<iframe>`, your `tab.php` file must be rendered as valid FBML, which is demonstrated by the following code by wrapping content within two `<fb:fbml>` tags:

```
<fb:fbml>
 <h1>Tab Page - Test Tube</h1>
 <p>Hello, World!</p>
</fb:fbml>
```

Figure 8.3   Example canvas page for the Test Tube application.

The `<fb:fbml>` tag has an optional `version` parameter that, if omitted, will render the content in the latest version of FBML. To view this number, you can use the `<fb:fbmlversion />` to render the version number within your application. After you've uploaded the `tab.php`, go back into your application's settings and enter a tab name and tab URL on the Profiles tab. In this instance, the tab URL should be set to `tab.php` to mirror the file you have just uploaded, and the tab name should be set appropriately. Once you have saved your settings, visit your own Facebook profile and, if you have installed your application, you should be able to click the plus sign (+) next to the Wall, Info, and Photos tabs and select the tab you just created, as illustrated in Figure 8.4.

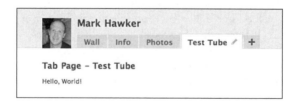

Figure 8.4   Example application tab for the
Test Tube application.

Up until now, the application tab contains only static content, and so the next section looks at how these tabs can be extended to add more personalized information tailored to its owner and viewers.

Extending an Application Tab

Before adding additional functionality, it is worth evaluating which Facebook parameters are contained within an application tab, both when viewing a friend's profile and when interacting with it (such as sending a message). When you are viewing a canvas page, the following parameters are exposed and can be accessed by using the `$facebook->fb_params` array:

- `in_canvas, added, in_profile_tab`, and `in_new_facebook`

    These parameters should all be set to a `1`, indicating that the profile owner has added the application and that the viewer is located within the "Profile" tab. The `in_new_facebook` parameter is used for legacy reasons when Facebook was transitioning between old and new layouts. If the `in_profile_tab` is not set to `1`, you should code in functionality to redirect the user to your application's canvas page or display an error message.

- `friends, locale, profile_update_time, profile_user, profile_id`, and `ext_perms`

    These parameters are associated with the profile owner and contain a comma-separated list of their friends alongside their identifiers and any extended permissions they have granted the host application.

- `request_method, time, expires, profile_session_key, api_key`, and `app_id`

    The final parameters are used when handling Facebook actions that require sessions, such as extracting the profile owner's friends. When you are using the official client libraries, parameters such as `api_key` are less important because the library handles much of its complexity for you.

These parameters are also accompanied by a signature that can be accessed by using `$_POST["fb_sig"]`. All the parameters above are made available whether the viewer has added the application or not. However, if users intend to interact with the application (for example, submitting a form) but they have not added your application, only the following parameters will be exposed within the `$facebook->fb_params` array: `profile`; `locale`; `in_new_facebook`; `sig_time`; `added`, which will be set to `0`; `api_key`; and `app_id`. In the instance, the identity of the viewer is not accessible to your application. If the viewer has added your application, this will expose the following additional parameters:

- `profile_update_time, expires, session_key`, and `ext_perms`, which were detailed earlier, although the `session_key` is linked with the profile viewer and not the owner.

- The viewer identifier is now also made available via the `user` parameter.

One of the great features about application tabs is their capability to utilize Mock AJAX calls to perform dynamic actions or to submit forms inline without having to redirect the user. In the remainder of this section, you learn how to create an application tab that enables viewers to leave a basic text comment for their friend to view. Figure 8.5 gives an example of what the final page should look like. It consists of a form that handles submissions using Mock AJAX, a comments box, and functionality to prompt users who have not already authorized your application to add it and grant extended permissions to write data to their stream.

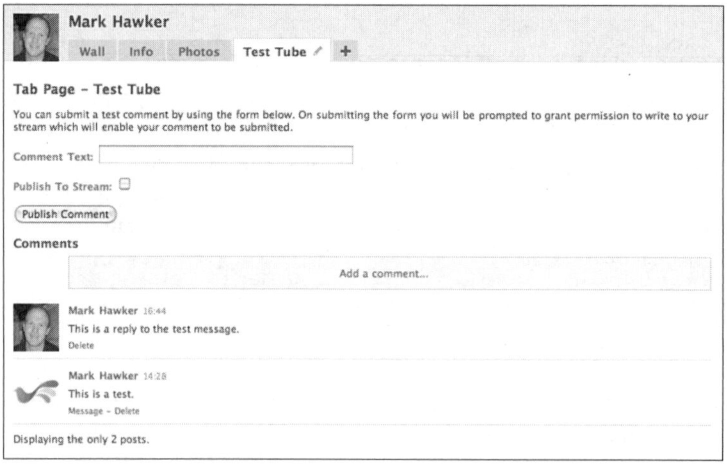

Figure 8.5   Extended application tab for the Test Tube application.

To create the application tab shown in Figure 8.5, you must amend tab.php and create a new file for handling the comment submissions called post.php. The first step is to create the skeleton of the application tab, which will include the Facebook API PHP client library. This library will be used to validate all parameters and to ensure that the user is, in fact, viewing from within Facebook. Because the canvas callback URL exists on your own web server, it is possible for users to type that file location into their web browser outside of Facebook, which means that they must be redirected back to Facebook to prevent any malicious access. This can be achieved by adding the code in Listing 8.2 to tab.php.

Listing 8.2   **Example for the tab.php File Demonstrating a Simple Application Tab**

```
1  <?php
2  include "../config.php";
3  include "../functions.php";
4  include "../facebook-platform/php/facebook.php";
5  $facebook = new Facebook(API_KEY, SECRET, $_POST["fb_sig_profile_
   session_key"]);
```

```
6  $facebook->require_frame();
7  $facebook_parameters = $facebook->get_valid_fb_params($_POST, null,
   "fb_sig");
8  $profile_user = $facebook_parameters["profile_user"];
9  if($facebook_parameters["in_profile_tab"] == 1) {
10 ?>
11 <fb:fbml>
12  // Your Application Logic Goes Here
13 </fb:fbml>
14 <?php
15 } else {
16  // Either redirect the user by setting $facebook->redirect(CANVAS_
   PAGE_URL); or by presenting them with a warning saying that they are
   not within an application tab.
17 }
18 ?>
```

On line 6, a function has been added that ensures that if users type in the URL to your tab on your domain in their web browser they will be redirected back to a Facebook-hosted page. Before you add any application logic, it is worth drafting out what use your new application tab should be able to handle. Because it will have been added by a user, it is known that the user has already authorized your application, and it is possible that you can use the user identifier or other details to extract data that you hold about that user from your database and display that on your tab. Because you are provided with a session key, a number of functions can be performed on the tab itself (for example, extracting the user's friends, photos, or events). However, you will not be able to publish to the user's stream or retrieve any protected data on the user's behalf. When a user's friends access your application tab, they will be in a "passive" mode. This means you cannot access their user identifier, and so cannot determine whether they have authorized your application. Facebook provides two mechanisms for handling this issue:

- Adding a `requirelogin="true"` parameter to all links. This will pop up a Facebook dialog box so that users can authorize your application before proceeding if they have not already.
- When using Mock AJAX, you can add an `ajax.requireLogin=1` parameter so that if viewers submit your comment form and they are not a user of your application, they will be prompted to authorize first before the comment is posted.

Both mechanisms should arrive at the same results. However, because you'll be learning about Mock AJAX in this example, the second option is used. When submitting their comment, viewers can also select whether they want to post their comment to their stream via the `comments.add` method. Note that you could post the response as a stream attachment or even via the Dashboard API (described earlier in this chapter). The `comments.add` method is used for convenience because a comments box can be placed on the application tab to show feedback to the user. Posting to their stream also requires that a viewer has granted the `publish_stream` extended permission, which will be prompted by the `Facebook.showPermissionDialog()` JavaScript function.

The comments form can be constructed using the following code, which you should use in place of the comment on line 12 of Listing 8.2:

```
1   <h1>Tab Page - Test Tube</h1>
2   <p id="comment_response">You can submit a test comment by using the
    form below. On submitting the form you will be prompted to grant
    permission to write to your stream which will enable your comment to
    be submitted.</p>
3   <form>
4   <p><label for="comment_text">Comment Text: </label><input type="text"
    name="comment_text" id="comment_text" value="" size="50"
    maxlength="140" /></p>
5   <p><label for="publish_comment">Publish To Stream: </label><input
    type="checkbox" name="publish_comment" id="publish_comment" /></p>
6   <p><input type="submit" value="Publish Comment" onclick="
    submit_form('comment_response'); return false;" onsumbit="return
    false;" /></p>
7   </form>
8   <h2>Comments</h2>
9   <div id="comments_box">
10  <fb:comments xid="c_<?php echo $profile_user; ?>" canpost="true"
    candelete="true"></fb:comments>
11  </div>
```

The code above displays a simple prompt to the user on line 2. This prompt will be replaced when the form is submitted by either a success or error response. The form itself is defined in lines 3 to 7. It does not include traditional `action` and `method` attributes because you will be using the `onclick` action of the Submit button to post a comment. Form elements include a mixture of `name` and `id` attributes because their values and states need to be evaluated for validation and submission. The comments box on line 10 is wrapped inside a `<div>` because when a user submits a comment there is no way of "refreshing" its contents without refreshing the application tab. The `xid` of the `<fb:comments>` FBML element is set to that of the profile owner and is prefixed by a `c_`, because Facebook sometimes has issues displaying comments boxes that are purely numeric.

The next element that needs to be created is the JavaScript function `submit_form()`, which includes the `id` of the element to update after submission. The JavaScript for this example is split into two parts. The first detects whether comment text was added and whether viewers have chosen to publish their comment to their stream. If both are true, they are presented with a Permissions dialog box to grant extended permissions. If permissions are granted, a successful callback will be triggered, and the comment will be posted to their stream. If denied, the comment will still be posted but will not appear in their stream. The second part is the Mock AJAX itself, which is used to submit the comment and update the user interface. The `submit_form()` function looks like this and should be placed inside a `<script type="text/javascript">` element:

```
1   function submit_form(form) {
2    comment_text = document.getElementById("comment_text").getValue();
3    if(!comment_text == "") {
4     publish_comment = document.getElementById("publish_comment").
     getChecked();
5     if(publish_comment) {
6      Facebook.showPermissionDialog(
7       "publish_stream",
8       function(response) {
9        if(response) { do_ajax(form, publish_comment); }
10       else {
11        do_ajax(form, false);
12        document.getElementById("publish_comment").setChecked(false);
13       }
14      }
15     );
16    } else {
17     do_ajax(form, false);
18    }
19   } else {
20    document.getElementById("comment_text").setStyle({color: "white",
     background: "red"});
21   }
22  }
```

Facebook's implementation of JavaScript, FBJS, is slightly different to JavaScript in handling variable names. In all instances, variables are prefixed by your application ID, which creates a more controlled and sandboxed environment that prevents malicious screen refreshes and other potentially dangerous scripting abilities. Some useful FBJS commands are shown on line 2 for getting the value of a text box, on lines 4 and 12 for getting and setting the state of a check box, and on line 20 for setting the style of a text field. Further details are available in the next section for how to add event listeners and other advanced functionalities to your application tab. The `Facebook.showPermissionDialog()` function on lines 6 to 15 is broken down as follows:

- Line 7 defines the extended permission or permissions that are being requested. In this instance, you require only the `publish_stream` permission, but multiple permissions can be requested by supplying a string of comma-separated values.
- Lines 8 to 14 are the `callback` function, which is invoked if the user allows the permission that leads to the call on line 9. If the user denies permission or closes the Permissions dialog box, the response will be `null`. This will still submit the

comment but will ensure that it does not attempt to publish to their stream. Because this function is being called as a result of the user checking the Publish Comment check box and then being denied, the check box is set to "unchecked" to improve user experience should the user attempt to submit again. Both callback paths will call a do_ajax() function (detailed below).

The remainder of the submit_form() function is to handle if users do not want to publish to their stream. Under this scenario, the do_ajax() function is called, much like if they deny the publish_stream extended permission. If they do not provide any comment text, the background of the text field will be set to red and the text to white. The do_ajax() functions should be placed below submit_form() and contains the following code:

```
1   function do_ajax(div, publish_comment) {
2     comment_text = document.getElementById("comment_text").getValue();
3     if(!comment_text == "") {
4       var ajax = new Ajax();
5       ajax.responseType = Ajax.JSON;
6       ajax.ondone = function(data) {
7         document.getElementById(div).setInnerFBML(data.fbml_response);
8         document.getElementById("comments_box").
          setInnerFBML(data.fbml_comments);
9         document.getElementById("comment_text").setValue("");
10        document.getElementById("comment_text").setStyle({
            color: "black", background: "white"
          });
11      }
12      ajax.onerror = function() {
13        document.getElementById(div).setInnerFBML('<fb:error message="There
          was an error submitting the form." />');
14      }
15      var params = {
16        "comment_text": comment_text,
17        "owner": <?php echo $profile_user; ?>,
18        "publish_comment": publish_comment
19      };
20      ajax.requireLogin = 1;
21      ajax.post("<?php echo CANVAS_CALLBACK_URL; ?>/post.php", params);
22    }
23  }
```

As with the submit_form() function, the do_ajax() function first tests to see that comment text has been entered. If it hasn't been, it will not submit any data to Facebook. On line 4, an AJAX object is created, and its responseType is set on line 5. The responseType can be set to Ajax.JSON, Ajax.RAW, or Ajax.FBML, which dictates the format in which the AJAX object expects data to be returned. The most flexible format is

Ajax.JSON, which will be demonstrated in the example in this chapter. Lines 7 and 8 use two JSON strings, fbml_reponse and fbml_comments, which will become clear after exploring the server-side file generating the response. There are two cases for AJAX requests, which are ajax.ondone and ajax.onerror for handling successful or other responses. The ajax.ondone function on lines 6 to 11 is used to update the comments_box and for resetting the Comments text field to its original state. The final part of the function is shown on lines 15 to 21, which are used to set up POST parameters, comment_text, owner, and publish_comment, to require that users have authorized the application and to actually post the data.

The <fb:js-string> FBML Element

When setting the innerFBML of an element, you might find that Facebook refuses to add the content that you specify. The <fb:js-string> FBML element is provided specifically for this case—another is for Facebook Dialogs—and contains a single var parameter, which is the name that it will be referenced by and will contain the FBML that you want to be added. The <fb:js-string> should be placed within an <fb:fbml> element and will not be displayed to users. The var should be passed as the single parameter to an innerFBML() function.

Your post.php is used to perform specific server-side Facebook functions and to return the response back to the do_ajax() function. The CANVAS_CALLBACK_URL parameter that was set within the config.php should include the canvas directory to ensure that the post.php file can be found. Listing 8.3 defines an example post.php file. This should be uploaded to your web server alongside tab.php and index.php.

Listing 8.3   Example **post.php** File Demonstrating Adding a Comment and Returning Data Back to an Application Tab

```
1   <?php
2   include "../config.php";
3   include "../functions.php";
4   include "../facebook-platform/php/facebook.php";
5   $facebook = new Facebook(API_KEY, SECRET);
6   $facebook_parameters = $facebook->get_valid_fb_params($_POST,
    null, "fb_sig");
7   if(empty($facebook_parameters)) {
8     $facebook->redirect(CANVAS_PAGE_URL);
9     exit;
10  }
11  if($facebook_parameters["is_ajax"] == 1) {
12    $owner = $_POST["owner"];
13  } else {
14    $owner = $facebook_parameters["profile"];
15  }
```

```
16 $viewer = $facebook_parameters["user"];
17 $comment_text = $_POST["comment_text"];
18 $publish_comment = $_POST["publish_comment"];
19 $facebook->set_user($viewer, $facebook_parameters["session_key"]);
20 $json = array();
21 $json["fbml_comments"] = '<p>The page <a href="http://www.facebook.com/
   profile.php?id='.$owner.'&v=app_'.$facebook_parameters["app_id"].'">
   must be refreshed</a> to view recently-submitted comments.</p>';
22 try {
23   $title = "Test Tube";
24   $url = CANVAS_PAGE_URL;
25   $comment = $facebook->api_client->comments_add("c_".$owner,
     $comment_text, $viewer, $title, $url, $publish_comment);
26   $json["fbml_response"] = '<fb:success message="Your comment was added
     and will be viewable the next time you visit this tab." />';
27 }
28 catch(Exception $e) {
29   $json["fbml_response"] = '<fb:error message="'.$e->getMessage().
     '" />';
30 }
31 echo json_encode($json);
32 ?>
```

As with the `tab.php` file, you must cater for the fact that your `post.php` file will be accessed externally, which is the reason for including lines 7 to 10. Because Mock AJAX is being used, Facebook adds another parameter called `is_ajax` but does not pass the profile parameter, which is why the owner POST parameter was set within the `do_ajax()` function. Other parameters are set on lines 16 to 18, and then the profile viewer is set as the active user on line 19. An empty array is created on line 20, which is finally converted to a JSON string on line 31 and which is returned to `do_ajax()`. As an example, line 21 is the text that replaces the initial `comments_box` container and is accessed within `do_ajax()` using `data.fbml_comments`. If you want to return data that is to be set using `setInnerFBML`, it must be prefixed with `fbml_` within the `$json` parameter. The `comments.add` method is called on line 25 using the `comment_text`, and the final parameter dictates whether the comment is published to the viewer's stream.

After you have created the `post.php` file, you should upload it to your web server, and you should be ready to test out your new application tab. From here, you could try out another publishing method such as `stream.publish` or add additional functionality such as listing the owner's friends who have commented or displaying richer comments that include images. The final section looks at how to use the FBJS, and in particular the Animation library, which can be used to create "tweening" CSS fading background colors and styles, to hide and show block-level elements, and to ease animations for smoother transitions.

Dynamic Content and the Facebook JavaScript (FBJS) Library

The Facebook JavaScript (FBJS) library is a solution prepared by Facebook to enable developers to execute JavaScript within their applications. Because allowing developers to perform the full range of JavaScript commands could lead to malicious use, FBJS attempts to provide a happy medium for providing access to simple animations and to utilizing event listeners and implementing Facebook dialog boxes. As you may have seen if you have tried to use JavaScript within Facebook before, all your variable names and functions are prefixed with an application ID. If your application ID is `1234567890` and you have a function named `foo()`, it becomes `a1234567890_foo()`. In the code for the application tab in the previous section, it was not possible to simply refresh the tab using `window.location.reload()` because of this, although you could use `document.setLocation()`, which is provided in the FBJS library. Because application tabs are the only way of enabling a user to showcase your application, it is important to add features such as Mock AJAX and animations to improve the usability of your work and to distinguish yourself from others.

Including JavaScript Files

If you have a rather large JavaScript file, you can use a `<script>` tag and set the `src` to include the remote file. As Facebook caches the file to reduce the burden on your own servers, you should suffix your files with a version number after each major update (for example, `foo.js?v=0.1`) to ensure that Facebook caches the new file.

The FBML Test Console (http://developers.facebook.com/tools.php?fbml) is a great resource for testing out your FBJS before deploying to an application tab (see Figure 8.6). It can also be used to test out a Facebook Platform application or to trial Facebook API methods before production.

You can set the Position drop-down menu to `tab` to ensure that the correct proportions are being shown onscreen. When previewing your application in the Test Console, you are presented with a preview of how your application tab will look, the contents of the HTML that Facebook will generate, and a simple list of errors (as well as the ability to view a profile from the perspective of another user by setting the Profile text field). The remainder of this section uses the FBML Test Console to experiment with the various features of the FBJS library.

Facebook Animation Library

Facebook provides an easy-to-use library for creating a richer user interface for your users via CSS both inside Facebook and outside through an animation library (http://developers.facebook.com/animation/). This library could therefore be used to create animations for other applications that are not Facebook driven but utilize basic animations such as

Figure 8.6   Screen shot of the FBML Test Console showing
an example application tab.

creating shading effects that "tween" between background or text colors or hiding and
showing page elements. These could be used to animate a particular element and can be
achieved in the following ways by populating the `onclick()` parameter of any element:

- `Animation(this).to("background', "#000").go();`

  This function will transition the element's current `background` color to black
  (`#000`) and is "executed" by supplying the final `.go()` method. The use of this
  ensures that the animation is performed on the current element but any other
  DOM object could also be passed into this function for manipulating elements in
  other areas of a page.

- `Animation(this).to("background", "#f00").to("color", "#fff").go();`

  You can string multiple styles together, such as `background` and `color`, as shown in
  the example. Both transitions will run smoothly in parallel, which means that as the
  background is changing color, so will the color of the text.

- `Animation(this).to("background", "#fff").from("#000").go();`

  To transition between two styles irrespective of the current style, you can use a
  `.from()` method. In this instance, this meant changing the `background` from white
  (`#fff`) to black (`#000`).

- `Animation(this).by("font-size", "1px").go();`

  The `.by()` method can be used to increment or decrement an attribute, such as
  `font-size`, `width`, `height`, or `left` or `right` positioning.

- `Animation(element).to("height", 0).to("opacity", 0).`
  `blind().hide().go();`

  By setting the `height` and `opacity` of a supplied `element`, you can automatically hide it from view. You should also set the element's `overflow` style to `hidden`, which will prevent images contained within the `element` from still being shown despite it having no size. The `.blind()` method is used to prevent automatic text wrapping from occurring while the `element` is being resized.

- `Animation(element).to("height", "auto").from(0). to("width",`
  `"auto").from(0).to("opacity", 1).`
  `from(0).blind().show().ease(Animation.ease.end).go();`

  Revealing elements that have a `display` style set to `none` works in a similar way to hiding them but requires both a `.to()` and `.from()` method as well as `.show()` in replace of `.hide()`. A final, `.ease()` method was added to the animation, which will mean the element will "ease" into being revealed. Other options are `Animation.ease.begin` and `Animation.ease.both`, which will start slow and end fast or start and end slow, respectively.

All the animations above will occur over a duration of 1,000 milliseconds (1 second), but you can add a `.duration()` method right before `.go()` should you want the animation to last a longer or shorter time. The code examples available for this chapter contain a few animations to demonstrate how they function on application tabs and how they could be implemented in your own applications. A final advanced feature of the Animation library is checkpoints. Checkpoints are useful if you want to build an animation that consists of two or more logical steps that are part of a single animation. Example could be first increasing a width and then increasing its height or increasing the size of an element and then changing its color. This can be demonstrated using a simple example:

```
<div id="test_1" style="display: none; border: 1px solid #ccc; padding:
5px;">
 <span>This is a test message which will first increase in width and
 then in height.</span>
</div>
<a href="#" onclick="Animation(document.getElementById('test_1')).
to('height', 0).from(0).to('width', 'auto').from(0).show().blind().
checkpoint().to('height', 'auto').blind().go(); return false;">Click
to Expand</a>.
```

It is also possible to "stagger" checkpoints so that an action can be executed midway through the first animation. To implement this feature, you can add an additional parameter to the `.checkpoint()` function, which must be a number that ranges from `0` to `1`, where `0` will not render the animation at all and a value of `1` will render the animation straight after the first has finished. For example, in the code above, you could set the checkpoint to `0.5` to start growing the `height` of the element halfway through its `width` increase. This can also be accompanied by a `.duration(500)` function just before `.go()`

to ensure that both animations finish at the same time. A trick to delay animations is to use the following:

```
Animation(element).duration(3000).checkpoint().to("width", "auto").go();
```

This code would pause for 3,000 milliseconds (3 seconds) and then adjust the width of the given `element`. A use case for this may be to present a message after a certain period of time to the user or to hide a message after a number of seconds has elapsed. The final advanced feature of checkpoints is to use callbacks within the `.checkpoint()` function for performing animations on other elements as well as the current `element`. This can be achieved by using `.checkpoint(1, function() { Animation(...); })` and nesting your animation within the two parentheses. Remember that you can also save these animation chains as functions and thus greatly reduce the amount of code you are typing and make it more readable if you call functions such as `expand()`, `contract()` or `growThenFadeToBlack()`.

Facebook Dialogs

The `<fb:dialog>` FBML Element

Facebook has a beta version of an `<fb:dialog>` element that is a condensed version of the FBJS equivalent discussed in this chapter. The element can be invoked by adding a `clicktoshowdialog` attribute to any element. It is recommended that you use the FBJS version until Facebook confirms the `<fb:dialog>` element, which is expected in mid-2010.

Facebook uses dialog boxes to alert users of messages that they have deleted and to alert them about errors and many other scenarios. To make your application blend in with their environment, they provide a `Dialog` object that can be manipulated to show a pop-up message called `Dialog.DIALOG_POP` or a contextual message called `Dialog.DIALOG_CONTEXTUAL`, which displays an inline dialog box rather than a pop-up. Both types of dialog work in similar ways, except that the contextual dialog can be displayed close to where the user's cursor is pointing or around a certain element. A simple dialog box can be created by using the following code:

```
<p><a href="#" onclick="new Dialog(Dialog.DIALOG_POP).showMessage('Test
Dialog Box', 'Hello, World!', 'Close'); return false;">Click to Test
Dialog Box</a></p>
```

The dialog box shows a message which has the title `Test Dialog Box`, the content set to `Hello, World!`, and its only button set to `Close`. The `.showMessage()` function could be replaced by `.showChoice()`, which accepts an additional parameter for allowing a cancel option. A more thorough example of using dialogs is to evaluate which action the user has chosen and to update an element:

```
1   <p>Do you like social programming? <a href="#" onclick="confirm('Do
    you like social programming?', this);">Click to Answer</a></p>
2   <p id="response">Unknown Response</p>
3   <script type="text/javascript">
4   <!--
```

```
5  function confirm(text, context) {
6   var dialog = new Dialog(Dialog.DIALOG_CONTEXTUAL);
7   dialog.setContext(context).showChoice("Social Programming", text,
    "Yes", "No");
8   dialog.onconfirm = function() {
9    document.getElementById("response").setTextValue("Yes, I do.");
10  };
11  dialog.oncancel = function() {
12   document.getElementById("response").setTextValue("No, I don't.");
13  };
14  return false;
15 }
16 //-->
17 </script>
```

In this example, the results of the dialog box lead to the `response` element being updated either on being confirmed (lines 8 to 10) or canceled (lines 11 to 13). You can also see how the `.setContext()` function was used to ensure the dialog appeared close to the `Click to Answer` text. The final example of dialogs makes use of the `<fb:js-string>` FBML element to show a rich select box to the user within a message and enables them to update a string of text based on the color that they select:

```
<p id="body_text">This is some standard text.</p>
<p><a href="#" onclick="update_text_color();">Update Text Color</a></p>
<fb:js-string var="color_picker">
 <p><b>What is your favorite color?</b></p>
 <p>
  <select id="color_select">
   <option value="black">Default</option>
   <option value="red">Red</option>
   <option value="green">Green</option>
   <option value="pink">Pink</option>
  </select>
 </p>
</fb:js-string>
<script type="text/javascript">
<!--
function update_text_color() {
 var dialog = new Dialog(Dialoh.DIALOG_POP).showChoice("Color Picker",
 color_picker, "Pick", "Cancel");
 dialog.onconfirm = function() {
  var color_text = document.getElementById("color_select").getValue();
  document.getElementById("body_text").setStyle({color: color_text});
 };
 return false;
}
//-->
</script>
```

The main difference in this example is that instead of passing a string of text into the .showChoice() function, the var of the <fb:js-string> element is used. This method can prove particularly effective if you intend to create a rich form that the user has to fill out or if you intend to include multimedia in your dialog box. The only methods that have not been explored are .hide(), which can be used to hide a dialog box if it is already opened (such as if you intend to open multiple dialog boxes or ensure that they are all properly closed), and .setStyle(), which can add styling to the dialog box.

Handling Events with an Event Listener

You might sometimes want to detect whether users have clicked an element on your application tab or moved their mouse over a text field or image. In these instances, you can set up an event listener that sits in the background of your code waiting for actions to occur. Facebook provides its own facilities to "listen" for events and has thus extended the W3C addEventListener() method. Event listeners are broken into three components:

- A string related to the event type that is being listened for, which includes mouse events such click, mousedown, mouseup, mouseover, mousemove, mouseout, or keyboard events like keyup, keydown, or keypress. To detect a particular key press, you can use the keyCode property of an Event object to perform specific functions dependent on keys. You can also use the Event object to detect whether the ctrlKey, shiftKey, or metaKey were pressed.

- A callback function that handles the event and triggers whatever functionality you want to implement. This could be updating a text box, adding text to row tables, or performing search "typeahead" functions. Two important functions can be set within this function: stopPropagation(), for preventing the listener from being added to any parent elements; and preventDefault(), for stopping an element's "normal" behavior (such as preventing clicking a link from directing the user). In the case of a link, you must also set its onclick attribute to return false;.

- The final parameter must be set and relates to a useCapture behavior, which should be set to false. This will prevent events being triggered for descendants of the element that triggers that particular listener.

You can use event listeners in two ways depending on what types of actions you want to capture. The first type of listener is used to encompass multiple elements and handle their logic within the callback function. For example, suppose you have a catalog of images and you want to update a text box to describe the image based on what product the user has rolled his mouse cursor over. You can do so using the following code:

```
<p id="product_description">Roll your mouse over an image to update this
description.</p>
<div id="products">
 <p id="image_1"><img src="..." ... /></p>
 <p id="image_2"><img src="..." ... /></p>
</div>
```

```
<script type="text/javascript">
<!--
function handler(event) {
 var product_description = document.getElementById("product_description");
 if (event.type == "mouseout") {
  product_description.setTextValue("Roll your mouse over an image to
  update this description.");
  return true;
 }
 var product_id = event.target.getId();
 var product_text = "";
 switch(product) {
  case "image_1":
   product_text = "This is the first product.";
   break;
  case "image_2":
   product_text = "This is the second product.";
   break;
  default:
   product_text = "This is an unknown product.";
 }
 product_description.setTextValue(product_text);
}
document.getElementById("image_1").addEventListener("mouseover", handler);
document.getElementById("image_1").addEventListener("mouseout", handler);
document.getElementById("image_2").addEventListener("mouseover", handler);
document.getElementById("image_2").addEventListener("mouseout", handler);
//-->
</script>
```

The code above would display two images and accompanying text and has two listeners, mouseover and mouseout, which will either update the product_description element with a product description or reset it to its default text. The event.target.getId() function ensures that the correct element is identified, and then the JavaScript logic is tailored to that identifier. Another way to add an event listener is to completely separate the code from your application tab content:

```
<div id="test" style="border: 1px solid #ccc; padding: 5px; height: 50px;
width: 100px;" onclick="return false;"></div>
<script type="text/javascript">
<!--
function random_number(low, high) {
 return Math.floor((Math.random() * (high - low)) + low);
}
function color(obj) {
 var red = random_number (0, 255);
 var blue = random_number(0, 255);
```

```
  var green = random_number(0, 255);
  var color = red + ", " + green + ", " + blue;
  obj.setStyle("color", "rgb(" + color + ")");
  }
function load() {
  var obj = document.getElementById("test");
  obj.addEventListener("click",
   function(event){
    color(obj);
    event.stopPropagation();
    event.preventDefault();
    return false;
   }, false);
  }
load();
//-->
</script>
```

The code above will display a box that is clickable and that will change to a random color generated by the `color()` function. The difference in this example is that a `click` event is being captured and so the `preventDefault()` function is called to prevent the usual action of clicking an object. Note that only this second event listener can be validated using the FBML Test Console and the previous example of the product catalog must be hosted on a live application tab. Event listeners are the final component of the FBJS library explored in this section and can be used in combination with the Animation library and Mock AJAX. You should now feel well enough equipped to create an interactive and dynamic application tab that will keep your users coming back and that will persuade their friends to add one of their own.

Summary

This chapter described how you can use dashboards in your Facebook Platform application through the Dashboard API. Through the Dashboard API, you can post news items to a user's dashboard, promote friends' activities, and utilize activity counters. The second part of this chapter focused on application tabs as a way of sharing your application's information with users and their friends. Following the deprecation of profile boxes, application tabs are the only mechanism for enabling users to personalize their profiles and showcase their favorite applications. You were shown how to configure and install an application tab and how to add Mock AJAX functionality. The final part of this chapter detailed the Facebook JavaScript (FBJS) library, which you can use to add animations, dialogs, and event listeners.

9

An Overview of Google Friend Connect

Google Search was their first venture, but now Google offers other products and services, such as e-mail, online mapping, video sharing, web browsing, and mobile operating systems (to name but a few). Google also invests a lot of time in social networking with their Facebook and MySpace competitor orkut and Google Friend Connect, enabling users to connect with friends on third-party social applications. With the Google Friend Connect JavaScript API, you can access content such as user profiles and friends and can generate "activities" from a Google Friend Connect site directly using JavaScript.

This chapter explores (through code snippets, discussion, and a sample application called Color Picker) the inner workings of the Google Friend Connect JavaScript API and demonstrates how it integrates with the OpenSocial API. At the end of this chapter, you should understand how to implement fully interactive Google Friend Connect JavaScript code into your website to create functionality such as site members list maintenance, activity generation, and persistent "app data" storage.

Components of Google Friend Connect

Google Friend Connect is a service that provides website owners with tools to add social features for community building and increasing engagement. These features are known as *gadgets* and *plug-ins* and are suitable for people with little or no programming experience. For example, the Members gadget enables visitors to join a website and see and interact with other members through comments, messages, and reviews. Google Friend Connect was developed to lower two barriers to entry:

- Many website owners want to add social features that enable their visitors to do things with their friends without necessarily wanting to become a social network. It is about helping the "long tail" of sites become more social as simply as possible so that they can publish their activities back to their social network, attracting even more visitors.

- People are tiring of needing to create new logins and profiles and of re-creating friend lists wherever they go online. Google Friend Connect offers a solution to this issue through partnering with networks such as OpenID, Twitter, and Yahoo!, enabling users to sign in using existing credentials. For larger publishers, this could be perceived negatively because site owners do not "own" users and their data like they would if Facebook or Twitter were used, but it does not preclude them from having direct relationships with gadget users on their sites.

The skill sets required to adopting Google Friend Connect range from basic copying and pasting code snippets known as gadgets and plug-ins into your website via wizard-like interfaces through to full client- and server-side integration using the Google Friend Connect JavaScript and OpenSocial APIs. Basic gadgets and plug-ins are not explored in detail because their usage is as simple as copying and pasting code into your website. What is explored is how to build your own gadgets to provide deeper integration into your site with Google Friend Connect. Several examples are available from Google (http://code.google.com/apis/friendconnect/code.html) demonstrating how to integrate Google Friend Connect with your website using the Google Friend Connect JavaScript API and server-side integration. You can use these alongside the Google AJAX API Playground (http://code.google.com/apis/ajax/playground/), which is useful for debugging code and exploring features before deployment.

Google Friend Connect Gadgets

Google Friend Connect gadgets are the simplest way to add social capabilities to websites without any programming experience. Gadgets allow visitors to sign in with OpenID and preexisting Google, Yahoo!, and other OpenID accounts; integrate existing profiles from social networks and services; discover existing friends from other linked social networks; and make friends across networks and interact with fully scalable and tested social gadgets created by Google and the broader OpenSocial development community. Current Google Friend Connect gadgets include the Social Bar and the Members gadget.

The Social Bar gives site visitors easy access to social features such as discovering new friends, reading and posting comments, and exploring new site activities. An example installation is available on this book's website at http://www.socialprogramming.info and shows how the Social Bar works and looks in a live environment (see Figure 9.1).

The Members gadget comes in two forms: a more feature-rich interactive gadget allowing visitors to join your site, sign in and out, see other members, invite friends, and use other social features; and a smaller gadget for signing in and out of your site (see Figure 9.2).

A Gadget Gallery (http://www.google.com/friendconnect/directory/) hosts other gadgets created by Google (for example, Comments, Ratings and Reviews, Events, and Recommendations). Other gadgets created by other social application developers are also contained in the Gadget Gallery.

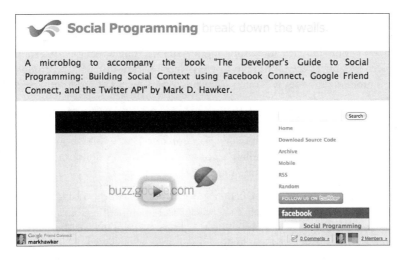

Figure 9.1   Demonstration of the Social Bar with comments enabled.

Figure 9.2   Demonstration of the Members
gadget with invitations enabled.

Google Friend Connect JavaScript API

The Google Friend Connect JavaScript API works in addition to the basic usage of
Google Friend Connect, where access to OpenSocial content is through the hosting of
gadgets or via server-side integration. The Google Friend Connect JavaScript API allows
you to directly access OpenSocial content from a Google Friend Connect site using
JavaScript. The `<iframe>` approach to design makes getting up and running with Google
Friend Connect fast and easy, but it keeps Google Friend Connect social data locked
inside of the `<iframe>` itself. This means that you can't call Google Friend Connect
JavaScript methods directly from your website.

Server-Side Integration

In combination with the Google Friend Connect JavaScript API, server-side integration
is possible through support for the OpenSocial RESTful and RPC protocols. As well as
running social gadgets on your website and displaying social information, Friend Connect

can be integrated with existing server-side code on any desktop, web, or mobile clients (see Chapter 10, "Server-Side Authentication and OpenSocial Integration"). As an example, integration could be with an existing login system, letting anyone with a supported Google Friend Connect account log in to your website without having to complete a registration process. Processes will differ from site to site, but most login integrations follow the same processes:

1. Give users an option to log in with Google Friend Connect, which you can do by adding a few lines of JavaScript code. You don't need to worry about customizing another user interface or handling a complicated authorization process because Google Friend Connect handles much of this centrally.

2. After users have joined your site, their information is made available through the Google Friend Connect server-to-server APIs. For authentication, a dynamically generated `fcauth` cookie is placed on the domain of the site; an alternative method is to use two-legged OAuth, which is discussed in Chapter 10.

3. Sites need to be able to check for logged-in Google Friend Connect users and integrate that data with existing accounts so they are treated as "just another" registered users. Data models need to be extended to keep track of a Google Friend Connect ID per account and pull profile fields from the server-to-server APIs because data cannot be persisted.

4. Google Friend Connect provides additional controls that will help users manage their settings on your site. These include linking to options for configuring their accounts, managing friends and un-joining your site, and for inviting friends to join your website.

5. Logging out can be as simple as a single JavaScript call, which can be problematic if you need to do server-side processing such as ending a session or clearing cookies.

6. Take some time to think how best to present your site's data in a social way. Through the login process, you have access to a "friendship model." Therefore, design considerations include whether friends might be interested in the content a user has just added or listing what activities their friends have been performing on your site (such as sharing reviews or posting high scores).

Several open source client libraries (http://wiki.opensocial.org/ index.php?title=Client_Libraries) written in popular programming languages such as PHP, Ruby, Java, and Python are available to make it easy to access the OpenSocial RESTful and RPC protocols.

Google Friend Connect Plug-ins

Third-party plug-ins are available for popular blogging, forum, and content management systems such as WordPress, Drupal, and phpBB. These make it easier for visitors to log in with a Google account, Yahoo! account, or to log in via any site that implements

OpenSocial 0.8 (such as Plaxo, hi5, and MySpace) and comment on material. Developing Google Friend Connect plug-ins can prove particularly rewarding if your work is used by a number of other users. For example, you could build a plug-in for a new blogging platform or content management system. This could then be reused by other users and extended by other developers. Remember when developing plug-ins that you should not include your own site ID and should allow users to customize every aspect of the design and functionality of the plug-in.

Using the Google Friend Connect JavaScript API

Every website that uses Google Friend Connect automatically becomes an OpenSocial container. This means that you can access people, activities, and persistence data (application data) through the Google Friend Connect JavaScript API, gadgets, and plug-ins, or via the OpenSocial RESTful and RPC protocols. Although gadgets can be copied and pasted easily into web pages, they are run inside an `<iframe>`, which means that data is locked inside that frame and cannot be accessed externally. The JavaScript Library provides a convenient way to access Google Friend Connect and OpenSocial methods, which you can embed directly into any HTML page.

Installing and Configuring the JavaScript Library

Before you can install the JavaScript Library, you must first register a new Google Friend Connect site (http://www.google.com/friendconnect/) by filling out the web form. Every Google Friend Connect site is allocated a unique identifier known as a site ID, which is the ticket that links interactions back to your container. You will find it by checking the `id` parameter in the URL when inside Google Friend Connect and having selected your application.

You can find the embeddable JavaScript API code under the Plug-ins & APIs section of the Google Friend Connect site. An example page is shown in Listing 9.1 and is used throughout this chapter.

Listing 9.1   **A Simple Google Friend Connect page.**

```
1   <!DOCTYPE html PUBLIC "-//W3C//DTD XHTML 1.0 Strict//EN"
2     "http://www.w3.org/TR/xhtml1/DTD/xhtml1-strict.dtd">
3   <html xmlns="http://www.w3.org/1999/xhtml" xml:lang="en" lang="en">
4   <head>
5   <title>Test Tube</title>
6   <!-- Load the Google AJAX API Loader //-->
7   <script type="text/javascript" src="http://www.google.com/jsapi">
    </script>
8   <!-- Load the Google Friend Connect javascript library. //-->
9   <script type="text/javascript">
10  google.load("friendconnect", "0.8");
```

```
11 </script>
12 </head>
12 <body>
13 <h1>Test Tube</h1>
14 <!-- Initialize the Google Friend Connect OpenSocial API. //-->
15 <script type="text/javascript">
16   google.friendconnect.container.setParentUrl("/");
17   google.friendconnect.container.initOpenSocialApi({
       site: "XXXXXXXXXXXXXXXXXXXX",
       onload: function(securityToken) { initAllData(); }
     });
19   function initAllData() {
20     alert("Hello, world!");
21   }
22   function onData(data) {}
23   function createActivity() {}
24 </script>
25 </body>
26 </html>
```

The two most important lines in this code snippet are the following:

1. For legacy applications, Google Friend Connect required that you uploaded two files to your web server for verification. Line 16 is the relative or absolute location of the rpc_relay.html and canvas.html files that needed to be uploaded. In newer installations, this line is now redundant because you no longer need to upload any files.

2. Line 17, which is already prepopulated with your site ID. In this instance, it has been removed for security reasons. The line also contains a reference to a callback function that is passed a security token so that Google Friend Connect data can be retrieved. This callback function is called every time the user's identity becomes known or changes. You will be populating the initAllData() function in the following section.

Save the code in Listing 9.1 and upload it to your web server as index.html, which should match the URL you provided when you first set up Google Friend Connect. If all was successful, when viewing the file in a web browser you should be greeted with a pop-up and the words "Hello, world!". If this wasn't the case, recheck that your site ID and callback function are correct. The three functions initAllData(), onData(), and createActivity() will be updated as you progress through this chapter; you are now ready to retrieve Google Friend Connect data.

Working with Google Friend Connect Data

Google Friend Connect data is accessed through two sets of methods: the Google Friend Connect JavaScript API, which is used to set up the container, initiate the OpenSocial API, handle sign-in and -out processes, and render other OpenSocial gadgets; and the OpenSocial API, for fetching and updating people, activities, and persistence. The OpenSocial v0.8 specification, which is the current standard for Google Friend Connect, is particularly extensive, so this section focuses on the most important methods and points you in the right direction to explore the finer details of the OpenSocial API at your leisure.

Google Friend Connect JavaScript API Methods

Methods in the Google Friend Connect JavaScript API fall into four categories: container setup, pre-registration, post-registration, and gadget interaction. For methods that support or require additional parameters, these take the form of a series of `"key"`: `"value"` pairs separated by a comma (,) and enclosed within curly parentheses ({}), which is one of the data structures supported by JSON.

Container Setup Methods

You have used the two container setup methods, `google.friendconnect.container.setParentUrl()` and `google.friendconnect.container.initOpenSocialApi()`, in the code in Listing 9.1. The first accepts a single `url` parameter that points to the location of `rpc_relay.html` and `canvas.html`. The second accepts two parameters: a required string called `site` containing the site ID; and `onload`, which is an optional parameter giving the name of the JavaScript callback function run every time the user's identity becomes known or changes.

Pre-Registration Methods

There are two pre-registration methods for prompting a user to sign in using Google Friend Connect:

- For visual consistency, Google offers several options for generating buttons for handling signing in to Google Friend Connect sites. To display a standard Google Friend Connect button, you can use the `google.friendconnect.renderSignInButton()` method, which accepts three parameters: `id` is a required string containing the HTML element identifier where the button will be rendered; `text` is an optional string containing the text to be displayed inside the button; and `style` is the button style that can be set to `standard`, `long`, or `text`. For more information about visual styles, visit the Google Friend Connect Buttons page (http://code.google.com/apis/friendconnect/gfc_buttons.html).

- Alternatively, you can use the `google.friendconnect.requestSignIn()` method to prompt a user to sign in using a link rather than a button. This method requires visible attribution of the words "`Friend Connect`" in proximity to the link. A typical usage is this: `<a href="#" onclick="google.friendconnect.requestSignIn();">Sign In with Google Friend Connect</a>`.

The pre-registration methods are part of a workflow of events, because you must change the content of pages when a user's identity becomes known or changes. For example, once signed in, you will no longer have to display the Sign In with Google Friend Connect button.

Post-Registration Methods

There are three post–registration methods. These are displayed only to signed-in users. In other words, the display of a button or link for signing in and the options presented by post-registration methods are binary. So, when one is on, the other should be off:

- A site becomes a lot more social with friends, and so the `google.friendconnect.requestInvite()` method gives users a convenient way to invite their friends to your site. With a single line of code, a highly interactive invitation pop-up window is created, which can be customized via an optional `opt_message` string for pre-populating the invitation message field.

- It is important that users have full control over their Google Friend Connect identity. The `google.friendconnect.requestSettings()` method enables users to manage their account and friends or un-join your site. Like the invitation method, the settings method opens up a pop-up window with a single line of code.

- The `google.friendconnect.requestSignOut()` method logs the user out of the Google Friend Connect site. As with signing in, the method then calls the `onload` handler when done. This can prove problematic if you need to perform any server-side processing, such as maintaining a session, and so utilizing a counter for the number of times the page has been loaded is a useful technique (see Chapter 10).

Although these methods are not mandated, they show good practice and are recommended to ensure users have full control over their Google Friend Connect profile. As an added bonus (and with little programming effort), the invitation method can promote your site to a wider audience if members share details with their friends.

Gadget Interaction Methods

None of the methods in this section can be used within gadgets, but the `google.friendconnect.container.renderOpenSocialGadget()` and `google.friendconnect.container.setNoCache()` methods are useful for testing gadgets in a Google Friend Connect environment. For example, you can combine ready-made gadgets such as Activities or Members with custom code on your website. To disable gadget caching, you just supply a `1` as the parameter, which is useful if you are debugging a gadget that is being continually updated (e.g., the `trunk` of version-controlled source code). If you explore any of the copy and paste gadgets from the Google Friend Connect Gadget Gallery, you will notice the use of the `renderOpenSocialGadget()` method. In some instances, Google has created specialized methods, such as `renderMembersGadget()` and `renderSocialBar()`, but the majority of gadgets do not use these specialized methods.

An Overview of the OpenSocial API

OpenSocial is a set of common APIs for social network applications developed by Google along with MySpace and a number of other social network partners. It is now maintained by the OpenSocial Foundation, a "non-profit, private foundation dedicated to the sustainable and open development of the OpenSocial initiative and related intellectual property."

OpenSocial Specifications

At the time of this writing, the most current version of OpenSocial is v0.9, which added a Lightweight JavaScript API using a new `osapi` namespace. This specification is used for gadgets, but the v0.8 specification is used for the Google Friend Connect JavaScript API.

OpenSocial enables applications, social networks known as "containers," and other clients such as web, desktop, and mobile devices to collaborate and share social data. Every OpenSocial container exposes the same set of APIs so that applications are portable across all social networks. What OpenSocial does is provide an easy way for developers to create applications that work across all social networks, in essence learning once and writing everywhere. The OpenSocial JavaScript API and other client libraries provide access to common concepts such as people and friends, activities, persistence (application data) and messages. Unlike the Facebook Platform, OpenSocial does not have its own markup language, but instead uses regular JavaScript and HTML so that developers are not locked into the Google platform.

Apache Shindig

For those interested in hosting your own OpenSocial container like LinkedIn, hi5, or Zing, check out Apache Shindig (http://shindig.apache.org/). Apache Shindig comprises of a JavaScript container and implementations of the back-end APIs and proxy required for hosting OpenSocial applications. Apache Shindig is built on code donated by Ning, Inc. based on their OpenSocial implementation.

For OpenSocial application developers, Google Friend Connect provides a whole new audience for applications. Now every site that adopts Google Friend Connect is also an OpenSocial container.

OpenSocial API Methods

The Google Friend Connect JavaScript Library provides "helper" methods for initiating requests, but you will need to use the OpenSocial API to fetch and update Google Friend Connect data. Two of the most popular methods from the `opensocial` namespace for interacting via Google Friend Connect are as follows:

- `opensocial.newDataRequest()`

- `opensocial.requestCreateActivity()`

A number of object "definitions," such as `opensocial.Person` and `opensocial.Activity`, provide references to the fields and types available for each object. For example, an `opensocial.Person` contains fields such as NAME, THUMBNAIL_URL, and CURRENT_LOCATION, which maps to an `opensocial.Address` object. In some instances, these fields are not returned by default and therefore need to be referenced manually via additional method parameters.

OpenSocial API Field Names

In the OpenSocial API documentation, many of the field names are listed in uppercase and are separated with an underscore (_). However, in all cases, these can be used interchangeably with a "camel case" version. For example, CURRENT_LOCATION becomes `currentLocation`. This is a matter of preference, and functionality will be the same whichever naming structure is chosen (although you should stick to a single convention).

If you want to dive straight in and experience some of the OpenSocial API or the Google Code AJAX APIs, Playground has an interactive sandbox for editing and debugging code. You can use your own site ID in examples to imitate the Google Friend Connect logic on your website. The remainder of this section focuses on the three popular methods and introduces how to handle errors and use OpenSocial API "identifier specifications" and parameters to customize methods.

The `DataRequest` Object

The best place to start is the `DataRequest` object, which is initiated via a call to the `opensocial.newDataRequest()` method. Although initiating the object does not request any OpenSocial data, it provides a mechanism for "attaching" other requests, which are then pooled so that you can retrieve all the information that you need by sending a single request rather than initiating multiple asynchronous requests and handling their responses individually. After a `DataRequest` object has been created, requests can be attached using the `add()` method and finally submitted via the `send()` method. This is best explained via an example, which should be added inside the `initAllData()` function that you have already created in Listing 9.1:

```
1  function initAllData() {
2   var req = opensocial.newDataRequest();
3   req.add(req.newFetchPersonRequest("VIEWER"), "viewer");
4   req.add(req.newFetchPersonRequest("OWNER"), "owner");
5   req.send(onData);
6  }
```

The `DataRequest` object is initiated in line 2 and is assigned to the `req` JavaScript variable. Lines 3 and 4 contain two requests for OpenSocial person data, which will be explained further in the "Fetching People and Profiles" section. The `add()` method requires two parameters to be set: the request itself, and a unique label for that request so that responses can be handled separately. Finally, the request is sent on line 5, which includes a parameter representing the JavaScript callback function to be executed after the request has been completed (with errors or not). All responses are packaged inside an opensocial.ResponseItem object, which provides methods for testing whether there was an error and for getting the data from within the response. To extend the example above, replace the onData() function in Listing 9.1 with the following code:

```
1  function onData(data) {
2   if (!data.get("viewer").hadError()) {
3    var viewer_data = data.get("viewer").getData();
4    alert(viewer_data.getDisplayName());
5   } else {
6    alert("Viewer is anonymous");
7   }
8   if (!data.get("owner").hadError()) {
9    // Process "owner" data
10  } else {
11   // Process "owner" error data
12  }
13 }
```

If you resave and upload the new index.html file to your web server, you should see an alert box containing either your Google Friend Connect display name if already logged in or an alert box saying Viewer is anonymous. In lines 2 and 8, you can see an example of the hadError() method of the opensocial.ResponseItem object, which also returns true for a null value such as the viewer not being signed in the code above. Line 3 demonstrates the getData() method, and line 4 the getDisplayName() method of the opensocial.Person object. The parameter in the get() method on lines 2, 3, and 8 is set to the unique labels for viewer and owner data.

Debugging with Firebug

If you use Mozilla Firefox, it is recommended that you install the Firebug developer plug-in for interrogating the JSON outputs of each of the methods. If you enable the console and browse to the Net tab and then look for the request beginning with POST rpc, you can analyze the response from the console.

The code snippet could be used for toggling between the pre- and post-registration controls from the Google Friend Connect JavaScript Library; if the viewer is not known, he or she could be requested to sign in with Google Friend Connect. Through the DataRequest object, you can request social information such as people, activities, and persistence, which will be explored in the remainder of this section. A full integration example provided by Google (http://ossamples.com/api/) demonstrates each of these methods should you want to edit the source and experiment with other parameters.

Fetching People and Profiles

You have already seen one of the people methods when calling
newFetchPersonRequest() with the VIEWER and OWNER parameters. In the context of a
Google Friend Connect site, the use of the OWNER parameter in this request returns the
site's profile information, and VIEWER returns the logged-in user. If you want to access the
site's owner and administrators, its members, or a user's friends who are also members of
the site, you use the newFetchPeopleRequest() and provide an opensocial.IdSpec to
define which you would like. For example:

```
1  function initAllData() {
2   var req = opensocial.newDataRequest();
3   var idspec = new opensocial.IdSpec({
4    "userId": "OWNER",
5    "groupId": "FRIENDS"
6   });
7   var params = {
8    "max": 8,
9    "profileDetail": [
10    opensocial.Person.Field.ID,
11    opensocial.Person.Field.NAME,
12    opensocial.Person.Field.THUMBNAIL_URL,
13    opensocial.Person.Field.PROFILE_URL
14   ],
15    "sortOrder": [
16    opensocial.DataRequest.SortOrder.NAME
17   ]
18   };
19   req.add(req.newFetchPeopleRequest(idspec, params), "members");
20   req.send(onData);
21  }
```

The userId can be one of OWNER or VIEWER depending on whether you want the site's
"friends" (members) or the viewers' friends. In most, but not all, instances, groupId can be
set to ADMINS, ALL, FRIENDS, or SELF. If the userId is set to OWNER and groupId to
ADMINS, you can display the site's owner and administrators. In the example above, parameters were used to request a maximum of eight members and additional profile information. Not all fields are returned by default, so PROFILE_URL needed to be included
manually. The fields that are available by default can be found in the opensocial.Person
documentation. In the code from "The DataRequest Object" section, you used the
getDisplayName() method, but if you had included PROFILE_URL in your parameters,
you could have added a call to getField("profileUrl") to get the profile URL of the
viewer. Other parameters can be found within the documentation for the DataRequest
object, including filters and sorting:

```
function onData(data) {
 members = data.get("members").getData();
 var member_list = document.getElementById("members");
```

```
member_list.innerHTML = "";
if (members.size() > 0) {
 members.each(
   function(member) {
     member_list.innerHTML += "<p>" + member.getDisplayName() + "</p>";
   }
 );
} else {
 member_list.innerHTML = "There are no site members";
 }
}
```

Inside the callback function, you can use a combination of the JavaScript `size()` and `each()` functions to iterate through the members and parse the data in any way you like. In this case, updating a predefined HTML element `<div id="members"></div>` for each member or displaying a paragraph "There are no site members" if no persons have added themselves to the site.

Fetching and Updating Activities

The OpenSocial API lets users share activities with their friends through an activity stream. An activity can be anything from modifying an application's state to writing an online book review. Google Friend Connect site members can specify whether they want their activities posted to other Google Friend Connect-enabled sites and linked in other social networks such as orkut or Twitter. Users can set this preference in their Google Friend Connect settings; this is not a default action. Site owners may want to offer this as a recommendation for their users by making them aware of that functionality.

Activities can be requested through the `DataRequest` object's `newFetchActivitiesRequest()` method but are created via the `opensocial.requestCreateActivity()` method. Table 9.1 summarizes the activities that can be requested via Google Friend Connect:

Table 9.1   **The Activities Fetched by the OpenSocial API**

Method	Data
`newFetchActivitiesRequest("OWNER")`	Not supported.

`newFetchActivitiesRequest(`
`new opensocial.IdSpec({`
`  "userId": "OWNER",`
`  "groupId": "FRIENDS"`
`})`
`)`
	Returns all the site member's activities.

Table 9.1   **The Activities Fetched by the OpenSocial API**

Method	Data
`newFetchActivitiesRequest("VIEWER")`	If the user is signed out, this returns `null`; otherwise, it returns the viewer's activities across all Google Friend Connect sites.

`newFetchActivitiesRequest(`
`new opensocial.IdSpec({`
`  "userId": "VIEWER",`
`  "groupId": "FRIENDS"`
`})`
`)`
	If the user is signed out, this returns `null`; otherwise, it returns the friends' activities of the viewer across all Google Friend Connect sites.

In addition to the activities automatically generated when users join a Google Friend Connect site to their profile, you can add your own activities through the `opensocial.requestCreateActivity()` method. The `opensocial.Activity` object contains both `title` and `body` parameters for specifying the primary text and an optional expanded version of an activity. For gadgets, it is suggested that Activity templates be used to support internationalization and that message variables be replaced (but that's not required in this instance). Using the code from Listing 9.1, you can now add the `createActivity()` function:

```
function createActivity() {
 var activity = opensocial.newActivity({
  title: viewer.getDisplayName() + " created an activity."
 });
 opensocial.requestCreateActivity(
  activity,
  "HIGH",
  function() { setTimeout(initAllData, 1000); }
 );
}
```

In the code example, an activity is constructed and then created via a call to the `opensocial.requestCreateActivity()` method. The `HIGH` parameter is the activity priority, which means it will be created even if it requires asking the user for permission. A `LOW` priority means it will not be created if the user has not given permission for the current application to create activities. Finally, a callback function is provided and will be run after 1,000ms. A simple way to test this function is to use a `<button onclick="createActivity();">Create Activity</button>`.

Fetching and Updating Persistence

The OpenSocial API defines a data store that applications can use to read and write per-user and per-application data known as *app data*. An in-depth view of The Persistence API is documented on the OpenSocial wiki (http://wiki.opensocial.org/index.php?title=The_Persistence_API), although this can be reduced to three primary functions of updating, fetching, and removing data. All functions utilize the `DataRequest` object explored earlier and use the `newUpdatePersonAppDataRequest()`, `newFetchPersonAppDataRequest()`, and `newRemovePersonAppDataRequest()` methods. The basic premise is that each piece of data contains a unique identifier for associating the stored data item with a particular user, a "key" for this data, and the data itself, which must be a formatted as a JSON string.

Translating JavaScript Values to JSON Strings

The `gadgets.json` object provides two utility methods for converting JavaScript values into JSON strings. The `stringify()` and `parse()` methods prove particularly useful when you are creating JSON for updating app data if you have more than one value that you want to update at once.

If you try to update a person's app data using a previously defined key, the new value will just replace the existing value. This means that you can set and reset app data as many times as you want. For example:

```
1  function initAllData() {
2    var currentTime = new Date().getTime().toString();
3    var currentDate = new Date().getDate().toString();
4    var dateAndTime = {
       "currentTime": currentTime,
       "currentDate": "<b>" + currentDate + "</b>"
     };
5    var json = gadgets.json.stringify(dateAndTime);
6    var req = opensocial.newDataRequest();
7    var idspec = new opensocial.IdSpec({
       "userId": "VIEWER",
       "groupId": "SELF"
     });
8    var params = {
       "escapeType": [
         opensocial.EscapeType.HTML_ESCAPE
       ]
     };
9    req.add(req.newUpdatePersonAppDataRequest("VIEWER", "time",
     json), "update");
10  // req.add(req.newFetchPersonRequest("VIEWER"), "viewer");
11  // req.add(req.newFetchPersonAppDataRequest(idspec, "time",
     params), "data");
12  // req.add(req.newRemovePersonAddDataRequest("VIEWER","time"));
13    req.send(onData);
14  }
```

An optional callback has been included to check whether an error has occurred, which is important for general OpenSocial applications because some containers do not support the persistence layer. A successful update does not return any data. The fetch data parameter can be set to HTML_ESCAPE or NONE and is used to HTML-escape outputs, which may corrupt the display or could even expose security vulnerabilities if left as NONE. If you choose to set the HTML_ESCAPE parameter, you must unescape the "stringified" JSON object before parsing. The gadgets.util object has an unescapeString() method that can be used as follows:

```
var unescaped_string = gadgets.util.unescapeString(json_data);
var json = gadgets.json.parse(unescaped_string);
```

If you comment out lines 2 to 9 and uncomment lines 10 and 11, you can add the following callback for fetching the app data:

```
function onData(data) {
 var viewer_data = data.get("viewer");
 var data_data = data.get("data");
 if (!viewer_data.hadError() && !data_data.hadError()) {
  var viewer = viewer_data.getData();
  var data = data_data.getData();
  var viewer_data = data[viewer.getId()];
  if (viewer_data) {
   var unescaped_string = gadgets.util.unescapeString(
   viewer_data["time"]);
   var json = gadgets.json.parse(unescaped_string);
   alert(json["currentTime"]);
   alert(json["currentDate"]);
  } else {
   alert("Time not found");
  }
 } else {
  // Process "viewer" and "data" error data
 }
}
```

The returned app data is contained in a JavaScript map indexed by a data key, which is in turn contained within another map indexed by an OpenSocial ID. To access the viewer's data, you also need the viewer's ID, which is why the viewer is also fetched. Because app data can be fetched for several individuals simultaneously, it is necessary to be contained within this structure. Using the method above, you can access each of the stored values via the json object, which is the parsed version of the unescaped string stored in the data store.

You might sometimes want to remove app data from the data store. Again, the DataRequest object is used, and a request is made to the newRemovePersonAppDataRequest() method, which accepts an OpenSocial ID as its first parameter and the name of a key or set of keys as the second parameter. If you uncomment line 12 in the code above, this will remove the time app data that you stored for the current viewer. Multiple keys can be removed by specifying ["key1", ..., "keyN"] in replace of the time parameter, and if you want to clear all keys simultaneously, you can use the asterisk (*) character.

Color Picker: A Google Friend Connect Application

Having explored some of the most popular methods of both the Google Friend Connect JavaScript API and the OpenSocial API, you should now be able to pool together all this knowledge into creating a simple Google Friend Connect application. Being a developer, sometimes the best way to learn something is to be able to dissect a worked example. For this, a sample site has been created to showcase Google Friend Connect in action: http://socprog.thebubblejungle.com/google/.

The example demonstrates how to access site member details, sign in with Google Friend Connect, publish and display activities, and store and fetch app data (see Figure 9.3).

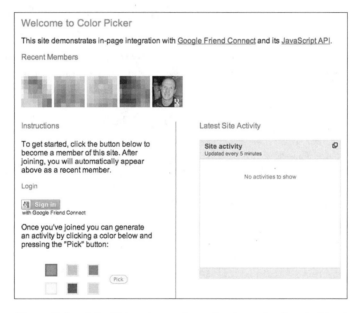

Figure 9.3   Color Picker: A sample application using Google Friend Connect.

Once signed in to Google Friend Connect, you can pick a color and it will automatically be created as an activity. The application also uses app data to store when users last logged in and displays the most recent members at the top of the application to demonstrate how users can be extracted, instead of using the embeddable Members gadget.

Known Limitations

At the time of this writing, the Google Friend Connect JavaScript Library does not function correctly in the Opera web browser. Two issues prevent gadgets from being rendered and sign-in functions working correctly (due to reported security errors). In time, these issues will most likely be resolved, and this will be reflected in the code examples.

You can get this example up and running on your own web server in three steps:

1. Register your site on the Google Friend Connect website and install and configure the JavaScript Library.

2. Download the HTML source code from the sample site, edit the variables SITE_ID and FILE_LOCATION to mirror your web server, save as index.html, and then upload the file to your web server.

3. Finally, visit your newly uploaded page in a web browser and test that you can sign in and pick a color. If you find that your page throws an error, double-check your SITE_ID and FILE_LOCATION.

The application construction can be broken into five associated phases: registering and configuring the Google Friend Connect library, enabling sign-in functionality, retrieving members, posting and retrieving activities, and storing (and retrieving) app data. These are explored in the remaining sections of this chapter. Along with the HTML code, you should also create the following CSS file containing all the styles used in the application:

```
body { font-family: Arial, sans-serif; text-align: center; }
h1 { color: #07c; font-size: 1.3em; font-weight: normal; }
h2 { color: #666; font-size: 1em; font-weight: normal; padding: 0 0 4px 0;
margin: 0; }
h3 { color: #666; font-size: 0.9em; font-weight: normal;
padding: 0 0 4px 0; margin: 0; }
.page { width: 700px; margin: 0 auto; padding: 5px; text-align:left; }
.left { float: left; width: 40%; border-right: 1px solid #666;
padding-right: 50px; }
.right { float: left; padding-left: 50px; width: 40%; }
.clear { clear: both; height: 5px; }
.footer { font-size: 0.8em; color: #666; text-align: center; }
#recentMembers { padding: 10px 0; }
#recentActivities { width: 300px; border: 1px solid #ddd; }
#colorTable { width: 100%; }
#colorPicker { margin: 20px 40px; }
#redCell { border: 3px solid #666666; }
.color { width: 20px; height: 20px; border: 3px solid #e5ecf9; }
.red { background-color: red; }
.orange { background-color: orange; }
.green { background-color: green; }
.yellow { background-color: yellow; }
```

```
.blue { background-color: blue; }
.pink { background-color: pink; }
.memberPhoto { width: 65px; height: 65px; border: 0; padding-right: 5px; }
```

This file should be saved as `style.css` and uploaded to your server alongside the HTML file, which should be named `index.html`.

Registering and Configuring Google Friend Connect

To get started, you must first register a new application by visiting http://www.google.com/friendconnect and clicking the "Add New Site" link, which is located in the lower left of the main window. The form requires a website name, "Color Picker", and website URL, which must be set to a location on your web server where the `style.css` and `index.html` are to be uploaded. After these two parameters have been saved, you should be able to input the site ID into line 14 of the code below, which will be shown as an `id` parameter in your browser's address bar:

```
1  <!DOCTYPE html PUBLIC "-//W3C//DTD XHTML 1.0 Strict//EN"
   "http://www.w3.org/TR/xhtml1/DTD/xhtml1-strict.dtd">
3  <html xmlns="http://www.w3.org/1999/xhtml" xml:lang="en" lang="en">
3  <head>
4  <meta http-equiv="Content-type" content="text/html;charset=UTF-8" />
5  <title>Color Picker</title>
6  <script type="text/javascript" src="http://www.google.com/jsapi">
   </script>
7  <script type="text/javascript">
8  /* <![CDATA[ */
9  google.load("friendconnect", "0.8");
10 /* ]]> */
11 </script>
12 <script type="text/javascript">
13 /* <![CDATA[ */
14 var SITE_ID = "ADD YOUR SITE ID HERE";
15 var FILE_LOCATION = "/";
16 google.friendconnect.container.setParentUrl(FILE_LOCATION);
17 google.friendconnect.container.initOpenSocialApi({
18   site: SITE_ID,
19   onload: function(securityToken) { initAllData(); }
20 });
21 /* ]]> */
22 </script>
23 <link href="style.css" media="screen" rel="stylesheet"
   type="text/css" />
24 </head>
```

With your new site ID added to line 14, the remainder of the `<head>` element contains Google Friend Connect initialization code. After the library has been initialized, a call is made to the `initAllData()` JavaScript function, which is described later in this section. The naming of this function is not fixed, but it is conventional to use this descriptor. If you have named the style sheet anything other than `style.css`, line 23 is where you reference your renamed file. With the header complete, it is time to move on to the document body:

```
25 <body>
26 <div class="page">
27  <h1>Welcome to <span id="siteName">this site</span></h1>
28  <p>This site demonstrates in-page integration with Google Friend
    Connect and its JavaScript API.</p>
29  <!-- Placeholder for Members HTML //-->
30  <div class="left">
31   <h2>Instructions</h2>
32   <p>To get started, click the button below to become a member of
     this site. After joining, you will automatically appear above as
     a recent member.</p>
33   <!-- Placeholder for Sign In HTML //-->
34   <!-- Placeholder for App Data HTML //-->
35   <!-- Placeholder for Activity HTML //-->
36  </div>
37  <div class="right">
38   <!-- Placeholder for Activity HTML //-->
39  </div>
40  <div class="clear"></div>
41  <div class="footer">
42   <p>Example inspired by "<a href="http://ossamples.com/api/">Color
     Picker</a>".</p>
43  </div>
44 </div>
```

The first part of the `<body>` element contains the HTML, which will be dynamically updated by JavaScript. For example, on line 27 the site name will be updated appropriately if it can be retrieved. Other placeholders, such as on lines 29, 33 to 35, and 38, are to be replaced during the remaining sections (for displaying a login button and site members, for instance). The second part of the `<body>` element contains the JavaScript for updating the HTML elements:

```
45 <script type="text/javascript">
46  /* <![CDATA[ */
47  var viewer, owner, members;
48  function initAllData() {
49   // var buttonHtml = document.getElementById("button").disabled
     = true;
50   var params = {
51    "max": 8,
52    "profileDetail": [
53      opensocial.Person.Field.ID, opensocial.Person.Field.NAME,
```

```
54      opensocial.Person.Field.THUMBNAIL_URL,
        opensocial.Person.Field.PROFILE_URL
55      ]
56    };
57    var idspecOwner = new opensocial.IdSpec({"userId": "OWNER",
      "groupId": "FRIENDS"});
58    var idspecViewer = new opensocial.IdSpec({"userId": "VIEWER",
      "groupId": "SELF"});
59    var req = opensocial.newDataRequest();
60    req.add(req.newFetchPersonRequest("OWNER", params), "owner");
61    req.add(req.newFetchPersonRequest("VIEWER", params), "viewer");
62    req.add(req.newFetchPeopleRequest(idspecOwner, params), "members");
63    req.add(req.newFetchPersonAppDataRequest(idspecViewer, "time",
      params), "data");
64    req.send(onData);
65  }
```

The JavaScript is split into two sections containing the `initAllData()` function for extracting OpenSocial data and the `onData()` function for parsing responses. To ensure that variables are available to all functions, `viewer`, `owner`, and `members` are defined on line 47. Data from lines 57, 58, and 61 to 63 are used later in this section for extracting details about the viewer of the site (a logged-in Google Friend Connect user), its members, and a user's app data. Finally, the batch of requests is sent on line 64, including the name of a callback function, which is defined on lines 66 to 78:

```
66  function onData(data) {
67    var siteNameHtml = document.getElementById("siteName");
68    if (!data.get("owner").hadError()) {
69     owner = data.get("owner").getData();
70     siteNameHtml.innerHTML = owner.getDisplayName();
71    } else {
72     siteNameHtml.innerHTML = "this site";
73    }
74    <!-- Placeholder for Sign In JavaScript //-->
75    <!-- Placeholder for Members JavaScript //-->
76    <!-- Placeholder for App Data JavaScript //-->
77    <!-- Placeholder for Activity JavaScript //-->
78  }
79  /* ]]> */
80  </script>
81  </body>
82  </html>
```

The `onData()` function will be expanded in later sections but already contains code to update the `siteName` `<span>` element on line 27. If there was an error retrieving this value, the text will be set to this site.

Enabling Sign-In Functionality

With the core of the application complete, it's time to start adding specific functionality. The first set of code is for enabling users to sign in using Google Friend Connect. This includes replacing the HTML on line 33 with the following:

```
<div id="viewerInfo"><h3>Login</h3></div><p id="gfcButton"></p>
```

This code will display a heading and element to be replaced by a rendered Google Friend Connect button. To enable this, you must update the JavaScript on line 74 to make use of the viewer data requested on line 61:

```
var viewerInfoHtml = document.getElementById("viewerInfo");
var gfcButtonHtml = document.getElementById("gfcButton");
if (data.get("viewer").hadError()) {
 google.friendconnect.renderSignInButton({
  "id": "gfcButton",
  "style": "standard"
 });
 gfcButtonHtml.style.display = "block";
 viewerInfoHtml.innerHTML = "<h3>Login</h3>";
} else {
 gfcButtonHtml.style.display = "none";
 viewer = data.get("viewer").getData();
 var html = '<img src="' + viewer.getField("thumbnailUrl") +
 '" height="65" width="65" alt="' + viewer.getDisplayName() +
 '" /><br />';
 html += "Hello, <b>" + viewer.getDisplayName() + "</b>.<br />";
 html += '<a href="#" onclick="google.friendconnect.requestSettings();">
 Settings</a> | ';
 html += '<a href="#" onclick="google.friendconnect.requestInvite();">
 Invite</a> | ';
 html += '<a href="#" onclick="google.friendconnect.requestSignOut();">
 Sign Out</a>';
 var buttonHtml = document.getElementById("button").disabled = false;
 viewerInfoHtml.innerHTML = html;
 // updateAppData();
}
```

This code first creates references to the two HTML elements, `viewerInfo` and `gfcButton`, which will be updated dynamically. If there was an error retrieving user data, such as if the user is not logged in, the Google Friend Connect login button will be shown; otherwise, the `gfcButton` element will be hidden, and `viewerInfo` replaced with the user's display name and three links to edit the user's settings, invite friends, and sign out. The final line, which references the `updateAppData()` function, has been commented out because it has not been created yet.

Retrieving Site Members

After allowing users to sign in, it is now possible to start retrieving a list of members and displaying them in the application. The first snippet of HTML replaces the original line 29:

```
<h2>Recent Members</h2><p id="recentMembers">Loading...</p>
```

The HTML element is supported by a block of JavaScript that parses the data requested on line 62, which replaces the placeholder on line 75:

```
var membersHtml = document.getElementById("recentMembers");
if (!data.get("members").hadError()) {
 members = data.get("members").getData();
 membersHtml.innerHTML = "";
 if (members.size() > 0) {
  members.each(
    function(member) {
     membersHtml.innerHTML += '<a href="' + member.getField("profileUrl") +
     '" title="' + member.getDisplayName() + '"><img class="memberPhoto"
     src="' + member.getField("thumbnailUrl") + '" height="65" width="65"
     alt="' + member.getDisplayName() + '" /></a>';
    }
  );
 } else { membersHtml.innerHTML += "There are no site members."; }
} else {
 membersHtml.innerHTML = "There was an error retrieving site members.";
}
```

The code first registers the link between the recentMembers HTML element to be updated dynamically with the retrieved data. If no members are available or there was an error gathering data, an appropriate error message is shown. Because the params on lines 50 to 56 define the fields and number of results to be returned, a maximum of eight members will be returned along with a profile URL, display name, and thumbnail URL. If these additional fields were not added as parameters, they would not be available to be displayed.

Posting and Retrieving Activities

After users have logged in, you can get them to create events on your site such as posting status updates, rating articles, or updating their mood. These interactions are stored by Google, but can also be sent to users' other social accounts (e.g., Twitter) if they have added them to their Google profile. To add activities to Color Picker, you should add the following HTML, which replaces line 35 of the code above:

```
<p>Once you've joined you can generate an activity by clicking a color
below and pressing the "Pick" button:</p>
<div id="colorPicker">
 <table id="colorTable" cellspacing="10">
  <tr>
```

```
    <td><div class="color red" onclick="pickColor(this, 'red');"
    id="redCell"></div></td>
    <td><div class="color orange" onclick="pickColor(this, 'orange');">
    </div></td>
    <td><div class="color green" onclick="pickColor(this, 'green');">
    </div></td>
    <td style="width: 10px;" rowspan="2"><button onclick="
    createActivity();" id="button" disabled="disabled">Pick</button></td>
   </tr>
   <tr>
    <td><div class="color yellow" onclick="pickColor(this, 'yellow');">
    </div></td>
    <td><div class="color blue" onclick="pickColor(this, 'blue');">
    </div></td>
    <td><div class="color pink" onclick="pickColor(this, 'pink');">
    </div></td>
   </tr>
  </table>
</div>
```

This HTML generates a selection palette of colors that executes a `pickColor()` JavaScript function that parses the color name and creates an activity. By default, the Submit button is disabled because when users first visit a page they will not be logged in. After they have logged in, it will execute the `createActivity()` function. Because this is the client-side version, all the event handling is in JavaScript. However, this functionality could also be executed server-side using AJAX if you want. Chapter 10 provides more information on the server-side implementation of Google Friend Connect and OpenSocial. The code below should replace the placeholder on line 77:

```
var color = "red";
var lastColorDiv = document.getElementById("redCell");
function pickColor(div, newColor) {
 color = newColor;
 div.style.border = "3px solid #666666";
 lastColorDiv.style.border = "3px solid #e5ecf9";
 lastColorDiv = div;
};
function createActivity() {
 if (viewer) {
  var activity = opensocial.newActivity({
   title: viewer.getDisplayName() + " picked " + color + " as
   their favorite color."
  });
  opensocial.requestCreateActivity(activity, "HIGH", function() {
   setTimeout(initAllData, 1000); });
  } else { alert("There was an error creating an activity"); }
}
```

The important part about this code is that it sets the first color, red, as the active element. This ensures that a value is always sent to the pickColor() function. The function updates the HTML depending on the color that the user has picked and highlights the particular color cell with a colored border. The createActivity() function tests to see whether the viewer parameter has been set and then creates a new Activity object. The activity itself will contain the user's display name along with the color that the user picked. The activity will then be created, and after 1,000ms the initAllData() callback function will be executed. This could also be used to update an element or display a success or failure message to the user:

```
<h2>Latest Site Activity</h2><p id="recentActivities"></p>
```

To display activities, the prebuilt Activities gadget will be used. To initiate the gadget, you are required to create a placeholder element that replaces line 38 of the code above. The gadget itself is created within the JavaScript code block, which should be appended underneath the pickColor() and createActivity() functions:

```
var skin = {};
skin["HEIGHT"] = "250";
skin["BORDER_COLOR"] = "#cccccc";
skin["ENDCAP_BG_COLOR"] = "#e0ecff";
skin["ENDCAP_TEXT_COLOR"] = "#333333";
skin["ENDCAP_LINK_COLOR"] = "#0000cc";
skin["ALTERNATE_BG_COLOR"] = "#ffffff";
skin["CONTENT_BG_COLOR"] = "#ffffff";
skin["CONTENT_LINK_COLOR"] = "#0000cc";
skin["CONTENT_TEXT_COLOR"] = "#333333";
skin["CONTENT_SECONDARY_LINK_COLOR"] = "#7777cc";
skin["CONTENT_SECONDARY_TEXT_COLOR"] = "#666666";
skin["CONTENT_HEADLINE_COLOR"] = "#333333";
google.friendconnect.container.renderOpenSocialGadget({
  id: "recentActivities",
  url: "http://www.google.com/friendconnect/gadgets/activities.xml",
  height: 250,
  site: SITE_ID,
  "view-params": {"scope": "SITE"}
}, skin);
```

The gadget itself scopes the whole site, but could also be set to FRIENDS, which would display activities that the viewer's friends have made. Feel free to change any of these parameters to change the colors of the gadget itself.

Storing and Retrieving Application Data

The final benefit of using Google Friend Connect is the ability to store user-level data via its application data store. This data must be JSON encoded and can contain anything from user preferences to new profile data. For this example, it is used to store the date that the user last logged in. Before delving into the details of this function, first uncomment the updateAppData() line used in the sign-in process. This line ensures that each time a user logs in, a new date is recorded. The following HTML replaces the placeholder on line 34 for displaying a simple text block:

```
<p id="date">Loading...</p>
```

Within the onData() function on line 76, the following code checks whether app data has already been set and then renders it to users. If this is the first time that they have logged in, no data will be available for their last login, which is displayed to them. In this code snippet, the date JSON, which contains two keys, currentTime and currentDate, is parsed and set using the toLocaleDateString() function:

```
var dateHtml = document.getElementById("date");
if (!data.get("data").hadError()) {
 var data = data.get("data").getData();
 var viewer_data = data[viewer.getId()];
 if (viewer_data) {
  var unescaped_string = gadgets.util.unescapeString(viewer_data["time"]);
  var json = gadgets.json.parse(unescaped_string);
  var date = new Date();
  date.setTime(json["currentTime"]);
  dateHtml.innerHTML = "Last Login Date: " + date.toLocaleDateString();
 } else {
  dateHtml.innerHTML = "Last Login Date: Not Available.";
 }
} else { dateHtml.innerHTML = ""; }
```

To update the app data for a user, add the following function to your JavaScript code block. It gets the current date and time and translates it into a JSON string. The string is then associated with the user and sent to storage:

```
function updateAppData() {
 var currentTime = new Date().getTime().toString();
 var currentDate = new Date().getDate().toString();
 var dateAndTime = {
  "currentTime": currentTime,
  "currentDate": "<b>" + currentDate + "</b>"
 };
 var json = gadgets.json.stringify(dateAndTime);
 var req = opensocial.newDataRequest();
 req.add(req.newUpdatePersonAppDataRequest("VIEWER", "time",
 json), "update");
 req.send();
}
```

With the code now complete, you can save the file as index.html and upload it alongside the style.css file to the location set in the Google Friend Connect settings page. Either using the sample site or the one that you have just created and uploaded, test out signing in and out or picking a color, and then investigate the "behind the scenes" interactions via a developer tool such as Firebug or the in-built developer tools in Internet Explorer, Google Chrome, or Apple Safari. Also, why not update the code by adding a new gadget, displaying more member information, or storing additional information via the data store?

Summary

The beauty of Google Friend Connect is its simplicity and extensibility. For example, its wizard-like interface is great for beginners who want a copy-and-paste solution to add interactivity to their website through gadgets and plug-ins. For developers, there are a wide range of options for adding interactivity through the client-side JavaScript API or server-side through utilizing the OpenSocial RESTful and RPC protocols. The Google Friend Connect JavaScript API and OpenSocial API provide you with a way of integrating social features into your website, such as profiles and friends and the ability to generate "activities." Some of the ways in which these can be used are for recording site members, registering comments, and providing login functionality. Because the libraries are client side, you can embed them directly into static pages without having to worry about creating complex server-side code. This chapter explored some of the most common methods contained within these libraries and ended with an example that brought together all the functions that were discussed. The next chapter examines server-side integration using OpenSocial and Google Friend Connect.

10

Server-Side Authentication and OpenSocial Integration

Chapter 9, "An Overview of Google Friend Connect," explored the Google Friend Connect JavaScript API and OpenSocial API for integrating social features directly into websites. However, what if you already have a login system and want to extend it to accept Google Friend Connect logins? Because Google Friend Connect supports the OpenSocial RESTful and RPC protocols, it is possible to access OpenSocial data from a website or any other Internet-enabled device outside of a gadget or a standard web page. With authentication and secure server-to-server communication handled through OAuth, and the `fcauth` authentication cookie or the security token for gadgets provided by Google Friend Connect, you can give users peace of mind that their data is being handled securely and safely away from prying eyes.

This chapter demonstrates how to use the PHP OpenSocial client library in conjunction with the skills learned in Chapter 9 for Google Friend Connect and OpenSocial server-side integration. This includes fetching site members and creating and fetching activities and app data. Many of the steps and advice should be transferable to any of the other available client libraries (including Java, Python, and Ruby).

Server-Side OpenSocial Protocols and Authentication Methods

Two major disadvantages for advanced developers of Google Friend Connect are that their application code is exposed to the public through viewing the source of their pages when using the client-side JavaScript libraries and that they cannot take advantage of fully integrating with their server-side systems (for example, linking a Google Friend Connect profile to an existing profile on your website so that data you have already stored can be displayed to the user). Working in conjunction with the client-side Google Friend Connect JavaScript API for authentication, you can soon start to build some complex applications using the knowledge you have already acquired via easy-to-use OpenSocial client libraries. Using the server-side implementation of these technologies, you can extend Google Friend Connect past websites and onto any Internet-enabled platform such as mobile phones or game consoles.

Both the OpenSocial RESTful and RPC protocols enable developers to access and update OpenSocial container data via HTTP through a number of URL-addressable endpoints. Google Friend Connect supports four such endpoints for accessing data: through GET (or POST in the case of the All RPC endpoint), updating through POST and PUT, and deleting through DELETE requests. In the case of Google Friend Connect, not all endpoints support all operations, as shown in Table 10.1. (All endpoints have the common http://www.google.com/friendconnect/api URL stub.)

Table 10.1   **Google Friend Connect OpenSocial RESTful and RPC Protocol Endpoints**

API	Endpoint	Supported Requests
People REST	/people/	GET
Activity REST	/activity/	GET, POST, DELETE, PUT
App Data REST	/appdata/	GET, POST, DELETE, PUT
All RPC	/rpc	POST

You may have noticed that when debugging your code in Chapter 9 that you came across requests that began with POST rpc. This was in fact a call to the All RPC endpoint with additional parameters supplied for the authentication method, which would have taken the form of a gadget security token (st) parameter. Three Google Friend Connect authentication methods are explored in the following section. To access data, you make a request using one of the endpoints either using cURL from the command line or inside your server-side code adding two additional parameters (userId such as @me) and groupId (such as @self or @friends). A typical request looks something like this:

```
http://www.google.com/friendconnect/api/people/@me/@self?fcauth=XXXX
```

Instead of handling requests in this raw form, you should use a specialized client library that has been purpose built to reduce the barrier to entry for developers new to OpenSocial. But first, let's look at the three authentication methods supported by Google Friend Connect: gadget security tokens, authentication cookies, and standard two-legged OAuth.

Google Friend Connect Authentication Methods

Google Friend Connect provides three authentication methods to apply in different scenarios. For example, the client-side example in Chapter 9 used a security token, which was passed via the onload parameter of the `google.friendconnect.container.initOpenSocialApi()` method without you even realizing. A security token is preferred for gadget developers because it provides a short-lived token that offers access to information about the site, gadget, and the viewer (which is discussed further in Chapter 11, "Developing OpenSocial Gadgets with Google Friend Connect"). Two additional authentication methods are provided for use by site owners for online and offline processing: the Friend Connect authentication cookie, and standard two-legged OAuth.

The Google Friend Connect Authentication Cookie

Whenever a user signs in using Google Friend Connect, an `fcauth` cookie is placed on the domain of the site named `fcauthXXXXXXXXXXXXXXXXXXXXX`, where XXXXXXXXXXXXXXXXXXXX should be replaced by the numeric site identifier found in the Google Friend Connect administration page for your site. The cookie is long-lived, meaning that it will expire after a number of days or until the user signs out of your site and is unique to the user who signed in. Using a developer plug-in such as Firecookie, you should be able to identify the `fcauth` cookie if you select the Cookies tab within the application. In PHP, this `fcauth` cookie can be retrieved using the following code:

```
$cookieIdentifier = "fcauthXXXXXXXXXXXXXXXXXXXXX";
$cookie = (isset($_COOKIE[$cookieIdentifier]) ?
$_COOKIE[$cookieIdentifier]
: null);
```

The code checks to see whether the `fcauth` cookie has been set, and if so, it assigns its value to the `$cookie` parameter; otherwise, `$cookie` is set to `null`. You now know that if a cookie is available, and more important valid, you can start requesting OpenSocial data. The advantage of this method is that the presence of a cookie can be checked every time a request is to be made, but the major disadvantage is that it is not suitable for offline processing through which actions are performed in the absence of the user. For this, you can utilize the standard two-legged OAuth authentication method.

Standard Two-Legged OAuth

There are two flavors of OAuth: two-legged authentication and three-legged authentication. When the term *OAuth* is used, it is most frequently used to describe the three-legged version through which users go through a "dance" when they start on an OAuth "consumer" site and are then redirected to the OAuth "provider," site where they are asked to approve access by the consumer site to their data. If approval is given, they are then bounced back to the OAuth consumer site, where it can start using their authenticated credentials to access data. Two-legged OAuth, on the other hand, does not require this dance. Instead, is can perform its "signed fetch" or "phone home" authentication without needing the additional steps for three-legged OAuth.

> **Two-Legged OAuth Request Anonymity**
>
> When you are requesting a specific user's details, such as using the `@me` syntax, you need to explicitly set the identity of the user who is requesting the data. In OAuth terms, this is done by setting the `xoauth_requestor_id` parameter to the user ID along with using the `@me` syntax or by replacing `@me` directly with the user ID. If the parameter is not set, it will execute as an anonymous user.

In Google Friend Connect, developers are provided with a consumer key and secret that they use to "sign" requests. You can find these under the REST API tab of the Plug-ins and APIs section within the main Google Friend Connect administration page for your site. These OAuth credentials never expire, but you will notice an option to regenerate your consumer secret should the security of your application become compromised. This makes OAuth ideal for requesting user data offline; all you need to store is their user ID and your consumer key and secret. This particular functionality is used in the walk-through described in Chapter 13, "Integrating Twitter, Facebook, and Google Friend Connect," to allow user activities to be created "offline."

While the creation of a valid OAuth request is quite complex because each request must be digitally signed by the container, this is handled elegantly via the OpenSocial client libraries. In comparison to the authentication cookie method, OAuth requires the storage of user IDs or for offline requests to be iterated over the site owner's friends (members) using the relevant OpenSocial API method. Any data that is stored about the user should be noted in your site's privacy policy. For security, it is recommended that this is limited to a single user ID, because other information such as name or URLs may change over time.

OpenSocial Client Libraries

A number of OpenSocial client libraries are available in PHP, Java, Ruby, and Python as an alternative to the OpenSocial JavaScript API. New libraries are also available for .NET and ActionScript 3.0 for Adobe Flex or Adobe Flash applications. Each library is open sourced under an Apache 2.0 license that welcomes and encourages user contributions and patch submissions. Both the Ruby and Python libraries include fully featured sample applications that you can customize and use as templates for your own containers. An issue tracker is also available, as are source downloads and SVN access. The OpenSocial Client Library Google group is also a great place to search for issues and through which to receive notifications about new SVN code submissions.

The client libraries provide a simple way to access the OpenSocial RESTful and RPC protocols by taking care of the complex authentication processes, creation of data models, and provision of services to fetch, update, and delete people, activities, and app data. For other OpenSocial containers, there is also support for other features such as groups, media items, and messages. It is recommended that you use the source code from your chosen client's SVN directory; this is generally a more up-to-date version than that provided in the Downloads section. For example, support for `fcauth` cookie does not exist in version

1.01 of the PHP client library. Through the Source Checkout functionality, you can view changes and browse the code before checking out the latest version.

Using the PHP OpenSocial Client Library with Google Friend Connect

The best way to understand the details of the server-side implementation of Google Friend Connect and OpenSocial is to work through a sample code snippet. Two main issues are faced: the changeover from the client-side login authentication provided by Google Friend Connect to the server-side requests made via OpenSocial; and the fact that Google Friend Connect does not function in the Opera web browser. The key to working with this transition is to understand the workflow of the client-side authentication process.

Google Friend Connect Authentication Workflow

You will remember that in Chapter 9 two container setup methods, `google.friendconnect.container.setParentUrl()` and `google.friendconnect.container.initOpenSocialApi()`, were used to initialize the Google Friend Connect JavaScript library. In the second method, an `onload` function was supplied. It was to be called every time a user's state changed, such as signing in or out. When updating the page dynamically using client-side JavaScript and `innerHTML`, it was sufficient that this page "refresh" did not affect the workflow of the application. However, if you want to perform server-side requests, you must act on this page refresh accordingly. This is made possible through a modified `onload` function, which would look like the following:

```
1  google.friendconnect.container.initOpenSocialApi({
2    site: "XXXXXXXXXXXXXXXXXXXX",
3    onload: function(securityToken) {
4      if (!window.timesloaded) {
5        window.timesloaded = 1;
6      } else {
7        window.timesloaded++;
8      }
9      if (window.timesloaded > 1) {
10       // User signed in or out
11     } else {
12       initAllData();
13     }
14   }
15 });
```

The use of the `window.timesloaded` counter means that when the page is initially loaded the counter is set to 1, and then subsequent refreshes which occur when a user signs in or out increment the counter. If the counter is greater than 1, the workflow begins on line 10. For now, this contains a simple comment. In production, however, this would contain a server redirect to an authentication page or function that handles the authentication process.

Setting Up a Server-Side Application

Let's begin by creating a new file called `test.php` that you'll upload to your web server under the same location as set in Chapter 9. Initially, this page will contain the following lines of PHP code:

```php
1  <?php
2  $SITE_ID = "XXXXXXXXXXXXXXXXXXXX";
3  $PARENT_URL = "/";
4  $FILE_NAME = "test.php";
5  if(isset($_REQUEST["authenticate"])) {
6   $request = $_REQUEST["authenticate"];
7   switch ($request) {
8    case "login":
9     header("Location: ".$PARENT_URL.$FILE_NAME."?loggedin");
10    break;
11   case "logout":
12    header("Location: ".$PARENT_URL.$FILE_NAME."?loggedout");
13    break;
14   default:
15    header("Location: ".$PARENT_URL.$FILE_NAME);
16  }
17 } else {
18  $cookieIdentifier = "fcauth".$SITE_ID;
19  $cookie = isset($_COOKIE[$cookieIdentifier]) ?
    $_COOKIE[$cookieIdentifier] : null;
20  $isLoggedIn = $cookie ? true : false;
21  $userAgent = $_SERVER["HTTP_USER_AGENT"];
22  $unsupportedBrowsers = array("Opera");
23  $isBrowserSupported = true;
24  foreach ($unsupportedBrowsers as $unsupportedBrowser) {
25   $isBrowserSupported = preg_match("/".$unsupportedBrowser."/i",
    $userAgent) ? false : true;
26  }
27 }
28 ?>
```

Line 5 tests to see whether the authenticate parameter has been set and branches appropriately depending on whether the application should redirect the user to the "logged in" or "logged out" page. On lines 18 to 20, you store three new variables: `$cookie`, containing the value of the authentication cookie; `$isLoggedIn`, which is a Boolean indicating whether a user is logged in; and `$isBrowserSupported`, which is another Boolean indicating whether the user's browser is supported by Google Friend

Connect. To extend the code above, you should also translate these server-side variables into client-side variables in the next HTML code snippet:

```
29 <!DOCTYPE html PUBLIC "-//W3C//DTD XHTML 1.0 Strict//EN"
30   "http://www.w3.org/TR/xhtml1/DTD/xhtml1-strict.dtd">
31 <html xmlns="http://www.w3.org/1999/xhtml" xml:lang="en" lang="en">
32 <head>
33 <title>My OpenSocial Test Page</title>
34 <!-- Load the Google AJAX API Loader //-->
35 <script type="text/javascript" src="http://www.google.com/jsapi">
   </script>
36 <!-- Load the Google Friend Connect javascript library. //-->
37 <script type="text/javascript">
38  google.load("friendconnect", "0.8");
39 </script>
40 <!-- Initialize the Google Friend Connect OpenSocial API. //-->
41 <script type="text/javascript">
42  <?php
43   if ($isBrowserSupported) { echo "var isBrowserSupported = true;"; }
      else { echo "var isBrowserSupported = false;"; }
44   if ($isLoggedIn) { echo " var isLoggedIn = true;"; } else {
      echo " var isLoggedIn = false;"; }
45  ?>
46  google.friendconnect.container.setParentUrl("<?php echo $PARENT_URL;
      ?>");
47  // Initialize OpenSocial
48 </script>
49 </head>
```

You can replace the comment on line 47 with the code created in the previous section, and you can also replace the line 10 comment from that snippet with the following:

```
window.location = '<?php echo $PARENT_URL.$FILE_NAME; ?>?
authenticate=<?php echo !$isLoggedIn ? "login" : "logout"; ?>';
```

What this line does is redirect users depending on whether they are logged in or not. If they are not logged in, the `authenticate` parameter will be set to `login`; otherwise, it will be set to `logout`. These two values correspond directly to the two `case` switches on lines 9 and 12 of the code above. Note also on lines 43 and 44 that the client-side variables `isLoggedIn` and `isBrowserSupported` are set to match the server-side code. You are now left with two final tasks to complete: defining the `<body>` HTML and creating the `initAllData()` JavaScript function. With these two tasks completed, you can then start exploring how to fetch and update data using the client library:

```
50 <body>
51 <h1>An OpenSocial Test Page</h1>
52 <div id="viewerControlPanel">
53   <p id="gfcButton"></p>
```

```
54 </div>
55 <?php
56 if($cookie) {
57   echo "<p>We have the Google Friend Connect authentication
     cookie.</p>";
58 } else {
59   echo "<p>We don't have the Google Friend Connect authentication
     cookie.</p>";
60 }
61 ?>
62 <script type="text/javascript">
63   function initAllData() { onData(); }
64   function onData() {}
65 </script>
66 </body>
67 </html>
```

To keep this OpenSocial example simple, there are just two <body> elements: the "viewer control panel" on lines 52 to 54, which will include the Google Friend Connect login button when not signed in and an edit settings and sign out links for when they are signed in; and a simple PHP echo statement on lines 55 to 61 indicating whether you have an authentication cookie. Remember, an authentication cookie exists only when a user is logged in. The initAllData() function points directly to the onData() function to remain consistent with code examples in Chapter 9. To reduce client-side server calls, the onData() function looks like this:

```
1  var viewerControlPanelHtml = document.getElementById(
   "viewerControlPanel");
2  if (isBrowserSupported) {
3    if (!isLoggedIn) {
4      viewerControlPanelHtml.innerHTML = '<p id="gfcButton"></p>';
5      google.friendconnect.renderSignInButton({
6        "id": "gfcButton",
7        "style": "standard"
8      });
9    } else {
10     html = "<p>";
11     html += '<a href="#" onclick="google.friendconnect.
       requestSettings();">Settings</a> | ';
12     html += '<a href="#" onclick="google.friendconnect.
       requestSignOut();">Sign Out</a>';
13     html += "</p>";
14     viewerControlPanelHtml.innerHTML = html;
15   }
16 } else {
17   viewerControlPanelHtml.innerHTML = "<p>We're sorry, but your
     current browser is not supported by Google Friend Connect.</p>";
18 }
```

Two conditional statements on lines 2 and 3 are used to test that the user's browser is supported and if the user is logged in or out. Because the authentication cookie is being used as a test of whether a user is logged in, you do not need to make any calls to the OpenSocial API to retrieve data. You will have noticed that as of yet there has been no real server-side processing of user data, just stating that you have access to an authentication cookie. The next section demonstrates how to use this authentication cookie to set up the Google Friend Connect provider object.

OpenSocial Data Extraction Principles

Having downloaded the PHP OpenSocial client library, you should find a directory called `osapi`. You want to upload this to a suitable location on your web server. For this example, it is placed in the same directory as the `test.php` file and can be loaded with the following code:

```
require_once "osapi/osapi.php";
```

To save on resources, it is recommended that this library be loaded only when you have an authentication cookie. In the code covered in the preceding section, you replace line 57, which contains a simple `echo` statement indicating that you had access to the authentication cookie. You can create the Google Friend Connect provider object with three lines of code:

```
1   $provider = new osapiFriendConnectProvider();
2   $authentication = new osapiFCAuth($cookie);
3   $opensocial = new osapi($provider, $authentication);
```

On line 2, an `$authentication` parameter is created that could also be an `osapiSecurityToken($securitytoken)` for gadgets or an `osapiOAuth2Legged($consumerKey, $consumerSecret, $userId)` for standard two-legged OAuth. The latter would be used for offline processing if you had stored a list of user identifiers or were programmatically iterating over your site's members. If you are unsure as to how to get the user ID for a Google Friend Connect user, you can use the cookie-based method to initially log the user in and then user `$viewer->getID()` to extract the user's parameter to be stored in your file store.

Inside the OpenSocial Client Directory

Within the `osapi` directory are several other directories that detail the supported authentication methods (`auth`), OpenSocial component definitions (`models` and `service`), and each of the supported providers (`providers`). The client library also supports a simple storage mechanism (`storage`) for XRDS and three-legged OAuth implementations.

With the `$opensocial` object created, you can now start accessing some data. You do this through a process whereby all requests are batched together, which is similar to client-side requests in Chapter 9. A batch is created using `$batch = $opensocial->newBatch();`, and then requests are added using `$batch->add($request, "key");`, where $request could be anything from getting all members or creating an activity to updating application data. The key is a placeholder for referencing the $request data after it has been returned. Finally, a $response = $batch->execute(); will execute all the requests and save them in a $response variable. It is important that if you are intending to use batching that you do not create the $batch parameter several times. You should be able to create it once, add all your requests that you require for the page, and then execute the command. To request the viewer's data, you may use the following code:

```
1  $batch = $opensocial->newBatch();
2  $viewerParameters = array(
3    "userId" => "@me",
4    "groupId" => "@self",
5    "fields" => "@all"
6  );
7  $getViewer = $opensocial->people->get($viewerParameters);
8  $batch->add($getViewer, "viewer");
9  $response = $batch->execute();
10 $viewer = $response["viewer"];
11 if ($viewer instanceof osapiError) {
12   $code = $viewer->getErrorCode();
13   $message = $viewer->getErrorMessage();
14   // Process OpenSocial API Error
15 } else {
16   $viewerName = htmlentities($viewer->getName());
17   $viewerThumbnailUrl = htmlentities($viewer->getThumbnailUrl());
18   echo "<p>Hello, ".$viewerName.".</p>";
19 }
```

Most of the code should appear familiar. The userId on line 3 is set to @me for the current viewer, but could also be set to a specific user ID. groupId on line 4 can be set to @self or @friends depending on whether you want to return a single person or group of people. fields is set to @all to retrieve all fields but could be set to an array of supported person fields, including the following:

```
id
name
displayName
profileUrl
thumbnailUrl
```

You will also find that within the $viewer parameter is the ability to access photos and URLs that the user has associated with his account. These can be accessed as follows:

```
echo "<p>Profile URL: ".$viewer->profileUrl."</p>";
echo "<p>Thumbnail URL: ".$viewer->thumbnailUrl."</p>";
echo "<h2>Photos</h2>";
echo "<ul>";
foreach($viewer->photos as $photo) {
```

```
 echo "<li>".$photo["type"].": ".$photo["value"]."</li>";
}
echo "</ul>";
echo "<h2>URLs</h2>";
echo "<ul>";
foreach($viewer->urls as $url) {
 echo "<li>".($url["type"] ? $url["type"] : "none").':
 <a href="'.$url["value"].'">'.(!empty($url["linkText"]) ?
 $url["linkText"] : "Unknown")."</a></li>";
}
echo "</ul>";
```

Optional parameters such as start and startIndex have been excluded but can be used for paging through multiple results. For example, if you want to extract the first three members of your site (fixed ordering by user ID), you can use the following code:

```
$batch = $opensocial->newBatch();
$memberParameters = array(
 "userId" => "@owner",
 "groupId" => "@friends",
 "fields" => "@all",
 "count" => 3,
 "startIndex" => "3"
);

$getMembers = $opensocial->people->get($memberParameters);
$batch->add($getMembers, "members");
$response = $batch->execute();
$members = $response["members"];
if ($members instanceof osapiError) {
 $code = $members->getErrorCode();
 $message = $members->getErrorMessage();
 // Process OpenSocial API Error
} else {
 echo "<ol>";
 foreach($members->list as $member) {
  echo "<li>".htmlentities($member->getName())."</li>";
 }
 echo "</ol>";
 echo "<p>Total Results: ".$members->totalResults."</p>";
}
```

The use of the count and startIndex parameters enables you to extract specific sets of users rather than returning the full list. The $members->totalResults value can then be used to display the total number of members on your site who have connected via Google Friend Connect. This number can then be used to ensure that you extract all users from the list. Unfortunately, the sortBy and sortOrder parameters do not appear to work with Google Friend Connect, although it could be used to sort the results by name or updated in ascending or descending order.

For fetching and creating activities or fetching, creating, updating, and deleting app data, the client library works slightly different than with people data. Table 10.2 summarizes the subtle differences in these methods, which are discussed in further detail using live code examples building on the Color Picker application created in Chapter 9.

Table 10.2   **Additional Parameters to `userId` and `groupId` Required by activities and App Data Requests (All requests must also use `"appId" => "@app"` to set the application identifier).**

Request	Required Parameters	Example
Fetch Activities	None	See Below
Create activity	activity	`$activity = new osapiActivity(null, null);` `$activity->setTitle("Test Title");` `$activity->setBody("This is a test.");`
Fetch and delete app data	fields	`array("key", ...)`
Create and update app data	data	`array(` `"key" => "value"` `)`

Successful responses to creating, updating, or deleting data are denoted by the response not being an instance of osapiError. Using the Color Picker application as an example from Chapter 9, you should be able to request the recent activities for the logged-in user by using the following code, which extends the test.php code described in the previous section, ensuring that the osapi library is included:

```php
$provider = new osapiFriendConnectProvider();
$authentication = new osapiFCAuth($cookie);
$opensocial = new osapi($provider, $authentication);
$batch = $opensocial->newBatch();
$viewerParameters = array(
  "userId" => "@me",
  "groupId" => "@self",
  "fields" => "@all"
);
$getActivities = $opensocial->activities->get($viewerParameters);
$batch->add($getActivities, "activities");
$response = $batch->execute();
```

```
$activities = $response["activities"];
if ($activities instanceof osapiError) {
 $code = $activities->getErrorCode();
 $message = $activities->getErrorMessage();
 // Process OpenSocial API Error
} else {
 echo "<ul>";
 foreach($activities->list as $activity) {
  echo "<li>".htmlentities($activity->getTitle())."</li>";
 }
 echo "</ul>";
}
```

This code shows how to retrieve a list of activities that a user has performed on your site. To iterate over results requires using the `list` element of the `$activities` object because multiple activities are being returned. After these results have been retrieved, you can then easily extract the title or body of the activity by using `$activity->getTitle()` or `$activity->getBody()`. Another potentially useful element of the Activity object is the post time, which you can retrieve via `$activity->getPostedTime()`, which returns a UNIX time stamp (which can then be reformatted).

Creating an activity is a similar process to that when using the client-side library: an Activity object is created, and then the activity creation method is called, passing in the object. To re-create a "dummy" choice of picking the color black, you could use the following code, which will be executed each time that you refresh the `test.php` page:

```
$activity = new osapiActivity(null, null);
$activity->setTitle("You picked black as your favorite color.");
$batch = $opensocial->newBatch();
$activityParameters = array(
 "userId" => "@me",
 "groupId" => "@self",
 "activity" => $activity
);
$setActivity = $opensocial->activities->create($activityParameters);
$batch->add($setActivity, "activity");
$response = $batch->execute();
$activity = $response["activity"];
if ($activity instanceof osapiError) {
 $code = $activity->getErrorCode();
 $message = $activity->getErrorMessage();
 // Process OpenSocial API Error
} else {
 echo "<p>The activity was created successfully.</p>";
}
```

The code adds the create activity request to the batch request, and if no errors occurred you can assume that the activity was created successfully. You should notice that if you save the new code and refresh the page, the fetch activities request now contains the new activity. Note that you cannot delete activities programmatically via the client library, but they can be removed via the Administration panel on the Google Friend Connect website.

Retrieving app data is similar to retrieving activities, apart from the fact that you must add a `fields` (if you require a specific field to be returned) and an `appId` parameter to the initial request, as follows:

```
$batch = $opensocial->newBatch();
$appDataParameters = array(
 "userId" => "@me",
 "groupId" => "@self",
 "appId" => "@app"
);
$getAppData = $opensocial->appdata->get($appDataParameters);
$batch->add($getAppData, "appdata");
$response = $batch->execute();
$appdata = $response["appdata"];
if ($appdata instanceof osapiError) {
 $code = $appdata->getErrorCode();
 $message = $appdata->getErrorMessage();
 // Process OpenSocial API Error
} else {
 // Process Returned App Data
}
```

Unfortunately, it appears that at the time of this writing the client-side and server-side versions of the Persistence API handle data in different ways for Google Friend Connect. This means that the two time fields that were stored in Chapter 9 are not retrieved by this method call. However, you can add your own server-side app data using the following code:

```
$batch = $opensocial->newBatch();
$appDataParameters = array(
 "userId" => "@me",
 "groupId" => "@self",
 "appId" => "@app",
 "data" => array(
  "test" => "1"
 )

);
$setAppData = $opensocial->appdata->create($appDataParameters);
$batch->add($setAppData, "appdata");
$response = $batch->execute();
$appdata = $response["appdata"];
if ($appdata instanceof osapiError) {
```

```
$code = $appdata->getErrorCode();
$message = $appdata->getErrorMessage();
// Process OpenSocial API Error
} else {
echo "<p>The App Data was stored successfully.</p>";
}
```

If, having stored this app data, you run the retrieval method again, you should have returned a multidimensional array containing the user ID as the key and an array of app data items. To retrieve this specific test item, you could add a `"fields" =>` `array("test")` parameter to `$appDataParameters` before retrieving the results. If you change the `userId` parameter to `@owner` and the `groupId` to `@friends`, you can retrieve all app data for the members of your site. Although you cannot delete app data, you can update it using the same method as adding data, except that you just replace the value of the key that you want to change with new data.

Summary

The client-side Google Friend Connect JavaScript API and OpenSocial API are not the only ways to access people, activity, and app data from OpenSocial containers. Server-side access through the OpenSocial RESTful and RPC protocols enables deep integration onto your Internet-enabled applications, where your code logic can be hidden away from site visitors. This chapter explored the workflow of a server-side Google Friend Connect implementation and the various ways that authentication is performed using authentication cookies and standard two-legged OAuth. And now that you've seen the principles of the PHP OpenSocial client library demonstrated, you should have enough knowledge to begin transforming your application into a fully functioning OpenSocial container. Chapter 11, "Developing OpenSocial Gadgets with Google Friend Connect," explores how to create an OpenSocial gadget with Google Friend Connect.

11

Developing OpenSocial Gadgets with Google Friend Connect

With your experience with the Google Friend Connect JavaScript API and OpenSocial API and server-side using the OpenSocial RESTful and RPC protocols, how about expanding your social reach even further through gadgets? Gadgets are self-contained applications that can be rendered on any Google Friend Connect container or in a standalone service like iGoogle. Data processing can be performed client side using JavaScript, or secure, authenticated requests can be made to retrieve server-side resources. Built-in JavaScript libraries make it easy to create gadgets that include tabs, Adobe Flash content, persistent storage, dynamic resizing, preferences, skins, and more. Gadgets promote the reach of your service because they can be installed by anyone and listed in the Google Friend Connect Gadget Directory.

This chapter explores the fundamentals of creating, testing, and submitting Google Friend Connect gadgets. Many of the skills you will learn in this chapter will draw on those you have already learned in Chapter 9, "An Overview of Google Friend Connect," and Chapter 10, "Server-Side Authentication and OpenSocial Integration." Being OpenSocial compatible, Google Friend Connect gadgets work in much the same way as ones from other containers, such as orkut, LinkedIn, and Ning. Therefore, once you grasp the fundamentals, they are transferable across all OpenSocial platforms with little modification. The best way to learn about gadgets is by exploring a worked example and being pointed to further resources for expansion and personalization.

An Overview of Google Gadgets

Google gadgets are applications that are built using HTML with JavaScript, Adobe Flash, or Microsoft Silverlight for dynamic features. They are structured as XML and can be made more interactive using feature extensions such as Maps, Calendar, and of course, OpenSocial which can be included in a gadget through the `<ModulePrefs>` tag. The simplest gadget comprises just a few lines of code:

```
<?xml version="1.0" encoding="UTF-8" ?>
<Module>
 <ModulePrefs title="Hello, World!">
  // Feature Extensions
  // User Preferences
 </ModulePrefs>
 <Content type="html" view="default">
  <![CDATA[
   Hello, World!
  ]]>
 </Content>
</Module>
```

This section explains what makes up a gadget and examines some of the features available. As with the majority of the examples in this book, it is impossible to cover the entire breadth of the subject, but this chapter touches on the fundamentals and provides references to resources to further your understanding.

Anatomy of an OpenSocial Google Gadget

Google gadgets contain several "compartments" that you can use to extend their functionality: module preferences, feature extensions, user preferences, and the content itself. The OpenSocial Gadgets API Specification, alongside the common Gadgets API Reference, describes the built-in features and core JavaScript API functionality, including processing inputs and outputs, JSON, tabbed content, and internationalization. The core JavaScript features are as follows:

- `gadgets.io` for retrieving remote content
- `gadgets.json` for translating objects to and from JSON
- `gadgets.Prefs` for handling and storing gadget preferences
- `gadgets.util` for providing utilities such as a HTML escaping a string via `gadgets.util.escapeString(<<STRING>>)` and un-escaping strings with `gadgets.util.unescapeString(<<STRING>>)`

The best way to explore these features is to use and experiment with them and understand how they can be implemented in different situations. This chapter will be focusing on the newer `gadgets.*` API and not on the deprecated Legacy API. All the JavaScript functionality should be used within `<Content>` sections, such as programmatically getting and setting user preferences.

Module Preferences

The `<ModulePrefs>` tag specifies characteristics of the gadget such as `title`, `title_url`, `author`, `author_email`, `description`, `screenshot`, and `thumbnail`. Users cannot change these attributes, although they can be automatically rendered using user preference substitution variables using the `__UP_userpref__` syntax within `<ModulePrefs>` or the `gadgets.Prefs()` JavaScript function within `<Content>` sections. For example:

```
<ModulePrefs title="__UP_title__" />
 <UserPref name="title" display_name="Title" default_value="Test" />
</ModulePrefs>
```

For clarity, if you submit to any of the gadget directories, you should also provide a `directory_title`, which is the default title for your gadget if you plan on allowing users to change titles. This can be set programmatically using the JavaScript `gadgets.window.setTitle(_hesc(newTitle))` function of the `gadgets.window` library and adding the `<Require feature="settitle" />` feature.

Top iGoogle Developers Directory

If you plan on submitting to the iGoogle Directory (http://www.google.com/ig/directory), you can also supply `author_photo` (a 70px by 100px image), `author_aboutme`, `author_link`, and `author_quote` parameters. Setting these will mean that you will also appear in the iGoogle Developers Directory (http://www.google.com/ig/directory?type=authors).

Other attributes such as `screenshot` and `thumbnail` have specific requirements such as being 280px wide and 120px by 60px, respectively. It is important when setting these attributes that special characters such as an ampersand (&) are HTML escaped and URLs encoded and that no ISO 8859-1 symbols are used. The `_hesc(string)` or `gadgets.util.escapeString(string)` JavaScript functions can be used to facilitate special HTML-character encoding, but this does not need to be performed within CDATA blocks.

The tag also serves as a container for other elements such as feature extensions, icons, OAuth, preloads, links, and locale.

Feature Extensions

Feature extensions are dependencies that can be loaded alongside the gadget to provide additional functionality. For example, you have already used the `<Require feature="settitle" />` tag to support the setting of the gadget title. Including these features loads an additional JavaScript library that is hidden away but that can be referenced using the supported methods of that feature. Two types of feature can be included using `<Require ... />` or `<Optional ... />` and must have a `name` attribute. The core `gadgets.*` API provides features such as `setprefs` for user preferences, `dynamic-height` for controlling the height of gadgets, `tabs` for tabbed content, `minimessage` for temporary messages, and `flash` for Adobe Flash rendering. Other third-party feature extensions also exist, including `skins`, which are supported by Google Friend Connect.

Skins

Skins are an essential feature that enables color personalization of your gadgets. This means that when users install your gadget, they can select which colors they want to use (or stick with the default palette). Using `<Optional feature="skins" />` will enable this func-tionality, which requires a number of skin parameters. Skin colors can be extracted by using `gadgets.skins.getProperty(property)`, where property is one of the available skin parameters, such as `CONTENT_TEXT_COLOR` or `CONTENT_BG_COLOR`. The Google Friend Connect version of the skins feature extends from the OpenSocial specification, which supports four parameters: `ANCHOR_COLOR`, `BG_COLOR`, `BG_IMAGE`, and `FONT_COLOR`.

User Preferences

For gadgets that require a bit of extra personalization, such as a weather gadget requesting a user's location, a `<UserPref>` can be used to support user input. User preferences require a unique `name` attribute, which is used as both the request reference and label that is dis-played to the user unless the `display_name` attribute is set. Other attributes include `datatype`, which can be one of `string`, `bool`, `enum`, `hidden` (users are not permitted to change these values) or `list`; `required`, which can be set to `true` or `false`; and `default_value`, for if no user value is set. User preferences can be retrieved and set using the JavaScript `gadgets.Prefs` class within `<Content>` sections. Using the `title` example, you could use the following:

```
var userPrefs = new gadgets.Prefs();
var title = userPrefs.getString("title");
```

Storing JSON Values as Strings

When storing user preferences, you can take advantage of the two `gadgets.json` functions for parsing (`parse`) and "stringifying" (`stringify`) values. Remember to convert back to JavaScript values for processing and note that OpenSocial performs automatic HTML escap-ing on app data, so you must "unescape" stringified JSON objects before parsing via `gadgets.util.unescapeString()`.

The `enum` and `list` data types function slightly differently to the `string`, `bool`, and `hidden` data types. The `enum` data type is presented to the user as a drop-down menu of choices, which are constructed within an `<EnumValue>`. For example:

```
<UserPref name="size" display_name="Drink Size" datatype="enum"
default_value="2">
 <EnumValue value="1" display_value="Small" />
 <EnumValue value="2" display_value="Medium" />
 <EnumValue value="3" display_value="Large" />
</UserPref>
```

Each `<EnumValue>` must contain a `value` attribute, and an optional `display_value` is used within the interface as a user-friendly name. Unlike the `list` data type, the `enum` should be used for predefined values because there is no method to programmatically change their values. The `list` data type should be used if you want to allow users to supply an arbitrary list of values, which can be retrieved as an array using the `userPrefs.getArray(list)` function or as a string where values are separated using the pipe (|) character using `userPrefs.getString(list)` if you were to use the `userPrefs` variable demonstrated earlier. By using `<Require feature="setprefs" />`, you can set this `list` by providing an array as the second parameter to the `userPrefs.` `setArray(name, list)` function. For example, here's a code snippet:

```
<UserPref name="destinations" display_name="Destinations" datatype="list"
default_value="Leeds|Sydney" />
</ModulePrefs>
<Content type="html">
var userPrefs = new gadgets.Prefs();
userPrefs.setArray("destinations", ["New York","London"]);
var destinations = userPrefs.getArray("destinations");
```

User preferences are also great for saving state, because by including `<Require feature="setprefs" />`, you can set preferences using the `userPrefs.set(key, value)` function. The only other important feature of user preferences is that they can be made shareable with other gadget users by including `<Optional feature="shareable-prefs" />`. For example, this could be used to define a "to do" list across a set of room-mates or to share a reading list across classmates. Adding the feature extension enables the user to share the gadget with friends and allows them to view and edit content dynamically. Note that this is available only to friends who have been authorized to edit user preferences.

Module Content and Views

Finally, `<Content>` sections are where the gadget attributes and user preferences are combined with programming logic to render the display to the user. These sections can either hold the content itself, which is set using the `type="html"` attribute, or can link to external content using the `type="url"` and setting the `href` attribute, or via proxied content, which is explored in the next section. It is possible to provide multiple `<Content>` sections, which are known as "views" and which have different characteristics, such as being shown on a default or canvas page. In Google Friend Connect, you can pass data into a gadget by using `<Require feature="views" />` and setting `"view-params": {"name": "value"}` within the `google.friendconnect.container.renderOpenSocialGadget()` method. These parameters can be accessed by using the following:

```
var params = gadgets.views.getParams();
var value = params["name"];
```

For Google Friend Connect, it is recommended that you stick to the single `type="html"` view because a special "lightbox" version of the `canvas` view is provided, although you could use the `canvas` and `default` views to navigate through the content should you want. The introduction of the lightbox is a move to simplify the Google Friend Connect install process for beginners, which used to require uploading two files (but that is now being phased out). If you want to use a custom `canvas.html` file, you can set the `useLightBoxForCanvas` attribute as `false` within the render method shown above. If you do not supply a default view, no content will be shown if you explicitly set a

canvas or default view. The best way around this is to either use `<Content
type="html">` on its own to cover all cases or to combine it with multiple views by using
`<Content type="html" view="canvas,default">`.

URL Content Types

The gadget content type can also be set to `url`, which means that any other content within
the `<Content>` tag is ignored. Use of this content type is similar to how a "ping" works in
network communications. The gadget assumes that all the programming logic is performed
server side, and so no actual response data will be rendered. This could prove useful if you
want to track any usage statistics of your gadget without using the `<Link>` tag.

If you include the `views` feature, you can navigate through them by using the following:

```
1  function getViewName() {
2    return gadgets.views.getCurrentView().getName();
3  }
4  function navigateTo(view, params) {
5    var supported_views = gadgets.views.getSupportedViews();
6    gadgets.views.requestNavigateTo(supported_views[view], params);
7  }
8  if (getViewName() == "canvas") {
9    document.write('<a href="javascript:navigateTo('default', null);">
10   Go To Default View</a>');
11 } else {
12   document.write('<a href="javascript:navigateTo('canvas', null);">
13   Go To Canvas View</a>');
14 }
```

By utilizing the `gadgets.views` class, you can easily navigate between views and also
pass data between instances. Because the `requestNavigateTo()` function on line 6
requires a view as its first parameter, you must use the `getSupportedViews()` function on
line 5 to extract all the views currently used in the container gadget. Note that Google
Friend Connect supports only the `canvas` and `default` views and not `profile`.

OpenSocial v0.9 Specification

The OpenSocial v0.8 specification is being used as of this writing because it is the current
version supported by Google Friend Connect. However, for gadgets, you can take advantage of the new features supported by the OpenSocial v0.9 specification, including the
following:

- A lightweight JavaScript API that makes requesting and parsing data simpler by
  making the code more intuitive and smaller. For example, to request the viewer, you
  use `osapi.people.getViewer().execute(callback)`. Batching is also supported,
  and so multiple requests can be strung together to reduce server calls. A separate
  namespace is used for backward compatibility and can be activated by using

`<Require feature="osapi">` or `<Require feature="opensocial-0.9">` for the old APIs.

- Proxied content, which reduces latency by enabling the display of an external web page within a gadget and thus eliminates the need to use excessive HTML and JavaScript to re-create content. Data can also be cached to provide minimum render time.

- Data pipelining eliminates the process whereby a gadget has to be loaded fully before data is requested from OpenSocial. In this instance, the user may receive a "Loading..." message while content is fetched. Data pipelining works hand in hand with proxied content and OpenSocial templates to make data available as soon as the gadget is loaded.

- OpenSocial templates provide a simpler mechanism for rendering data within gadgets using OpenSocial Markup Language (OSML) tags. OSML is also extensible, which means that developers can also create their own tags for use in their applications and gadgets.

Other minor additions can be found in the OpenSocial Specification Release Notes and include content rewriting, upload support, international formatting, and messaging support. There are no incompatible changes from the OpenSocial v0.8 specification, and so it should be fairly painless to update a gadget to support this new specification. When newer versions of OpenSocial become available, the Release Notes provide a useful overview and pointers for finding out information about changes and issues that may affect your legacy applications. Unfortunately, at the time of this writing, Google Friend Connect did not support this version of the specification, and so some elements such as data pipelining will not function correctly.

The final addition to OpenSocial is the release of the OpenSocial App Directory (http://directory.opensocial.org/gadgets/directory), which is a centralized container for developers to submit, review, and share OpenSocial applications. There is no specific Google Friend Connect category because this is provided externally by Google, but all of the gadget specifications are made available should you want to explore the inner workings of the most popular gadgets. This highlights an important issue: gadgets are public by their nature, and so you shouldn't store any sensitive information such as passwords within your specification. If you want your gadget to remain as elusive as possible (for example, for testing), do not submit it to any directories or link to it from an external web page.

Proxied Content

In its simplest form, proxied content enables the gadget developer to specify an external URL to be rendered for a `<Content>` section. For example:

```
<Content view="canvas" href="http://example.com/canvas.html"></Content>
```

Setting the `refreshInterval` attribute to the number of seconds you want your content to be cached can prove useful in development if set to 0, but for production-level applications, caching provides significant benefits for scaling and latency. Proxied content can also be used to make unsigned requests to content (as discussed later in this chapter in the "Advanced OpenSocial Gadget Development" section). Because Google Friend Connect does not always having access to the viewer of the gadget, this means that signed requests using data pipelining cannot be performed.

Data Pipelining and OpenSocial Templates

Data pipelining is a declarative syntax for OpenSocial data requests that you can use to retrieve proxied content for sending a POST request to a third-party server or OpenSocial data such as owners, viewers, and activities, which can be rendered through OpenSocial templates or the OpenSocial JavaScript API. Data pipelining reduces the number of requests to your server, thus reducing the render time of gadgets. A simple process flow is shown in Figure 11.1: A client requests an application view from a container (1), which sends social data to the remote server (2), which combines the social data with application data and returns it back to the container (3), ready to be rendered by the client (4).

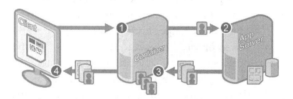

Figure 11.1   The four stages of a data pipelining
and proxied content request for OpenSocial data.

A data pipelining example of retrieving a list of songs for use in the OpenSocial template detailed below is as follows:

```
<script type="text/os-data" xmlns:os="http://ns.opensocial.org/
2008/markup">
 <os:HttpRequest key="songs" href="http://example.com/songs.json"
 format="json" />
</script>
```

At the time of this writing, many of the data pipelining features were still in draft and were not fully implemented in Google Friend Connect containers. For this reason, it will not be used for accessing social data, although it will be an essential feature in the future. The alternative is to use the OpenSocial JavaScript API methods for batches and requests. Their use requires a `<Require feature="osapi" />` feature extension in place of `<Require feature="opensocial-data" />`. However, data pipelining can be used alongside OpenSocial templates for external application data using authentication and signed requests (as detailed in the next section).

OpenSocial templates are a way of generating a user interface without manipulating a DOM element's `innerHTML` and/or dynamically creating elements. The feature can be added using `<Require feature="opensocial-templates" />` and works inside any `content` section. By separating markup and programming logic, OpenSocial templates create cleaner code that is more streamlined, reusable, and much easier to maintain. OpenSocial templates support looping and conditional display, giving you the flexibility to create more elaborate elements with less code. For example, if you have an array of songs requested using data pipelining, you can use a template to iterate and render them onscreen:

```
1  <script type="text/os-template" xmlns:os="http://ns.opensocial.org/
   2008/markup" require="songs">
2   <ul>
3    <li repeat="${songs.content}" var="song">
4     <img src="${song.albumThumbnail}" />
       ${song.title} by ${song.artist} from ${song.album}
5    </li>
6   </ul>
7  </script>
```

In this example, the `repeat` function was used on line 3, and each subsequent reference was prefixed by `song`, which was set by the `var` parameter. An alternative to the OpenSocial template approach is to use `opensocial.data.getDataContext().getDataSet("songs")` to take advantage of the OpenSocial JavaScript API to handle the requested data. It is a matter of preference which you use (although OpenSocial templates are the preferred method because of their render speed).

Advanced OpenSocial Gadget Development

With the basics under your belt, it's time to start looking at the more advanced features supported by Google gadgets. Up until now, you have not looked at how to extract any OpenSocial data or work with remote content.

Working with OpenSocial Data

Google Friend Connect enables you to work with people, activities, and app data within gadgets just like the client- and server-side applications explored in Chapters 9 and 10. This data can be accessed via data pipelining (currently not supported) or via OpenSocial JavaScript API requests. A request to retrieve the owner of the gadget can be made by using `<Require feature="osapi" />` and the following code inside a `<Content>` section:

```
1  <p id="owner"></p>
2  <script type="text/javascript">
3   gadgets.util.registerOnLoadHandler(init);
4   function init() {
```

```
5    initAllData();
6   }
7   function initAllData() {
8    var batch = osapi.newBatch();
9    batch.add("owner", osapi.people.getOwner());
10   batch.execute(onData);
11  }
12  function onData(data) {
13   if(!data.owner.error) {
14    var owner = data.owner;
15    var ownerName = owner.displayName;
16    document.getElementById("owner").innerHTML = ownerName;
17   } else {
18    // Process Error
19   }
20  }
21 </script>
```

Line 3 registers the `init()` callback function to be executed when the gadget is
loaded, which in this instance calls another function `initAllData()` on line 5, which
contains data-retrieval commands. The `init()` function is a useful place to call other functions, such as setting your gadget's skin or requesting other external data. It is often useful
to separate out all your functions so that they can be called individually when required.

Google Friend Connect Owner and Viewer

Unlike other containers, in Google Friend Connect the owner represents the site's profile information and not the owner who created it. Site administrators can be extracted by setting the
`groupId` to `ADMINS`. Remember that unlike containers such as orkut, often your gadget viewers will not be logged in, and so your gadget should be capable of dealing with this use case.

Inside the `initAllData()` function, an `osapi.BatchRequest` is created to retrieve the
owner data, which is the most efficient way to request data because multiple requests can
be executed within the batch. On line 10, the request is executed and data is fed back into
the `onData()` function. The `displayName` of the `owner` is then extracted on lines 15 and
6, and rendered inside the `<p>` tag on line 1.

Working with Remote Content

You may want your gadget to request or manipulate data that is held externally where
some server-side processing is performed and data is returned back to the viewer. In cases
where you want to send identifiers to your server, it is imperative that you "sign" requests,
because they could be vulnerable to manipulation by malicious gadget users. For example,
a user could execute an external `gadgets.io.makeRequest()` method passing custom
`opensocial_owner_id` and `opensocial_viewer_id` parameters to spoof those used in
your application. OpenSocial provides a convenient way to sign requests in a way that

transmits these values via OAuth to your server-side code. For this, you will require a server-side validation file called `sign.php` and available within this book's resources that signs requests and client-side JavaScript to invoke that script. The validation file uses a file that is contained within the PHP OpenSocial client library (http://code.google.com/p/ opensocial-php-client/), so it is assumed that this file exists in your directory structure along with the `osapi` client directory. The contents of `sign.php` are as follows:

```php
1  <?php
2  require_once("osapi/external/OAuth.php");
3  class FriendConnectSignatureMethod extends
   OAuthSignatureMethod_RSA_SHA1 {
4   protected function fetch_public_cert(&$request) {
5    return <<<EOD
6    -----BEGIN CERTIFICATE-----
7    MIICSjCCAb...
8    ...Pq1pUdWig=
9    -----END CERTIFICATE-----
10   EOD;
11  }
12 }
13 $request = OAuthRequest::from_request(null, null, array_merge(
   $_GET, $_POST));
14 $signature_method = new FriendConnectSignatureMethod();
15 @$signature_valid = $signature_method->check_signature($request,
   null, null, $_GET["oauth_signature"]);
16 $payload = array();
17 if ($signature_valid == true) {
18  $payload["validated"] = true;
19 } else {
20  $payload["validated"] = false;
21 }
22 $payload["query"] = array_merge($_GET, $_POST);
23 $payload["rawpost"] = file_get_contents("php://input");
24 print(json_encode($payload));
25 ?>
```

On line 7, you need to paste in the remainder of the Google Friend Connect signed request public key (http://www.google.com/friendconnect/certs/friendconnect.pem), which has been cut out from the code. Lines 12 to 14 are used to validate the request, and this is passed as the `$payload["validated"]` parameter back to the application. The code on lines 21 and 22 is used for debugging and returns the concatenation of GET and POST requests along with the raw POST data. Instead of passing all of these values back to the gadget, you could also do some further processing using the `$_POST["token"]` gadget authentication token parameter, such as creating an OpenSocial object to update app data or an activity. You could also look to pass back an entire view to display inline. In the client-side code, this would be invoked by using the following code:

```
1   var token = shindig.auth.getSecurityToken();
2   makeRequest("http://example.com/sign.php", {"token" : token});
3   function makeRequest(url, postdata) {
4     var postdata = gadgets.io.encodeValues(postdata);
5     var params = {};
6     params[gadgets.io.RequestParameters.AUTHORIZATION] =
        gadgets.io.AuthorizationType.SIGNED;
7     params[gadgets.io.RequestParameters.CONTENT_TYPE] =
        gadgets.io.ContentType.JSON;
8     params[gadgets.io.RequestParameters.METHOD] =
        gadgets.io.MethodType.POST;
9     params[gadgets.io.RequestParameters.POST_DATA]= postdata;
10    params[gadgets.io.RequestParameters.REFRESH_INTERVAL] = 60;
11    gadgets.io.makeRequest(url, response, params);
12  }
13  function response(payload) {
14    alert(payload.data.validated);
15  }
```

The code on line 1 extracts the gadget authentication token, which is passed as a parameter to the `makeRequest()` function on line 2, where the POST data is encoded on line 4. The `response` parameter is the name of the callback function, which accepts the data request, and this just creates an alert box stating whether the request was validated. You can optimize your call by adding the URL to your sign request to a `<Preload>` tag within module preferences:

```
<Preload href="http://www.example.com/sign.php" authz="signed"
sign_owner="true" sign_viewer="true" views="canvas" />
```

If you do not need to use owner or viewer details, you can prevent sending them during the signing process by setting the `sign_owner` or `sign_viewer` parameters to `false`. You can restrict preloads to specific views by setting the `views` parameter. In this instance, data is preloaded only for the `canvas`. Preloads that do not take advantage of signed requests can omit the `authz` parameter or replace `signed` with `none`.

"Don't Be Evil"

When debugging your `makeRequest`, you might come across the following response: `throw 1; < "don't be evil" >`, which suffixes your data calls. This is known as an "Unparseable Cruft" and is used to create an illegal JavaScript syntax that defeats XSRF attacks and does not affect your code.

As you will appreciate, there are multiple ways to access data, such as data pipelining, proxied content, and using the OpenSocial JavaScript API with the `gadgets.io.makeRequest()` method. It is recommended that if you are working with any OpenSocial data such as people, activities, or app data that you use the OpenSocial JavaScript API as Google Friend Connect doesn't support some of the more advanced data-retrieval features. Therefore, any signed requests must also use this method. Any unsigned requests such as retrieving standard data could be made using data pipelining, OpenSocial templates, and proxied content.

Gadget Internationalization (i18n) and Localization (L10n)

Because your gadget may be used worldwide, English might not be your user's first language. Translations are achieved fairly easily using message bundles for all your user-visible text and are stored as external XML files that support UTF-8 encoding. Internationalization is the process of structuring your gadgets so that they can be localized. Localization is the process of making your gadget accessible based on a user's country/language. A sample message bundle would look like this:

```
<?xml version="1.0" encoding="UTF-8" ?>
<messagebundle>
 <msg name="red">Red</msg>
 <msg name="orange">Orange</msg>
 <msg name="green">Green</msg>
</messagebundle>
```

Each message bundle should contain only a single language translation and should be stored using a `<<LANGUAGE>>_<<COUNTRY>>.xml` naming convention. For example, `en_ALL.xml` applies to all English-speaking users independent of their country. The default or "fallback" message bundle is set to `ALL_ALL.xml` if no exact match can be found. Languages should be one of the two-character ISO 639-1 codes, and countries should be one of the two-character ISO 3166-1-apha-2 codes. You initialize a message bundle by setting the `<Locale>` tag inside `<ModulePrefs>`, as follows:

```
<Locale messages="http://example.com/ALL_ALL.xml" />
<Locale lang="en" messages="http://example.com/en_ALL.xml" />
```

An optional country attribute can be set for cases such as distinguishing U.K. or U.S. English. Using the colors message bundle, you can use substitution variables, and thus `<p>__MSG_red__</p>` would display the "Red" text within a paragraph. Alternatively, you can use a `gadgets.Prefs` object:

```
var prefs = new gadgets.Prefs();
var red = prefs.getMsg("red");
var orange = prefs.getMsg("orange");
var green = prefs.getMsg("green");
```

You can use a message as your gadget's title, but remember that if you allow the user to set this manually, you may lose out on this functionality. Consider localizing the `directory_title` instead, because this is the one that will appear if you submit to the gadget directory. You should also consider localizing your gadget `description`. It might be best to get a native speaker to translate this for you, instead of relying on an online translation tool.

Detecting Country and Language

You can detect a user's country and language by using a `gadgets.Prefs` object and then calling the `prefs.getCountry()` or `prefs.getLanguage()` methods. These can prove useful if sent as POST variables for server-side processing and rendering.

Gadgets also support bidirectional text, which reads from right to left (for languages such as Hebrew and Arabic). This is achieved by specifying a `language_direction="rtl"` attribute within `<Locale>` for the specific language. Four special substitution variables are made available by the BIDI (Bi-Directional) API and can prove useful for setting padding and alignment of characters: `__BIDI_START_EDGE__` and `__BIDI_END_EDGE__`, which represent the start and endpoints of the letters that are set to left or right; and `__BIDI_DIR__` and `__BIDI_REVERSE_DIR__`, which are set to rtl or ltr for the two modes. To set the margin of an element you could use the following style element:

```
style="margin-__BIDI_START_EDGE__: 10px;"
```

Because the `__BIDI_START_EDGE__` will be updated to reflect the user's preference, this will change either the right or the left margin.

Creating a Google Gadget

To bring this chapter together, a simple OpenSocial gadget has been created that does some basic retrieval of social data using some of the techniques explored in this chapter. The Color Picker application that was created in Chapter 9 has been adapted to suit a gadget container. The client-side implementation of Google Friend Connect enabled viewers to pick their favorite color, which was then submitted as a site activity. The gadget also displays a section with the five most recent members, along with their thumbnail photos. This section also includes some tips for testing and submitting your gadget and for adding Google Analytics for user tracking.

Color Picker, Revisited

The quickest and easiest way to get your gadget up and running is to use the Google Gadget Editor (http://gadgeteditor.appspot.com/editor) created by Arne Roomann-Kurrik. It provides a convenient place for testing your gadget with Google Friend Connect and other containers (see Figure 11.2). (The link requires a Google account to access.) Although not suited for production gadget storage, it will give you a good idea of how your gadget will function in the Google Friend Connect environment.

The gadget source code (`gadget.xml`) is split into several pieces, which can be edited directly in a new Google Gadget Editor page:

```
1   <?xml version="1.0" encoding="utf-8"?>
2   <Module>
3     <ModulePrefs author="Mark Hawker" author_email="mark@example.com"
        description="A test Google Gadget." title="Color Picker"
        directory_title="Color Picker" height="100" scrolling="true">
4       <Require feature="opensocial-0.9" />
```

```
5    <Require feature="osapi" />
6    <Require feature="dynamic-height" />
7    <Optional feature="skins" />
8    </ModulePrefs>
```

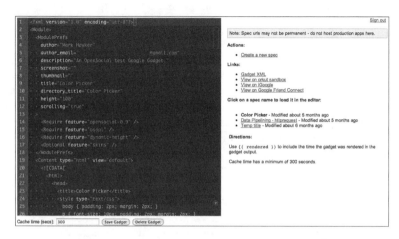

Figure 11.2   The Google Gadget Editor.

Every Google gadget is initiated via a `<Module>` element, which must contain `<ModulePrefs>` and `<Content>` child elements. Inside the module preferences are details such as the author's name and e-mail address along with information about the gadget such as its name and description. Specific gadget requirements are also set in this opening code block, which is for including the OpenSocial libraries and skin capabilities. With all the preferences now set, you can start building the gadget content:

```
9     <Content type="html" view="default">
10    <![CDATA[
11    <html>
12     <head>
13      <title>Color Picker</title>
14      <style type="text/css">
15       body { padding: 2px; margin: 2px; }
16       p { font-size: 10px; padding: 2px; margin: 2px; }
17       h1 { font-size: 12px; }
18       h2 { font-size: 11px; }
19       h3 { font-size: 10px; }
20       #gadget { width: 250px; }
21       #colorTable { width: 100%; }
22       #colorPicker { margin: 20px 40px; }
23       #redCell { border: 3px solid #666666; }
24       .color { width: 20px; height: 20px; border: 3px solid #e5ecf9; }
25       .red { background-color: red; }
26       .orange { background-color: orange; }
```

```
27    .green { background-color: green; }
28    .yellow { background-color: yellow; }
29    .blue { background-color: blue; }
30    .pink { background-color: pink; }
31    .memberPhoto { width: 46px; height: 46px; border: 0;
      padding-right: 2px; }
32    </style>
33    </head>
```

This initial code block sets the header of the gadget, which utilizes the `default` view and includes a number of style sheet elements. Instead of referencing an external file, they have been included inline, but it is possible that you could use an external style sheet if required. The next block of code is for displaying a welcome message to the gadget viewers and enables those who have logged in to Google Friend Connect to pick a color for submission:

```
34    <body>
35    <div id="gadget">
36    <h1>Welcome to <span id="owner"></span></h1>
37    <p>This application demonstrates <a href="http://www.google.com/
      friendconnect/">Google Friend Connect</a> and its Google Gadget
38    capabilities.</p>
39    <h2>Recent Members</h2>
40    <p id="recentMembers"></p>
41    <p>Once you've signed in you can generate an activity by clicking
      a color below and pressing the "Pick" button:</p>
42    <div id="colorPicker">
43     <table id="colorTable" cellspacing="10">
44      <tr>
45       <td><div class="color red" onclick="pickColor(this, 'red');"
         id="redCell"></div></td>
46       <td><div class="color orange" onclick="pickColor(this,
         'orange');"></div></td>
47       <td><div class="color green" onclick="pickColor(this,
         'green');"></div></td>
48       <td style="width: 10px;" rowspan="2"><button
         onclick="createActivity();" id="button" disabled="disabled">
         Pick</button></td>
49      </tr>
50      <tr>
51       <td><div class="color yellow" onclick="pickColor(this,
         'yellow');"></div></td>
52       <td><div class="color blue" onclick="pickColor(this, 'blue');">
         </div></td>
53       <td><div class="color pink" onclick="pickColor(this, 'pink');">
         </div></td>
54      </tr>
```

```
55      </table>
56      </div>
57      <h2>Recent Activities</h2>
58      <p id="recentActivities"></p>
59      </div>
```

The code above is very similar to that discussed in Chapter 9, in that it contains a placeholder on line 40 for displaying recent members, a color picker between lines 42 and 56, and recent activities to be rendered on line 58. The Submit button is initially disabled on line 48 because you cannot guarantee that you'll have a logged-in viewer available. Clicking each of the colors will run the `pickColor()` function, which is created on lines 152 to 157 below. No further content is to be shown to the viewer of the gadget, so the remainder of the code is to define specific JavaScript functionalities of Color Picker:

```
60      <script type="text/javascript">
61      var viewer;
62      gadgets.util.registerOnLoadHandler(init);
63      function init() { skin(); initAllData(); }
64      function skin() {
65      var borderColor = gadgets.skins.getProperty("BORDER_COLOR");
66      var endcapBgColor = gadgets.skins.getProperty("ENDCAP_BG_COLOR");
67      var endcapTextColor = gadgets.skins.getProperty(
        "ENDCAP_TEXT_COLOR");
68      var endcapLinkColor = gadgets.skins.getProperty(
        "ENDCAP_LINK_COLOR");
69      var alternateBgColor = gadgets.skins.getProperty(
        "ALTERNATE_BG_COLOR");
70      var contentBgColor = gadgets.skins.getProperty(
        "CONTENT_BG_COLOR");
71      var contentLinkColor = gadgets.skins.getProperty(
        "CONTENT_LINK_COLOR");
72      var contentTextColor = gadgets.skins.getProperty(
        "CONTENT_TEXT_COLOR");
73      var contentSecondaryLinkColor = gadgets.skins.getProperty(
        "CONTENT_SECONDARY_LINK_COLOR");
74      var contentSecondaryTextColor = gadgets.skins.getProperty(
        "CONTENT_SECONDARY_TEXT_COLOR");
75      var contentHeadlineColor = gadgets.skins.getProperty(
        "CONTENT_HEADLINE_COLOR");
76      html = new Array();
77      html.push('<style type="text/css">');
78      html.push(' body { color: " + contentTextColor + ';
        background-color: " + contentBgColor + "; }');
79      html.push("</style>");
80      document.write(html.join(""));
81      }
```

As with previous Google Friend Connect examples, the main functionality of the application is contained within the `initAllData()` and `onData()` functions, which gather and render data. However, unlike web pages, which can load JavaScript when a page is loaded, you need to explicitly tell a Google gadget to execute a function on load. This is achieved by setting the code on line 62 that executes the `init()` callback function on line 63. The `init()` function calls two functions for constructing the gadget's skin and for extracting data. The `skin()` function accepts the colors that a user has set when rendering the gadget on the user's site (for example, in the following JavaScript, which could be rendered on another web page):

```
var skin = {};
skin["CONTENT_BG_COLOR"] = "#ffffff";
skin["CONTENT_TEXT_COLOR"] = "#333333";
google.friendconnect.container.renderOpenSocialGadget({
 id: "colorPicker",
 url: ".../gadget.xml",
 height: 250,
 site: SITE_ID,
}, skin);
```

The `url` given in the example above is not complete and should point to the absolute reference to your gadget hosted on your server. Note that only a few of these properties are actually rendered as gadget styles on lines 76 to 80, and you could've used any number of them in your own gadgets:

```
82      function initAllData() {
83       var buttonHtml = document.getElementById("button").
         disabled = true;
84       var batch = osapi.newBatch();
85       var viewerParams = {"fields": [opensocial.Person.Field.NAME]};
86       var membersParams = {
87        "count": 5,
88        "fields": [
          opensocial.Person.Field.ID,
          opensocial.Person.Field.NAME,
          opensocial.Person.Field.THUMBNAIL_URL,
          opensocial.Person.Field.PROFILE_URL
          ]
89       };
90       var activitiesParams = {
91        "userId": "@owner",
92        "groupId": "@friends",
93        "count": 2
94       }
95       batch.add("owner", osapi.people.getOwner());
96       batch.add("viewer", osapi.people.getViewer(viewerParams));
97       batch.add("members", osapi.people.getOwnerFriends(
```

```
         membersParams));
98       batch.add("activities", osapi.activities.get(activitiesParams));
99       batch.execute(onData);
100      }
```

The initAllData() function is used to collect all the data to be rendered by the gadget. The parameters for a viewer and members are set on lines 85 to 89, which define which fields to return, and those for an activity are set on lines 90 to 94, ensuring that only two activities for the site's members are shown by the gadget. The request batch is split into owner, viewer, members, and activities data, which are executed and passed to the callback function on line 99. The content of the onData() function have been split into groupings that parse each of the batch requests:

```
101      function onData(data) {
102        if(!data.owner.error) {
103          var owner = data.owner;
104          var ownerName = owner.displayName;
105          document.getElementById("owner").innerHTML = ownerName;
106        } else {
107          document.getElementById("owner").innerHTML = "this site";
108        }
```

The owner is the one parameter that should be available irrespective of whether users are signed in with Google Friend Connect. This parameter will set the name of the site in which the gadget is placed or will use a standard placeholder if an error has occurred:

```
109      if(!data.viewer.error) {
110        viewer = data.viewer;
111        var buttonHtml = document.getElementById("button").
           disabled = false;
112      } else {
113        // data.viewer.error.code
114        // data.viewer.error.message
115      }
```

The viewer parameter will return an error if the user is not logged in. In this case, no further processing is required. However, you could use the space on lines 113 and 114 to display a warning message to the user. If the viewer is available, the Submit button on line 48 can be enabled.

```
116      var membersHtml = document.getElementById("recentMembers");
117      if (!data.members.error) {
118        var members = data.members;
119        membersHtml.innerHTML = "";
120        if (members.totalResults > 0) {
121          for (var i in members.list) {
122            membersHtml.innerHTML += '<a href="' +
               members.list[i].profileUrl + '" title="' +
               members.list[i].displayName + '"><img class="memberPhoto"
```

```
             src="' + members.list[i].thumbnailUrl + '" height="65"
             width="65" alt="' + members.list[i].displayName + '" />
             </a>';
123        }
124      } else {
125        membersHtml.innerHTML = "There are no site members.";
126      }
127    } else {
128      membersHtml.innerHTML = "There was an error retrieving
           members.";
129    }
```

The members data set is slightly more complex that owner and viewer in that it contains an array of elements. A test is made on line 120 to determine whether the gadget has any members associated with it. If so, the list is iterated over, and a link is created on line 122 containing the member's name, thumbnail photo, and profile URL. The members are sent automatically to the HTML element created on line 40, along with appropriate error messages if no members were returned or if there was an exception. The final JavaScript code that needs to be created is for handling activities:

```
130      var recentActivitiesHtml = document.getElementById(
           "recentActivities");
131      if (!data.activities.error) {
132        var activities = data.activities;
133        recentActivitiesHtml.innerHTML = "";
134        if (activities.totalResults > 0) {
135          var title, body;
136          for (var i in activities.list) {
137            title = unescape(activities.list[i].title);
138            body = unescape(activities.list[i].body);
139            recentActivitiesHtml.innerHTML += "<p>" + title + body +
               "</p>";
140          }
141        } else {
142          recentActivitiesHtml.innerHTML = "There are no site
             activities.";
143        }
144      } else {
145        recentActivitiesHtml.innerHTML = "There was an error retrieving
           site activities.";
146      }
147      adjustHeight();
148    }
149    function adjustHeight() { gadgets.window.adjustHeight(); }
```

On line 130, the activities are associated with the HTML element on line 58, which iterates over the two requested activities and displays their `title` and `body` values. All that remains to do is to create a new activity via the gadget itself:

```
150    var color = "red";
151    var lastColorDiv = document.getElementById("redCell");
152    function pickColor(div, newColor) {
153     color = newColor;
154     div.style.border = "3px solid #666666";
155     lastColorDiv.style.border = "3px solid #e5ecf9";
156     lastColorDiv = div;
157    }
158    function createActivity() {
159     if (viewer) {
160      var activity = opensocial.newActivity({
           "title": viewer.displayName + " picked " + color + " as their
           favorite color."
          });
161      opensocial.requestCreateActivity(activity, "HIGH",
           function() { setTimeout(initAllData, 1000); });
162     } else {
163      alert("There was an error creating an activity.");
164     }
165    }
166   </script>
167  </body>
168  </html>
169  ]]>
170 </Content>
171 </Module>
```

The code on line 150 and 151 ensures that the red cell is selected by default, which can then be used by the `pickColor()` function. An activity is created in much the same way as via the client-side and server-side libraries. This activity consists of creating an `Activity` object on line 160 and sending the request on line 161. On success, the `initAllData()` function is called, but could also be used to update other gadget elements or to display a message to the user depending on whether the activity was created successfully or not. The final part of this code is for closing the appropriate `<Content>` and `<Module>` elements ready for the gadget to be saved.

Click "Save Gadget", and then click the "View on Google Friend Connect" link. You should see a developer's sandbox that enables you to sign up to the container and then test out the gadget's functionalities for both an anonymous and named viewer (see Figure 11.3).

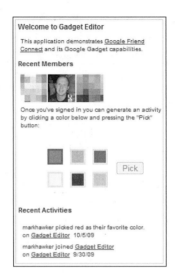

Figure 11.3   The completed Color Picker
Google gadget.

Because you are writing to the site's activities register, it's possible that if the site administrators have other gadgets running that they, too, will be added to the activity stream. Why not implement the Color Picker functionality using app data instead? Or add internationalization? Or add a different canvas page view showing what colors the viewer's friends have picked? The possibilities are endless.

Testing, Tracking, and Directory Submission

Before submitting your gadget to a directory, test it for common coding errors and ensure that is it optimized for heavy traffic. A common misconception with Google Friend Connect gadgets is that you will always have the viewer details. You should test your gadgets both with and without the viewer details available using a browser extension such as Firebug or with other similar development tools. You can use these tools to test gadget latency in many interesting ways.

Google Gadget Checker

Google has its own Gadget Checker, which runs inside iGoogle and checks for common errors such as client-side latency, correct syntax, and XML well-formedness. This is useful for checking the simpler bugs within your gadgets and offers quick fixes to the issues it identifies.

The Google Speed project (http://code.google.com/speed/) provides some useful tips for ensuring your gadget is as optimized as possible for high traffic. This includes "minifying" your internal JavaScript and CSS and reducing the number of browser fetches of content by combining JavaScript files. You could also use image "sprites" to combine multiple images together, distribute connections across multiple servers, and use cache tools such as the `gadgets.io.getProxyUrl()` method. This method works by passing in the URL of an image or JavaScript file, which will return the cached URL of the file. For example:

```
var imgUrl = "http://example.com/logo.png";
var cachedImgUrl = gadgets.io.getProxyUrl(imgUrl);
```

Adobe Flash developers can also use the `gadgets.flashembedCachedFlash()` method to achieve the same effect with their content.

Google AJAX Libraries API

If you want to use dynamic content libraries such as jQuery or Prototype, it is recommended that you include them using the methods provided by the Google AJAX Libraries API (http://code.google.com/apis/ajaxlibs/). Not only do they provide minified versions of each library, but the API also handles caching and loading automatically.

A great resource for general information about gadget publishing is the Google Gadget Center (http://www.google.com/webmasters/gadgets/about/), which provides details about promoting, tracking, and optimizing your gadget.

Installing and Configuring Gadget Analytics

For in-depth analytics, you can install the Google Analytics feature for Google gadgets. Unlike with regular websites, gadgets are all hosted as a subdomain of `gmodules.com`. Therefore, for each gadget that you are tracking, you need a unique Google Analytics identifier. Creating an identifier requires you to visit https://www.google.com/analytics/ and either sign up for a new account or log in using an existing account. You should then proceed to add a new site profile. The required website URL is only a string that the Google Analytics software pairs with the identifier, and so this URL can be set to any valid URL string, whether fabricated or real. An appropriate URL may be your domain if you have not already created a Google Analytics account for that URL. Because you are installing the tracking code on a gadget and not a web page, you will not need access to the website URL that you set. After completing the registration process, you will be given a web property ID that will be in the form `UA-123456789-1` and should be stored within your gadget. To enable Google Analytics using the Color Picker example above, you must make the following changes:

- Add a `<Require feature="com.google.gadgets.analytics" />` element within the module's preferences to enable tracking.

- Create the Tracker object by adding a `var ga = new _IG_GA("UA-123456789-1");` line at the top of the JavaScript code block. This should be your own web property ID because the example is simply a placeholder.

Google Analytics provides two ways to track user interactions for different situations: virtual URL, for gadget statistics such as special page views; and event tracking. When you are using virtual URL, each call is recorded as a page request for the string that you provide as a parameter to the method. This is typically a fabricated string that can be used if you have multiple gadgets or want to track separate views by using different string parameters. You can use event tracking to log user interactions (for example, the user picking a color or submitting a new activity). At the time of this writing, this feature was in closed beta. So, until this has been fully released, you should use the virtual URL method. Here are a few examples of using the virtual URL method within the Color Picker gadget:

```
ga.reportPageview("/view/colorPicker");
```

This method call would be placed right underneath the creation of the tracker object and would be called each time the gadget was rendered. If you want to track when a user submits his choice of color, you can update the `createActivity()` function to include the following:

```
ga.reportPageview("/colorpicker/link/submit");
```

Using the event tracking method, you can track which colors are being clicked the most by adding the following to the `pickColor()` method:

```
ga.reportEvent("Color Picker", "Pick", color);
```

It is best practice to set the first parameter as the name of your gadget and then the action as the second parameter. The final parameter is for adding another categorical layer to events so that you can then segment by color. For example, if you also have an "Unpick" action, this would group both events together for each color. These parameters are just guides, and you can actually use any string combination within your event reporting, but it does help if you apply the relevant groupings shown.

Submitting Your Google Gadget

Remember that you do not have to publish your gadget anywhere! You can use it privately without letting anybody know where to find it. But, if you want to submit your creation, you can use either the iGoogle Directory (http://www.google.com/ig/directory) or the Google Friend Connect Directory (http://www.google.com/friendconnect/submitgadget) and thus allow others to see, build upon, and use your gadget. With the iGoogle Directory, you must integrate specific Google Friend Connect functionality into your gadget, such as signing in, because a user's iGoogle home page does not include that facility.

When submitting to the Google Friend Connect Directory, you must ensure that you have set the `title`, `description`, `author`, `author_email`, `screenshot`, `thumbnail`, and `directory_title` elements in the module preferences and ensure that your gadget handles having a viewer's details both available and unavailable.

Summary

Google gadgets present another opportunity to showcase your newly found skills with Google Friend Connect and OpenSocial. The applications are limited only by your imagination, and this chapter just scratches the surface of what is possible with the extensible format afforded by the various gadget specifications. This chapter explored the anatomy of a Google gadget, including setting gadget and user preferences, and discussed feature extensions such as skinning and dynamic heights. The chapter also explored content types and views and then looked at more advanced features provided by the OpenSocial v0.9 specification. Although data pipelining, proxied content, and OpenSocial templates do not work perfectly using Google Friend Connect, they will be a major feature in the future. Remote content using signed requests was explored, and then some internationalization features for creating multilanguage gadgets were highlighted. The Color Picker example from Chapter 9 was revisited and transformed into a gadget, and to conclude, gadget testing and analytics were referenced and developed.

12

Building a Microblog Tool Using CodeIgniter

In Part I, you were given an overview of Twitter and how it can be used for user authentication via "Sign in with Twitter," which allows you to post updates, send direct messages, and perform other functionalities on behalf of a user. In Part II, Facebook Platform integration for websites was described, which you can use for user authentication, content sharing, commenting, and stream publishing. Google Friend Connect was explored in Part III, using client- and server-side technologies. It can be used for posting activities, storing application data, and fetching people and profiles. In isolation, each of these technologies can make an application more social, but when used together, you can create rich solutions that are more accessible and interactive for your users and their friends.

In this chapter, you will learn how to create a "social programming microblog" called Sprog from scratch using a PHP framework called CodeIgniter. The final version of Sprog will implement many of the features that have been described in this book, including user authentication, status updates, commenting, "likes," and social context through Twitter, Facebook, and Google Friend Connect integration. This chapter is split into two sections: looking at elements of the CodeIgniter framework, and building the bare bones of the microblog. Chapter 13, "Integrating Twitter, Facebook, and Google Friend Connect," incorporates many of the social features described in Parts I, II, and III of this book.

An Overview of CodeIgniter

CodeIgniter (http://codeigniter.com/) is a community-driven PHP framework with a very small footprint and is built for programmers who need a simple and elegant toolkit to create rich web applications. The beauty of CodeIgniter lies in its vibrant user community and extensive help documentation, which enables you to focus on creating your applications rather than struggling with messy command-line solutions. You will also find a wealth of video tutorials on the CodeIgniter website (http://codeigniter.com/tutorials/) containing many more features than are discussed in this chapter. These features include sending e-mails to users, working with images, performing unit tests, and uploading files.

Handling GET Parameters

The one downside to using CodeIgniter is its inability to handle GET parameters without seriously affecting the complexity of the framework. This is particularly important when using Twitter because it sends an `oauth_token` parameter back to your applications. A workaround will be used that just reformats the Twitter callback as a POST parameter to work with inside your applications.

CodeIgniter uses the Model-View-Controller (MVC) architectural pattern, which separates application logic from presentation and database extraction. In case you have not used MVC before, this section includes a brief overview with examples and prompts of how to set up the first stages of Sprog. Even for beginners, it will take only a matter of hours before you start to appreciate the benefits of MVC and wonder why you have never used it before! For experienced programmers, you can use the more advanced features of CodeIgniter, such as benchmarking, File Transfer Protocol (FTP), and caching, to increase performance of large-scale applications.

The Model-View-Controller Architectural Design

The MVC pattern is one of the most commonly used architectures used in web applications today. The clearest benefit of MVC is its separation of presentation and application logic, which is akin to the separation of HTML and CSS. For example, although your data-retrieval functionality might be the same you may want to present content to a number of devices from laptops to cell phones. What MVC enables is the ability to make maximum reuse of existing code that is easier to test and build upon. Applications are divided into three components:

- The **model** (or **models**) is the conduit between a controller and your application's data store.

- The **controller** (or **controllers**) manages user requests such as GET or POST operations and in turn requests data from a model and then sends it to a view for presentation. In practice, a controller will contain all the logic for handling form inputs or requests to view specific pages. You may want to use a master controller, which connects to multiple other controllers to handle requests from multiple devices.

- The **view** (or **views**) handles data passed via the controller, and then presents the data onscreen or to the requesting device. A view should be parsing only prefetched data and should not make requests to your data store (because that is the role of a model). Often, you can use a template engine such as Smarty (http://www.smarty.net/) to promote greater reuse of views across multiple devices.

The remainder of this chapter and Chapter 13 focus on MVC using a web application framework called CodeIgniter. The benefits of a framework are that most of the complexity of using common features such as working with databases, sessions, and form handling are already coded for you. All that you then need to do is configure the framework to your specific needs without worrying about creating your own potentially error-prone functions. Many of the frameworks available today have been tested extensively and are updated continually when new vulnerabilities are discovered.

Installing, Configuring, and Exploring CodeIgniter

You can download CodeIgniter from http://codeigniter.com/downloads/. It requires PHP 4.3.2+ and supports MySQL (4.1+), MySQLi, MS SQL, Postgres, Oracle, SQLite, and ODBC database platforms. Because you are using the twitter-async library, it is assumed that you are working with PHP 5.2+. The latest version of CodeIgniter at the time of this writing, and that is included with source code examples, is 1.7.2. After you have downloaded the framework, unzipped it to a location of your choice, and renamed the base folder to `codeigniter`, you will notice a directory structure similar to the following:

- **`system`**

  The `system` directory contains all the files required to make CodeIgniter work. It includes directories for saving an application cache, for storing logs, and for storing core helpers and libraries. Each helper file is just a collection of functions in a particular category that help you with specific tasks. For example, URL Helpers assist with creating links, Form Helpers help you create form elements, and Text Helpers perform various text-formatting routines. Libraries, on the other hand, are suites of functions that perform tasks such as maintaining a database, uploading files, and sending e-mails. You will also see a `plug-in` directory, which is used for installing code created by the CodeIgniter community to use in your applications.

- **`system\application`**

  One of the most important directories in `system` is `application`. This directory stores all the models, views, and controllers used in your applications. It also stores configuration and error page details. Although not explored in this book, it is possible to have multiple applications running from a single CodeIgniter installation.

- **`user_guide`**

  The `user_guide` directory should be exactly the same as the one that can be found at http://codeigniter.com/user_guide/, and so you can delete this if you want to save space on your web server.

- **`index.php`**

  This is the main file that runs all the CodeIgniter functions and is where you can change the names of the `system` and `application` directories for enhanced security.

- **`license.txt`**

  The license associated that must be adhered to when using the framework.

The `system` directory contains all the CodeIgniter functionality, such as libraries and helpers, which are explored later in this section. You will also notice an `application` directory, which is where all the models, views, and controllers are stored. For security reasons, this directory should be moved up one level alongside the `system` and `user_guide` directories. Because you cannot place static files such as images, JavaScript, or CSS within the `application` directory, you should create another directory called `static` to be used to host such files in the future. Your new directory structure should look like this:

- `application`
- `static`
- `system`
- `index.php`
- `license.txt`

For added security, you might also consider renaming the `system` directory and updating `$system_folder` variable within the `index.php` file with the new name you've chosen. For the examples in this chapter, this will remain as `system`. If you upload all the CodeIgniter files to your server and then visit the URL of your new `codeigniter` folder, you should be prompted with a screen similar to that shown in Figure 12.1.

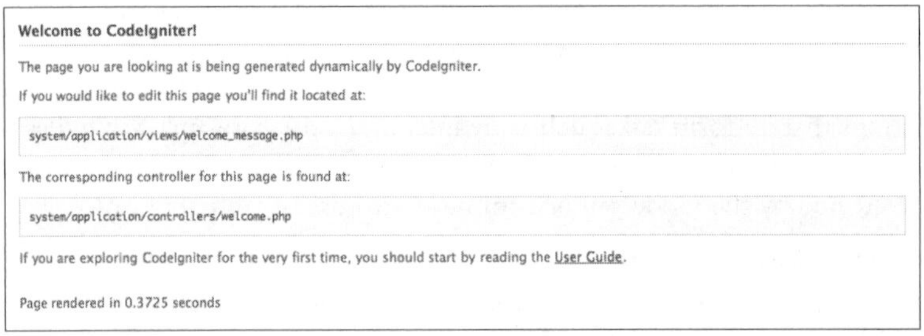

Welcome to CodeIgniter!

The page you are looking at is being generated dynamically by CodeIgniter.

If you would like to edit this page you'll find it located at:

system/application/views/welcome_message.php

The corresponding controller for this page is found at:

system/application/controllers/welcome.php

If you are exploring CodeIgniter for the very first time, you should start by reading the User Guide.

Page rendered in 0.3725 seconds

Figure 12.1   Screen shot of the default CodeIgniter application.

With the framework successfully installed on your web server, you can open the two local files `application\controllers\welcome.php` and `application\views\welcome_message.php` to glimpse at what a simple CodeIgniter application looks like. This is explained in more detail in the "Building the Basic Sprog Application" section, and so you are not expected to look at these files in too much detail (although they should be self-explanatory). The next section covers how to set your application configuration, such as your base URL and database settings.

You can find the CodeIgniter configuration within the `application\config\config.php` file. It contains a number of important settings related to your application or applications. This includes setting your base URL, so if you uploaded to http://sprog.com/codeigniter/, that is what this parameter should be set to. Although you could theoretically use a `localhost` connection for the initial steps within this chapter, it will not be suitable when interacting with the Twitter, Facebook, and Google Friend Connect resources. In this case, it is recommended that you install CodeIgniter in a "world-facing" location.

Removing `index.php` from Site URLs

CodeIgniter prefixes all URLs with `index.php`. Therefore, if you create a new directory called `sprog` on the domain http://sprog.com/codeigniter/, its URL will be http://sprog.com/codeigniter/index.php/sprog/. If your web server supports `mod_rewrite`, you can fix this by ensuring the `$config["index_page"]` parameter is blank and adding the following to an `.htaccess` file and uploading it to the `codeigniter` directory:

```
DirectoryIndex index.php
RewriteEngine on
RewriteCond $1 !^(index\.php|static)
RewriteCond %{REQUEST_FILENAME} !-f
RewriteCond %{REQUEST_FILENAME} !-d
RewriteRule ^(.*)$ ./index.php/$1 [L,QSA]
```

This `.htaccess` file should work for almost every Apache web server irrespective of whether your application is placed within a subdomain or across multiple directories.

You can also use this configuration file if you want to enable encryption or control cookie or session data. You may also want to set the `$config["global_xss_filtering"]` parameter to TRUE, which will enable XSS filtering on all user inputs. Other configuration files located within the `application\config` directory that you may want to modify include the following:

- **`autoload.php`**

    When an application is loaded, you can also set CodeIgniter to include libraries, helpers, and plug-ins automatically. In this chapter, the main libraries that are used are `database`, `pagination`, and `session`, which should be added to the `$autoload["libraries"]` array. As for helpers, the `url` and `form` helpers will be essential for handling inputs and URL parsing. You can also load models automatically, as well as multiple configuration files, if you have more than one application using CodeIgniter.

- **`constants.php`**

    This file contains parameters that are addressable within your applications. For example, a Twitter consumer key and consumer secret could be added to this file alongside your Facebook API key and other details added to the `config.php` file used in Chapters 5–8. In the sample code for this chapter, prompts in this file remind you of what parameters you should be adding.

- **`database.php`**

    All database parameters should be added in this file to be used by CodeIgniter to connect to your database. It is possible to add multiple database connections to this file if you intend to use a local and production database by following the array naming conventions and updating the `$active_group` parameter to the appropriate array. For this chapter, you will be required to create a database and ensure that you can connect to it through CodeIgniter.

- `routes.php`

  The final important configuration file is used for loading the default controller and setting up URI routing. You may have noticed that when you navigated to your live CodeIgniter folder that you were redirected to the Welcome page. This can be found within the `$route["default_controller"]` parameter, which corresponds to `application/controllers/welcome.php`. This parameter will be modified later in this chapter to point to Sprog. URI routing is explored in a little more detail in the "URI Class" section and more within this chapter's sample code.

Before starting on the Sprog application, it is worth first exploring some of the libraries and helpers provided by CodeIgniter. The next two sections are not meant to be extensive, but should give you an impression of the extensibility of the framework and how simple it is to perform tasks that would be very mundane to have to create from scratch.

CodeIgniter Libraries

Libraries contain a suite of functions for performing tasks such as uploading files, validating forms and handling sessions. In the CodeIgniter User Guide these can be found in the Class Reference section. The four libraries that will be used within the Sprog application are the Database Class, URI Class, Pagination Class, and the Session Class. Most libraries need to be loaded explicitly via `autoload.php` with the exception of a handful of core libraries such as the URI Class, Config Class, and Loader Class. It is assumed that you have loaded the `database`, `pagination` and `session` classes within the `$autoload["libraries"]` array.

Database Class

The Database class can be used to perform the four CRUD (create, read, update, and delete) operations and to handle transactions and caching. There are three ways in which you can manipulate records using the Database class:

- Standard Structured Query Language (SQL) can be used to formulate requests and then execute them based on your query parameters.

- A technique known as *query binding* can be used. It combines standard SQL with PHP variables that are automatically escaped by CodeIgniter. This is required if you want to execute safe queries in your applications. An example query is to set a `$sql` variable to "`SELECT * FROM test WHERE id = ?`" and then use `$this->db->query($sql, array(3))` to extract the user whose id was set to the number 3.

- The Active Records class enables you to formulate queries using PHP-like methods for performing each of the CRUD operations. Using active records means that SQL is generated "on-the-fly" and is customized depending on which database platform you are using. As with query binding, all queries are automatically escaped.

In this chapter, active records are used because they provide the greatest flexibility and are structured in a logical manner. Here are some examples assuming the database table structure shown in Table 12.1 and that you have correctly set your database parameters in `database.php`. Copy the data into your own database and save the table as `test`.

Table 12.1   **Sample data Used to Demonstrate Functionality of Active Records**

id	screen_name	full_name
1	johndoe	John Doe
2	janedoe	Jane Doe
3	richardroe	Richard Roe

The simplest way to retrieve results from the `test` table is to use the following:

```
$query = $this->db->get("test", 2, 0);
if ($query->num_rows() > 0) {
 foreach($query->result() as $row) {
  echo $row->screen_name;
  echo $row->full_name;
 }
}
```

The `$query` variable will return results from the `test` table and has had optional `LIMIT` and `OFFSET` parameters added. Using the data from Table 12.1, the code above would echo the `screen_name` and `full_name` of John and Jane Doe. The `$query->num_rows()` method is used to test whether results have been received; otherwise, the `$query->result()` object is iterated over. To retrieve specific fields from a table, you use this:

```
$this->db->select("screen_name");
```

This would be placed above the `$this->db->get("<<TABLE>>")` method and could also be set to `select_max("<<FIELD>>")`, `select_min("<<FIELD>>")`, `select_sum ("<<FIELD>>")` or `select_avg("<<FIELD>>")` to perform arithmetic operations on numeric fields. Specifying `$this->db->distinct()` before running a query will only return unique rows from your database. If you have multiple tables, you can also perform joins by using a combination of `$this->db->from("<<TABLE 1>>")` and `$this->db->join("<<TABLE 2>>", "<<TABLE 1>>.<<ID>> = <<TABLE 2>>.<<ID>>")` methods to amalgamate results based on a shared identifier.

Query Helper Functions

A number of "query helper" functions exist for extracting the number of rows within a table by using `$this->db->count_all("<<TABLE>>")`, within a returned query using `$this->db->num_rows()` or `$this->db->affected_rows()` to count the number of rows affected by an insert, update, or delete operation. To free up system memory, you can also call the `$query->free_result()` method after processing query results, which deletes the result's associated PHP resource ID.

To select a particular record you can use the `$this->db->get_where("<<TABLE>>", array("<<FIELD>>" => "<<VALUE>>"))` method. This requires an array just after the table name such as `array("id" => 1)` and is followed by the `LIMIT` and `OFFSET` parameters. It is also possible to use `$this->db->where("id", 3)` to perform the same function. In this instance, however, you can use `id !=` to find users whose `id` was not equal to `3` or to combine multiple methods to combine results with an `AND`. Other restriction methods include `or_where()`, `where_in()`, `or_where_in()`, `where_not_in()`, `or_where_not_in()`, `like()`, `or_like()`, `not_like()`, `or_not_like()`, `group_by("<<FIELD>>")`, `having("<<FIELD>>", "<<VALUE>>")`, `or_having("<<FIELD>>", "<<VALUE>>")`, and `order_by("<<FIELD>>", "<<DIRECTION>>")`. In the `order_by()` method, you can use either `asc`, `desc`, or `random` to order your results randomly.

Inserting data into a table can be achieved by using the following:

```
$data = array(
 "screen_name" => "babydoe",
 "full_name" => "Baby Doe",
);
$this->db->insert("test", $data);
echo $this->db->insert_id();
```

This query could also be assembled using the `set("<<FIELD>>", "<<VALUE>>")` method:

```
$this->db->set("screen_name", "babydoe");
$this->db->set("full_name", "Baby Doe");
$this->db->insert("test");
```

Updating works in a similar way to the first insert example except that a `$this->db->where()` method is first called and then the `$data` array is passed into a `$this->db->update("<<TABLE>>", <<DATA>>)` method. Finally, data can be deleted in three ways:

- You can use the `$this->db->delete("<<TABLE>>", array("<<FIELD>>" => "<<VALUE>>"))` or use a combination of `$this->db->where()` methods to first specify what data should be deleted and then call `$this->db->delete()` method omitting the second parameter.

- If you want to delete the same identifier from multiple tables, you can use a combination of `$this->db->where()` methods and specify an array of tables as the only parameter to the `$this->db->delete()` method.

- Deleting all the data from a table can be achieved by using either `$this->db->empty_table("<<TABLE>>")` or `$this->db->truncate("<<TABLE>>")`. If the `TRUNCATE` operation is not available on the database platform that you are using, a `DELETE` operation will be performed.

As you can see, even for a seemingly simple function of manipulating data in a database, multiple use cases are available. CodeIgniter aims to satisfy all these use cases and more. Don't worry if you think you've missed some of the finer details of the Database class; some of these methods are used in practice when we create the Sprog application.

URI Class

By default, CodeIgniter uses segmenting to link a URL to a corresponding controller class/function. For example, the URL http://sprog.com/codeigniter/sprog/profile/ johndoe would call the `profile()` function of the `test` controller passing in `johndoe` as the identifier. The URI class can be used to extract the identifier component of the URL through `$this->uri->segment(3, "unknown")`. The second parameter sets the default value for the method call if the segment does not exist. If you want to override the default mapping between the URL and functions, you can use the `routes.php` configuration file to assign new mappings. For example, the link above could be changed to http://sprog. com/codeigniter/profile/johndoe and set `$route["profile/(:any)"] = "sprog/ profile_lookup/$1"` to call the `profile_lookup` function of the `sprog` controller passing in the value `johndoe`. In this instance, you would use `$this->uri->rsegment(3, "unknown")` to extract the `screen_name`. The sample code and example for this chapter use the URI class, so its uses will become more apparent.

Pagination Class

Pagination is used to split database records into "chunks" that can be navigated using fully customizable links. CodeIgniter provides a Pagination class that makes this as simple as specifying three parameters and that can be integrated with the Database and Table classes as follows:

```
$this->load->library("table");
$config["base_url"] = site_url("/sprog/members");
$config["total_rows"] = $this->db->get("test")->num_rows();
$config["per_page"] = 2;
$this->pagination->initialize($config);
$results = $this->db->get("test", $config["per_page"],
$this->uri->segment(3, 0));
echo $this->table->generate($results);
echo $this->pagination->create_links();
```

The `$config["base_url"]` includes the `site_url()` of the application, which will be appended with the page that is currently being viewed, so this would be the `members` function of the `sprog` controller. For example, if the user has clicked the third page, this would produce `sprog/members/3`. The `$config["total_rows"]` parameter is set to the total number of rows in the `test` table, and the `$config["per_page"]` parameter dictates how many results are shown per "page." The `$results` variable is where the appropriate results are extracted from your database and uses the LIMIT and OFFSET parameters to extract the appropriate number of records. The records are then passed into the Table class to generate a table of results, which is then followed by the pagination links. A number of optional configuration options for the Pagination class can be used:

- `$config["num_links"]`

  Sets the number of "digit" links you would like before and after the selected page number. For example, the number 2 will place two digits on either side.

- `$config["full_tag_open"]` and `$config["full_tag_close"]`

  If you would like to surround the entire pagination with some markup, you can set this here (for example, wrapping the pagination inside a `<div>` or `<p>`).

- `$config["first_link"]`, `$config["first_tag_open"]`, `$config["first_tag_close"]`, `$config["last_link"]`, `$config["last_tag_open"]`, `$config["last_tag_close"]`, `$config["next_link"]`, `$config["next_tag_open"]`, `$config["next_tag_close"]`, `$config["prev_link"]`, `$config["prev_tag_open"]` and `$config["prev_tag_close"]`

  These parameters can be used to customize the "first," "last," "next," and "previous" links and related opening and closing tags.

- `$config["cur_tag_open"]`, `$config["cur_tag_close"]`, `$config["num_tag_open"]` and `$config["num_tag_open"]`

  To customize the display of the current page or other numbers, you can wrap them with tags supplied in these parameters.

Note that this sample code has not been introduced into the MVC architecture and is demonstrated in the "Building the Basic Sprog Application" section.

Session Class

CodeIgniter provides a Session class that permits you to maintain a users' "state" and track their activity while they browse your site. Session information is serialized (and optionally encrypted) within a cookie. You can also store the session data in a database for added security by matching the session ID in the cookie to one stored in your database. By default, only the cookie is saved. If you choose to use the database option, you must create the session table as indicated in the CodeIgniter User Guide for the Session class (http://codeigniter.com/user_guide/libraries/sessions.html).

Session Cookies Update Time

Session cookies are updated only every five minutes to reduce processor load, even if a page is repeatedly reloaded. If you want to update this more regularly, you can set `$config["time_to_update"]` in the `config.php` file.

Within a session you have access to four variables alongside any others that you want to store: `session_id`; `ip_address`; `user_agent`; and `last_activity`, which is a time stamp when the cookie was last written. For added security, you can load the Encryption class and set the `$config["encryption_key"]` within the `config.php` file. This encryption key should be at least 32 characters in length and is very similar to the keys provided by Twitter and Facebook. You can then use `$this->encrypt->encode(<<TEXT>>)` and `$this->encrypt->decode(<<ENCRYPTED TEXT>>)` to reveal the original text. If you have enabled encryption, you access session data as follows:

```
$session_id = $this->encrypt->decode($this->session->
userdata("session_id"));
```

Sometimes you might want to store custom session data, such as a user's e-mail address, username, or logged-in status. You can do so as follows:

```
$user = array(
 "username" => $this->encrypt->encode("johndoe"),
 "logged_in" => true
);
$this->session->set_userdata($user);
```

To "unset" or remove session data, you can use `$this->session->unset_user-data(<<KEY>>)`, where `<<KEY>>` in the example above would be `username` or `logged_in`. If you want to destroy all data at once, you can use the `$this->session->sess_destroy()` (for example, when a user logs out of your application). CodeIgniter also supports "flashdata," which is session data that will be available only for the next server request and is then automatically cleared. These can be manipulated using three methods:

- `$this->session->set_flashdata("<<KEY>", "<<VALUE>>");`
- `$this->session->flashdata("<<KEY>>");`
- `$this->session->keep_flashdata("<<KEY>>");`

The example in this chapter uses sessions and encryption.

CodeIgniter Helpers

Helpers are sets of functions that perform a particular task such as working with URLs or forms. You have already come across one of the methods of the URL Helper, which gathered your `site_url()`. Unlike libraries, you don't need to use the `$this` syntax to initialize helper methods. The URL Helper also includes these useful methods:

- `base_url()`.
- `current_url()`.
- `uri_string()`, which returns the segments after the `base_url()`.
- For creating links, you can use `anchor("sprog/profile/johndoe", "John Doe", array("title" => "John Doe's Profile"))` to render a hyperlink.

The URL Helper contains a number of other methods, which you can find in the CodeIgniter User Guide (http://codeigniter.com/user_guide/helpers/url_helper.html).

The Form Helper, as the name suggests, can be used to create form elements such as input boxes, hidden fields, and buttons. The following example uses most of the methods from the Form Helper:

```
$this->load->helper("form");
$hidden = array("time" => microtime());
echo form_open("sprog/login", array("id" => "login"), $hidden);
$username_input = array(
 "name" => "username",
 "id" => "username",
 "maxlength" => 128,
 "style" => "width: 50%;"
);
echo form_input($username_input);
echo form_password("password");
echo form_submit("submit", "Log In", 'onsubmit="function() {}"');
echo form_close();
```

This generates the following in HTML:

```
<form action="sprog/login" method="post" id="login">
 <input type="hidden" name="time" value="0.06839700 1267274117" />
 <input type="text" name="username" value="" id="username" maxlength="128"
 style="width: 50%;" />
 <input type="password" name="password" value="" />
 <input type="submit" name="submit" value="Log In" onsubmit="function() {}"
 />
</form>
```

The Form Helper contains a number of other methods, which you can find in the CodeIgniter User Guide (http://codeigniter.com/user_guide/helpers/form_helper.html). The example in this chapter uses both of these helpers and some of their associated methods.

Building the Basic Sprog Application

Now that you understand a bit about CodeIgniter and some of its libraries and helpers, it is time to start creating our Sprog application. The application itself will be similar to Twitter (and other microblog tools) in functionality and will contain the following core components:

- It will enable users to register an account and sign in using a Sprog username and password, or to authenticate using their Twitter, Facebook, or Google Friend Connect credentials.

- It will enable users to post short status updates. In later sections, these updates will also be posted to their Twitter/Facebook or linked to Google accounts.

- It will enable users to post a comment on or "like" another user's status updates from a profile page.

The aim of this section is to build a simple prototype that satisfies these basic applications, which will be extended when adding Twitter, Facebook, and Google Friend Connect functionality in Chapter 13. The prototype will adhere as closely as possible to the MVC architectural pattern to ensure that presentation, application logic, and data extraction and manipulation are separated (which increases scalability and code reusability). Models are used to interact with your database or other file store, reading and writing to files, and many other tasks that manipulate data. Views, on the other hand, are used to present data back to your users and should not contain any data processing at all apart from iterating over a results set. The logic that binds these two components together is the controller. The controller is the main hub of your application. It requests data from the model and then "feeds" it into a view. It is possible to have more than one controller for your applications, although in this example only one will be used. Multiple models will be defined for specific functionalities for Twitter, Facebook, and Google Friend Connect.

Stage 1: Creating the Registration, Login, and Home Pages

First, we must set up the CodeIgniter environment to support the new Sprog application. To do this, you will need to complete the following:

1. Using the CodeIgniter files that you downloaded earlier, edit `autoload.php` to load the following libraries: `database`, `session`, `pagination`, `table`, and `encrypt`; the `url` and `form` helpers; and a `sprog_model` model, which will be created later in this section. Your `config.php` should have the full path to your web server added to `$config["base_url"]`, and if you intend to use the `.htaccess` "fix" to remove `index.php` from URLs, you should ensure that `$config["index_page"]` is blank. In this file, you should also set your `$config["encryption_key"]` to at least a 32-character random string and ensure that `$config["global_xss_filtering"]` and `$config["sess_encrypt_cookie"]` are set to TRUE. You should add your database configuration to the `database.php` file, which will be used throughout the remainder of this chapter. Finally, set the `$route["default_controller"]` variable in `routes.php` to `sprog`, which will be created shortly.

2. Add empty Sprog model and controller files, named `sprog_model.php` and `sprog.php`, to the `application\controllers` and `application\models` directories. In the `application\views` directory, add a new directory called `sprog`.

3. Ensure that you have a `static` directory located in the root of your server alongside your `application` and `system` directories.

4. Upload the new files to your web server and visit your CodeIgniter URL.
    For example, if you have uploaded your files to a local host, you would use
    http://localhost/codeigniter/. Because no further data has been added to the
    controller, a "404 Page Not Found" error will display.

The first page that will be created is the index page and will look something like
Figure 12.2, which shows a logo, header, and a log in or create a new account prompt.
A page will also be created for a new user to register, and a simple page will be generated
upon successful login. Other features that will be added include form validation, storing
values inside a session, database manipulation, and exception handling.

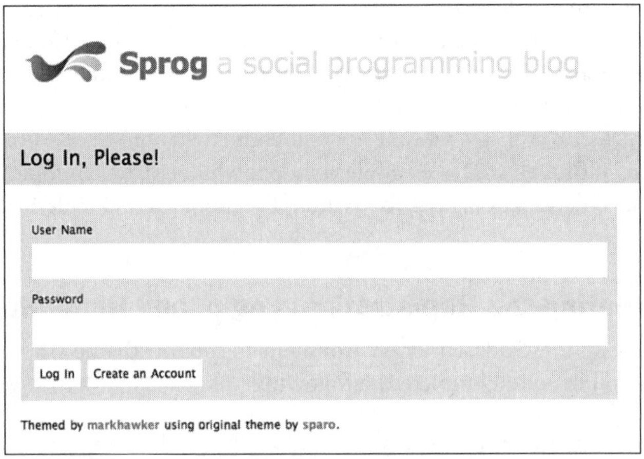

Figure 12.2   Screen shot of the Sprog index page.

A number of steps will lead you to the application shown in Figure 12.2, which is only
the beginning. The first step is to create a template that contains standard header and
footer code for your application. Navigate to the application\views\sprog\ directory
and create a directory in there called includes. Inside the includes directory, create
three new files: templates.php, header.php, and footer.php. The templates.php
should contain the following code:

```php
<?php
$data["title"] = $title;
$this->load->view("sprog/includes/header", $data);
$this->load->view($content);
$this->load->view("sprog/includes/footer");
?>
```

Both the $title and $content variables are explained later because these are passed
from the application controller. You can see that three views are loaded. These correspond

to `header.php`, `footer.php`, and a variable tat is used to pass in dynamic content that will enable the reuse of this template. Again, this is explored further by way of example. Your `header.php` file should contain the following code, which accepts a `$data` array that contains a `title` variable:

```
<!DOCTYPE html PUBLIC "-//W3C//DTD XHTML 1.0 Strict//EN"
 "http://www.w3.org/TR/xhtml1/DTD/xhtml1-strict.dtd">
<html xmlns="http://www.w3.org/1999/xhtml">
<head>
 <title><?php echo $title; ?> - Sprog</title>
 <link rel="stylesheet" href="<?php echo base_url(); ?>static/style.css"
 type="text/css" />
</head>
<body>
<div id="header">
 <h1 class="title"><img src="<?php echo base_url(); ?>static/logo.png" />
 Sprog <span>a social programming blog</span></h1>
 <div id="description">
  <p><?php echo $title; ?></p>
 </div>
</div>
<div id="wrap">
 <div id="content">
```

Notice that the `title` element is now accessed via the `$title` variable and used as both the title of the window and is displayed in the description bar shown in Figure 12.2 with the text "Log In, Please!" A reference is also made to an external style sheet, `style.css`, which is located inside the `static` directory. You can find the contents of this file in this book's code repository. The corresponding `footer.php` file, which is located in the `includes` directory alongside `template.php` and `header.php`, should contain the following code:

```
</div>
 <div id="footer">
  <p>Themed by <a href="http://markhawker.tumblr.com">markhawker</a> using
  original theme by <a href="http://www.tumblr.com/themes/by/
  sparo">sparo</a>.</p>
 </div>
</div>
</body>
</html>
```

This file simply closes the content `<div>` element and displays some standard footer information. Upload the new `includes` directory, and then we're on to creating the Welcome screen, which displays a form and a button to create a new account. The first thing to do is to create the register view. The register view is what users see when they first visit the application and is supported by a simple controller. You should store this view inside the application\views\sprog directory and name it login.php. This file contains the code for constructing a username and password input box and two buttons for submitting the form and creating a new account and utilizes the Form helper:

```
<div id="login">
<?php
if(!empty($error)) { echo '<p class="error">'.$error."</p>"; }
echo form_open("sprog/login");
echo form_label("User Name", "username");
echo form_input("username");
echo form_label("Password", "password");
echo form_password("password");
echo form_submit("submit", "Log In");
echo anchor("sprog/register", "Create an Account");
echo form_close();
?>
</div>
```

The $error variable is utilized if a user supplies invalid login credentials or leaves the form blank. The form submits to the login() function, which must be created inside the sprog.php file alongside the register() function. The contents of this file are wrapped inside the template, so that is why no header and footer information is required. Finally, you should open the sprog.php file located within application\controllers and add the code in Listing 12.1, which includes the index() function (the default controller).

Listing 12.1   The **sprog.php** File Demonstrating the Default **index()** Function

```
1   <?php
2   class Sprog extends Controller {
3    function Sprog() {
5     parent::Controller();
6    }
7    function index($error = false) {
8     $data["error"] = ($error == "error" ? "The username or password
      you supplied was incorrect, please try again." : false);
9     $data["content"] = "sprog/login";
10    $data['title'] = "Log In, Please!";
11    $this->load->view("sprog/includes/template", $data);
12   }
13  }
14  ?>
```

The code in Listing 12.1 shows a standard CodeIgniter controller architecture, which is initiated on lines 2 to 6. Note that the class name and constructor *must* be the same name as your filename, which in this instance is sprog.php. Lines 7 to 12 define the index() function, which sets up three variables to add to the $data array: error, content, and `title`. These variables are then passed to the template view for parsing. In particular, the `content` is used to render the `application\views\sprog\login.php` file. If you save `sprog.php` and upload it to your web server within `application\ controllers`, you should be presented with the page illustrated in Figure 12.2, assuming that you have also added `style.css` and `logo.png` to the static directory. Clicking either of the "Log In" or "Create an Account" options should present you with a warning message from CodeIgniter (because these controllers have not been set up yet).

Before we continue and add the `login()` and `register()` functions, a database table should be created that will contain all the user data. This can be created with the following SQL:

```
CREATE TABLE IF NOT EXISTS "user" (
 "username" varchar(24) NOT NULL,
 "password" varchar(32) NOT NULL,
 "fullname" varchar(64) NOT NULL
 PRIMARY KEY ("username")
);
```

Because passwords are to be encrypted using an `md5()`, this will give a length of 32 characters, and the `username` and `fullname` fields are to be restricted via the front-end code to the appropriate lengths. After your database has been created, you're ready to add the first bit of advanced functionality: inserting a user to the database. Inside the `sprog.php` file, add the following code, which is similar to the `index()` function:

```
function register($error = false) {
 $data["error"] = ($error == "error" ? "The username you supplied already
 exists, please choose another." : false);
 $data["content"] = "sprog/register";
 $data["title"] = "Register, Please!";
 $this->load->view("sprog/includes/template", $data);
}
```

The only difference here is that the error message has been updated and a reference is made to a `sprog/register` view, which hasn't been created yet. This view should look something like Figure 12.3.

The main features of the registration page will be form validation using the Form Helper, which can be used to perform multiple checks on the submitted data. Because the XSS filtering option has already been set, this is something that does not have to be checked in your application. As with the index page, the Form Helper is used to construct a form that also uses its `set_value()` methods in case there are validation errors and the form needs to be prepopulated with data that the user previously submitted:

```
<div id="register">
<?php
if(!empty($error)) { echo '<p class="error">'.$error."</p>"; }
echo validation_errors('<p class="error">');
echo form_open("sprog/create");
```

```
echo form_label("User Name", "username");
echo form_input(array("name" => "username", "value" =>
set_value("username")));
echo form_label("Full Name", "fullname");
echo form_input(array("name" => "fullname", "value" =>
set_value("fullname")));
echo form_label("Password", "password");
echo form_password(array("name" => "password", "value" =>
set_value("password")));
echo form_label("Confirm Password", "confirm_password");
echo form_password(array("name" => "confirm_password", "value" =>
set_value("confirm_password")));
echo form_submit("submit", "Create Account");
echo anchor("sprog/index", "Cancel");
echo form_close();
?>
</div>
```

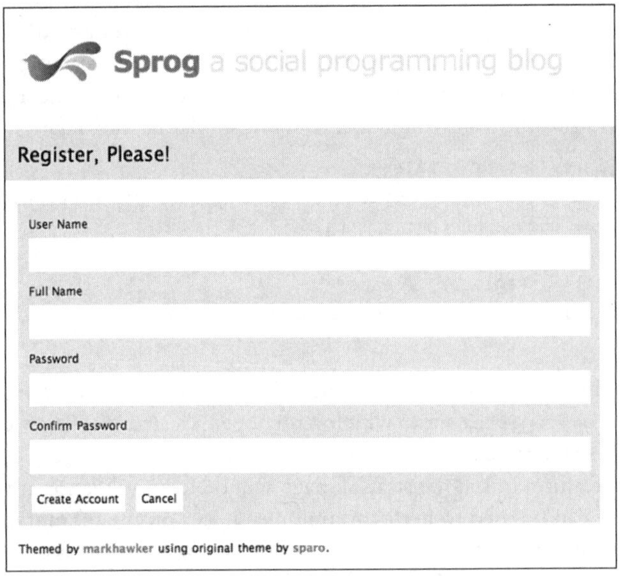

Figure 12.3   The Sprog registration page.

The code above constructs appropriate form labels and inputs that post to the create() function, which has not been created yet. Another feature is the validation_ errors() method. This method shows any errors with the form input and is initiated from within the controller as per the rules of MVC. Save this code as register.php within application\views\sprog and upload it to your web server. You should now be able to visit your home page and navigate to the registration page, as shown in Figure 12.3. The create() function will be the first instance in which the sprog_model is initiated to insert a record into the database but also to validate form output, update a user's session data with encrypted details, and redirect to the home page. Listing 12.2 shows the code for this function.

Listing 12.2   **The create() Function within the Main Controller**

```
1   function create() {
2     $this->load->library("form_validation");
3     $this->form_validation->set_rules("username", "User Name",
      "trim|required|min_length[4]|max_length[24]");
4     $this->form_validation->set_rules("fullname", "Full Name",
      "trim|required|max_length[64]");
5     $this->form_validation->set_rules("password", "Password",
      "trim|required|min_length[4]|max_length[32]");
6     $this->form_validation->set_rules("confirm_password", "Confirm
      Password", "trim|required|matches[password]");
7     if($this->form_validation->run() == false) {
8       $this->register();
9     } else {
10      $username = $this->input->post("username");
11      $fullname = $this->input->post("fullname");
12      $password = md5($this->input->post("password"));
13      $user = $this->sprog_model->create($username, $fullname, $password);
14      if(!empty($user)) {
15        $data = array(
16          "username" => $this->encrypt->encode($user["username"]),
17          "fullname" => $this->encrypt->encode($user["fullname"]),
18          "is_logged_in" => true,
19          "source" => $this->encrypt->encode("s")
20        );
21        $this->session->set_userdata($data);
22        redirect("sprog/home");
23      } else {
24        $this->register("error");
25      }
26    }
27  }
```

The complexity of this controller lies in the multiple paths that need to be covered from all data being correct and a value being added to the database to invalid details or attempts to re-register an existing username. Form validation is performed on lines 3 to 6 on each of the input fields after first loading the Form Validation Helper on line 2. The first parameter of the set_rules() method corresponds to the input field name, the second its "friendly" name, and the third is the validation to be performed. In the examples in Listing 12.2, this includes trimming whitespace, testing required elements, maximum and minimum length, and checking that the confirm_password matches the password field. The validation is then executed on line 7. true is returned if there are none, and false if any have been found. If errors are found, the registration page is reloaded, and the errors will be shown by the validation_errors() method.

On lines 10 to 12, the data from the form is extracted and the password is hashed. These fields are then passed into the create() function, which is shown in Listing 12.3. On success, the function returns an array of a username and fullname, which is encrypted alongside is_logged_in and source parameters, which are stored in a session on lines 15 to 21. The source parameter will be important in the future because it stores the authentication mechanism used to log in. The user is then redirected to the home page, or, if the create() function is unsuccessful, the user is redirected to the registration page, where an error will be shown. The contents of the home page, which you want to upload to application\views\sprog as home.php, will simply contain the following, which will be extended in the next section:

```
<h1>Success!</h1>
<p><?php echo anchor("sprog/logout", "Logout"); ?></p>
```

In the sprog.php file, a controller should be added for both logout() and home(), as shown here:

```
function home() {
 $this->is_logged_in();
 $fullname = $this->encrypt->decode($this->session->userdata("fullname"));
 $data["content"] = "sprog/home";
 $data["title"] = "Welcome, ".$fullname."!";
 $this->load->view("sprog/includes/template", $data);
}
function logout() {
 $this->session->sess_destroy();
 redirect("sprog/index");
}
function is_logged_in() {
 $is_logged_in = $this->session->userdata("is_logged_in");
 $uri_segment = $this->uri->segment(2);
 if((isset($is_logged_in) && $is_logged_in == true) &&
 ($uri_segment == "index" || $uri_segment == "register")) {
  redirect("sprog/home");
 }
 elseif((!isset($is_logged_in) || $is_logged_in != true) &&
 $uri_segment != "index" && $uri_segment != "register") {
  redirect("sprog/index");
 }
}
```

Because you do not want users who are not logged in to access the home page, an extra is_logged_in() function has been included that tests for the existence of the session value. If the session value does not exist, the user is redirected to the index. You should also add a $this->is_logged_in() call to the first line of the index() and register() controllers, because if users have already logged in and they visit these pages, they should be redirected to the home page. The home page decodes the fullname variable, which is stored within the session, and also presents a logout link to destroy the session and return the user to the index page. In your application\views\sprog folder, add a new file called home.php and which contains the following code:

```
<div id="update">
 <p>You are logged in!</p>
</div>
<p><?php echo anchor("sprog/logout", "Logout"); ?></p>
```

This code above just presents a message to the user saying that he or she has logged in (alongside a link to log out). In the next section, this is greatly extended. Just as with the controller, setting up a model requires a constructor and class name that match the name of the file, sprog_model.php, and must be named differently to your controller. Listing 12.3 shows the create() function, which tests whether a username is already stored in the database on line 7, and if so, the function returns false on line 25. Otherwise, a $user array is created consisting of the variables passed to the function from the controller and then inserted into the database.

Listing 12.3   **The Sprog Model and the create() Function**

```
1   <?php
2   class Sprog_Model extends Model {
3    function Sprog_Model() {
4     parent::Model();
5    }
6    function create($username, $fullname, $password) {
7     $query = $this->db->get_where("user", array("username" =>
      $username));
8    if($query->num_rows() == 0) {
9     $user = array(
10      "username" => $username,
11      "fullname" => $fullname,
12      "password" => $password
13     );
14     $query = $this->db->insert("user", $user);
15     if($query) {
16      $data = array(
17       "username" => $username,
18       "fullname" => $fullname
19      );
```

```
20    return $data;
21  } else {
22    return false;
23  }
24  } else {
25    return false;
26  }
27  }
28 }
```

The result of the query will return `true` or `false`, and if `true`, a `$data` array is constructed containing the `username` and `fullname`, which is processed by the controller. Again, this function will return `false` if there was an error. If you save the `sprog_model.php` into the `application\models` directory and upload it to your web server, you should now be able to register your own account! Test that validation works as expected and that when you register an account the appropriate data is being added to your database. The final part of this section is to create the `login()` function of the index page for returning users. The `login()` function takes some of its code from the registration controller because you want to test whether the user exists in your database and redirect as appropriate. Add the following code to the `sprog.php` controller:

```php
function login() {
 $username = $this->input->post("username");
 $password = md5($this->input->post("password"));
 $user = $this->sprog_model->validate($username, $password);
 if(!empty($user)) {
  $data = array(
    "username" => $this->encrypt->encode($user["username"]),
    "fullname" => $this->encrypt->encode($user["fullname"]),
    "is_logged_in" => true,
    "source" => $this->encrypt->encode("s")
  );
  $this->session->set_userdata($data);
  redirect("sprog/home");
 } else {
  $this->index("error");
 }
}
```

The difference in this code is that it calls the `validate()` function of the model before storing the user data within a session and redirecting as appropriate. This final model function consists of the following code:

```php
function validate($username, $password) {
 $this->db->where("username", $username);
 $this->db->where("password", $password);
 $query = $this->db->get("user");
```

```
if($query->num_rows() == 1) {
 $data = array(
  "username" => $query->row()->username,
  "fullname" => $query->row()->fullname
 );
 return $data;
} else {
 return false;
}
}
```

In this code, the $username and $password are cross-checked against the database. If a match is found, the user's username and fullname is passed back to the controller; otherwise, the function returns false. This final piece of code should be saved within the sprog_model.php file and uploaded to your web server alongside all the files that have been modified in this section, which are also available within the stageone directory of the code repository. This directory should be renamed codeigniter and include your customized configuration files. If all is well, you should have created the following files and functions and added the static directory, which includes logo.png and style.css from the code repository:

- applications\controllers\sprog.php: index(), login(), register(), create(), home(), logout(), and is_logged_in()

- applications\models\sprog_model.php: create() and validate()

- applications\views\sprog\includes\header.php

- applications\views\sprog\includes\footer.php

- applications\views\sprog\includes\template.php

- applications\views\sprog\home.php

- applications\views\sprog\login.php

- applications\views\sprog\register.php

The next section extends the Sprog application to include the ability to post status updates, view profiles, comment, and "like" other user's updates.

Stage 2: Extending the Sprog Application with Updates, Comments, and Likes

The next step in creating the Sprog application is to add the functionality that enables users to post and delete short updates, comment on updates, and "like" updates. To keep this application fairly simple, users will not be able to "unlike" or delete their comments, but will be able to delete their updates. Users will also be given a simple profile with their latest updates listed. By the end of this section, you should have something resembling the home page shown in Figure 12.4.

Figure 12.4   The Sprog home page.

In addition to the home page, there will be a page listing all the updates made by all users; this page can be commented on or liked. In the future, you could add the ability to search for updates or other users. Before getting started on coding the application, you need to create three new database tables:

- **update**

    This table will store all the updates made by users and contains five fields: id, which is a BIGINT(30) and is set to auto_increment; text, which is a TEXT field that contains the update text; datetime, containing the date and time that the update was made; username, for storing the user who posted the update; and source, for storing which method was used to post the update, which is a CHAR(1) and which can be set to s for Sprog, t for Twitter, f for Facebook, and g for Google Friend Connect.

- **comment**

    This table is almost identical to update except that a new field is added called update_id, which is a BIGINT(30) and is used to link comments to an original update.

- **like**

    The like table contains only two fields: an update_id that references the update table; and a count, which is a simple INT(12) for counting the number of times an update is liked.

You can create these tables using the following SQL:

```sql
CREATE TABLE IF NOT EXISTS "update" (
 "id" bigint(20) NOT NULL auto_increment,
 "text" text NOT NULL,
 "datetime" datetime NOT NULL default "0000-00-00 00:00:00",
 "username" varchar(12) NOT NULL,
 "source" char(1) NOT NULL,
  PRIMARY KEY ("id")
)
CREATE TABLE IF NOT EXISTS `comment` (
 "id" bigint(20) NOT NULL auto_increment,
 "update_id" bigint(20) NOT NULL default "0",
 "text" text NOT NULL,
 "datetime" datetime NOT NULL default "0000-00-00 00:00:00",
 "username" varchar(12) NOT NULL,
 "source" char(1) NOT NULL,
 PRIMARY KEY ("id")
)
CREATE TABLE IF NOT EXISTS "like" (
 "update_id" bigint(20) NOT NULL default "0",
 "count" int(12) NOT NULL default "0",
 PRIMARY KEY ("update_id")
);
```

There is no need to add any records to these tables yet because methods will be created to insert, update, and delete values. This section focuses on the creation of four new views, which should be stored within application\views\sprog and which will perform the following functions:

- The home.php view will display an update form which will be validated and posts to the update table. This view will also display the user's latest update, which can be deleted alongside the user's recent comments. This page will also contain links to the user's profile and to the global page for user updates.

- The latest.php view displays the latest updates made by all users and grants the ability to like and comment on updates. Unlike home.php, this view will not let users delete their updates.

- The profile.php is very similar to the latest.php view, although it will be used to display a specific user's updates. For now, no further profile information is supplied to this view.

- The comments.php view presents users with a form to submit their comment and to view other comments. This form will be validated and will redirect the commenter back to the home.php view on success.

These four new views are supported by various controller methods that make further use of the application's mode. In all cases, there is a corresponding controller that will be added to `sprog.php` and some helper functions for updating and deleting an update, liking, and commenting. The accompanying style sheet for this new stage will be included within the source code for this chapter and is not included here. The best place to start this section is with the hub of our application, `home()`, where you should add the following code to the `sprog.php` controller:

```
1   function home() {
2       $this->is_logged_in();
3       $fullname = $this->encrypt->decode($this->session->
        userdata("fullname"));
4       $username = $this->encrypt->decode($this->session->
        userdata("username"));
5       $config["base_url"] = site_url("/sprog/home");
6       $config["total_rows"] = $this->db->get_where("update", array(
        "username" => $username))->num_rows();
7       $config["per_page"] = 15;
8       $config["full_tag_open"] = '<div id="pagination">';
9       $config["full_tag_close"] = "</div>";
10      $this->pagination->initialize($config);
11      $data["updates"] = $this->sprog_model->updates($username,
        $config["per_page"], $this->uri->segment(3, 0));
12      $data["comments"] = $this->sprog_model->my_comments($username);
13      $data["pagination"] = $this->pagination->create_links();
14      $data["username"] = $username;
15      $data["content"] = "sprog/home";
16      $data["title"] = "Welcome, ".$fullname."!";
17      $this->load->view("sprog/includes/template", $data);
18  }
```

This function first makes sure that issuers are logged in and then extracts their username and full name from the encrypted session on lines 3 and 4. Because you don't want to show all the user's updates at once, the Pagination class is initiated on lines 5 to 10 and passed to the view on line 13. To ensure that the page links can be styled using the external style sheet, you just wrap the pagination controls within a `<div>`. The next two lines call specific functions within the `sprog_model.php` file, which extracts a user's updates, passing in the pagination variables, and extracts the user's comments, which are then stored in the `$data` array passed to the template view. Listing 12.4 shows these two functions.

Listing 12.4 **The `updates()` and `my_comments()` Functions**

```
1   function updates($username, $limit, $offset) {
2       $this->db->select("*")->from("update")->join("like", "like.update_id =
        update.id", "left")->where("username", $username)->order_by(
        "datetime", "desc")->limit($limit, $offset);
3       $query = $this->db->get();
```

```
4    if($query->num_rows() > 0) {
5      $updates = array();
6      foreach($query->result() as $row) {
7        $comment_count = $this->comment_count($row->id);
8        $updates[] = array("id" => $row->id, "text" => $row->text,
         "source" => $row->source, "time" => strtotime($row->datetime),
         "like_count" => $row->count, "comment_count" => $comment_count);
9      }
10     return $updates;
11   } else {
12     return array(array("id" => -1, "text" => "There are no updates,
       yet.", "source" => "n", "time" => -1, "like_count" => -1,
       "comment_count" => -1));
13   }
14 }
15 function my_comments($username) {
16   $this->db->where("username", $username)->order_by("datetime",
       "desc")->limit(10, 0);
17   $query = $this->db->get("comment");
18   if($query->num_rows() > 0) {
19     $my_comments = array();
20     foreach($query->result() as $row) {
21       $my_comments[] = array("id" => $row->update_id, "text" =>
         $row->text, "source" => $row->source, "time" => strtotime(
         $row->datetime));
22     }
23     return $my_comments;
24   } else {
25     return array(array("id" => -1, "text" => "There are no comments,
       yet.", "source" => "n", "time" => -1));
26   }
27 }
```

Both functions shown in Listing 12.4 demonstrate how the Database class can be used to extract data from your database. "Chaining" is used to string together the components of the query, which is then tested using the `$query->num_rows()` method on lines 4 and 18. The `updates()` function also iterates over each update and searches for related comments, on line 7, which contains the following code:

```
function comment_count($update_id) {
 $query = $this->db->get_where("comment", array("update_id" =>
 $update_id));
 return $query->num_rows();
}
```

Results from the `updates()` and `my_comments()` functions are stored within arrays, which are then passed back to the controller. If no updates or comments are found, a

dummy array is created with appropriate error messages. You should update the
`sprog_model.php` and `sprog.php` files and save them to the `application\models` and
`application\controllers` directories. Before you can run the application, update the
`home.php` view to correspond to the data that has just been added to the controller:

```php
<div id="update">
<?php
echo validation_errors('<p class="error">');
echo form_open("sprog/update");
echo form_label("Update Me?", "update", array("style" => "font-size:
2em;"));
echo form_input(array("name" => "update"));
echo form_submit("submit", "Update");
echo form_close();
?>
</div>
```

This first section constructs the update form, which requires the creation of the
`update()` function in the main controller, which is shown in Table 12.2 below, alongside
its corresponding model functions:

```php
<div id="latest">
 <h2>My Updates</h2>
 <?php
 foreach($updates as $update) {
  echo '<div class="update '.$update["source"].'">';
  echo "<p>".($update["time"] != -1 ? '<span class="date">'.date("m-d-Y",
  $update["time"])."</span>" : " ").$update["text"]."</p>";
  echo '<div class="controls">';
  if($update["like_count"] != -1) {
   echo '<span class="like_count">Likes: '.($update["like_count"] ?
   $update["like_count"] : 0)."</span>";
  }
  if($update["comment_count"] != -1) {
   echo '<span class="comment_count">Comments: '.($update["comment_count"]
   ? $update["comment_count"] : 0)."</span>";
  }
  if($update["id"] != -1) {
   echo '<span class="delete">'.anchor("sprog/delete/".$update["id"],
   "Delete")."</span>";
  }
  echo "</div>";
  echo "</div>";
 }
 echo $pagination;
 ?>
 <h2>My Latest Comments</h2>
```

```php
<?php
foreach($comments as $comment) {
  echo '<div class="update '.$comment["source"].'">';
  echo "<p>".($comment["time"] != -1 ? '<span class="date">'.date("m-d-Y",
  $comment["time"])."</span>" : " ").($comment["id"] != -1 ?
  anchor("sprog/view_comment/".$comment["id"], $comment["text"]) :
  $comment["text"])."</p>";
  echo "</div>";
 }
?>
</div>
<p><?php echo anchor("sprog/profile/".$username, "My Profile"); ?> |
<?php echo anchor("sprog/latest", "Latest Updates"); ?> | <?php echo
anchor("sprog/logout", "Logout"); ?></p>
```

Table 12.2   **Controller and Model Functions for Deleting and Posting an Update**

Controller	Model
| ```php
function update() {
 $this->load->library(
 "form_validation");
 $this->form_validation->
 set_rules("update",
 "Update", "trim|
 required");
 if($this->
 form_validation->
 run() == false) {
  $this->home();
 } else {
  $username = $this->
  encrypt->decode(
  $this->session->
  userdata("username"));
  $update = $this->input->
  post("update");
  $source = $this->
  encrypt->decode(
  $this->session->
  userdata("source"));
  $this->sprog_model->
  update($username,
  $update, $source);
  redirect("sprog/home");
 }
}
``` | ```php
function update($username,
$update, $source) {
 $data = array(
  "id" => null,
  "text" => $update,
  "datetime" => date(
  "Y-m-d H:i:s",
  time()),
  "username" =>
  $username,
  "source" => $source
);
 $this->db->insert(
 "update", $data);
 return $this->db->
 insert_id();
}
``` |

Table 12.2   **Controller and Model Functions for Deleting and Posting an Update**

Controller	Model
``function delete() {
$update_id = $this->uri->
segment(3);
$this->sprog_model->
delete($update_id);
redirect("sprog/home");
}```	```function delete(
$update_id) {
$this->db->where(
"id", $update_id);
$this->db->delete(
"update");
$tables = array(
"like", "comment");
$this->db->where(
"update_id",
$update_id);
$this->db->delete(
$tables);
return true;
}```

The remainder of this code is used to iterate over both the `$updates` and `$comments` variables and to display links to the `delete()` function and to redirect users to the `profile` and `latest` views. Save this code as `home.php` and upload it to your web server, where you should be able to log in and view this page.

The three views that still need to be created are `profile` and `latest`, plus a `comments` view for submitting responses to updates. These are saved in the `application\views\sprog` directory as `profile.php`, `latest.php`, and `comments.php`. Because these views contain similar methods and controllers, these are not described in detail here, but are included in the sample code for this chapter. The latest updates view is shown in Figure 12.5, which, unlike the home page, allows a user to like an update and links to the comments view. The code for this page is produced by the `latest()` controller function, supported by the `like()` function and model functions `latest_updates()` and `like()`.

Latest Updates

02-28-2010 This is a test message posted from Sprog. via markhawker

Likes: 0   Comments: 0

Home

Figure 12.5   The Sprog Latest Updates page.

The final comments view is shown in Figure 12.6, which shows a comments box and the latest comments posted by other users. This view is supported by the `view_comment()` controller function, which requires the `get_comments()` model function, alongside the `comment()` controller function, for posting a comment, which requires the `post_comment()` model function and `get_original()` for retrieving the details of an update.

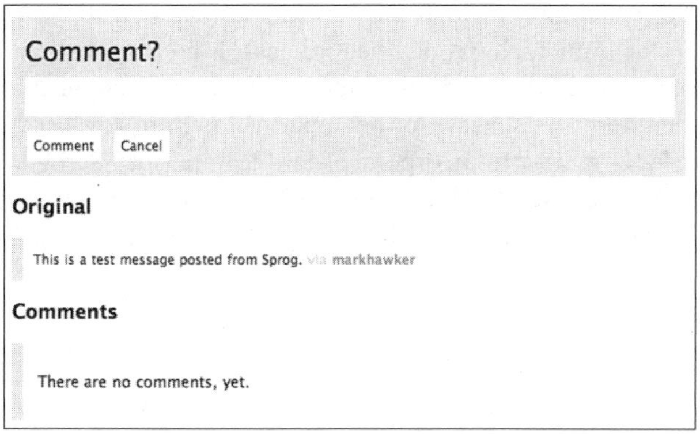

Figure 12.6   The Sprog Comments page.

After saving the newly created controller, model, and views files to your web server and ensuring that you have created the specified databases, you should be able to visit your fully functional Sprog application. You can find the files in the github code repository inside the `stagetwo` directory. This directory should be renamed `codeigniter` and include your customized configuration files. If all is well, you should have created or modified the following files and functions and updated the `static` directory with the new `style.css` file from the repository:

- `applications\controllers\sprog.php`: `home()`, `update()`, `delete()`, `profile()`, `latest()`, `like()`, `comment()`, and `view_comment()`.

- `applications\models\sprog_model.php`: `updates()`, `my_comments()`, `comment_count()`, `update()`, `delete()`, `latest_updates()`, `like()`, `get_comments()`, `post_comment()`, and `get_original()`.

- `applications\views\sprog\comment.php`

- `applications\views\sprog\latest.php`

- `applications\views\sprog\profile.php`

- `applications\views\sprog\home.php`

- `applications\views\sprog\login.php`

- `applications\views\sprog\register.php`

With the framework for the microblog tool complete, the next chapter looks at how to add Twitter, Facebook, and Google Friend Connect functionality to the Sprog application.

Summary

This chapter described how you can use the CodeIgniter web application framework to create your very own microblog tool. The tool enables users to register, log in, post updates, leave comments, and "like" updates. The extensibility and simplicity of CodeIgniter makes it an excellent resource suitable for beginners through to advanced programmers. The next chapter looks at how to incorporate social features into Sprog, such as authentication via Twitter, Facebook, and Google Friend Connect, as well how to post updates, comments, and likes to each of the services.

Integrating Twitter, Facebook, and Google Friend Connect

This chapter extends Chapter 12, "Building a Microblog Tool Using CodeIgniter," which built a "social programming microblog" from scratch using CodeIgniter. The final version of Sprog, which you will build in this chapter, will implement some of the features that have been described in this book, including user authentication, status updates, commenting, and "likes" through Twitter, Facebook, and Google Friend Connect. The chapter is split into three sections for each technology platform, giving examples of how to first integrate them with CodeIgniter and then how to extend the functionality that was created in Chapter 12. At the end of this chapter, you will understand how to incorporate social features into your own web applications. However, don't think of this sample application as production ready. You would still need to modify it appropriately to ensure that it was secure enough to be released in the wild. The best strategy to adopt while developing is to continually test it with your own Twitter, Facebook, and Google accounts to gauge how it will function in the real world.

As with all code examples in this book, be aware that any one of the Twitter, Facebook, or Google Friend Connect services could update their libraries to add or remove features. Following the appropriate developer forums and blogs will help you identify the breaking changes to your applications. You should also follow the book's blog http://www.socialprogramming.info/ and code repository, which will be updated with new code as time progresses.

Implementing Twitter Functionality

The two main ways in which Twitter will be used is to provide login functionality using "Sign in with Twitter," which will create a new user account or will update an existing account with Twitter credentials, and to post updates to their stream. For this to work, another table needs to be created in your database, twitter, which will store the user's

Twitter ID, access token, and token secret, plus a reference to a record in the user table (if one already exists). To create the twitter table, just execute the following SQL:

```
CREATE TABLE IF NOT EXISTS "twitter" (
 "id" bigint NOT NULL,
 "access_token" varchar(50) NOT NULL,
 "token_secret" varchar(50) NOT NULL,
 "user_username" varchar(24) NULL,
 PRIMARY KEY ("id")
);
```

For users who already have a Sprog account, once they have logged in with Twitter they will be prompted to link their accounts. Those users who do not already have a Sprog account are prompted to create one after authenticating with Twitter. Other changes that will be required are adding a twitter_id field to the update table. This will store the status ID of an update posted when logged in via Twitter and is required to be a bigint. For this example, comments are not included (but would function in exactly the same way as regular updates).

Setting Up Twitter and Twitter-async Support

Before proceeding, you must first register a Sprog application on Twitter by visiting http://twitter.com/apps/new and submitting the following:

- **Application icon:** This can be any image of your choosing, but you could use the logo.png located within the static directory.

- **Application Name:** An appropriate name for this application would be Sprog, although this can be anything that you want.

- **Description:** This can be left blank or you could add the following: 'A test application for @markhawker's book entitled: "The Developer's Guide to Social Programming"'.

- **Application Website:** You can set this to your own URL or use the book's URL, which is http://www.socialprogramming.info/.

- **Organization and Website:** These can be set to your own company name and URL, if required.

- **Application Type:** For this example, this should be set to "Browser."

- **Callback URL:** As CodeIgniter does not readily support GET operations, which are how Twitter responds to a successful authentication. This should be set to a URL outside of the application directory. For now, set this to point to your static directory in a new subdirectory called php. For example, if your URL is http://sprog.com/codeigniter/, this should be set to http://sprog.com/codeigniter/static/php/. Create a new file in this directory called index.php and add the following code:

  ```php
  <?php header("Location: http://sprog.com/codeigniter/sprog/twitter/".
  $_GET["oauth_token"]); ?>
  ```

This code should redirect the user back inside your application to the `twitter` function of the `sprog` controller, which will expect a token appended to the URL. Note that this URL should be located on your own server!

- **Default Access Type:**Because this application will be updating a user's Twitter profile, this will need to be set to "Read & Write" so that we can support this functionality.

- **Use Twitter for Login:**Again, because "Sign in with Twitter" is to be used, you should check this option.

After all of these details have been submitted, you are given a consumer key and consumer secret. These should be added to your `constants.php` configuration file using the following names:

```php
define("TWITTER_CONSUMER_KEY", "XXXXXXXXXXXXXXXXXXXXXX");
define("TWITTER_CONSUMER_SECRET", "XXXXXXXXXXXXXXXXXXXXXX");
```

By adding these two constants you ensure that they are both addressable within the application, instead of having to worry about storing them as an external reference. The final step is to download the twitter-async library from http://github.com/jmathai/twitter-async and upload it to the `application\libraries` directory. To make this a pseudo-CodeIgniter library, a `twitter.php` class must be created that will include the twitter-async library and includes some standard functions such as creating an EpiTwitter Object and checking responses, which were explored in Chapter 3, "Authentication with Twitter OAuth," when creating the Test Tube application:

```php
<?php if (!defined("BASEPATH")) exit("No direct script access allowed");
include "twitter-async/EpiCurl.php";
include "twitter-async/EpiOAuth.php";
include "twitter-async/EpiTwitter.php";
class Twitter {
 function init($oauth_token = null, $oauth_token_secret = null) {
  return new EpiTwitter(TWITTER_CONSUMER_KEY, TWITTER_CONSUMER_SECRET,
  $oauth_token, $oauth_token_secret);
 }
 function get_url() {
  $twitter = $this->init();
  try {
   return $twitter->getAuthenticateUrl(null, array("force_login" =>
   true));
  }
  catch(EpiOAuthException $e) { return "oauthexception"; }
  catch(EpiTwitterException $e) { return "twitterexception"; }
 }
 function verify($twitter) {
  if (is_object($twitter)) {
   $response = $twitter->get_accountVerify_credentials();
```

```
    return $this->check($response);
  } else {
  return false;
  }
 }
 function check($payload) { return ($payload->code == 200) ? $payload :
false; }
}
?>
```

Within this file, you directly import the twitter-async library so that whenever the `$this->load->library("twitter")` method is called, these files are immediately loaded. By constructing the library in this way, you can then access `$this->twitter->init()` to initialize a session as well as the `get_url()`, `verify()`, and `check()` functions. Because you will be using this library throughout the application, it should be loaded automatically by adding `twitter` to the `$autoload["libraries"]` variable in `autoload.php`. You can create any number of libraries in the way that was just described, which is the basis for the Facebook and Google Friend Connect sections.

Stage 3: Extending the Sprog Application with Twitter Functionality

This stage builds on the two previous stages from Chapter 12, which included creating the skeleton of the Sprog application using CodeIgniter. You might want to revisit that chapter to refresh your mind on the basic functionalities of Sprog and use the CodeIgniter references if any of the libraries or helper functions are not readily apparent to you.

The goal of adding Twitter functionality is to enable users to log in using Twitter credentials so that they can post their Sprog updates to their Twitter stream easily and conveniently. There is one major issue in how this needs to be implemented, which is illustrated via an example scenario. Suppose a user has created an account, "markhawker," via Sprog, but then wants to log in via Twitter, too. The user will click the "Sign in with Twitter" button, shown in Figure 13.1, authenticate, and then be returned to the callback URL that has already been set.

Which username would you use? Suppose that the user logged in using the Twitter account "markhawker." Would you assume that this account was held by the user who created the markhawker Sprog login? In this event, you can't assume that these two are linked, and so an intermediate stage needs to be added that acknowledges that a user has logged in via Twitter but it is unknown which Sprog account is the user's (or even whether the user has created one). This will occur only once because as soon as the user's accounts have been linked, you will have stored this in your database for future reference. Although this might sound complex, it can be achieved by modifying the original Sprog files to account for having a Twitter login.

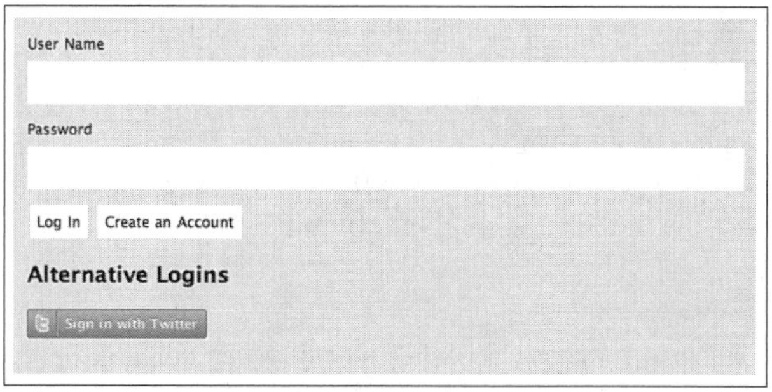

Figure 13.1   Screen shot of the Sprog index page with
Twitter functionality.

The first step that needs to be addressed is populating the `twitter()` function inside the main `sprog.php` controller, which was referenced via the callback URL and which appends an access token to the third segment of the URL. This function is similar to `login()` function created in Chapter 3, in that the token is parsed and if available an EpiTwitter Object is created and initialized. The difference in this function is that the access token and token secret are being stored in encrypted sessions rather than simple cookies:

```
1  function twitter() {
2    $token = $this->uri->segment(3);
3    $oauth_token = $this->encrypt->decode(
       $this->session->userdata("oauth_token")
     );
4    $oauth_token_secret = $this->encrypt->decode(
       $this->session->userdata("oauth_token_secret")
     );
5    if (!empty($token)) {
6      $session = $this->twitter_model->set_tokens($token);
7      $this->check_link(
         $this->encrypt->decode($session["oauth_token"]),
         $this->encrypt->decode($session["oauth_token_secret"])
       );
8    } else if(empty($oauth_token) && empty($oauth_token_secret)) {
9      $this->session->set_userdata("oauth_token", "");
10     $this->session->set_userdata("oauth_token_secret", "");
11     redirect("sprog/index");
12   } else {
13     $this->check_link($oauth_token, $oauth_token_secret);
14   }
15 }
```

Lines 3 and 4 are used just in case a user has already been authenticated, which will execute the `check_link()` function on line 13 using the stored credentials. If a token is available, the branch on lines 5 to 7 is executed. This sets the tokens using a function that needs to be created in a new `twitter_model.php` model file and that then parses its output and executes the `check_link()` function. If neither of the tokens is available, the user is redirected back to the index page on line 11.

Autoloading Models

Don't forget to autoload commonly accessed models within the `autoload.php` configuration file (for example, `twitter_model`) that is created in this section. This ensures all available functions within the model are accessible to your application.

Create a new `twitter_model.php` file. This will be stored alongside `sprog_model.php` in the `application\models` directory and should be autoloaded by your application. This model will host the specific functionality for interacting with the twitter library and updating Twitter-specific tables. The first function that is required is `set_tokens()`, which accepts the `oauth_token` sent from Twitter as its only parameter:

```php
<?php
class Twitter_Model extends Model {
 function Twitter_Model() {
  parent::Model();
 }
 function set_tokens($oauth_token) {
  $twitter = $this->twitter->init();
  try {
   $twitter->setToken($oauth_token);
   $token = $twitter->getAccessToken();
   $twitter->setToken($token->oauth_token, $token->oauth_token_secret);
   $data = array(
     "oauth_token" => $this->encrypt->encode($token->oauth_token),
     "oauth_token_secret" => $this->encrypt->encode(
     $token->oauth_token_secret)
   );
   $this->session->set_userdata($data);
   return $data;
  }
  catch(EpiOAuthException $e) { redirect("sprog/index/oauthexception"); }
  catch(EpiTwitterException $e) { redirect("sprog/index/
  twitterexception"); }
 }
}
```

The `set_tokens()` function is used to extract the access token and token secret for the authenticated user, which is then stored within an encrypted session. These two variables will be accessible for the duration of the time that the user is logged in and will be used to access the numerous Twitter methods. If an error occurs during processing of the token, the user is redirected to the `index` page. The next step in this process now that a user's tokens have been stored is to validate the user's Twitter credentials and to check (via the `check_link()` function within the main controller) whether the user has already created a Sprog account. If so, the user is redirected to the home page with the source parameter set to "t" for Twitter. If not, the user is redirected to the home page, but this time you will have saved the user's account ID and tokens within a session so that the user can be "remembered" when the application is linking accounts:

```
function check_link($oauth_token, $oauth_token_secret) {
 $twitter = $this->twitter->init($oauth_token, $oauth_token_secret);
 $twitter_user = $this->twitter_model->get_user($twitter);
 $check_user = $this->twitter_model->check_user($twitter_user["id"]);
 if(!$twitter_user) {
  redirect("sprog/index/twitterexception");
 } else {
  $this->session->set_userdata("twitter_id",
   $this->encrypt->encode($twitter_user["id"])
  );
  if($check_user) {
   $data = array(
    "username" => $this->encrypt->encode($check_user["user_username"]),
    "fullname" => $this->encrypt->encode($twitter_user["fullname"]),
    "is_logged_in" => true,
    "source" => $this->encrypt->encode("t")
   );
   $this->session->set_userdata($data);
   redirect("sprog/home");
  } else {
   redirect("sprog/index");
  }
 }
}
```

The aim of this function is to extract the User object of authenticated users and to check whether they already exist in the database. If they do, their details are stored in the session, and they are redirected to the home page. If they have not authenticated, they are redirected to the home page, where they must create a Sprog account or log in as normal. Remember, because the twitter_id has been stored within the session, it is accessible in other methods when linking accounts. The `get_user()` and `check_user()` should be placed within the `twitter_model.php` model file and contain the following code:

```
function get_user($twitter) {
 $twitter_user = $this->twitter->verify($twitter);
 if (!empty($twitter_user)) {
  $user = array(
   "id" => $twitter_user->id,
```

```
   "fullname" => $twitter_user->name
  );
  return $user;
 } else {
  return false;
 }
}
function check_user($id) {
 $query = $this->db->get_where("twitter", array(
  "id" => $id, "user_username !=" => ""
 );
 if($query->num_rows() == 0) {
  return false;
 } else {
  return array("id" => $id, "user_username" => $query->
  row()->user_username);
 }
}
```

These two functions make use of the Twitter library as well as the Database class for extracting user details from the `twitter` table. The next step is to reconfigure the `index` page to acknowledge that users have authenticated via Twitter so that when they log in or register, an entry is added to both the `user` table and the `twitter` table. Your `index()` function should be updated to include the following lines, which create an authenticate URL and display a simple message to the user:

```
$data["twitter_url"] = $this->twitter->get_url();
if($this->session->userdata("twitter_id")) {
 $data["has_twitter"] = "You are signed in with Twitter, but you must
 login or register with us to link accounts. You will only have to do
 this once.";
}
```

In the `login.php` view, you then need to toggle this message and either show or hide the "Sign in with Twitter" button (depending on whether you have an active session):

```
if(!empty($has_twitter)) { echo '<p class="twitter_message">'.
$has_twitter."</p>"; }
if(empty($has_twitter)) {
 echo "<h2>Alternative Logins</h2>";
 echo '<p><a href="'.$twitter_url.'"><img src="'.base_url().
 'static/siwt-darker.png" height="24" width="151" alt="Sign in with
 Twitter" />
 </a></p>';
}
```

Similar code should be added to the `register()` function in the controller and the `register` view to show the information message. No "Sign in with Twitter" button should be shown on this page, and the authentication URL is also not required. The final steps in this process are to validate the user details against your database and to link both of the accounts. After all this has been completed the details are stored within the session. The modified query within the `validate()` method of the `sprog_model.php` file should be as follows:

```
$this->db->select("*")->from("user")->join("twitter",
"twitter.user_username = user.username", "left");
```

This query is used to join the `user` and `twitter` tables, and also return all results from the `user` table that do not have a related record in the `twitter` table. This is important because not all of your users will have linked a Twitter account. What also needs to be added within this function is to return users' access tokens and token secrets within the `$data` array so that if they log in via their Sprog account, their Twitter credentials will be automatically included:

```
"oauth_token" => $query->row()->access_token,
"oauth_token_secret" => $query->row()->token_secret
```

The new `login()` function within the main controller now contains the following:

```
1   function login() {
2     $username = $this->input->post("username");
3     $password = md5($this->input->post("password"));
4     $user = $this->sprog_model->validate($username, $password);
5     if(!empty($user)) {
6       $source = "s";
7       $data = array();
8       if($this->session->userdata("twitter_id")) {
9         $this->twitter_model->link($this->session->userdata("twitter_id"),
          $username);
10        $source = "t";
11      } else {
12        $data["oauth_token"] = $this->encrypt->encode($user["oauth_token"]);
13        $data["oauth_token_secret"] = $this->encrypt->encode(
          $user["oauth_token_secret"]);
14      }
15      $data["username"] = $this->encrypt->encode($user["username"]);
16      $data["fullname"] = $this->encrypt->encode($user["fullname"]);
17      $data["is_logged_in"] = true;
18      $data["source"] = $this->encrypt->encode($source);
19      $this->session->set_userdata($data);
20      redirect("sprog/home");
21    } else {
22      $this->index("error");
23    }
24  }
```

This modified `login()` function now enables the `$source` variable to be changed to either an "s" or a "t," depending on the authentication model, which is then encoded on line 18. If the user has already authenticated with Twitter, on line 8, their details are linked using the `link()` method, which needs to be created in the `twitter_model.php` file. Otherwise, the user's pre-existing tokens are stored on lines 12 and 13, which are then set within the session on line 19. Within the `create()` function of the main controller, lines 6 and 8 to 11 should be added within the `if(!empty($user))` conditional. On line 8, however, you don't need to open the else case because you already have the user's Twitter tokens stored within a session.

The final method, `link()`, is the method that actually stores a user's credentials within a database:

```
function link($id, $username) {
 $id = $this->encrypt->decode($id);
 $oauth_token = $this->encrypt->decode($this->session->
 userdata("oauth_token"));
 $oauth_token_secret = $this->encrypt->decode(
  $this->session->userdata("oauth_token_secret")
 );
 $user = array(
  "id" => $id,
  "access_token" => $oauth_token,
  "token_secret" => $oauth_token_secret,
  "user_username" => $username
 );
 $query = $this->db->insert("twitter", $user);
 return true;
}
```

Now that the Twitter login process has been tweaked to enable users to link their Twitter and Sprog accounts together, it's time to allow them to post updates to their newly linked accounts.

Updating a User's Twitter Account

The ability to post updates to a user's Twitter account is much simpler than the authentication process. This is because you already have access to an access token and token secret, which can now be passed into the `init()` function of the Twitter library. First, the `home()` function in the main controller needs to be updated to test whether a user has linked a Twitter account. You can do so by adding the following line:

```
$data["has_twitter"] = $this->twitter_model->has_twitter($username);
```

The associated model function is as follows:

```
function has_twitter($username) {
 $query = $this->db->get_where("twitter", array("user_username" =>
```

```
$username));
return ($query->num_rows() > 0 ? true : false);
}
```

This simple function tests whether a user can be found in the `twitter` table and returns either `true` or `false`. Within the `sprog\home` view, the following can then be added within the form. It will display a check box with which users can choose whether to also post the update to their Twitter account:

```
if($has_twitter) {
echo form_label("Post to Twitter?", "twitter");
echo form_checkbox("twitter", 1, true);
echo "<br /><br />";
}
```

When the user submits the form, a `twitter` parameter is passed to the `update()` function of the main controller, which must be modified to include the following:

```
$id = $this->sprog_model->update($username, $update, $source);
if($this->input->post("twitter") == 1) {
$this->twitter_model->update($update, $id);
}
```

This addition stores the recently added update identifier to the `$id` variable, which is then passed a new function called `update()` in the `twitter_model.php` file. The reason for this is to set the value of the newly created Twitter status to a new field in the `update` table called `twitter_id`, which must be a `bigint`. By doing this, it is then possible to reference an update to a Twitter status seamlessly. The `update()` function should be as follows:

```
function update($text, $id) {
$oauth_token = $this->encrypt->decode($this->session->
userdata("oauth_token"));
$oauth_token_secret = $this->encrypt->decode(
 $this->session->userdata("oauth_token_secret")
);
$twitter = $this->twitter->init($oauth_token, $oauth_token_secret);
$response = $twitter->post_statusesUpdate(array("status" => $text));
if($this->twitter->check($response)) {
 $this->db->set("twitter_id", $response->id);
 $this->db->where("id", $id);
 $this->db->update("update");
 }
}
```

In this function, the `statuses/update` Twitter method is called, and then the identifier of the Status object is set to the `update` table. Figure 13.2 shows an example of a status posted to Twitter.

Figure 13.2   Screen shot of Sprog update posted to
Twitter.

It is also important that when users logs out of Sprog their Twitter session should also
be terminated. You can achieve this by extending the `logout()` function in the controller
to include the following:

```
$oauth_token = $this->encrypt->decode($this->session->
userdata("oauth_token"));
$oauth_token_secret = $this->encrypt->decode(
 $this->session->userdata("oauth_token_secret")
);
if(!empty($oauth_token) && !empty($oauth_token_secret)) {
 $this->twitter_model->logout($oauth_token, $oauth_token_secret);
}
```

And change the `logout()` function of the `twitter_model.php` file to the following:

```
function logout($oauth_token, $oauth_token_secret) {
 $twitter = $this->twitter->init($oauth_token, $oauth_token_secret);
 $twitter->post_accountEnd_session();
}
```

You can find the files for this section in the online github code repository inside the
`stagethree` directory. This directory should be renamed `codeigniter` and include your
customized configuration files. If all is well, you should have created or modified the following files and functions and updated the `static` directory with the new `style.css` file
and added the `siwt-darker.png` image and the `static\php\index.php` file from the
code repository:

- `applications\controllers\sprog.php`: `twitter()`, `check_link()`, `index()`,
  `register()`, `login()`, `create()`, `home()`, `update()` and `logout()`

- `applications\models\sprog_model.php`: `validate()`.

- `applications\models\twitter_model.php`: `set_tokens()`, `get_user()`,
  `check_user()`, `link()`, `has_twitter()`, `update()` and `logout()`

- `applications\views\sprog\home.php`

- `applications\views\sprog\login.php`

- `applications\views\sprog\register.php`

In addition, you should have also uploaded the twitter-async library to `application\`
`libraries\twitter-async` and added the `twitter.php` file. Extensions to this code
would be to also post comments to Twitter that link back to the original update, handling
when users revoke access to your application and providing support for "liking" updates,
which would add them as a Twitter favorite. The possibilities are almost limitless. The next
section looks at how to add Facebook functionality alongside Twitter to increase the
reach of your application even further.

Implementing Facebook Functionality

Because Facebook uses a JavaScript library to detect status, this makes the implementation
of this technology slightly easier than Twitter. This section details how to add the functionality to sign in using Facebook, link accounts, and then post updates, comments, and
likes back to Facebook. You will also add a little more social context through highlighting
what a user's friends have updated on Sprog. As with the "Implementing Twitter
Functionality" section, you will have to create a new table in your database, `facebook`, for
storing user credentials, but also extend other tables to include Facebook functionality,
such as tying an update to a Facebook update. The Facebook PHP client library will also
be translated to work with CodeIgniter, and a new model will be created,
`facebook_model.php`, to contain code specific to Facebook.

The `facebook` table will store the user's Facebook ID and session key plus a reference
to a record in the `user` table (if one already exists). The following SQL should be executed to create this table:

```
CREATE TABLE IF NOT EXISTS "facebook" (
 "id" bigint NOT NULL,
 "session_key" varchar(50) NOT NULL,
 "user_username" varchar(24) NULL,
 PRIMARY KEY ("id")
);
```

For users who already have a Sprog account, after they have logged in with Facebook
they are prompted to link their accounts. If users do not already have a Sprog account,
they will be prompted to create one after authenticating with Facebook. Other tables will
be modified, as indicated throughout this section. The next stage is to register an application with Facebook and to reference the various Facebook libraries within Sprog.

Registering a Facebook Application and Adding Facebook Support

Before proceeding, you must first register a Sprog application on Facebook by visiting
http://www.facebook.com/developers/createapp.php and submitting the following:

- **Application Name:** An appropriate name for this application would be Sprog,
  although this can be anything that you want.

- **Description:** This can be left blank or you could add the following: 'A test application for @markhawker's book entitled: "The Developer's Guide to Social Programming"'.

- **Icon and Logo:** A sample application icon and logo have been included in the static directory but these can be modified as appropriate.

- **Post-Authorize Callback URL and Post-Remove Callback URL:** These parameters are located within the Authentication tab and should reference your CodeIgniter base URL plus `sprog/facebook/authorize` and `sprog/facebook/remove`, which are functions that need to be created within the main controller.

- **Connect URL:** This parameter is located in the "Connect" tab and should be set to your CodeIgniter base URL plus `sprog`.

- **Base Domain:** If your CodeIgniter base URL were http://sprog.com/codeigniter/, the base domain would be sprog.com. This parameter will vary depending on whether you have installed CodeIgniter on a subdomain or not.

- **Facebook Logo:** As with the icon and logo, a logo has been included in the `static` directory or can be left blank for this example.

After all these details have been saved, you will be given an application ID, API key, and secret alongside the path to your `xd_receiver.htm` file, which should be added to your `constants.php` configuration file using the following names:

```
define("APP_ID", "XXXXXXXXXXXX");
define("API_KEY", "XXXXXXXXXXXXXXXXXXXXXXXX");
define("SECRET", "XXXXXXXXXXXXXXXXXXXXXXXX");
define("XD_RECEIVER", "...\xd_receiver.htm");
```

By adding these constants, you ensure that they are addressable within the application, instead of having to worry about storing them as an external reference. Note that this application is going to utilize just a subset of the entire Facebook library, so possible extensions include adding a canvas page, application tab, or a Publisher interface.

The final step is to download Facebook PHP client library and upload it to the `application\libraries` directory. To make this a pseudo-CodeIgniter library, a `facebook_library.php` class will need to be created that will include the library plus some standard functions, such as creating the Facebook object:

```php
<?php if (!defined("BASEPATH")) exit("No direct script access allowed");
include "facebook-platform/php/facebook.php";
class Facebook_Library {
 function get_facebook() {
  return new Facebook(API_KEY, SECRET);
 }
}
?>
```

Within this file, you directly import the library so that whenever the `$this->load->library("facebook_library")` method is called, these files are immediately loaded. By constructing the library in this way, you can then access `$this->facebook_library->get_facebook()` to initialize a Facebook session. Because you will be using this library throughout the application, it should be loaded automatically by adding `facebook_library` to the `$autoload["libraries"]` variable in `autoload.php`.

Stage 4: Extending the Sprog Application with Facebook Functionality

The goal of adding Facebook functionality is to enable users to log in using their Facebook credentials so that they can post their Sprog updates to their Facebook stream easily and conveniently. As with the complexities encountered in adding Twitter functionality, you have to handle cases in which users already have a Sprog account and want to "link" this with their Facebook account. In this instance, it is required that they log in via Facebook and then log in using their Sprog credentials to create the link that will then be automatic the next time they authenticate. The first hurdle is to add the Facebook library to the template files to ensure that they are loaded on each page. Inside the `application\views\sprog\includes` directory, you should open the global template file, `template.php`, and add the following:

```
$source = $this->encrypt->decode($this->session->userdata("source"));
switch($source) {
 case "s":
  $data["via"] = "<b>Sprog</b>";
  break;
 case "t":
  $data["via"] = "<b>Twitter</b>";
  break;
 case "f":
  $data["via"] = "<b>Facebook</b>";
  break;
 case "g":
  $data["via"] = "<b>Google Friend Connect</b>";
  break;
 default:
  $data["via"] = false;
}
```

This code snippet will pass a variable to the `header.php` that will be used to display a simple prompt to users letting them know which authentication mechanism was used to log them in. This is important because if users have not logged out from Facebook and visit your site, they will automatically be logged in. The code to display the prompt inside `header.php` should be placed just below the description container:

```
<?php if($via) { ?>
<div id="logged_in_via">
 <p>You are currently logged in via <?php echo $via; ?>.</p>
</div>
<?php } ?>
```

As with all the styles used in this chapter, the accompanying `style.css` file is included within the code repository. The final template file that needs to be modified is `footer.php`, which will contain the references to the Facebook library. These should be placed just above the closing `</body>` tag:

```
<script src="http://static.ak.connect.facebook.com/js/api_lib/v0.4/
FeatureLoader.js.php" type="text/javascript"></script>
<script type="text/javascript">
 FB.init("<?php echo API_KEY; ?>", "<?php echo XD_RECEIVER; ?>",
 {"reloadIfSessionStateChanged":true});
</script>
```

This addition makes use of the constants that were saved earlier and should reference the `xd_receiver.htm` file, which should be uploaded to the `static` directory and given `644` permissions. So far, all that has been achieved is to reference the Facebook files and not to detect whether users have authenticated or linked their account to Sprog. To begin, the main controller should be updated with the reference to the `facebook()` function to support the post-authorize and post-remove callback URLs:

```
function facebook() {
 $function = $this->uri->segment(3);
 switch($function) {
  case "authorize":
   break;
  case "remove":
   $this->facebook_model->remove();
   break;
  case "logout":
   $this->session->set_userdata("facebook_logout", true);
   redirect("sprog/index");
   break;
 }
}
```

In this application, the first authorize case is not used because it is already part of the process to add a user's details to the database. Because Facebook simply "pings" this function, you could use it to store authorization attempts to your database if you suspect that a user might not fully complete the linking of their accounts. The remove case accesses a `remove()` function, which needs to be created within a new model, `facebook_model.php`, and which will contain all your Facebook functionality. The final case is used to clear a Facebook-specific session variable that will be created after a user has logged in to detect his status. Your initial `facebook_model.php` should be stored within `application\models` and will contain the single `remove()` function for deleting a user from the `facebook` table:

```php
<?php
class Facebook_Model extends Model {
 function Facebook_Model() {
  parent::Model();
 }
 function remove() {
  $facebook = $this->facebook_library->get_facebook();
  $facebook_parameters = $facebook->get_valid_fb_params($_POST, null,
  "fb_sig");
  if (!empty($facebook_parameters) && $facebook->fb_params['uninstall']
  == 1) {
   $this->db->delete("facebook", array("id" => $facebook->
   fb_params["user"]));
  }
 }
}
?>
```

The two main view files that need to be modified are `login.php` and `register.php`, which must be able to detect Facebook connectivity. Their related controller functions, `index()` and `register()`, should include the following two code blocks, which should be placed at the top of each function:

```php
$this->facebook_model->is_facebook_logged_in();
if($this->facebook_model->get_user()) {
 $data["has_facebook"] = "You are signed in with Facebook, but you
 must log in or register with us to link accounts. You will only have
 to do this once.";
}
```

As with the `$data["has_twitter"]` variables, a related entry should be added to the two views for displaying the message itself:

```php
if(!empty($has_facebook)) {
 echo "<p class=\"facebook_message\">".$has_facebook."</p>";
}
```

Within the `login.php` file, you also want to show the Facebook login button as an alternative login option alongside the "Sign in with Twitter" button created in the "Implementing Twitter Functionality" section, earlier in the chapter:

```php
if(empty($has_twitter) && empty($has_facebook)) {
 echo "<h2>Alternative Logins</h2>";
 echo '<p><a href="'.$twitter_url.'"><img src="'.base_url().
```

```
'static/siwt-darker.png" height="24" width="151" alt="Sign in with
Twitter" /></a> <fb:login-button></fb:login-button></p>';
}
```

Before you can run your application, the `facebook_model.php` needs to be updated with the `is_facebook_logged_in()`, `get_user()` and related methods. These methods are used to test whether a Facebook session has been initiated and to check whether the users have already linked their Facebook and Sprog accounts. Of course, this functionality has not been added yet, and so they will not be able to log in fully but will be shown the message that they have authenticated via Facebook.

```
function get_user() {
 $facebook = $this->facebook_library->get_facebook();
 return $facebook->get_loggedin_user();
}
```

This helper method is used to test whether a Facebook ID is available via the client library. Remember, both the client-side and server-side Facebook libraries work in unison, and so if issuers are logged in via clicking the Facebook button, their session will be made available to you:

```
function check_user($facebook_id) {
 $this->db->select("*")->from("user")->join("facebook",
 "facebook.user_username = user.username", "left");
 $this->db->where("id", $facebook_id);
 $query = $this->db->get();
 if($query->num_rows() == 0) {
  return false;
 } else {
  $user = $query->row();
  $data = array(
   "username" => $this->encrypt->encode($user->username),
   "fullname" => $this->encrypt->encode($user->fullname),
   "is_logged_in" => true,
   "source" => $this->encrypt->encode("f")
  );
  $this->session->set_userdata($data);
  return true;
 }
}
```

Another helper method, this will check whether users have already authenticated their account and will store their details within the active session if they have. These two helper methods are tied together in the main `is_facebook_logged_in()` method:

```
function is_facebook_logged_in() {
 $is_logged_in = $this->session->userdata("is_logged_in");
 $facebook_logout = $this->session->userdata("facebook_logout");
 $facebook_user = $this->get_user();
```

```
if($facebook_user && !$is_logged_in && !$facebook_logout) {
 $this->check_user($facebook_user);
}
$this->session->set_userdata("facebook_logout", false);
}
```

This function tests whether issuers are already logged in or have just logged out of the application and will update their session accordingly. After saving this model and uploading it with the amended views and controller, you should be able to click the Facebook button and be presented with the message stating that you have logged in via Facebook. This final step is to integrate this within the `login()` and `create()` controller functions so that details are stored within the database and made accessible in future sessions. Both functions require the following code to be added within the `if(!empty($user))` conditional:

```
if($this->facebook_model->get_user()) {
 $this->facebook_model->link($this->facebook_model->get_user(), $user
name);
 $source = "f";
}
```

This simple addition shows the true power of the MVC architecture in that no major changes were required to customize the login functionality. All that remains is to create the `link()` method within the model:

```
function link($facebook_id, $username) {
 $query = $this->db->get_where("facebook", array("id" => $facebook_id));
 if($query->num_rows() == 0) {
  $user = array(
   "id" => $facebook_id,
   "session_key" => "",
   "user_username" => $username
  );
  $query = $this->db->insert("facebook", $user);
  return true;
 } else {
  return false;
 }
}
```

This method is simple, in that all that needs to be done is to check whether users have already been added to the `facebook` table. If not, they should be added as appropriate. The rest of the functionality has already been created in previous iterations to handle other complexities. The final addition is to flesh out the `logout()` function within the controller to log a user out of Facebook, too, which can be achieved by using the following:

```
if($this->facebook_model->get_user()) {
 $this->facebook_library->get_facebook()->logout(
 base_url()."sprog/facebook/logout");
```

```
} else {
  redirect("sprog/index");
}
```

This code tests whether a Facebook user is present, and if so, the `logout()` method of the client library is executed, which requires a parameter instructing Facebook where to redirect the user after he or she has been logged out (in this instance, referencing the `facebook()` function detailed at the beginning of this section). Now that you have access to Facebook users' credentials, it's time to add some functionality to post updates, comments, and likes to their stream, which requires three extended permissions: `read_stream`, `publish_stream`, and `offline_access`.

When users visit their home page for the first time, they will be prompted with the message shown in Figure 13.3, which will invite them to grant Sprog access to their stream and an "infinite" session key. To achieve this, you need to add a mixture of client-side code to prompt them for the permissions and server-side code for displaying controls based on what permissions they have granted. When they click the link to grant permissions, the `FB.Connect.showPermissionDialog()` function will be called and open a dialog box for them to confirm the application's access to their stream. They will not be shown the message on subsequent visits to this page because their permissions will have already been retrieved from Facebook.

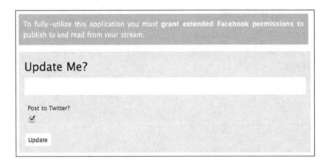

Figure 13.3   Screen shot of Sprog home page with Facebook permissions prompt.

The first edit that needs to be made is within the JavaScript inside `footer.php`. A new function will need to be created called `get_permissions()` with a callback function `parse_permissions()`, which will check to see that all three were granted and will refresh the page. This code should be placed just after the `FB.init()` call:

```
function get_permissions() {
  FB_RequireFeatures(["Connect"],
    function() {
      FB.Connect.showPermissionDialog("publish_stream,read_stream,
      offline_access", parse_permissions, false, null);
```

```
    }
  );
}
function parse_permissions(response) {
 var permissions = new Array();
 permissions = response.split(",");
 if(permissions.length == 3) {
  document.getElementById("facebook_permissions").style.display = "none";
  window.location.reload();
 }
}
```

The `parse_permissions()` function splits the string returned by the `get_permissions()` function and tests whether it has three elements. If so, the prompt is hidden and the page is refreshed. The next step is to update the `home.php` view file, but first the `home()` function within the main controller needs to be updated with two new `$data` items:

```
$data["has_facebook"] = $this->facebook_model->has_facebook($username);
$data["has_facebook_permissions"] = $this->facebook_model->
has_permissions($username);
```

These two items first check that the users have connected their Facebook details and then will check that they have allowed access to the three permissions requested in the call to `FB.Connect.showPermissionDialog()` above. Both requests utilize a username to look up values from your database and return Boolean `true` or `false` values. The two functions should be added to `facebook_model.php`:

```
function has_facebook($username) {
 $query = $this->db->get_where("facebook", array("user_username" =>
 $username));
 return ($query->num_rows() > 0 ? true : false);
}
function has_permissions($username) {
 $facebook = $this->facebook_library->get_facebook();
 $user = $facebook->get_loggedin_user();
 if($user) {
  try {
   $data = $facebook->api_client->fql_query(
   'SELECT uid, publish_stream, read_stream, offline_access FROM
   permissions WHERE uid = "'.$user.'"');
   if(is_array($data)) {
    $permissions = array(
     "publish_stream" => $data[0]["publish_stream"],
     "read_stream" => $data[0]["read_stream"],
     "offline_access" => $data[0]["offline_access"]
    );
   }
```

```
  if($permissions["publish_stream"] && $permissions["read_stream"] &&
  $permissions["offline_access"]) {
    $session_key = (isset($_COOKIE[API_KEY."_session_key"]) ?
    $_COOKIE[API_KEY."_session_key"] : false);
    $expires = (isset($_COOKIE[API_KEY."_expires"]) ?
    $_COOKIE[API_KEY."_expires"] : -1);
    if($expires == 0 && $session_key) {
      $this->db->set("session_key", $session_key);
      $this->db->where("id", $user);
      $this->db->update("facebook");
    }
    return true;
  } else { return false; }
  }
  catch (Exception $e) { return false; }
} else {
  $query = $this->db->get_where("facebook", array("user_username" =>
  $username, "session_key !=" => ""));
  return ($query->num_rows() == 1 ? true : false);
  }
}
```

The complexity of the `has_permissions()` function is due to the fact that you want to display the option to post to Facebook even if users have not logged in via Facebook (for example, if they have linked accounts and then logged in via Twitter). By granting the `offline_access` permission, you are able to retrieve the session key located within the Facebook cookie and then store it within your database. This session key will remain valid unless they revoke access to your application, which would be an extension for this application because in this example it is not checked. The results of both functions are then passed to the `home.php` view for displaying the permissions prompt but also the option to post to Facebook:

```
<?php if($has_facebook && !$has_facebook_permissions) { ?>
  <p id="facebook_permissions">To fully-utilize this application you must
  <a href="#" onclick="get_permissions();">grant extended Facebook
  permissions</a> to publish to and read from your stream.</p>
<?php } ?>
```

The option to post to Facebook should be placed alongside the option to post to Twitter and can be added with the following code:

```
echo "<table><tr>";
if($has_twitter) {
  echo "<td>";
  echo form_label("Post to Twitter?", "twitter");
  echo form_checkbox("twitter", 1, true);
  echo "</td>";
}
```

```
if($has_facebook && $has_facebook_permissions) {
 echo "<td>";
 echo form_label("Post to Facebook?", "facebook");
 echo form_checkbox("facebook", 1, true);
 echo "</td>";
}
echo "</tr></table>";
```

This simple addition will send a value within the form as to whether to post to Facebook or not. The next function that needs to be amended is update() within the controller. It will check for this value and then execute the update() function of the Facebook model. This test should be placed within the controller just underneath the test for the twitter value:

```
if($this->input->post("facebook") == 1) {
 $this->facebook_model->update($username, $update, $id);
}
```

The associated update() function within facebook_model.php has to extract the user's Facebook details from the database, set the correct session, post the update, and then set the returned Facebook identifier to a new facebook_id field within the update table. The field should be a varchar(64) and can be NULL (because not all updates relate to Facebook):

```
function update($username, $update, $id) {
 $query = $this->db->get_where("facebook", array("user_username" =>
 $username));
 $user = $query->row();
 $facebook = $this->facebook_library->get_facebook();
 $facebook->set_user($user->id, $user->session_key);
 try {
  $post_id = $facebook->api_client->stream_publish($update);
  $this->db->set("facebook_id", $post_id);
  $this->db->where("id", $id);
  $this->db->update("update");
  return true;
 }
 catch (Exception $e) { return false; }
}
```

The $facebook->set_user() method is extremely useful because you can mimic the "presence" of users irrespective of how they have logged in. The update is published to their stream and the record is updated. The reason why the Facebook identifier is stored is that you can then extract the post from Facebook and get its likes and comments. In this application, you will only be posting data to Facebook rather than extracting data from it, which could be an addition, should you want to show comments made inside Facebook in your applications.

The like() and comment() functions within the main controller need to be updated so that they are also posted to Facebook. Both functions require you to test whether the user has appropriate permissions but also to extract the relevant Facebook identifier (if available) for an update:

```
$has_facebook_permissions = $this->facebook_model-
>has_permissions($username);
$facebook_id = $this->facebook_model->get_facebook_id($update_id);
```

The like() function then requires an if($has_facebook_permissions && $facebook_id) { $this->facebook_model->like($facebook_id); } to be added which calls the like() function within the Facebook model:

```
function like($facebook_id) {
 $facebook = $this->facebook_library->get_facebook();
 $user = $facebook->get_loggedin_user();
 if($user) {
  try {
   $like = $facebook->api_client->stream_addLike($facebook_id);
   return $like;
  }
  catch (Exception $e) { return false; }
 } else { return false; }
}
```

Because this function requires a valid Facebook identifier, this can be extracted from $update_id within the following function:

```
function get_facebook_id($update_id) {
 $query = $this->db->get_where("update", array("id" => $update_id,
 "facebook_id !=" => ""));
 return ($query->num_rows() == 1 ? $query->row()->facebook_id : false);
}
```

Comments are slightly more complex, in that it's good practice to store the returned Facebook identifier within your database, and so the controller function should be modified with this code:

```
if($has_facebook_permissions && $facebook_id) {
 $comment_id = $this->facebook_model->comment($facebook_id, $comment);
} else {
 $comment_id = null;
}
$this->sprog_model->post_comment($update_id, $username, $comment, $source,
$comment_id);
```

Here, the returned Facebook identifier is passed into the post_comment() function, which should be updated to accommodate the final parameter. Again, the comment table should be updated with a facebook_id field, which is a varchar(64). The comment()

function within the Facebook model is similar to the `like()` function, although uses the `$facebook->api_client->stream_addComment($facebook_id, $comment)` method. If all is successful and you submit an update, comment, or like to Facebook, you should be greeted with a screen shot similar to Figure 13.4.

Figure 13.4   Screen shot of an update, comment, and like submitted to Facebook.

You can find the files for this section in the online github code repository inside the `stagefour` directory. This directory should be renamed `codeigniter` and include your customized configuration files. If all is well, you should have created or modified the following files and functions and updated the `static` directory with the new `style.css` file and added the `xd_receiver.htm` file and updated the following files and functions:

- `applications\controllers\sprog.php`: `facebook()`, `index()`, `register()`, `login()`, `create()`, `home()`, `update()`, `logout()`, `like()` and `comment()`

- `applications\models\sprog_model.php`: `post_comment()`

- `applications\models\facebook_model.php`: `remove()`, `get_user()`, `check_user()`, `is_facebook_logged_in()`, `link()`, `has_facebook()`, `has_permissions()`, `update()`, `get_facebook_id()`, `like()` and `comment()`.

- `applications\views\sprog\home.php`

- `applications\views\sprog\login.php`

- `applications\views\sprog\register.php`

- `applications\views\sprog\includes\header.php`

- `applications\views\sprog\includes\footer.php`

- `applications\views\sprog\includes\template.php`

In addition, you should have also uploaded the Facebook API PHP client library to `application\libraries\facebook-platform` and added the `facebook_library.php` file. Extensions to this code would be to retrieve comments and likes from Facebook, display a user's friends' updates and comments more prominently using `$facebook->api_client->friends_getAppUsers()`, and more efficient handle details of whether users revoke access to their account. The final section shows how to add Google Friend Connect functionality alongside Twitter and Facebook to increase the reach of your application further.

Implementing Google Friend Connect Functionality

As with Twitter and Facebook, you can use Google Friend Connect to authenticate users and to post updates. Widgets such as Comments and the Social Bar can be used to good effect to maintain a members list but also to surface updates and replies to users who do not have a Sprog account. The combination of client-side and server-side technologies makes the integration of Google Friend Connect similar to that of Facebook, where you can use a combination of cookie-based authentication and OAuth for "offline" updates. A new table needs to be created in your database, `google`, for storing user credentials. The OpenSocial client library will also be translated to work with CodeIgniter, and a new model will be created, `google_model.php`, to contain code specific to Google Friend Connect.

The `google` table will store the user's Google account ID plus a reference to a record in the `user` table (if one already exists). Because Google Friend Connect uses only two-legged OAuth, no other keys are required to authenticate a user. The following SQL should be executed to create this table:

```
CREATE TABLE IF NOT EXISTS "google" (
 "id" bigint NOT NULL,
 "user_username" varchar(24) NULL,
 PRIMARY KEY ("id")
);
```

For users who already have a Sprog account, after they have logged in with Google Friend Connect they will be prompted to link their accounts. If users do not already have a Sprog account, they will be prompted to create one after authenticating with Google Friend Connect. The next stage is to register an application with Google and to reference the client- and server-side OpenSocial libraries within Sprog.

Registering and Adding Google Friend Connect Support

Before you can add Google Friend Connect functionality, you must first register a Sprog application by logging in to your Google account and visiting http://www.google.com/friendconnect/admin/site/setup and entering the following details:

- **Website Name:** An appropriate name for this application would be Sprog, although this can be anything that you want.
- **Website URL:** This should be set to the domain (or subdomain) where you have installed CodeIgniter. For example, if you have installed your application at http://sprog.com/codeigniter/, this should be set to http://sprog.com/.

After all these details have been saved, you will be able to access a site ID from the address bar and a consumer key and secret within the REST API tab of the Plug-ins & APIs section. You should add these to your `constants.php` configuration file using the following names:

```
define("GFC_SITE_ID", "XXXXXXXXXXXX");
define("GFC_CONSUMER_KEY", "XXXXXXXXXXXXXXXXXXXXXXXXX");
define("GFC_CONSUMER_SECRET", "XXXXXXXXXXXXXXXXXXXXXXXX");
define("GFC_PARENT_URL", "/");
```

By adding these constants, you ensure that they are addressable within the application, instead of having to worry about storing them as an external reference. In particular, if the `GFC_PARENT_URL` is set incorrectly, the Google Friend Connect gadgets will not be loaded. Therefore, you must ensure that this is configured appropriately. In the examples in this section, this should be set to "/" because your domain (or subdomain) was set as the website URL.

The final step is to download OpenSocial PHP client library and upload it to the `application\libraries` directory. To make this a pseudo-CodeIgniter library, a `google.php` class will need to be created that will include the library plus some standard functions such as creating the OpenSocial object:

```php
<?php if (!defined("BASEPATH")) exit("No direct script access allowed");
include "osapi/osapi.php";
class Google {
 function get_google_oauth($userId) {
  $provider = new osapiFriendConnectProvider();
  $authentication = new osapiOAuth2Legged(GFC_CONSUMER_KEY,
  GFC_CONSUMER_SECRET, $userId);
  return new osapi($provider, $authentication);
 }
 function get_google_cookie($cookie) {
  $provider = new osapiFriendConnectProvider();
  $authentication = new osapiFCAuth($cookie);
  return new osapi($provider, $authentication);
 }
}?>
```

Within this file, you import the library so that whenever the `$this->load->library` `("google")` method is called, these files are immediately loaded. By constructing the library in this way, you can then initialize a Google Friend Connect session via either an authentication cookie or via OAuth. Because you will be using this library throughout the application, it should be loaded automatically by adding `google` to the `$autoload["libraries"]` variable in `autoload.php`.

Stage 5: Extending the Sprog Application with Google Friend Connect Functionality

As with Facebook, the Google Friend Connect workflow can be handled using client-side code to display the sign-in button and then via server-side code to detect the presence of login credentials such as an authentication cookie. The first two files that need to be modified are the `header.php` and `footer.php` views, which will include the client-side library and attempt to extract user data. In the `header.php` file, you should add the following code into the `<head>` element of the page:

```
<script type="text/javascript" src="http://www.google.com/jsapi"></script>
<script type="text/javascript">
 google.load("friendconnect", "0.8");
</script>
<script type="text/javascript">
 google.friendconnect.container.setParentUrl("<?php echo
GFC_PARENT_URL; ?>");
 google.friendconnect.container.initOpenSocialApi({
  site: "<?php echo GFC_SITE_ID; ?>",
  onload: function(securityToken) { initAllData(); }
 });
</script>
```

This simple snippet includes the library using the constants that were defined in the section above and finally calls the `initAllData()` function, which should be placed within `footer.php`:

```
<script type="text/javascript">
 var viewer;
 function initAllData() {
  var params = {
   "profileDetail": [opensocial.Person.Field.ID,
   opensocial.Person.Field.NAME, opensocial.Person.Field.THUMBNAIL_URL,
   opensocial.Person.Field.PROFILE_URL]
  };
  var req = opensocial.newDataRequest();
  req.add(req.newFetchPersonRequest("VIEWER", params), "viewer");
  req.send(onData);
 }
 function onData(data) {
  var gfcButtonHtml = document.getElementById("gfcButton");
  if (data.get("viewer").hadError()) {
   google.friendconnect.renderSignInButton({
    "id": "gfcButton",
    "style": "standard"
   });
   gfcButtonHtml.style.display = "block";
```

```
  } else {
    gfcButtonHtml.style.display = "none";
    window.location.reload();
  }
 }
</script>
```

The code above is used to try to retrieve a Google Friend Connect viewer's details and will then show or hide the sign-in button depending on whether the request is successful or not. If successful, the button is hidden and the page is then refreshed, where the authentication cookie can then be extracted. The final modification in terms of views is to add the `gfcButton` element to the `index` page, which will produce the screen shot shown in Figure 13.5.

Figure 13.5   Screen shot of the index page with
Google Friend Connect button.

Like the code added to the `login.php` view for authenticating via Twitter and Facebook, a message needs to be displayed if a user has signed in to Google Friend Connect but not linked his accounts. You can do so as follows:

```
if(!empty($has_google)) {
  echo '<p class="google_message">'.$has_google."</p>";
}
```

The small snippet of code above should also be added to the `register.php` view. The conditional for displaying the alternative login options should also be updated to include the following:

```
if(empty($has_twitter) && empty($has_facebook) && empty($has_google)) {
  ...
  $userAgent = $_SERVER["HTTP_USER_AGENT"];
  $unsupportedBrowsers = array("Opera");
  $isBrowserSupported = true;
```

```
foreach ($unsupportedBrowsers as $unsupportedBrowser) {
 $isBrowserSupported = preg_match("/".$unsupportedBrowser."/i",
 $userAgent) ? false : true;
 }
 if($isBrowserSupported) { echo '<p id="gfcButton"></p>'; }
}
```

Because the Google Friend Connect functionality doesn't appear to work correctly within the Opera browser, it must be omitted as an option for those users. The code to create the $has_twitter variable should be added to both the index() and register() functions of the main controller, which reference a Google model, which is created next:

```
if($this->google_model->get_viewer()) {
 $data["has_google"] = "You are signed in with Google Friend Connect, but
 you must log in or register with us to link accounts. You will only have
 to do this once.";
}
```

This conditional calls the get_viewer() function of the Google model, which will return a viewer's details if successful and return false if not. Create a new file called google_model.php and save it into application\models and add it to the autoload.php configuration file:

```
<?php
class Google_Model extends Model {
 function Google_Model() {
  parent::Model();
 }
 function get_viewer() {
  $cookieIdentifier = "fcauth".GFC_SITE_ID;
  $cookie = isset($_COOKIE[$cookieIdentifier]) ?
  $_COOKIE[$cookieIdentifier] :
 null;
  if ($cookie) {
  $opensocial = $this->google->get_google_cookie($cookie);
  $batch = $opensocial->newBatch();
  $viewerParameters = array("userId" => "@me", "groupId" => "@self",
  "fields" => "@all");
  $getViewer = $opensocial->people->get($viewerParameters);
  $batch->add($getViewer, "viewer");
  $response = $batch->execute();
  $data = $response["viewer"];
  if ($data instanceof osapiError) { return false; }
  else {
  $data = array("id" => $data->getId(), "name" => htmlentities(
  $data->getName()), "thumbnailUrl" => htmlentities($data->
  getThumbnailUrl()));
  return $data;
```

```
    }
  } else { return false; }
 }
}
?>
```

This code attempts to extract the authentication cookie using the site ID parameter and then creates the OpenSocial object to access a user's details. These details are then returned via a `$data` array; otherwise, the function will return `false`. One of the benefits of Google Friend Connect and the OpenSocial library is that you can create the OpenSocial object either via the authentication cookie or via two-legged OAuth. With the cookie, you can then store the user's identifier within the database for future use. This next step is supported by the is_google_logged_in() function within the model, which is called right at the top of index() and register():

```
function is_google_logged_in() {
 $is_logged_in = $this->session->userdata("is_logged_in");
 $google_user = $this->get_viewer();
 if($google_user && !$is_logged_in) {
  return $this->check_user($google_user);
  } else { return false; }
}
```

This method calls the check_user() function, passing in a user's Google Friend Connect details, which are then verified against your database to check whether users have previously authenticated their account. If so, their session is saved and they are logged in, otherwise they are prompted to link their accounts:

```
function check_user($google_user) {
 $this->db->select("*")->from("user")->join("google",
 "google.user_username = user.username", "left");
 $this->db->where("id", $google_user["id"]);
 $query = $this->db->get();
 if($query->num_rows() == 0) { return false; }
 else {
  $user = $query->row();
  $data = array(
   "username" => $this->encrypt->encode($user->username),
   "fullname" => $this->encrypt->encode($user->fullname),
   "is_logged_in" => true,
   "source" => $this->encrypt->encode("g")
  );
  $this->session->set_userdata($data);
  return true;
 }
}
```

The next step is to add code to both the `login()` and `create()` controller methods to link a user's accounts together, which is achieved by adding the following just below where the Facebook code was added:

```
if($this->google_model->get_viewer()) {
 $this->google_model->link($this->google_model->get_viewer(), $username);
 $source = "g";
}
```

The final step in the authentication process is to create the `link()` function within `google_model.php`, which creates a reference in the `google` table in your database:

```
function link($google_user, $username) {
 $query = $this->db->get_where("google", array("id" =>
 $google_user["id"]));
 if($query->num_rows() == 0) {
  $user = array("id" => $google_user["id"], "user_username" => $username);
  $query = $this->db->insert("google", $user);
  return true;
 } else { return false; }
}
```

You will notice that only a single identifier is required for a Google Friend Connect user because two-legged OAuth requests their individual identifier. If you save and upload the following files to your web server, you should now be able to sign in via Google Friend Connect:

- `applications\controllers\sprog.php`: `index()`, `register()`, `login()` and `create()`

- `applications\models\google_model.php`: `get_viewer()`, `is_google_logged_in()`, `check_user()` and `link()`

- `applications\views\sprog\login.php`

- `applications\views\sprog\register.php`

- `applications\views\sprog\includes\header.php`

- `applications\views\sprog\includes\footer.php`

In addition, you should have also uploaded the OpenSocial PHP client library to `application\libraries\google` and added the `google.php` file. Now that you have an authenticated user, you can now add a Comments gadget for users to reply to updates and also post original updates to their Google Friend Connect accounts. The first addition requires a new parameter to be added to the `view_comment()` controller function:

```
$data["is_google"] = ($this->encrypt->decode($this->session->
userdata("source")) == "g" ? true : false);
```

With this piece of additional information, a user will be shown a Google Friend Connect Comments gadget rather than the standard comments form in the comments.php view. Alongside the conditional test, you also need to add a snippet of JavaScript to render the gadget:

```php
<?php if($is_google) { ?>
 <div id="google_comments" style="width: 610px; border: 1px solid
#ccc;"></div>
<?php } else { ?>
<div id="comment">
...
</div>
<?php } ?>
<script type="text/javascript">
 var skin = {};
 skin["BORDER_COLOR"] = "#cccccc";
 skin["ENDCAP_BG_COLOR"] = "#e0ecff";
 skin["ENDCAP_TEXT_COLOR"] = "#333333";
 skin["ENDCAP_LINK_COLOR"] = "#0000cc";
 skin["ALTERNATE_BG_COLOR"] = "#ffffff";
 skin["CONTENT_BG_COLOR"] = "#ffffff";
 skin["CONTENT_LINK_COLOR"] = "#0000cc";
 skin["CONTENT_TEXT_COLOR"] = "#333333";
 skin["CONTENT_SECONDARY_LINK_COLOR"] = "#7777cc";
 skin["CONTENT_SECONDARY_TEXT_COLOR"] = "#666666";
 skin["CONTENT_HEADLINE_COLOR"] = "#333333";
 skin["DEFAULT_COMMENT_TEXT"] = "- add your comment here -";
 skin["HEADER_TEXT"] = "Comments";
 skin["POSTS_PER_PAGE"] = "5";
 google.friendconnect.container.renderWallGadget({
  id: "google_comments",
  site: "<?php echo GFC_SITE_ID; ?>",
  "view-params":{
   "disableMinMax":"true", "scope":"PAGE", "features":"video,comment",
   "startMaximized":"true"
  }
 }, skin);
</script>
```

By using the Comments gadget, you do not have to store any of the comments in your own database, which makes this quite a useful replacement for those who log in via Google Friend Connect. However, for original updates, you might want them to be stored and posted as activities to a user's linked Google accounts. This can be achieved by updating the update() controller function, which then points to the Google model to execute the update:

```php
$has_google_id = $this->google_model->get_google_id($username);
if($has_google_id) { $this->google_model->update($username, $update, $id);
}
```

The code that must be added to `google_model.php` consists of the `get_google_id()` function for extracting a user's connected Google identifier as well as the `update()` function itself:

```php
function get_google_id($username) {
 $query = $this->db->get_where("google", array("user_username" =>
 $username));
 return ($query->num_rows() == 1 ? $query->row()->id : false);
}
function update($username, $update, $id) {
 $google_id = $this->get_google_id($username);
 $opensocial = $this->google->get_google_oauth($google_id);
 $batch = $opensocial->newBatch();
 $activity = new osapiActivity($id, $google_id);
 $activity->setTitle($username);
 $activity->setBody($update);
 $parameters = array("userId" => "@me", "groupId" => "@self",
 "activity" => $activity);
 $addActivity = $opensocial->activities->create($parameters);
 $batch->add($addActivity, "activity");
 $response = $batch->execute();
 $data = $response["activity"];
 return ($data instanceof osapiError ? false : true);
}
```

The `update()` function attempts to construct an OAuth session and then create an Activity object, which must be passed a unique identifier (`$id`) plus the user's identifier (`$google_id`). The title of the activity is set to their username, and the body is the update itself. On success, an activity will be published, and then the function will return true. Alongside comments, you can view activities and members by adding the Social Bar to `footer.php`, as shown in Figure 13.6.

The final addition to the code is to modify the logout anchor in `home.php` to also sign a user out of Google Friend Connect by adding `array("onclick" => "google.friendconnect.requestSignOut();")` as the third parameter to the anchor() helper function. As with the additions of Twitter and Facebook, only a small portion of the many Google Friend Connect functionalities is demonstrated by this application. Additions could include posting likes as activities; improving user profiles by prepopulating them with data available via each of the services; adding handling for expired accounts and removals; and highlighting updates, comments, and likes specific to a user's social graph. The opportunities for building on top of the Sprog application are endless. As with the other sections, code for this section is available from the online code repository within the `stagefive` directory. This directory should be renamed `codeigniter` and include your customized configuration files.

Figure 13.6   Screen shot of the home page demonstrating the
Social Bar with comments, members, and activities.

Summary

This final chapter, along with Chapter 12, provided an example of how to integrate Twitter, Facebook, and Google Friend Connect into a real-world web application. By incorporating the authentication workflows of each platform, you can then quickly and easily build social features on top of a preexisting infrastructure. Through building a sample application, you should have picked up how this can be achieved easily and be left with numerous ideas about how to improve it!

Index

A

accessing responses, Test Tube application (Twitter), 51

accessor methods, Twitter API, 3-5

account methods, Twitter API, 3-5

accounts, Twitter, updating, 276-279

action links, Open Stream API, 125-126

activities

Color Picker sample application, posting and retrieving, 187-189

Google Friend Connect, fetching, 177

activity streams, Dashboard API, 139-143

administration methods, Facebook Platform, 86-87

animation library, Facebook, 157-160

Apache Shindig, OpenSocial API, 173

API methods, FQL (Facebook Query Language), 95

APIs (Application Programming Interface), 1

Facebook, 77-97

Open Stream API, 123-134

Google Friend Connect

JavaScript API, 167-173

OpenSocial API, 173-177

Twitter, 1-19

accessing, 11-19

authorized connections, 12

direct message objects, 28-29

error handling, 18-19

extending, 61–62

Geolocation API, 68–71

hash objects, 33

ID objects, 30–31

Lists API, 2–3, 61–68

location-based APIs, 61

methods, 3–33

parameters, 6–10

rate limiting, 17

relationship objects, 31–32

response objects, 32

REST (Representational State Transfer) API, 2–14

return formats, 10–11

Retweets API, 61–64

saved search objects, 29–30

Search API, 3–43

status objects, 26–28

Streaming API, 74–75

user objects, 22–26

versioning, 3

application data, Color Picker sample application, storing and retrieving, 189-190

Application Edit page (Facebook Platform), 79-81

application tabs

configuring and installing, 146–147

extending, 149–156

applications

Color Picker sample application (Google Friend Connect), 181–191

configuring, 183–185

creating, 222–233

posting and retrieving activities, 187–189

registering, 183–185

retrieving site members, 187

sign-in functionality, 186

storing and retrieving application data, 189–190

Facebook

referencing, 81–82

registering, 79–81

tags, 145–156

Sprog application, building, 246–266

building, 246–266

comments, 257–266

create() function, 253

Facebook, 279–292

Google Friend Connect, 292–300

home pages, 247–257

index() function, 250

index page, 248

likes, 257–266

logins, 247–257

registering, 247–257

Twitter, 268–279

Updates, 257–266

Test Tube application (Twitter), 50

class methods, 50–51

Translations for Facebook, preparing, 111–113

entry elements, 36–37

feed elements, 35–36

Atom syndication format

Search API (Twitter), 34-38

versus JSON, 37–38

authentication, 45

Facebook, 99–107

Facebook Platform, 87

Google Friend Connect, 194–196

cookies, 195

standard two-legged OAuth, 195–196

Twitter, OAuth, 45–59

Authentication tab (Application Edit page), 80

authentication workflow, Google Friend Connect, 197-198

authorized connections, Twitter API, 12

B

Basic Authentication, twitter-async client library, 16-17

Basic tab (Application Edit page), 80

block methods, Twitter API, 4-5

C

callback parameter (Twitter API), 8

character limit, Twitter, 2

class methods, twitter-async client library, 50-51

client libraries

OpenSocial client libraries, 196-197

PHP OpenSocial client library, Google Friend Connect, 197-207

code listings

3.1 (functions.php file), 52

3.2 (index.php file), 53-54

3.3 (master.php file), 55-56

4.1 (printRetweets function), 63

4.2 (printFollowers function), 72

5.1 (Simple Facebook Platform Page), 82

6.1 (Sample Facebook Page), 103-104

6.2 (Sample Facebook Post-Authorize Callback URL), 107

6.3 (Sample Facebook Post-Remove Callback URL), 108

7.1 (get_write_permission method), 128

8.1 (index.php File Demonstrating a Simple Facebook Canvas Page), 147

8.2 (Example for the tab.php File Demonstrating a Simple Application Tab), 150

8.3 (Example post.php File Demonstrating Adding a Comment and Returning Data Back to an Application Tab), 155

12.1 (sprog.php File Demonstrating the Default index() Function), 250

12.2 (create() Function within the Main Controller), 253

12.3 (Sprog Model and create() Function), 255

12.4 (updates() and my_comments() Function,)264

CodeIgniter, 235-266

configuring, 237-240

directory structue, 237-238

GET parameters, handling, 236

helpers, 245-246

installing, 237-240

libraries, 240-244

Database class, 240-243

pagination class, 243-244

session class, 244-245

URI class, 243

MVC (Model View Controller) architectural design, 236-237

Sprog application

building, 246-266

comments, 257-266

create() function, 253

home pages, 247-257

index() function, 250

index page, 248

likes, 257-266

logins, 247-257

registering, 247-257

updates, 257-266

Color Picker sample application (Google Friend Connect), **181-191**

activities, posting and retrieving, 187–189

application data, storing and retrieving, 189–190

configuring, 183–185

creation, 222–233

registering, 183–185

sign–in functionality, 186

site members, retrieving, 187

commands, cURL, REST API access, **12-14**

comments

Open Stream API, adding and removing, 129

Sprog application, 257–266

Comments Box widget (Facebook), **120-123**

communities, Twitter, **71**

future directions, 74–76

platform translations, 71

spam reporting, 72–74

configuration

application tabs, 146–147

CodeIgniter, 237–240

Color Picker sample application (Google Friend Connect), 183–185

JavaScript Library, Google Friend Connect, 169–170

Twitter, 268–270

Connect tab (Application Edit page), **81**

connecting Facebook friends, **109-110**

consumers, OAuth, **47**

container setup methods, Google Friend Connect, **171**

content types, URLs, **214**

content-sharing, Facebook, **115-120**

contributions, Twitter, **75-76**

cookies, Google Friend Connect, **195**

count parameter (Twitter API), **8**

counters, Games and Application counters, **143-144**

coverage, Twitter API parameters, **7**

create() Function within the Main Controller listing (**12.2**), **253**

cURL, Twitter API, accessing, **12-14**

cursor parameter (Twitter API), **9**

custom tags API methods, Facebook Platform, **93**

D

Dashboard API, **137-164**

methods, Facebook Platform, 89

naming conventions, 140

news and activity streams, 139–143

data extraction principles, OpenSocial, **201-207**

Database class, CodeIgniter, **240-243**

DataRequest object, OpenSocial API, **174-175**

data-retrieval methods, Facebook Platform, **87**

depreciation

Twitter API methods, 21–22

Twitter API parameters, 7

description parameter (Twitter API), **7**

dialogs, Facebook, **160-162**

direct message objects, Twitter API, **28-29**

direct messages methods, Twitter API, **4-6**

direct publishing, Open Stream API, **127-129**

directory structure, CodeIgniter, **237-238**

disconnecting, Facebook accounts, **107-109**

dynamic content, FBJS (Facebook JavaScript), **157-164**

E

email parameter (Twitter API), 7

entry elements, Atom syndication format, 36-37

error handling, Twitter API, 18-19

Event Listener (FBJS), handling events, 162-164

events, handling, FBJS Event Listener, 162-164

events API methods, Facebook Platform, 90-93

Example for the tab.php File Demonstrating a Simple Application Tab listing (8.2), 150

Example post.php File Demonstrating Adding a Comment and Returning Data Back to an Application Tab listing (8.3), 155

extending

application tabs, 149-156

Sprog application

Facebook, 281-292

Google Friend Connect, 294-300

Twitter, 270-276

F

Facebook

adding support, 279-281

animation library, 158-160

API, 77-97

Open Stream API, 123-134

applications

registering, 79-81

tabs, 145-156

content-sharing, 115-120

dashboards, Games and Application dashboard, 139-143

dialogs, 160-162

disconnecting accounts, 107-109

Facebook Platform, 77-98

developers, 77-78

Open Stream API, 123-134

referencing applications, 81-84

website integration, 78-84

Facebook Share, 116-118

FQL (Facebook Query Language), 118

multimedia content, 117

Facebook Widgets, 119-120

Comments Box widget, 120-123

FQL (Facebook Query Language), 77-97

friends, connecting and inviting, 109-110

functionality, 279-292

implementing, 279

live conversation, 115-120

logging out accounts, 107-109

Open Graph, 85-86

reclaiming accounts, 107-109

Sprog application

extending, 281-292

registering with, 279-281

state changes, detecting and handling, 102-105

status detection, 101-107

Translations for Facebook, 111-114

administering and accessing translations, 113-114

preparing applications, 111-113

registering text, 111-113

user authentication, 99-107

user registration, post-authorize callback URL, 105-107

XFBML (Facebook Markup Language), 77-98

Facebook JavaScript (FBJS). *See* FBJS
(Facebook JavaScript)

Facebook Markup Language (XFBML),
77-98

Facebook Platform, 77-98. *See also*
Facebook

administration methods, 86-87

Application Edit page, 79-81

applications, referencing, 81-84

authentication methods, 87

custom tags API methods, 93

Dashboard API, 137-144

   methods, 89

   news and activity streams, 139-143

data-retrieval methods, 87

developers, 77-78

events API methods, 90-93

FQL (Facebook Query Language),
93-97

friends, connecting and inviting,
109-110

login methods, 87

mobile methods, 89

Open Stream API, 123-134

   action links, 125-126

   adding and removing comments,
   129

   direct publishing, 127-129

   feed forms, 127-129

   Publisher, 131-134

   reading data from streams, 130-134

   removing stream posts, 128

   stream attachments, 125-126

   writing data to stream, 125

photos API methods, 89-90

publishing methods, 88

Translations for Facebook, 111-114

user authentication, 99-107

website integration, 78-84

XFBML (Facebook Markup
Language), 97-98

Facebook Query Language (FQL). *See* FQL
(Facebook Query Language)

Facebook Share, 116-118

FQL (Facebook Query
Language), 118

multimedia content, 117

Facebook Widgets, 119-120

Comments Box widget, 120-123

favorites methods, Twitter API, 4-6

FBJS (Facebook JavaScript), 137-164

animation library, 158-160

dialogs, 160-162

dynamic content, 157-164

Event Listener, handling events,
162-164

Test Console, 158

FBML (Facebook Markup Language),
elements, adding application tabs to, 145

feature extensions, OpenSocial gadgets, 211

feed elements, Atom syndication format,
35-36

feed forms, Open Stream API, 127-129

field names, Open Stream API, 174

follow parameter (Twitter API), 7

FQL (Facebook Query Language), 85-97

API methods, relationships, 95

Facebook Share, 118

friends, connecting and inviting, Facebook,
109-110

friendships methods, Twitter API, 4-6

functionality

Facebook, implementing, 279-292

Google Friend Connect,
implementing, 292-300

Twitter, implementing, 267-279

functions

create( ), 253

index( ), 250

functions.php file listings (3.1), 52

G

gadget-interaction methods, Google Friend Connect, 172

gadgets

Google Friend Connet, 166

Google gadgets, 209-233

creating, 222-233

submitting, 232-233

testing, 230-233

OpenSocial gadgets, developing, 209

Games and Application dashboard (Facebook), 139-143

Geolocation API (Twitter), 68-71

GET parameters, CodeIgniter, handling, 236

get_write_permission() method listing (7.1), 128

Google. *See also* **Google Friend Connect**

gadgets, 209-233

creating, 222-233

submitting, 232-233

testing, 230-233

iGoogle Directory, 211

Google Friend Connect, 165-193

authentication methods, 194-196

cookies, 195

standard two-legged OAuth, 195-196

authentication workflow, 197-198

Color Picker sample application, 181-191

configuring, 183-185

posting and retrieving activities, 187-189

registering, 183-185

retrieving site members, 187

sign-in functionality, 186

storing and retrieving application data, 189-190

container setup methods, 171

functionality, implementing, 292-300

gadget-interaction methods, 172

gadgets, 166

index page, 295

JavaScript API, 167-173

methods, 171

JavaScript Library, installing and configuring, 169-170

OpenSocial API, 173-177

DataRequest object, 174-175

fetching activities, 177

fetching persistence, 178-181

fetching profiles, 176-177

field names, 174

methods, 173-174

OpenSocial client libraries, 196-197

OpenSocial gadgets, 210-214

creating, 222-233

developing, 209

feature extensions, 211

gadget internationalization and localization, 221-222

module content, 213-214

module preferences, 210-211

module views, 213-214

OpenSocial v.0.9 specification, 214-217

remote content, 218-221

skins, 212

user preferences, 212-213

working with data, 217-218

OpenSocial RESTful endpoints, 194

PHP OpenSocial client library, 197-207

    data extraction principles, 201-207

    setting up server-side applications, 198-201

plug-ins, 169

post-registration methods, 172

pre-registration methods, 171-172

RPC protocol endpoints, 194

server-side integration, 167-169

server-side OpenSocial protocols, 193-197

Sprog application

    adding support, 292-293

    extending, 294-300

    registering, 292-293

Google Gadget Editor, 223-230

Google Gadget Tester, 230

H

hash objects, Twitter API, 33

help methods, Twitter API, 4

helpers, CodeIgniter, 245-246

home pages, Sprog application, 247-257

HTTP operation, Lists API, 2

I

ID objects, Twitter API, 30-31

id parameter (Twitter API), 9

iGoogle Directory, 211

image parameter (Twitter API), 7

in_reply_to_status_id parameter (Twitter API), 7

index() function, Sprog application, 250

index page, Sprog application, 248

index.php File Demonstrating a Simple Facebook Canvas Page listing (8.1), 147

index.php file listings (3.2), 53-54

installing

    application tabs, 146-147

    CodeIgniter, 237-240

    JavaScript Library, Google Friend Connect, 169-170

internationalization, Google gadgets, 221-222

inviting, Facebook friends, 109-110

J

JavaScript API, Google Friend Connect, 167-173

    methods, 171

JavaScript Library, Google Friend Connect, installing and configuring, 169-170

JSON (JavaScript Object Notation)

    versus Atom, 37-38

    strings, saving values as, 212

    Twitter API, 10

L

landing pages

    Test Tube application (Twitter), creating, 53-54

lang parameter (Twitter API), 9

lat parameter (Twitter API), 8-9

libraries, CodeIgniter, 240-244

    Database class, 240-243

    pagination class, 243-244

    session class, 244-245

    URI class, 243

like box, Facebook Widgets, 119

likes

Open Stream API, adding and removing, 129

Sprog application, 257-266

listings

3.1 (functions.php file), 52

3.2 (index.php file), 53-54

3.3 (master.php file), 55-56

4.1 (printRetweets function), 63

4.2 (printFollowers function), 72

5.1 (Simple Facebook Platform Page), 82

6.1 (Sample Facebook Page), 103-104

6.2 (Sample Facebook Post-Authorize Callback URL), 107

6.3 (Sample Facebook Post-Remove Callback URL), 108

7.1 (get_write_permission method), 128

8.1 (index.php File Demonstrating a Simple Facebook Canvas Page), 147

8.2 (Example for the tab.php File Demonstrating a Simple Application Tab), 150

8.3 (Example post.php File Demonstrating Adding a Comment and Returning Data Back to an Application Ta), 155

12.1 (sprog.php File Demonstrating the Default index() Function), 250

12.2 (create() Function within the Main Controller), 253

12.3 (Sprog Model and create() Function), 255

12.4 (updates() and my_comments() Function), 260

Lists API (Twitter), 2-3, 61-68

live conversation, Facebook, 115-120

live stream box, Facebook Widgets, 119-120

localization, Google gadgets, 221-222

location parameter (Twitter API), 7

location-based APIs, Twitter, 61

logging out, Facebook accounts, 107-109

login methods, Facebook Platform, 87

logins

Facebook, authentication, 101-107

Sprog application, 247-257

long parameter (Twitter API), 8

M

mas_id parameter (Twitter API), 9

master page, Test Tube application (Twitter), creating, 55-57

methods

container setup methods, 171

Facebook Platform

administration methods, 86-87

authentication methods, 87

custom tags API methods, 93

dashboard API methods, 89

data-retrieval methods, 87

events API methods, 90-93

login methods, 87

mobile methods, 89

photos API methods, 89-90

publishing methods, 88

gadget-interaction methods, 172

Google Friend Connect, 173-174

authentication, 194-196

JavaScript API, 171

OpenSocial API (Google Friend Connect), 173-174

post-registration methods, 172

pre-registration methods, 171

Twitter API, 3-33

accessor methods, 3-5

depreciation, 21-22

mutator methods, 5-6

Search API, 38-43

microblog tools. *See* Sprog application

Migrations tab (Application Edit page), 81

mobile methods, Facebook Platform, 89

module content, OpenSocial gadgets, 213-214

module preferences, OpenSocial gadgets, 210-211

module views, OpenSocial gadgets, 213-214

multimedia content, Facebook Share, 117

mutator methods, Twitter API, 5-6

MVC (Model View Controller) architectural design, CodeIgniter, 236-237

N

name parameter (Twitter API), 7

naming conventions, Dashboard API, 140

news streams, Dashboard API, 139-143

notifications methods, Twitter API, 6

O

OAuth

Google Friend Connect, 195-196

Twitter, 45-59

benefits, 46

consumers, 47

implementing, 48-57

protected resources, 47

protocol parameters, 47

service providers, 47

Test Tube application, 50-57

Test Tube application (Twitter), 57-58

tokens, 47

users, 47

workflow, 48-50

twitter-async client library, 14-15

objects, Twitter API

direct message objects, 28-29

hash objects, 33

ID objects, 30-31

relationship objects, 31-32

response objects, 32

saved search objects, 29-30

status objects, 26-28

user objects, 22-26

Open Graph, Facebook, 85-86

Open Stream API (Facebook), 123-134

action links, 125-126

comments, adding and removing, 129

direct publishing, 127-129

feed forms, 127-129

Publisher, 131-134

stream attachments, 125-126

stream posts, removing programatically, 128

streams

reading data from, 130-134

writing data to, 125

OpenSocial, v.0.9 specifications, 214-217

OpenSocial API (Google Friend Connect), 173-177

DataRequest object, 174-175

fetching

activities, 177

persistence, 178-181

profiles, 176-177

field names, 174

methods, 173-174

OpenSocial client libraries, Google Friend Connect, 196-197

OpenSocial gadgets, Google Friend Connect, 210-214

creating, 222-233

developing, 209

feature extensions, 211

gadget internationalization and localization, 221-222

module content, 213-214

module preferences, 210-211

module views, 213-214

OpenSocial v.0.9 specification, 214-217

remote content, 218-221

skins, 212

user preferences, 212-213

working with data, 217-218

OpenSocial RESTful endpoints, Google Friend Connect, 194

P

page parameter (Twitter API), 8

pagination class, CodeIgniter, 243-244

parameters, Twitter API, 6-10

coverage, 7

depreciation, 7

people, Google Friend Connect, fetching, 176-177

per page parameter (Twitter API), 9

persistence, Google Friend Connect, fetching and updating, 178-181

photos API methods, Facebook Platform, 89-90

PHP OpenSocial client library, Google Friend Connect, 197-207

data extraction principles, 201-207

setting up server-side applications, 198-201

platform translations, Twitter, 71

plug-ins, Google Friend Connect, 169

post-authorize callback URL, user registration, Facebook, 105-107

posting activites, Color Picker sample application (Google Friend Connect), 187-189

post-registration methods, Google Friend Connect, 172

pre-registration methods, Google Friend Connect, 171-172

printFollowers() function listing (4.2), 72

printRetweets() function listing (4.1), 63

profile_background_color parameter (Twitter API), 8

profile_link_color parameter (Twitter API), 8

profile_sidebar_border parameter (Twitter API), 8

profile_text_border parameter (Twitter API), 8

profiles, Google Friend Connect, fetching, 176-177

Profiles tab (Application Edit page), 81

protected resources, OAuth, 47

protocol parameters, OAuth, 47

Publisher (Facebook Platform), 131-134

publishing methods, Facebook Platform, 88

PUT operation, Lists API, 2

Q

q parameter (Twitter API), 9

query parameter (Twitter API), 8

R

rate limiting, Twitter API, 17

Really Simple Syndication (RSS), Twitter API, 10

reclaiming, Facebook accounts, 107-109

referencing, Facebook Platform applications, 81-84

registering

Color Picker sample application (Google Friend Connect), 183-185

Facebook applications, 79–81

Sprog application, Google Friend Connect, 292–293

Facebook, 279–281

Twitter, 268–270

Test Tube application (Twitter), 52–53

relationship objects, Twitter API, 31-32

remote content, OpenSocial gadgets, 218-221

response objects, Twitter API, 32

responses, accessing, Test Tube application (Twitter), 51

REST (Representational State Transfer) API, Twitter, 2-3

CURL commands, 12–14

return formats, Twitter API, 10-11

Retweets API (Twitter), 61-64

RPC protocol endpoints, Google Friend Connect, 194

RSS (Really Simple Syndication), Twitter API, 10

S

Sample Facebook Page listing (6.1), 103-104

Sample Facebook Post-Authorize Callback URL listing (6.2), 107

Sample Facebook Post-Remove Callback URL listing (6.3), 108

saved search objects, Twitter API, 29-30

saved searches methods, Twitter API, 4-6

screen_name parameter (Twitter API), 10

Search API (Twitter), 3-43

Atom syndication format, 34–38

entry elements, 36–37

feed elements, 35–36

JSON (JavaScript Object Notation) outputs, 37–38

methods, 38–43

search methods

Search API (Twitter), 38–40

Twitter API, 4

server-side applications, Google Friend Connect, setting up, 198-201

server-side integration, Google Friend Connect, 167-169

server-side OpenSocial protocols, Google Friend Connect, 193-197

service providers, OAuth, 47

session class, CodeIgniter, 244-245

show_user parameter (Twitter API), 10

sign-in functionality, Color Picker sample application (Google Friend Connect), 186

Simple Facebook Platform Page listing (5.1), 82

site members, Color Picker sample application (Google Friend Connect), retrieving, 187

skins, OpenSocial gadgets, 212

social graph methods, Twitter API, 4

source parameter (Twitter API), 8

source_id parameter (Twitter API), 10

spam reporting, Twitter, 72-74

Sprog application

building, CodeIgniter, 246–266

comments, 257–266

Facebook

adding support, 279–281

extending, 281–292

registering with, 279–281

Google Friend Connect

adding support, 292–293

extending, 294–300

registering, 292–293

home pages, 247–257

index() function, 250

index page, 248

likes, 257–266

logins, 247–257

main controller, create() function, 253

registering, 247–257

Twitter

extending with, 270–276

registering with, 268–270

updating accounts, 276–279

updates, 257–266

Sprog Model and create() Function listing (12.3), 255

sprog.php File Demonstrating the Default index() Function listing (12.1), 250

standard two-legged OAuth, Google Friend Connect, 195–196

state changes, Facebook, detecting and handling, 102–105

status detection, Facebook, 101–107

status methods, Twitter API, 4

status objects, Twitter API, 26–28

status parameter (Twitter API), 8

statuses methods, Twitter API, 6

storing application data, Color Picker sample application, 189–190

stream attachments, Open Stream API, 125–126

Streaming API (Twitter), 74–75

streams

Dashboard API, news and activity streams, 139–143

reading data from, Open Stream API, 130–134

strings, JSON (JavaScript Object Notation), saving values as, 212

submitting, Google gadgets, 232–233

support, Facebook, 279–281

T

tabs, Facebook applications, 145-156

configuring and installing, 146–147

extending, 149–156

Test Console (FBJS), 158

Test Tube application (Twitter), 50

accessing responses, 51

creating, 51–52

landing pages, creating, 53–54

master page, creating, 55–57

registering, 52–53

testing, 58

testing

Google gadgets, 230–233

Test Tube application (Twitter), 58

text, registering, Translations for Facebook, 111-113

text parameter (Twitter API), 8

tile parameter (Twitter API), 8

timeline methods, Twitter API, 4

tokens, OAuth, 47

Translations for Facebook, 111-114

applications, preparing, 111–113

registering text, 111–113

translations, administering and accessing, 113–114

trends methods

Search API (Twitter), 40–43

Twitter API, 5

Twitter, 76

accounts, updating, 276–279

API, 1–19

accessing, 11–19

authorized connections, 12

direct message objects, 28–29

error handling, 18–19

extending, 61–62

Geolocation API, 68–71

hash objects, 33

ID objects, 30–31

Lists API, 2–3, 61–68

location-based APIs, 61

methods, 3–6, 21–33

parameters, 6–10

rate limiting, 17

relationship objects, 31–32

response objects, 32

REST (Representational State Transfer) API, 2–14

return formats, 10–11

Retweets API, 61–64

saved search objects, 29–30

Search API, 3, 34–43

status objects, 26–28

Streaming API, 74–75

user objects, 22–26

versioning, 3

character limit, 2

community, 71

future directions, 74–76

spam reporting, 72–74

configuring, 268–270

contributions, 75–76

functionality, implementing, 267–279

Geolocation API, 68–71

Lists API, 61–68

location-based APIs, 61

OAuth, 45–59

benefits, 46

consumers, 47

implementing, 48–57

protected resources, 47

protocol parameters, 47

service providers, 47

tokens, 47

users, 47

workflow, 48–50

platform translations, 71

Retweets API, 61–64

Search API

Atom syndication format, 34–38

methods, 38–43

Sprog application

extending with, 270–276

registration, 268–270

Streaming API, 74–75

Test Tube application, 50

accessing responses, 51

class methods, 50–51

creating, 51–52

landing pages, 53–54

master page, 55–57

registering, 52–53

testing, 58

Twitter @anywhere, 76

twitter-async client library

accessing responses, 51

class methods, 50–51

configuring, 268–270

creating, 51–52

registering, 52–53

two-legged OAuth, Google Friend Connect, 195-196

U

updates, Sprog application, 257-266

updates() and my_comments() Function listing (12.4), 264

updating

> activities, Google Friend Connect, 177
>
> persistence, Google Friend Connect, 178-181
>
> Twitter accounts, 276-279

URI class, CodeIgniter, 243

url parameter (Twitter API), 7

URLs, content types, 214

user authentication, Facebook, 99-107

user methods, Twitter API, 5

user objects, Twitter API, 22-26

user preferences, OpenSocial gadgets, 212-213

user registration

> Facebook, post-authorize callback URL, 105-107

V

values, JSON (JavaScript Object Notation), saving as strings, 212

versioning, Twitter API, 3

W

website integration, Facebook Platform, 78-84

Widgets tab (Application Edit page), 81

woeid parameter (Twitter API), 10

workflow, OAuth, 48-50

X

XFBML (Facebook Markup Language), 77-98

XML (eXtensible Markup Language), Twitter API, 11

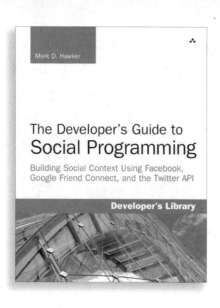